CRAFTING THE WOMAN PROFESSIONAL IN THE LONG NINETEENTH CENTURY

Over the course of the nineteenth century, women in Britain participated in diverse and prolific forms of artistic labour. As they created objects and commodities that blurred the boundaries between domestic and fine art production, they crafted subjectivities for themselves as creative workers. By bringing together work by scholars of literature, painting, music, craft and the plastic arts, this collection argues that the constructed and contested nature of the female artistic professional was a notable aspect of debates about aesthetic value and the impact of industrial technologies. All the essays in this volume set up a productive inter-art dialogue that complicates conventional binary divisions such as amateur and professional, public and private, artistry and industry in order to provide a more nuanced understanding of the relationship between gender, artistic labour and creativity in the period. Tracing how women engaged with the pragmatics of the work they did in vocations, trades and professions in the literary market-place and related art industries, this volume reveals the ideological positions surrounding the transition from industrious amateurism to professional artistry.

*Kyriaki Hadjiafxendi is Senior Lecturer at Bath Spa University, UK, and Patricia Zakreski is Lecturer at the University of Exeter, UK.*

*For my dad*
*whose τέχνη has helped make*
*artistry and industry a principle in my life*

*(Κυριακή Χριστάκη Χατζηαυξέντη)*

*For Joe*
*whose patience and support*
*has helped this professional woman thrive*

*(Patricia Zakreski)*

# Crafting the Woman Professional in the Long Nineteenth Century

## Artistry and Industry in Britain

---

Edited by
Kyriaki Hadjiafxendi and Patricia Zakreski

---

ASHGATE

Published by
Ashgate Publishing Limited
Wey Court East
Union Road
Farnham
Surrey, GU9 7PT
England

Ashgate Publishing Company
110 Cherry Street
Suite 3-1
Burlington, VT 05401-3818
USA

www.ashgate.com

**British Library Cataloguing in Publication Data**
A catalogue record for this book is available from the British Library

**The Library of Congress has cataloged the printed edition as follows:**
Crafting the woman professional in the long nineteenth century-artistry and industry in Britain / edited by Kyriaki Hadjiafxendi and Patricia Zakreski.
pages cm
Includes bibliographical references and index.
ISBN 978-1-4724-0896-9 (hardcover) -- ISBN 978-1-4724-0897-6 (ebook) -- ISBN 978-1-4724-0898-3 (epub) 1. Middle class women--Employment--Great Britain--History--19th century. 2. Handicraft--Great Britain--History--19th century. I. Hadjiafxendi, Kyriaki, 1976- II. Zakreski, Patricia.
HQ1597.C753 2013
305.48'22094109034--dc23

2013003636

ISBN 9781472408969 (hbk)
ISBN 9781472408976 (ebk – PDF)
ISBN 9781472408983 (ebk – ePub)

MIX
Paper from responsible sources
FSC www.fsc.org FSC® C013985

Printed in the United Kingdom by Henry Ling Limited, at the Dorset Press, Dorchester, DT1 1HD

# Contents

## PART II: THE ARTISTIC CAREER



## PART III: THE CRAFT OF SELF-FASHIONING

# List of Illustrations

## About the Contributors

ANNE ANDERSON is an international speaker, broadcaster and writer. She was Senior Lecturer in the History of Art and Design at Southampton Solent University for 14 years. She has authored many academic papers in leading journals and contributed papers to *Rethinking the Interior c.1867–1896: Aestheticism and the Arts and Crafts* (Ashgate 2010) and *Fashion, Interior Design and the Contours of Modern Identity* (Ashgate 2010). As exhibition curator at Southampton City Art Gallery, she toured two national exhibitions: *Ancient Landscapes, Pastoral Visions* (2008) and *The Truth about Faeries* (2009–11). In 2010 Anne worked on *Closer to Home*, the reopening exhibition at Leighton House Museum, South Kensington.

ALICE BARNABY is Lecturer in English Literature at the University of Bedfordshire. Her publications include *Light Touches: Cultural Practices of Illumination, London 1800–1900* (Routledge forthcoming 2015), 'Surface Recognition: Light and Surface in Drawing Rooms, 1800–1850' in *Surface Tensions: Surface, Finish and the Meanings of Objects* (Manchester University Press 2013) and 'Top-lighting in Exhibition Spaces: 1780–1860' in *Museum Media: The Handbook of Museum Studies* (Blackwell 2013).

CATHERINE FLOOD is Prints Curator in the Word and Image Department at the Victoria and Albert Museum where she specialises in graphics, posters and ephemeral print. She is the author of *British Posters: Advertising, Art and Activism* (V&A Publishing 2012) and has also published on London Transport posters and aspects of nineteenth-century print culture. She has curated exhibitions and displays on propaganda posters, Victorian sentimentality and fashion satire. She is currently working on a number of projects concerning protest graphics and activist objects.

KYRIAKI HADJIAFXENDI is Senior Lecturer in English Literature at Bath Spa University. Her publications include *Authorship in Context: From the Theoretical to the Material* (Palgrave 2007), *'What is a Woman to Do?' A Reader on Women, Work and Art, c.1830–1890* (Peter Lang 2011) and, as guest editor, a special issue of *George Eliot-George Henry Lewes Studies* on The Cultural Place of George Eliot's Poetry (2011). She is currently working towards completing her monograph on George Eliot, the literary market-place and sympathy and has recently embarked on a new book-length project on women, cultural exchange and Europe in the nineteenth century.

ANDREW KING is Professor of English Literature and Literary Studies at the University of Greenwich. His publications – including several essays on Ouida, a critical edition of her novel *The Massarenes* (Pickering & Chatto 2011) and a monograph on *The London Journal 1845–1883* (Ashgate 2004) – ask readers to reconsider the marginal: mainly neglected but once culturally significant Victorian periodicals and popular women's writing. He is currently co-editing *The Ashgate Research Companion to Nineteenth-Century British Periodicals* and writing a monograph on Ouida.

ELIZABETH MORGAN is Assistant Professor of Music at Saint Joseph's University in Philadelphia, where she teaches courses in music history and piano performance. Her research interests include keyboard and chamber music of the late eighteenth and early nineteenth centuries, music and the body, virtuosity, and music and gender. She completed a Doctor of Musical Arts degree in piano concurrently with her PhD in music history at UCLA, where she wrote a dissertation on amateur women pianists in late Georgian-era England. As a pianist, Elizabeth has performed throughout the US, as well as abroad; she is best known for her recital programme of keyboard works related to Jane Austen, which she has performed at venues internationally. She recently published an article entitled 'The Accompanied Sonata and the Domestic Novel in Britain at the Turn of the Nineteenth Century' in *19th-Century Music*.

PAMELA GERRISH NUNN, independent scholar and Adjunct Professor at the University of Adelaide, specialises in the histories of women artists of the nineteenth and early twentieth centuries. She has published widely in this field since 1978. She has curated the work of women artists between 1850 and 1930 for venues including Manchester City Art Gallery, Tate Britain and the Lady Lever Art Gallery. Her most recent publication is *A Pre-Raphaelite Journey: the Art of Eleanor Fortescue-Brickdale* (Liverpool University Press 2012).

LINDA H. PETERSON is Niel Gray, Jr. Professor of English at Yale University and author, most recently, of *Becoming a Woman of Letters: Myths of Authorship and Facts of the Victorian Market* (Princeton University Press 2009). She has also published articles and monographs on life writing, including *Victorian*

*Autobiography* (Yale University Press 1986) and *Traditions of Victorian Women's Autobiography* (University of Virginia Press 1999), and edited *The Autobiography and Letters of Margaret Oliphant* (Pickering & Chatto 2012), *Harriet Martineau's Autobiography* (Broadview 2007) and *The Life of Charlotte Brontë* by Elizabeth Gaskell (Pickering & Chatto 2006).

John Plunkett is Associate Professor in the Department of English at the University of Exeter. He is the author of *Queen Victoria – First Media Monarch* (Oxford University Press 2003), and editor of *Victorian Print Media: A Reader,* with Andrew King (Oxford University Press 2005), *Palgrave Sourcebook to Victorian Literature,* with Ana Parejo Vadillo et al. (Palgrave 2011) and *Popular Exhibitions, Science and Showmanship,* with Joe Kember and Jill Sullivan (Pickering & Chatto 2012). He is working on a book on popular visual and optical exhibitions 1820–1914, covering the exhibitions of panoramas, dioramas, magic lanterns and other optical devices.

Valerie Sanders is Professor of English and Director of the Graduate School at the University of Hull. Her most recent publications include *The Tragi-Comedy of Victorian Fatherhood* (Cambridge University Press 2009), *The Brother–Sister Culture in Nineteenth-Century Literature* (Palgrave 2002), three edited volumes of the ongoing *Selected Works of Margaret Oliphant* (Pickering & Chatto 2011–13) and articles and book chapters on fatherhood in Charles Dickens, George Eliot and Charles Kingsley. She has recently completed a second volume of *Records of Girlhood, An Anthology of Nineteenth-Century Women's Childhoods* (Ashgate 2012).

Talia Schaffer is Professor of English at Queens College and the Graduate Center, City University of New York. Her books include *Novel Craft: Victorian Domestic Handicraft & Nineteenth-Century Fiction* (Oxford University Press 2011), *The Forgotten Female Aesthetes: Literary Culture in Late-Victorian England* (University of Virginia Press 2001), *Women and British Aestheticism,* with Kathy A. Psomiades (University of Virginia Press 1999), an edition of Lucas Malet's 1901 novel *The History of Sir Richard Calmady* (University of Birmingham Press 2004) and a reader, *Literature and Culture at the Fin de Siècle* (Longman 2007). She has published widely on late-Victorian non-canonical novels, women's writing and material culture.

Ana Parejo Vadillo is Senior Lecturer in Victorian Literature and Culture at Birkbeck, University of London. Her publications include *Women Poets and Urban Aestheticism: Passengers of Modernity* (Palgrave 2005), *Michael Field, The Poet: Published and Manuscript Materials,* with Marion Thain (Broadview 2009) and *Victorian Literature: A Sourcebook,* with John Plunkett et al. (Palgrave 2012). She is also co-editor of the special issues on Literary Culture and Women

Poets for *Journal of Victorian Literature and Culture* (2006) (with Marion Thain) and Science, Literature and the Darwin Legacy for *19: Interdisciplinary Studies in the Long Nineteenth Century* (2010) (with Carolyn Burdett and Paul White).

PATRICIA ZAKRESKI is Lecturer in Victorian Literature and Culture at the University of Exeter. She is the author of *Representing Female Artistic Labour, 1848–1890: Refining Work for the Middle-Class Woman* (Ashgate 2006). She is co-editor, with Kyriaki Hadjiafxendi, of *'What is a Woman to Do?' A Reader on Women, Work and Art, c.1830–1890* (Peter Lang 2011). Her current project includes articles and a monograph on nineteenth-century design, the decorative arts and women's writing.

# Acknowledgements

There are many people we would like to thank who helped in the preparation of this volume but chief among them are our contributors, who provided us with such excellent material to work with, and our editor at Ashgate, Ann Donahue, for showing great patience with us as we brought it all together. Our very special thanks go to Karen Edwards, Regenia Gagnier, Joe Kember and John Plunkett for their unwavering support and encouragement that exceeded the conceptual advancement of this project. We are also grateful to our many colleagues and friends who have acted as careful and insightful readers; among those who have sustained our efforts in crafting this volume are Patrizia di Bello, Katie Halsey, Michael Kramp, Kate Newey, Pamela Gerrish Nunn, Adeline Johns-Putra, Vike Plock, Valerie Sanders, Susan Wolfson and Susan Zlotnick.

This volume was enriched by a conference held at the University of Exeter in 2008, under the auspices of the Centre of Victorian Studies, with the title *Artistry and Industry: Representations of Creative Labour in Literature and the Visual Arts c.1830–1900*. We would like to thank our conference co-organisers, Sunie Fletcher and Sally-Anne Huxtable, and all the delegates who contributed to what was an inspiring event, sponsored by the British Association of Victorian Studies and the Bristol Institute for Research in the Humanities and Arts. We would also like to thank the University of Exeter for providing us with an editorial assistant, Charlotte Campton, and Bath Spa University for clearing copyright permissions and reproduction rights on our behalf. Finally, we would like to thank Oxford University Press for permission to reproduce Talia Schaffer's chapter which is a revised extract of Chapter 1 of her recent monograph *Novel Craft: Victorian Domestic Handicraft & Nineteenth-Century Fiction* (2011).

# Foreword

*Linda H. Peterson*

The scholarly narrative of nineteenth-century women artists and authors has tended to emphasise their struggle for professional status and their increasing success in the fields of art, music, literature, journalism and publishing. *Crafting the Woman Professional* complicates this narrative by exploring the boundary between the amateur and the professional, revealing how fluid it often was and how it shifted during the course of the century. Contributors highlight the cultural values associated with amateurism in the arts, the desires of some (though not all) women to assert their professionalism and the strategies of self-education and self-presentation that they enacted to succeed. What emerges is a more nuanced account of the rise of the woman artist from 1790 to 1910, and a challenge to future scholars to consider the choices that individual women made in relation to professionalisation in their fields.

Two decades ago, when art historian Susan Casteras and I mounted an exhibition of the work of Victorian women artists and authors, our emphasis fell on the obstacles they confronted. As the catalogue title, *A Struggle for Fame,* attests, we highlighted women who 'against considerable odds, created many cultural levels and varieties of art – high, medium, and low' and whose work 'clearly affirms the existence of an important female tradition of making art that flourished in England, despite formidable obstacles' (9).[1] Today, this broad narrative requires more historical specification with attention to opportunities as well as obstacles. As several contributors suggest, especially Pamela Nunn in 'Dorothy's Career and Other Cautionary Tales', social resistance to women artists continued throughout the century, despite the known facts of their achievement in commercial and high art. Even so, the opportunities for women artists varied significantly from field to field, as did their artistic self-conceptions and career choices. In Chapter 4, 'Dresses and Drapery: Female Self-Fashioning in Muslin, 1800–1850', Alice Barnaby shows, for example, that in interior decoration, the amateur artist was highly valued in the early decades of the century and was indistinguishable from the professional – given that professional design emerged as a female (or male) activity only in the 1870s: 'amateurism had not yet come to denote a lack of quality, but rather a plenitude of it in the possession and expression of personal, polite accomplishments'. In arts such as china painting, the line between amateur and professional continued to be fluid throughout the century – as Anne Anderson documents in Chapter 6, 'The China Painter: Amateur Celebrities and Professional Stars at Howell and James's "Royal Academy of China Painting"'.

This collection reminds us, then, of the continuing need to situate research on women artists and authors historically, and of the original insights that emerge in so doing. Betty Schellenberg's study, *The Professionalization of Women Writers in Eighteenth-Century Britain*, emphasised the various approaches that women of the prior century took in their literary careers, arguing that women constructed their authorial identities self-consciously and diversely (76–7, 97). This collection affirms similar principles and practices for the nineteenth century. In the heyday of 'separate spheres', women often justified their movement into professional territory as an extension of their work within the domestic sphere.[2] Later, with the rise of the middle-class professions and the proliferation of professional institutions, women turned to other status markers, including formal education and elite training, financial reward and commercial success, and membership in professional groups such as the Society of Authors or the Royal Academy. As Catherine Flood demonstrates in Chapter 5, 'Contrary to the Habits of Their Sex? Women Drawing on Wood and the Careers of Florence and Adelaide Claxton', women artists could establish their professionalism as illustrators by perfecting the skill of drawing and cutting on woodblocks. Women designers learned not only the principles of industrial design in newly established schools of practical art, but also gained essential experience in the commercial workplace. Reflecting trends in the workaday world, mid-century fiction writers, as Patricia Zakreski suggests in Chapter 7, 'Creative Industry: Design, Art Education and the Woman Professional', celebrated women artists' professional progress (perhaps over-optimistically) and projected 'a parable of female development that place[d] design and paid labour at the centre of woman's moral and social progression'.

As the markers of professionalism changed, so too did women's public self-presentations in print and in society. In the 1830s, *Fraser's Magazine* ran a series of portraits, visual and verbal, of prominent women authors, showing them in domestic settings, praising their feminine virtues and chastising those who deviated from the norm. By the mid to late century, women had learned the importance of controlling their public portraits – a key insight of Part III, 'The Craft of Self-Fashioning'. In Chapter 12, 'Living Art: Michael Field, Aestheticism and Dress', Ana Parejo Vadillo shows how the poets

'Michael Field' (Katherine Bradley and Edith Cooper) used 'aesthetic' dress to express their oppositional stance to mass culture and crass professionalism and, more broadly, to enact their belief that dress 'was essential to achieve the aesthetes' aim of bringing art to every aspect of life'. Kyriaki Hadjiafxendi demonstrates in Chapter 9, 'Negotiating Fame: Mid-Victorian Women Writers and the Romantic Myth of the Gentlemanly Reviewer' that George Eliot and Mary Elizabeth Braddon invoked the 'gentlemanly' reviewers of the 1820s and 1830s to shape their authorial practice and to deploy an affective discourse that helped them negotiate distasteful aspects of literary celebrity. Yet these two women authors did so for quite different purposes: Eliot to encourage sympathy with characters rather than intimacy with herself, Braddon to perform a 'gentlemanliness' lacking in the male reviewers who criticised her sensation fiction. Eliot thus presented herself as a highbrow author resistant to a publicity-hungry culture, whereas Braddon used nostalgia to protest a gendered literary field that devalued her work. Interestingly, by invoking the 'gentlemanly' values of the past, Eliot and Braddon were de facto praising the pre- or semi-professional writers who wrote from intellectual interest more than for financial gain, even as they crafted models of modern, professional authorship that they wished to embody.

This collection reminds us, finally, that women's professionalism in the arts emerged alongside that of men's – as a broad trend within the nineteenth century that professionalised the fields of art and literature. As Julie Codell has argued in *The Victorian Artist*, male artists used a wide range of auto/biographical genres – including celebrity interviews, mini-biographies in periodicals, and entries in biographical dictionaries and histories of art – to distinguish themselves from less desirable artistic stereotypes (the failed Romantic genius, the bohemian, the degenerate) and to achieve parity with other middle-class professions like law and medicine. If, unfortunately, some men expressed their desire for professional status by denigrating women artists as amateurs, this aspect of the cultural field was only that – one small aspect of a much larger picture. *Crafting the Woman Professional* reveals that women artists were equally savvy in their use of interviews, mini-biographies and other auto/biographical genres for professional ends. The collection underscores the various ways in which the discourses of amateurism and professionalism were engaged by nineteenth-century women to conceptualise their work and to achieve the recognition that they individually and collectively desired.

## Works Cited

Casteras, Susan P., and Linda H. Peterson, eds. *A Struggle for Fame: Victorian Women Artists and Authors*. New Haven: Yale Center for British Art, 1994.

Codell, Julie F. *The Victorian Artist: Artists' Lifewritings in Britain, ca. 1870–1910*. Cambridge: Cambridge University Press, 2003.

Peterson, Linda H. *Becoming a Woman of Letters: Myths of Authorship and Facts of the Victorian Market*. Princeton: Princeton University Press, 2009.

Schellenberg, Betty A. *The Professionalization of Women Writers in Eighteenth-Century Britain.* Cambridge: Cambridge University Press, 2005.

## Notes

1 We took the title of the catalogue from Charlotte Riddell's novel, *A Struggle for Fame* (Richard Bentley & Son 1883).

2 For a discussion of this rationale in the literary realm, see Peterson 13–49.

# Introduction: Artistry and Industry – The Process of Female Professionalisation

*Kyriaki Hadjiafxendi and Patricia Zakreski*

> Here are women demanding of us employment whereby they may earn their livelihood: what shall we give them to do? … Art is the profession in which, more than all others, women may be expected to excel. (Purnell 107–8)

According to Thomas Purnell, artistic professions were the answer to one of the most pressing problems of the Woman Question. What kind of paid work could be done by middle-class women who needed to, or wanted to earn a living? The essays in this volume analyse the range of art work taken up by women in the long nineteenth century. Middle-class women continued in large numbers to populate traditionally feminine occupations such as teaching and nursing, yet they became increasingly aware of the opportunities for remunerative work with the expansion of the literary market-place and related 'art industries' (a specific term coined for a variety of manufactories such as textiles, pottery, engraving and metalwork, which combined artistic principles with the creation of consumer goods). *Crafting the Woman Professional* details the ways in which the aesthetics, practices and economics of creative labour shaped women's employment and self-expression and, in so doing, their subjectivities. The various types of art work undertaken are an index to the changing perception of what constituted women's proper activity; moreover, this collection argues that the constructed and contested nature of the female artistic professional was a notable aspect of debates about aesthetic value and the impact of industrial technologies.

Traditionally, the professions were limited to the masculine preserves of medicine, the church and the law which, according to Jennifer Ruth, 'drew on both the gentry and the upper middle classes but did not produce men who clearly identified themselves as a distinct class' (3). As the nineteenth century progressed, however, the number, type and perceived importance of professionals increased markedly and, thanks to the campaign for women's rights, became more inclusive to women who were no longer satisfied with pursuing their artistic occupations as enthusiastic amateurs. In 1857, Dinah Mulock Craik defined the art professions accessible to women as literature, painting, art or 'the vocation of public entertainment – including actresses, singers, musicians, and the like' (42). Craik's distinction was far from neutral in that it typified the way in which female artistic professions distinguished themselves from the rich tradition of domestic handicrafts, even as they emerged out of it. Indeed, the relationship between amateur and professional became something of an over-determined proxy for a range of debates concerning not only women's role but also the relationship between aesthetics and economics, artistry and industry.

*Crafting the Woman Professional* focuses on female employment in the creative arts rather than professionalism per se. Fields of labour connected to the arts were offered as a means of resolving the tension between domesticity, work and respectability, which challenged the middle-class feminine ideal within a commercial society increasingly organised around market relations. However, the extent to which women could be considered professionals remained a contested issue up until the end of the century. As Louisa Starr told the International Council of Women in 1899, 'when a woman has a profession, it means in most cases that she has two professions' (quoted in Cherry 33). This volume seeks to build on this insight so as to fashion a more nuanced picture of women's professional development in the creative arts than that current in Victorian scholarship. Amateur and professional; art, handicraft and industry; creativity and mass production; aesthetic and remunerative value – all existed in overlapping yet dialectical relationships, and this collection explores the interconnectedness of these paradigms. Its chronological scope is 1790–1910, beginning with the way a nascent leisure industry promoted creative accomplishments for genteel women and ending with the formalisation of women's professional engagement in a variety of artistic occupations.

W.J. Reader has claimed that 'The professions as we know them are very much a Victorian creation' (2). However, the volume's extended view across the long nineteenth century is key to our attempt to develop an understanding of how debates about female creativity and professionalisation were defined by the changing relationship between artistry and industry. Drawing on recent work on the literary professional (see Fergus; Prescott; Schellenberg; Siskin), this collection aims to nudge the discussion of the 'rise' of female professionalism from the 1830s back to the late eighteenth century, when industrious amateurs did not regard their artistic work merely as genteel accomplishments but as productions through which they could achieve a status akin to professional recognition. Of particular relevance here is

Betty Schellenberg's sociological study of female authorship, which charts how eighteenth-century female writers achieved not only respectable incomes but also professional authorial identities. In addition to their remuneration, commitment to their work and literary associations, their professionalism also involved 'structural and institutional aspects' such as 'critical reviews and the Royal Literary Fund', as well as the professional's claims to offer a specialized set of skills to meet a defined need of society at large, and to be deserving of certain status and economic rewards as a result' (13).

Whereas there is extensive scholarly work on women's involvement in authorship (see Batchelor; Labbe; Peterson; Turner), painting (see Bermingham; Nunn), music (see Hall-Witt; Weliver) or performance (see Davis; Gale; Marshall; Powell), as well as other working- or lower middle-class identified occupations such as needlework and shopkeeping (see Boos; Cluckie; Harris; Sanders; Young), it is only recently that the growth of the art industries and their prominent role in the professional advancement of middle-class women has received significant critical attention (see Elliott and Helland; Zakreski). *Crafting the Woman Professional* responds to Linda Peterson's call for a more comprehensive examination of the changing discourses of professionalism in regards to authorship by extending it to these related art industries. It is the contention of this volume that the process of 'becoming', which, according to Peterson, highlights the indeterminate and insecure professional status of women of letters, is more widely applicable. What it meant to be professional was a slippery and tantalising rhetoric and the subject of much debate in the nineteenth-century periodical press. Examining women's specific engagements with material culture and the strategies and techniques they used, this collection as a whole maps how they crafted artefacts, themselves and the world around them. We have chosen the term 'crafting' for two reasons. Firstly, this collection emphasises professionalism's historical debts to handicraft and amateurism. While the figure of the female amateur is often posited as the precursor to the woman professional, this volume offers up a series of essays that detail the intertwined development of these two categories. Secondly, the term crafting avoids implying that a stable notion of the professional woman artist ever appeared fully formed. Instead, what this volume traces is the state of being in process, 'of always seeking yet never quite achieving secure professional status' (Peterson 9).

Crafting is a constructive activity, one which involves the skilled organisation of varied components into an ordered, expressive whole. In part, this notion of crafting therefore depended strongly upon notions of female management, drawn largely from models of middle-class domestic arrangement in which women were routinely regarded, according to Elizabeth Langland, as the organising power that introduced harmony to a scattered assemblage of financial and household components. Also, crafting suggests something in excess of such organisational skills, which meant that the assembly of these various components could also become an act of transformation, elevating them from the status of the mundane or the patchwork to become more than the sum of their parts. Women's creative faculty, expressed through crafting, therefore took hold of the very material of the everyday to create objects without the immediate invocation of spirit or genius and thereby granted women a unique ability to combine art and commonplace life.

The originality of this collection is, we hope, two-fold; firstly, its essays demonstrate the range of women's engagement with the creative industries, ranging from different forms of craftwork, handicraft practices and music making to engraving, pattern design and literary production. What this range reveals are both the specificities and similarities in the way that female artistry was conceptualised and executed, and the role that it played in the overall emergence of female professionalism as it was increasingly taken up and pursued as an industry. Moreover, even where female industriousness went into handicrafts or other suitable genteel accomplishments – often in ways that marked an implicit rejection or appropriation of commodity culture and delineated a sphere outside that of paid labour – the artistry involved often required replicating professional techniques or using artefacts produced by an embryonic leisure industry devoted to filling women's spare time.

Art and industry had been constructed as opposing terms within eighteenth-century aesthetics, and the faultline between them continued to run deep in nineteenth-century culture. At one level, the dominance exerted by the industrial revolution continued to make them divisive rather than complementary. As Gustave Planche put it in 'La journée d'un journaliste' (1832), 'par une singulière application de la théorie d'Adam Smith sur la division du travail, il y a aujourd'hui deux parts bien distinctes dans la littérature, l'art et l'industrie' (149).[1] Many other examples could be given of how this antagonism fed into broader oppositions and debates about the impact of industrialisation. In Elizabeth Gaskell's *North and South* (1855), for example, Margaret and Thornton embody not only work versus leisure, aesthetics versus industry, past versus present but also the conflict between genders and regions, as exemplified by the comments of Thornton's mother in Chapter 15:

> 'I have no doubt the classics are very desirable for people who have leisure. But, I confess, it was against my judgment that my son renewed his study of them. The time and place in which he lives, seem to me to require all his energy and attention. Classics may do very well for men who loiter away their lives in the country or in colleges; but Milton men ought to have their thoughts and powers absorbed in the work of to-day. ...' (113)

Although artistry and industry were often seen as opposing discourses, attempts to overcome this opposition and unite them are nonetheless evident throughout the nineteenth century. Perhaps paradoxically, concerns about the place of Britain's manufacturers in the growing global trade market were one of the reasons why such a separation was questioned. As early as 1836, the Report of the Select Committee on Arts and Manufacturers argued for a greater linking of art and industry:

> [For] a peculiarly manufacturing nation [like Britain], the connexion between art and manufactures is most important ... since it is admitted that the cultivation of the more exalted branches of design tends to advance the humblest pursuits of industry, while the connexion of art with manufacture has often developed the genius of the greatest masters in design. (iii)

By applying artistic principles to the design and ornamentation of industrially manufactured goods, the desirability of the items produced could be improved. The Select Committee Report was keen to stress how industry could aid the development of genius through the increased opportunities for training in connoisseurship and craft production that would be afforded by governmental investment in a system of art schools throughout the country. In the light of these debates, *Crafting the Woman Professional* asks: what were the specific opportunities and constraints that the convergence of art and industry offered to women?

This volume joins a number of key studies that have recently begun to uncover the variety of contexts in which the convergence between artistry and industry was promoted rather than denied over the course of the century (see Kriegel; Pergam). Of course, women were not alone in working in the creative art industries, and a comparable analysis that concentrates on masculinity can be found in Tim Barringer's *Men at Work*. Nonetheless, what marks out the essays in this volume is the way female creative labour, which occupied a 'paradoxical position inside and outside the market – at once complicit and transcendent' (Ruth 22), interacted in a distinct way with the similarly liminal discourses of artistry and industry. Whether this was work in translation (see Scholl), print media and journalism (see Demoor; Easley; Gray; Liddle; Waters), or interior design (see Ferry; Lees-Maffei), it was participation in the public economic world that empowered women to claim for themselves a professional identity.

As Clare Pettitt has shown, claims for the superiority of work created through the combination of artistry and industry were drawn into debates about the purpose and value of literature in order to aver a professional status for authorship. In his seminal article on literature as a profession, 'The Condition of Authors in England, Germany, and France' (1847), George Henry Lewes declared that 'Talent commands a price; industry is not unrewarded' (292). Building on this maxim, Charles Dickens, alongside others such as Augustus Egg and Edward Bulwer Lytton, further stressed this connection between artistry and industry by their creation of the Guild of Literature and Art, which sought to provide pensions and annuities to writers and artists no longer able to support themselves. The broader growth of institutions, societies and guilds was key to the creation of professional identities and status; women benefited from bodies such as the Society of Women Artists (founded 1855) and the Society of Women Writers and Journalists (founded 1894). According to Harold Perkin, such structures are organised 'around career hierarchies rather than classes; a professional society is one in which people find their place according to trained expertise and the service they provide rather than the possession or lack of inherited wealth or acquired capital' (359). As well as societies, these structures included the Schools of Design, the Department of Science and Art, and the South Kensington Museum, the creation of which was funded by the proceeds of the Great Exhibition; all of which contributed to the professional recognition of their members by affirming their status, controlling their fees and protecting their labour.

The question of how art could be aided by industry, however, was contested throughout the century because of the vexed focus on the corrupting influence of the market-place on artistic beauty and taste. While the status of the relationship of use value to beauty fluctuated over the course of the century, the long-running, cultural project to reconcile artistry and industry continued even when aesthetic discourses began to reject mid-Victorian conceptions of art's moral and social purpose. In his 1878 chapter on 'Industrial Art' for *Great Industries of Great Britain*, the writer, painter and actor John Forbes-Robertson argued that the greatest achievements for the artist were to be found in the art industries: 'A thing of beauty may have no immediate practical use, a thing of use no appreciable beauty; but in their union the creative genius of man finds its highest and divinest expression' (21).

The connection between artistry and industry, as Pettitt claims, was ultimately a thorny one for the male author, one which 'risked dismantling the construction of "transcendent" literary value' associated with notions of genius and the Romantic image of the writer (158). However, for female authors the story was different: 'While it was difficult for women to appropriate androcentric Romantic male models of creativity, ... some women writers [were] less anxious about participation in the marketplace than their male counterparts' (Pettitt 28). Pettitt draws specifically on the legal principle of coverture, in which a married woman and all her possessions were legally defined as the property of her husband, as one of the reasons why women artists were less affected by their participation in the market-place (28). For male authors, the relationship between artistry and industry threatened to alienate them from their creative work as they sold the product of their genius for profit. But within the legal and ideological structures of mid-Victorian gender politics, women were already alienated from the products of their labour and therefore did not experience the alienating effects of capitalism in the same way as their male counterparts (a situation brought to the fore in the case of Caroline Norton, who, after separating from her abusive husband in 1836, found that he also claimed her earnings from her writings as his own). In fact, as the essays in this collection make evident, arguments for the compatibility of artistry and industry, though sometimes made in somewhat oblique ways, were particularly profitable for the professional advancement of women in the long nineteenth century. Discussing the problems of the older systems of art tuition for the female artist which limited training in art to a small number of those who could afford private tuition, John Cordy Jeaffreson elaborated on how women benefited from the opening of the schools of art, which, subsidised by public monies, offered affordable education from the 1830s onwards. As Jeaffreson argues:

> [W]oman's position in art may have been less favourable than some of her less generous censors imagine. Is it clear that the studios and best art teachers have been no less accessible to her than her masculine competitors? … it cannot be maintained that the girls of past generations had the same facilities as young men for procuring artistic instruction (30).

By the 1860s suitable employment for women acquired new meanings in that it was extended to involve not only profitability and usefulness but also the possibility of professional development. Many periodical articles such as 'Lithographic Employment for Women' (1864) or 'Photography as an Employment for Women' (1867) argued for the importance of proper training so that feminine accomplishments could be developed into professions. 'If she had been properly taught', as the *Englishwoman's Review* claims, 'she might have established a business for herself, and so have supported her children, but during that long time she had learned only to "touch" and mount, for which but little remuneration is given' ('Photography' 220).

Such training would not only convince women of their powers and familiarise them with all the branches of the profession, but, more importantly, it would rescue them from the drudgery of unskilled labour. According to an article 'What Is There I Can Do?' in the *Woman's Gazette*, 'The best definition of skilled labour is, perhaps, that it is work which either requires some education and intelligence in the worker, or is the result of long and careful training' (99). Women's transformation into skilled labourers defined the value of their work which was both monetary and symbolic. While skilled women earned less than most unskilled male labourers (Alexander 20), the symbolic capital that their work carried was maintained

> by the aesthetic knowledge attached to art and to the institutions developed to train artists and educate the public about art. … Industrial or commercial art was, therefore, a way for women to enter the marketplace as autonomous laborers and still have socially meaningful, well-paid work. (Masten 5–6)

Repeated arguments for the compatibility of artistry and industry encouraged a shift in the character of the debates around the Woman Question: the focus turned towards the opportunities that the expansion of the literary marketplace and the development of the art industries offered; their impact was not limited to the benefits they conferred on those women who became creative practitioners. As Antonia Losano has noted, while a number of studies explore how female artists' subjectivities were influenced by discourses of aesthetics, fewer 'consider the impact of gender on the changing aesthetic theories of the period' (19).

The construction of a specific type of female artistry could be a means of mediating between the competing demands of genius and the market. In his article describing the importance and good work of the Female School of Design, for instance, Thomas Purnell attempted to mitigate the conflict between the differing values of artistry and industry by appealing to the concomitant discourses of femininity and sympathy. For Purnell, art was a profession in which women could be expected to excel because of 'their quick perception of the laws of harmony and contrast of colour, their fineness of hand, their powers of arrangement, and their natural good taste' (108). Purnell describes a genteel conception of artistic production, one that usefully combines the remunerative with the respectable. Such a conception works very well to promote the art industries as suitable employment for women, but it also works to reorient the popular perception of what art is and how it should be produced. Purnell's general conception of art encompasses a feminised notion of creative activity, as it substitutes industry for inspiration and cultivation for a redefined notion of genius inclusive to women. The qualities that are seen to make the good artist are synonymous with the supposedly 'natural' feminine capabilities of harmony, delicacy, taste and management. In demanding sympathy for the woman forced by necessity to earn a livelihood through art work, Purnell extends this protection to all artistry which is also industry:

> We shall be suspected of no disrespect to Art by confessing ourselves to be not of those who are disposed to consider it as something sacred – as a holy of holies, to be approached only by the sanctified, and those who come with fear and trembling. In Art, no less than in Music and Poetry, the most successful cultivators have not been ashamed to make a purveyor of their profession … Surely we have advanced argument sufficient to arouse sympathy with the object we desire to promote: it is in this case, less the advancement of Art, – though we would advocate it also on specific grounds, – than the useful and honourable employment of those who are unhappily compelled to labour in order that they may live … (108)

For male artists, who in theory could do any kind of work in order to earn money, the choice to use their creative ability to earn money rather than to advance art could be seen as more suspect. But for women, whose choices for respectable employment were limited, there was also more freedom. Within the discourse of female creativity there was room for both ideas of genius and the market. Rather than being in opposition to female artistry, money was often seen as the spur, the motive that could overcome women's natural resistance to public and remunerative work and bring to light hidden or undeveloped talents. What could have languished in the obscurity of accomplishment, amateurism or handicraft could, through necessity, be made into the professional.

*Crafting the Woman Professional* is divided into three parts that reflect key conceptual issues while providing a genealogy of the process of female professionalisation in the literary market-place and related art industries. Part I focuses on different types of industrious amateurism – varying from window transparencies and music making to practices of interior design – in the period 1790–1850 in an attempt to recover the submerged role of amateurism in the history of female professionalism. Part II focuses on the development of the artistic career which emerged from the growing distinction between professional craft and amateur handicraft in the second half of the nineteenth century. Part III examines the self-fashioning strategies of individual Victorian women as they negotiated the complex relationship between art, professional recognition, respectability, fame and notoriety.

**Part I: Industrious Amateurism**

The tradition of female education in the accomplishments constructed for feminine artistry a model of industrious amateurism. While women were encouraged to engage in a number of genteel and superficial pursuits ranging from sketching, singing and playing the piano to conversing, drawing and doing needlework, they were not expected to occupy themselves with these artistic activities on a professional basis. For a woman to be well-accomplished suggested that she would be a good wife, and through the exhibition of her accomplishments she could advertise herself as an eligible and desirable match. In the early part of the century, the list of what comprised these accomplishments is neatly summarised by Caroline Bingley in Jane Austen's *Pride and Prejudice* (1813), when she argues that:

> '... A woman must have a thorough knowledge of music, singing, drawing, dancing, and the modern languages, to deserve the word; and besides all this, she must possess a certain something in her air and manner of walking, the tone of her voice, her address and expressions, or the word will be but half deserved.' (39)

Although Caroline's definition of the accomplishments is an advance on her brother's ideas that to be accomplished means to 'paint tables, cover skreens, and net purses', her notion of 'thorough knowledge' still signifies a form of superficial learning, a point Austen drives home through Darcy's suggestion that 'she must yet add something more substantial, in the improvement of her mind by extensive reading' (Austen 38–9).

As Charles Bingley's list suggests, the accomplishments were often considered to be frivolous and decorative pursuits, the kinds of activities women engaged in so as to embellish their domestic spaces and occupy copious amounts of free time. With such a reputation, the accomplishments were often criticised as a waste of time and, more seriously, as instruments of female oppression. Sarah Lewis, in her moderate conduct manual, *Woman's Mission* (1839), condemned the accomplishments as a 'risible' and 'painful subject' (58) because, she argued, they train women's hands rather than their minds:

> Into the cultivation of the arts, disguised under the hackneyed name of accomplishments, does one particle of intellectuality creep? Would not many of their ablest professors and most intelligent practitioners stare, with unfeigned wonder, at the supposition, that the five hours per diem devoted to the piano and the easel, had any other object than to accomplish the fingers? The idea of their influencing the head would be ridiculous! of their improving the heart, preposterous! (59)

While masculine creative production, associated with the mind and the imagination, constructed the notion of artistic genius, the feminine came to be associated with the artisanal hand, the decorative, and the imitative arts.

The four essays in this part present a nuanced picture of education in the accomplishments by mapping the ways it brought together the fine arts with the burgeoning commerce of leisure, enabling, as Talia Schaffer argues, 'women to practise the same skills that the British economy was built on'. It seeks to deconstruct and challenge some of the critiques that were used by the mid-Victorians, whose own agenda led them to dismiss previous modes of amateurism, obscuring aspects of their richness. Perhaps the most famous of these critiques is by Elizabeth Barrett Browning, who mocks the pedagogical demands of industrious amateurism in the list of accomplishments that Aurora Leigh learns under the direction of her aunt:

> I learnt much music – …
> … – fine sleights of hand
> And unimagined fingering, shuffling off
> The hearer's soul through hurricanes of notes
> To a noisy Tophet; and I drew…costumes
> From French engravings, nereids neatly draped
> (With smirks of simmering godship) – I washed in
> Landscapes from nature (rather say, washed out). (I.415, 417–23)

Aurora suggests that her accomplishments, along with the rest of her feminine education, are frivolous and superficial – painting, drawing and music making join embroidered footstools and stuffed birds as the irritating and irrelevant product of women's work. In this description, Barrett Browning highlights how training in the accomplishments worked to regulate and contain femininity within the structures of the amateur and the domestic. Judgments such as Barrett Browning's and Lewis's have contributed to the conventional critical narrative of women's efforts to move from amateur to professional as one of struggle, in which the female amateur's route to professionalism is traced as a move from private to public spheres, from 'feminine' to 'masculine' artwork, and from leisure activities to the world of remunerative labour. In her study of women's participation in nineteenth-century print media, *First-Person Anonymous,* Alexis Easley, for instance, notes that it is her intention in the book to draw 'attention to the ways women were able to capitalize upon the conventions of journalistic and literary print media as a way of making their way in a male-dominated profession' (1). Such narratives of women making their way in male-dominated professions have been highly productive and have permitted a systematic critique of the discursive operations that constituted the gendering of the professions.

In casting the image of women's professional development in such terms, these narratives also reflect the terms some Victorian women themselves used when representing this progress to themselves. The women's rights campaigner Bessie Rayner Parkes employed such imagery in her 1865 *Essays on Woman's Work,* when she noted with optimism:

> One profession after another responds to the pressure from without, and opens its enclosure to the gentle demand. Sometimes the gates are slowly forced back with an almost imperceptible movement, at other times suddenly unclose, as when a Florence Nightingale or a Rosa Bonheur gives to society the result of long hidden labours, to posterity the echo of a hitherto unknown name. (118)

Traditionally histories of female artists, designers and writers in the nineteenth century trace narratives of increasing professionalisation; these tended, like Parkes's, to imagine professions in the nineteenth century as enclaves that exist outside the spheres in which women tend to move, as walls they need to breach or boundaries they need to cross (see Casteras and Peterson; Rose; Sebba). Metaphors of movement figure women as moving out of the domestic sphere and into the professions, pushing at gates that finally open and allow them to enter. This move towards professionalisation is seen as the result of a variety of economic and cultural factors, including the growth of print culture and the rise of the periodical press; the establishment of educational and vocational bodies such as female art schools and exhibiting societies; the advent of organisations like the Society of Women Writers and Journalists and changing notions of women's role in the public sphere and work.

Such narratives reflect the real expansion of professional opportunities and the widespread work of women in paid occupations in the second half of the century; yet, such a focus on the need for women to attain 'that recognised position which is necessary [...] to clear a new and beautiful field of labour for women' is often at the expense of notions of the domestic and the amateur (Parkes 126). A struggle for opportunity, after all, needs something to struggle against: a movement into one sphere means another sphere must be left behind. The chapters in this part work together to nuance this narrative, tracing the complex and surprising links between women's accomplishments and commercial enterprise.

While women's amateur artwork is shown to nurture and sustain the development of domestic ideology, the work of the amateur – for all its associations with secluded drawing rooms and the domestic ideal – also offered opportunities for women to develop and refine the skills that were needed to participate in commercial enterprises and the public world of work. The figure of the industrious amateur, which provided the paradigm within and against which to work out what professionalism meant, is defined, in Talia Schaffer's words, by 'this complex activity – marginalizing yet ubiquitous, modern yet historical, critiquing yet emulating the mainstream economy' (59). Schaffer's chapter in this part describes some of the contradictions between the language and practice of some mechanical and imitative handicrafts. Female handicrafts were seen as an extension of the woman herself, and hence as anti-commodities because of their status as private objects, yet their relationship to the consumer economy was far more complex. Schaffer's chapter shows how handicraft was driven by the Victorians' need to retain an alternative to mainstream capitalism, which would allow women to envision themselves as makers but within a domestic, amateur and leisure framework.

In 'Light Work: Leisure and the Making of Transparencies', John Plunkett continues Schaffer's exploration of the relationship between women's decorative handicrafts and the world of industrial production with his focus on one of the most popular artistic feminine accomplishments of the late eighteenth century. Focussing particularly on transparencies, paper-based designs meant to refract and diffuse light for aesthetic effect, Plunkett builds on Schaffer's reading of domestic handicraft as a privileged locus of realism because, as transparencies demonstrate, they could be the thing, not mere representations. He argues that what was important was not the value of the ephemeral end product, the transparency, but the artistic experimentation and freedom that recreation activities afforded women. Noting how women writers such as Jane Austen, Mary Howitt, Jane Carlyle and Elizabeth Barrett Browning wrote about transparencies, Plunkett suggests links between the creation of female artistic subjectivity and the transparencies' aesthetic effect of mediation and transformation.

Following from Plunkett's discussion of transparencies, Elizabeth Morgan draws on yet another feminine accomplishment as an embodied practice in order to suggest how women's training in this amateur work could lead to professional aptitude. While Plunkett details the way transparencies helped to shape the sensory environment of the drawing-room, Morgan similarly argues that the etude, a form of music developed in the early nineteenth century as a pedagogical tool for female amateurs, literally transformed women's bodies by developing their physical technique, training their fingers to play the complex forms and combinations that signified masculine virtuosity. Morgan links this notion of training with the rhetoric of conduct manuals to show the difference between women's education in the ideal and in practice. Arguing that, in practice, this education could encourage virtuosity, Morgan shows how women actively engaged with, and sometime subverted, the pedagogical tools put in place within the rhetoric of female conduct.

In the last chapter of Part I, Alice Barnaby details the opportunities for sensory knowledge that interior design offered by exploring the uses to which muslin was put. She argues that though muslin would seem to encapsulate the relationship between the feminine, the accomplishments and the domestic interior, the aesthetic and phenomenological properties of this material gave women a way to manage the introduction of the public sphere into the private domain and arrange their homes, bodies and identities for exhibition. Describing women's management of light in the domestic interior, Barnaby suggests a continuation between the work that individual women did in arranging and crafting muslin and the development of the profession of interior design in the second half of the nineteenth century when women entered the industry.

## Part II: The Artistic Career

Whereas the chapters in Part I examine how women's artistic occupations helped them to negotiate the boundaries of woman's sphere, Part II traces the development of the artistic career. The artistic legitimacy of the skilled handiwork practised by female designers and craftswomen was crucial to the developing notion of the professional. The tension between handicraft, which by the 1860s signified an older form of domestic femininity, and emerging professional structures is described by the historian Hannah Lawrance in 1870, who claims that women's professional artistic success relies on their active participation in the market-place:

> [I]n the two highest departments of intellectual exertion – literature and the arts – women occupy precisely the same position as men … Now, how have women obtained this proud vantage-ground? Solely by their own exertions. No society was ever formed to purchase copyrights of women's manuscripts, and then push them into the publishing market. No society was every formed to commission the painting of so many pictures by women at a remunerative price. Unassisted in either case, the authoress went simply into the book market, proffered her work, and received a certain sum, and the female artist placed her painting in some picture-gallery, and sold it to the highest bidder. And what has been the result? (47)

For Lawrance, art as a remunerative profession involves more than the production of manuscripts or paintings that can be then sold for profit. The standardisation of professional artistry included industry; that is, the institutions and practices of the economic sphere in which these commodities traded.

In Lawrance's formulation, not only did the professional woman artist have to earn money from her work, but she also needed to remain independent of the numerous structures put in place to mediate between the woman artist and the market-place in order to preserve her amateur status and protect her from the degradations of the economic sphere, even as she earned money for her work. These structures included the employment of a male relative to act as an intermediary between the woman artist and the public commercial world – a situation, favoured by novels with artist heroines such as Anne Brontë's *The Tenant of Wildfell Hall* (1848), which allowed the woman's work to enter the public sphere as a commodity while the woman herself remained in the private, separate from male economic transactions. Another structure which mystified women's relation to the market-place was the charity bazaar; its reputation for inflating the prices of inferior and trivial articles of fancy work for the benefit of reduced gentlewomen made it the source of much ridicule and not a venue for serious work (see Prochaska 49–51).

Charitable assistance and male mediation could be seen to undermine women's professional status by tying women's art to the ideologies of amateurism, leisure and the private sphere and its historical roots in conventional bourgeois training in the accomplishments. The chapters in this part provide examples of how women themselves engaged with the structures that defined artistry as professional such as education, exhibition and remuneration. Catherine Flood, for instance, examines the careers of Florence and Adelaide Claxton in order to trace how they forged a professional career in drawing on wood. Flood identifies the Claxton sisters as pioneers of women's professionalism in commercial illustration not only through their appropriation of masculine fields of work, but also through their willingness to adapt their work to take advantage of a range of commercial opportunities.

Anne Anderson's chapter focuses on Howell and James's 'Royal Academy of China Painting' in order to explore the role that public exhibition played in legitimating creative work as art. Anderson's chapter describes how part of the appeal for painting on china was its aura of uniqueness and womanly care for domestic decoration. China painting was akin to domestic handicrafts in that it enabled women to transform the products of industrial manufacture; but, unlike handicrafts which were produced primarily for domestic decoration, painting on china supported female participation in the public world of art exhibition and society. Although, as Anderson notes, the Howell and James exhibition was technically not for profit, the opportunity it gave women china painters to display their skill opened one route to professional recognition and success.

Whereas Flood and Anderson are case studies of the way art industries superseded handicraft values, Patricia Zakreski and Pamela Nunn explore the significance of education in women's professionalisation. According to Gaye Tuchman and Nina E. Fortin's sociological study of female authorship, between 1750 and 1865 only 15 per cent of women born before 1815 and 25 per cent of those born later experienced schooling outside the home. Given this fact, the *Women's Gazette* claimed in 'What Is There I Can Do?' that the question that arose was:

> [W]hether a Society claiming to be benevolent as well as commercial, should be satisfied with training its workers to mechanical perfection alone, and should not rather seek to give to every one of them the means of rising out of the category of mere mechanics into that of artists? (51)

Focussing on the art education developed for the national system of Schools of Design, Zakreski argues that the principles of pattern designing that were taught in the schools comprised a unique aesthetic that placed the relationship between artistry and industry at its heart.

According to Zakreski, these principles of design provided a useful framework for popular women writers who claimed for their fiction a form of artistic workmanship distinct from ideas of both amateur feminine writing and genius. By analysing the way that authorship drew on discourses of design, Zakreski describes how design was a vital locus for discussions of women's self-determination, professional mastery and social equality more generally. Pamela Nunn also explores the institutions of nineteenth century art education; she focuses on the Royal Academy Schools and the supposedly lynchpin year of 1894 in which the Academy granted life study to its female students. Noting how this institutional event is often read as a signifier of progress in feminist art history and the reification of the female art professional, Nunn argues that in fact the figure of the female amateur continued to hold a powerful place in the cultural imagination. Examining a number of late-century narratives, Nunn points out that while there was growing social and institutional acceptance of the professional female artist, the image of the female amateur was still being used to question the legitimacy of female artists entering the masculine domain of painting.

## Part III: The Craft of Self-Fashioning

In 1841, the British census recorded 278 women who self-identified as artists; in 1871, this figure had grown to 1,069. This history of women creating art and doing so professionally goes hand in hand with their changing relationship to the public sphere. One of the meanings of professionalism is the process through which the artist asks recognition for the public value of his/her work.

Our question is: how did the woman professional negotiate and perform the public identities she crafted? In her introduction to *Women in the Victorian Art World,* Clarissa Campbell Orr has argued that women's struggle for professional recognition was 'not just a question of being admitted to art schools or the Royal Academy, but of challenging the whole notion of what an artist was' (7). The third and final part of this collection sets out to explore how women's professional agency was formed through their exploration of art, form and lived experience. The production and consumption of gendered artistic personae is evident in their biographical construction in the periodical press, the spaces in which they exhibited as well as the discussions of art and aesthetics within their works.

The chapters in Part III are all case studies of individual artists, seeking to recover the complexities of their careers. They draw upon the recent scholarly revival in biographical and memory studies (see Junod; Margadant; Rigney). These studies make evident how the biographical converges with social, historical or formal approaches to the work of art. Karen Junod, for example, has pointed out that the ways in which Michel Foucault identified the author-function 'posits biography as instrumental in defining the "mode of existence" and "circulation", as well as the self-fashioning and positioning of artists within a specific field of art' (3). Similarly, Pierre Bourdieu's work, Junod continues, suggests 'that it is precisely this artificiality and malleability of the genre that make biography a crucial instrument in the construction of artists' reputations and promotion within a specific artistic field, because they allow writers to tailor their subject's talents and genius to the needs and expectations of the art markets' (3). Building on the theoretical insights of Bourdieu and Foucault, critics have detailed the profusion of Victorian artists' auto/biographies and demonstrated their importance in shaping the public image of the artist. Thus, Julie Codell has argued that, while there was varied typology of artists ranging over the autochthonous, prelapsarian, bohemian, romantic and decadent, artists increasingly self-fashioned themselves as professionals in the final quarter of the nineteenth century (1–10).

The growth of professional training schools, large studios and public art galleries, as well as developments in popular culture such as the rise of New Journalism, allowed female artistic labourers to become increasingly visible in the literary market-place and related art industries. The more men and women became auto/biographical subjects, the more the tendency of the public (and reviewers) to read artistic personalities as key to their work was simultaneously popularised and questioned as a valid tool of criticism. In evaluating the function and economic importance of the biographical genre in the nineteenth century, Codell has argued that the success of artists' biographies was closely related to the changing material conditions of their works and practices. 'The rise of British artists' celebrity', Codell claims, made evident that 'British public taste had improved and that artists were thoroughly socialized, not alienated and suffering in garrets', and as 'models of success … and, ultimately, of Britishness' were 'all intended for public consumption' (2–3). Part III thus moves the collection forward by exploring issues of canonisation and women's position in critical histories both in the nineteenth century and beyond. The chapters on George Eliot, Ouida, Marian Huxley Collier and Michael Field demonstrate the contrasting ways that these individuals turned their lives into art and their art into lived experience, or, alternatively, how they struggled to disassociate life and art because of the difficulties the former posed in creating a professional reputation.

Kyriaki Hadjiafxendi's chapter typifies the way in which Part III examines what Ann Rigney has called 'procreativity': that is, the ability of an author's works to generate new versions of itself in other people's acts of productive remembrance (50). Hadjiafxendi analyses the self-fashioning of George Eliot and Mary Elizabeth Braddon as they sought to forge identities as professional women writers in the face of difficulties caused by their long-term unmarried relationships; revealingly, both authors looked back to Romantic models of authorship from the 1820s in order to legitimate their professional status. Yet the 'gentlemanly' authorship they evoked signified an opposition to the more commercial models of authorship that were becoming increasingly prevalent in the contemporary literary market-place; Hadjiafxendi explores the paradoxes created by Braddon and Eliot's use of pseudonyms, which, while seeking to secure and protect their professional identities, nonetheless opened them up to charges of treating their art as if it were no more than an industry.

Andrew King's chapter extends Hadjiafxendi's focus on female professional authorship through his chapter on the late Victorian popular novelist, Ouida. King focuses on a group of novels in which art and artistry form a key concern, *Pascarèl* (1873), *Signa* (1875) and *Ariadnê: The Story of a Dream* (1877). The plots of these three novels respectively centre on an itinerant actor, a male peasant composer and a female peasant sculptor; they are also deeply influenced by Ouida's move to Italy. King's chapter has a conjoined focus on the image of Ouida as a woman artist and a discussion of *Ariadnê: The Story of a Dream*, a text where a female sculptor is the protagonist, in order to argue that a close reading of the latter can shed new light upon a writer whose mass-market reputation has mitigated scholarly consideration of her own artistry and her interest in aesthetic debates. *Ariadnê: The Story of a Dream*, which looks back to classical myths of Ariadne as female weaver, reflects Ouida's move away from a commercial notion of art to one where art was a selfless intervention in society; the political and ethical function of artistry in her work parallels her own move towards social activism.

Valerie Sanders's chapter on the painter Marian Huxley Collier is akin to that of King's in excavating the complexities and contradictions in her career. Her attempt to recover a sense of Huxley's relevance suggests that remembering is inseparable from forgetting. Marian Huxley Collier was the gifted second daughter of Thomas Huxley and wife of the society portrait painter, John Collier. In spite of training at the Slade and exhibiting at the Royal Academy and Grosvenor Galleries, Collier struggled to achieve professional recognition; her reputation is further complicated by her work as a sketch artist within the Huxley household; her drawings included informal portraits of her father and Charles Darwin. As with Hadjiafxendi's treatment of Eliot and Braddon, Sanders highlights how difficult it was for women artists to fashion their own reputations. Sanders details how the pressures of her double status as both wife and artist fed through into her paintings. Just as Collier's career shuttles between amateur and professional, her work shifts between a masculine public world and a feminine private one.

The use of artistry to create a reputation is given a final twist in Ana Parejo Vadillo's chapter on Katharine Bradley and Edith Cooper, the aunt and niece who wrote together under the joint pseudonym of 'Michael Field'. Art, literature and design were deeply connected for them, as were their life and work, and Vadillo demonstrates the way that they used dress to simultaneously display their Aesthetic style and build their reputation. Through their appreciation of the aesthetic in dress, Michael Field explored what it meant to create an object of beauty by bringing into focus the double role of the creator as consumer and the integrity of the materials used. Drawing on unpublished letters and diaries as well as responses from other Aesthetes, Vadillo shows how Michael Field exercised cultural influence at the *fin de siècle* through turning themselves into artistic objects.

## Conclusion

The chapters in this collection survey the materials of everyday life that were available for women to craft. What becomes clear, though, is that these materials were much more than curtains, china, blocks of wood and literary creations. At the same time that they crafted items and commodities, women crafted subjectivities and professional roles for themselves in a pragmatic fashion, building them from a range of identities, among them, wife, mother, angel, artist, creator, designer, expert, genius, operative and hand. This sense of 'crafting' as an ongoing, constructive process of management and transformation is described by Talia Schaffer in her contribution to this collection: the craft aesthetic is the process through which objects which were considered dangerous, exotic, or 'outside' were ordered, shaped and made safe through the creative energies of female artistry. Crafting thus implies that women artists created works of art across different media that spoke of themselves as creators as safe and ordered regardless of their questionable presence in public, paid and professional labour. The crafting of the work therefore took place at the same time as the crafting of the female artist's identity, and this complex process tended to blur the boundary between amateur and professional labour, between the crafted product and the industrial commodity. *Crafting the Woman Professional* does not wish to obscure the gendered divide that existed between binaries of public and private, craft and commodity, or domestic and industrial, but does seek to convey how these ideological binaries were muddied, unravelled and challenged by the actual aesthetic practices of industrious women.

**Works Cited**


Alexander, Lynn. *Women, Work and Representation: Needlewomen in Victorian Art and Literature*. Athens: Ohio University Press, 2003.

Austen, Jane. *Pride and Prejudice*. London: Penguin, 1996.

Barringer, Tim. *Men at Work: Art and Labour in Victorian Britain*. New Haven: Yale University Press, 2005.

Batchelor, Jennie. *Women's Work: Labour, Gender, Authorship, 1750–1830*. Manchester: Manchester University Press, 2010.

Bermingham, Ann. *Learning to Draw: Studies in the Cultural History of a Polite and Useful Art*. New Haven: Yale University Press, 2000.

Boos, Florence, ed. *Working-Class Women Poets in Victorian Britain: An Anthology*. Peterborough: Broadview, 2008.

Bourdieu, Pierre. 'L'Illusion biographique'. *Actes de la recherche en sciences sociales* 62–3 (1986): 69–72.

Briggs, Asa. *Victorian Things*. Chicago: University of Chicago Press, 1988.

Browning, Elizabeth Barrett. *Aurora Leigh*. Ed. Kerry McSweeney. Oxford: Oxford University Press, 1993.

Casteras, Susan P., and Linda H. Peterson, eds. *A Struggle for Fame: Victorian Women Artists and Authors*. New Haven: Yale Center for British Art, 1994.

Cherry, Deborah. *Painting Women: Victorian Women Artists*. London: Routledge, 1993.

Cluckie, Linda. *The Rise and Fall of Art Needlework: Its Socio-Economic and Cultural Aspects*. Bury St. Edmunds: Arena Books, 2008.

Codell, Julie F. *The Victorian Artist: Artists' Lifewritings in Britain, ca. 1870–1910*. Cambridge: Cambridge University Press, 2003.

[Craik, Dinah]. *A Woman's Thoughts about Women*. London: Hurst and Blackett, 1858.

Daston, Lorraine, ed. *Things That Talk: Object Lessons from Art and Science*. Brooklyn, NY: Zone, 2004.

Davis, Tracy C. *Actresses as Working Women: Their Social Identity in Victorian Culture*. New York: Routledge, 1991.

Demoor, Marysa, ed. *Marketing the Author: Authorial Personae, Narrative Selves and Self-Fashioning, 1880–1930*. Basingstoke: Palgrave, 2004.

Easley, Alexis. *First-Person Anonymous: Women Writers and Victorian Print Media, 1830–1870*. Aldershot: Ashgate, 2004.

Elliott, Bridget, and Janice Helland, eds. *Women Artists and the Decorative Arts, 1880–1935: The Gender of Ornament*. Aldershot: Ashgate, 2002.

Fergus, Jan. 'The Professional Woman Writer'. *The Cambridge Companion to Jane Austen*. Ed. Edward Copeland and Juliet McMaster. Cambridge: Cambridge University Press, 2011. 1–20.

Ferry, Emma. '"Decorators May be Compared to Doctors": An Analysis of Rhoda and Agnes Garrett's *Suggestions for House Decoration in Painting, Woodwork and Furniture* (1876)'. *Journal of Design History* 16.1 (2003): 15–33.

Forbes-Robertson, John. 'Industrial Art–I '. *Great Industries of Great Britain*. 3 vols. London: Cassell, Petter, Galpin & Co, 1884. II.21–3.

Foucault, Michel. 'What is an Author?' *Language, Counter-Memory, Practice*. Trans. Donald F. Bouchard. Ithaca, NY: Cornell University Press, 1977. 113–38.

Gale, Maggie B., and Viv Gardner, eds. *Women, Theatre and Performance: New Histories, New Historiographies*. Manchester: Manchester University Press, 2000.

Gaskell, Elizabeth. *North and South*. Oxford: Oxford University Press, 1982.

Gray, F. Elizabeth, ed. *Women in Journalism at the Fin de Siècle: 'Making a Name for Herself'*. Basingstoke: Palgrave, 2012.

Hall-Witt, Jennifer. *Fashionable Acts: Opera and Elite Culture in London, 1780–1880*. Lebanon, NH: University of New Hampshire Press, 2007.

Harris, Beth, ed. *Famine and Fashion: Needlewomen in the Nineteenth Century*. Aldershot: Ashgate, 2005.

Jeaffreson, J. Cordy. 'Female Artists and Art-Schools of England'. *Art Pictorial and Industrial* 1 (1870): 25–30, 50–52, 70–73.

Junod, Karen. *'Writing the Lives of Painters': Biography and Artistic Identity in Britain 1760–1810*. Oxford: Oxford University Press, 2011.

Kriegel, Lara. *Grand Designs: Labor, Empire, and the Museum in Victorian Culture*. Durham, NC: Duke University Press, 2007.

Labbe, Jacqueline M., ed. *The History of British Women's Writing, 1750–1830*. Basingstoke: Palgrave, 2010.

Langland, Elizabeth. *Nobody's Angels: Middle-Class Women and Domestic Ideology in Victorian Culture*. Ithaca, NY: Cornell University Press, 1995.

[Lawrance, Hannah]. 'The Education and Employment of Women'. *British Quarterly Review* 52.103 (1870): 31–57.

Lees-Maffei, Grace, ed. 'Special Issue: Professionalizing Interior Design 1870–1970'. *Journal of Design History* 21.1 (2008).

[Lewes, George Henry]. 'The Condition of Authors in England, Germany, and France'. *Fraser's Magazine for Town and Country* 35.207 (1847): 285–95.

[Lewis, Sarah]. *Woman's Mission*. London: John W. Parker, 1839.

Liddle, Dallas. *The Dynamics of Genre: Journalism and the Practice of Literature in Mid-Victorian Britain*. Charlottesville: University of Virginia Press, 2009.

'Lithographic Employment for Women'. *Alexandra Magazine*, 1 July 1864: 183.

Losano, Antonia. *The Woman Painter in Victorian Literature*. Columbus: Ohio State University Press, 2008.

Margadant, Jo Burr, ed. *The New Biography: Performing Femininity in Nineteenth-Century France*. Berkeley: University of California Press, 2000.

Marshall, Gail. *Actresses on the Victorian Stage: Feminine Performance and the Galatea Myth*. Cambridge: Cambridge University Press, 1998.

Masten, April F. *Art Work: Women Artists and Democracy in Mid-Nineteenth-Century New York*. Philadelphia: University of Pennsylvania Press, 2008.

Nunn, Pamela Gerrish. *Victorian Women Artists*. London: The Women's Press, 1987.

'On the Adoption of Professional Life by Women'. *English Woman's Journal* 7 (1858): 1–12.

Orr, Clarissa Campbell. 'Introduction'. *Women in the Victorian Art World*. Manchester: Manchester University Press, 1995. 1–32.

Parkes, Bessie Rayner. *Essays on Woman's Work*. London: Alexander Strahan, 1865.

Pergam, Elizabeth A. *The Manchester Art Treasures Exhibition of 1857: Entrepreneurs, Connoisseurs and the Public*. Farnham: Ashgate, 2010.

Perkin, Harold. *The Rise of Professional Society: England since 1880*. New York: Routledge, 2002.

Peterson, Linda H. *Becoming a Woman of Letters: Myths of Authorship and Facts of the Victorian Market*. Princeton: Princeton University Press, 2009.

Pettitt, Clare. *Patent Inventions: Intellectual Property and the Victorian Novel*. Oxford: Oxford University Press, 2004.

'Photography as an Employment for Women'. *Englishwoman's Review* (July 1867): 219–23.

Planche, Gustave. 'La journée d'un journaliste'. *Paris, ou le livre des cent-et-un*. 15 vols. Paris: Ladvocat, 1831–34. VI.133–55.

Powell, Kerry. *Women and Victorian Theatre*. Cambridge: Cambridge University Press, 1997.

Prescott, Sarah. *Women, Authorship and Literary Culture, 1690–1740*. Basingstoke: Palgrave, 2003.

Prochaska, F.K. *Women and Philanthropy in Nineteenth-Century England*. Oxford: Clarendon, 1980.

Purnell, Thomas. 'Woman, and Art: The Female School of Design'. *Art Journal* 76 (1861): 107–8.

Reader, W.J. *Professional Men: The Rise of the Professional Classes in Nineteenth-Century England*. London: Weidenfeld & Nicolson, 1966.

'Report from the Select Committee on Arts and their Connexion with Manufactures'. House of Commons Papers; Reports of Committees 9.1 (1836). Parliamentary Papers Online.

Rigney, Ann. *The Afterlives of Walter Scott: Memory on the Move*. Oxford: Oxford University Press, 2012.

Rose, Sonya O. *Limited Livelihoods: Gender and Class in Nineteenth-Century England*. London: Routledge, 1992.

Ruth, Jennifer. *Novel Professions: Interested Disinterest and the Making of the Professional in the Victorian Novel*. Columbus: Ohio State University Press, 2006.

Sanders, Lise. *Consuming Fantasies: Labor, Leisure, and the London Shopgirl, 1880–1920*. Columbus: Ohio State University Press, 2006.

Schaffer, Talia. *Novel Craft: Victorian Domestic Handicraft & Nineteenth-Century Fiction*. Oxford: Oxford University Press, 2011.

Schellenberg, Betty A. *The Professionalization of Women Writes in Eighteenth-Century Britain*. Cambridge: Cambridge University Press, 2005.

Scholl, Lesa. *Translation, Authorship and the Victorian Professional Woman: Charlotte Brontë, Harriet Martineau and George Eliot*. Aldershot: Ashgate, 2011.

Sebba, Anne. *Battling for News: The Rise of the Woman Reporter*. London: Hodder & Stoughton, 1993.

Siskin, Clifford. *The Work of Writing: Literature and Social Change in Britain 1700–1830*. Baltimore: Johns Hopkins University Press, 1998.

Tuchman, Gaye, and Nina E. Forntin. *Edging Women Out: Victorian Novelists, Publishers, and Social Change*. New Haven: Yale University Press, 1989.

Turner, Cheryl. *Living by the Pen: Women Writers in the Eighteenth Century*. London and New York: Routledge, 1992.

Waters, Mary A., ed. *British Women Writers and the Profession of Literary Criticism, 1789–1832*. Basingstoke: Palgrave, 2004.
Weliver, Phyllis. *Women Musicians in Victorian Fiction, 1860–1900: Representations of Music, Science and Gender in the Leisured Home*. Aldershot: Ashgate, 2000.
'What Is There I Can Do?' *The Woman's Gazette* 2.4,7 (1877): 51–3, 99–100.
Young, Arlene. *Culture, Class, Gender in the Victorian Novel: Gentlemen, Gents and Working Women*. Basingstoke: Macmillan, 1999.
Zakreski, Patricia. *Representing Female Artistic Labour, 1848–1890: Refining Work for the Middle-Class Woman*. Aldershot: Ashgate, 2006.

## Notes

1 Translation (our own): 'Thanks to a unique application of Adam Smith's theory of the division of labour, there are nowadays two distinct areas in literature, art and industry'.

# PART I

# Industrious Amateurism

1

# Women's Work: The History of the Victorian Domestic Handicraft

*Talia Schaffer*

> By the way,
> The works of women are symbolical.
> We sew, sew, prick our fingers, dull our sight,
> Producing what? ... (Barrett Browning I.455–8)

This chapter aims to answer Aurora Leigh's famous question: what exactly were the 'works of women', the wax flowers, doilies, cardboard brackets, shell-encrusted boxes, leather-leaf frames, and embroidered slippers of the mid-Victorian era? Although this enormously popular hobby dominated middle-class women's domestic life through much of the nineteenth century, its history has received little attention.[1] I explore the history of the movement, looking at the way it expressed dominant cultural interests at different moments in the nineteenth century. Women wanted to make such artefacts because the objects articulated a certain position regarding issues central to Victorian life: nature, industrialism, economics and aesthetics. By tracking the development of the Victorian domestic handicraft movement, we can see what these humble ornaments really meant for their makers. We can also see what craft meant in a period when it was assumed to be an amateur pursuit before it became professionalised.

In the early nineteenth century, the domestic handicraft movement emerged as people began composing decorations by arranging found natural artefacts like shells, seaweed, pressed flowers, dried leaves and colourful sand. These new forms may have been inspired by the Romantic adoration of nature and a desire to introduce into the home what one manual called the 'ornaments which nature presents in the vegetable kingdom' (Parkes 99). Yet it was crucial that the space of interior culture exert a disciplining and ordering effect on these wild imports. Mary W. Helms has argued that in craft-making societies,

> the safe, civilized, ordered, moral, domesticated life of the home society where people live in the here-and-now is contrasted either with a dangerous, chaotic, immoral or amoral, pre-civilized natural world outside or with the outside as a mystically powerful place of sacred superiority. (46)

The function of crafts is to transform objects from this exciting but dangerous 'outside' into an acceptable component of the 'inside'. Crafting, then, is 'the creation of form, shape, order, and refinement from that which is formless, shapeless, chaotic, and unrefined' (Helms 25). Helms's argument explains why, in eighteenth- and early nineteenth-century crafts, the natural object is never presented in anything remotely like its natural setting. Natural objects would be gilded, shellacked, wrapped in foil, dipped in wax, pierced, glued together, wrapped in fabric or incorporated into larger geometrical patterns. Crafts do not in fact display the Romantic adoration of nature. Rather, they show the need to dominate nature, processing it into mere decoration. The domestic handicraft is the opposite of the sublime. Instead of the thrill of feeling overpowered by vast, infinite, dangerous nature, it is the smug satisfaction of putting a miniature, prettified bit of nature into its proper place (usually under glass).

Aurora Leigh gives us an example of these early nineteenth-century crafts. Although Aurora obediently does crochet (I.1035–52), the new craze invented in 1838, most of her work fulfils her aunt's preference for preservationist crafts (Caulfield and Saward 102). Aurora's aunt practises the arts of her youth when she produces seaweed collages, pricking the dried fronds into patterns with a pin (I.380–4)). Aurora herself 'spun glass, stuffed birds, and modelled flowers in wax, / Because she liked accomplishments in girls' (I.425–6). Taxidermy and wax flowers worked to produce a sense of permanence, to turn the decaying bird's corpse or the already-blown flowers into something that would last forever, radiant, orderly, scentless, protected under glass. In this respect, the handicrafts occupy the same kind of cultural role as Nash's orderly architectural squares, or Capability Brown's gardens that edited nature into carefully picturesque landscapes. Shell and seaweed pictures are diminutive decorative parallels to the important work of topographic reorganisation undertaken in the public sphere.

Handicrafts that incorporate natural objects also, crucially, participate in the industrial era's pleasure in producing a man-made world whose power and precision subdue nature itself. In her important study of Victorian interiors, Thad Logan argues that the nineteenth-century craze for aquariums and Wardian cases (glass cases filled with ferns) derives in part from a fascination with small enclosed spaces in which great natural forces could be domesticated (154–7):

> When the 'natural' appeared in the parlour, it always did so as cleaner, more wrought, more contained, or more organized than it would have been in its original

condition. The middle-class parlour functioned, in fact, as a symbolic and practical switchpoint, transforming the natural into the cultural. (Logan 159)

The craftswoman improved on nature by preserving, cleansing, arranging and fixing the materials that nature had left in chaos.

Coincidentally, this period also saw an explosion of consumer goods, which provided a plenitude of raw materials for textile crafts in particular. Cotton went from being a luxury textile to a popular and affordable material at the end of the eighteenth century. New kinds of cotton included sheeting, plaids, and corduroys, mixed worsted and cotton blends. But there were also new fibres like alpaca and new technology for textile printing which inspired craftswomen to develop new ways of salvaging and combining them (see Lemire; Styles). The class associations of handicraft altered by the middle of the nineteenth century. Prior to the nineteenth century, needlework had been a high-status activity, associated with aristocratic practitioners. But in the early nineteenth century, handicraft was increasingly identified with a middle-class sensibility, as a thrifty, skilful mode of domestic management. This does not mean handicraft was limited to the middle class; on the contrary, needlework continued to be popular with upper-class women, while domestic ornamentation was prized even by the very poor.[2] But handicraft now signified the moral, managerial virtues of the bourgeoisie, not aristocratic leisure, and consequently members of other classes were emulating these middle-class ideals when they did craftwork. In the nineteenth century, when high-art venues were largely closed off to women, they channelled their creative urges into the world around them, using the elements most readily available (see Davidoff and Hall). This kind of domestic decoration was also sanctioned because it added to the comforts of the home, whereas more ambitious high art was condemned as a selfish use of time taken away from the family.

Indeed, by the mid-nineteenth century, the handicraft's most visible and urgent function was to signify womanhood. Craft items were made by the home's female inhabitant, and thus appeared to be an extension of her body, as well as carrying the signs of her taste and skill. The woman's hands had held it, her mind had planned it, her eyes had gauged it, and she had communicated something of her intangible subjectivity to the completed object. For the Victorians, then, women were ensconced in a cocoon of items of their own manufacture, representing otherwise invisible aspects of their identity. This is the image behind Ruskin's famous claim that 'wherever a true wife comes, this home is always around her' (152). The craft was frequently described as 'pretty' or 'elegant', qualities that elided the object with its maker's own body. The craft was the woman's household skills made concrete, a tangible trace of her household labour that was all the more valuable for having been produced in leisure hours, for it showed that labour was leisure, that she never stopped working to improve the domestic abode. Its finished appearance also testified to the neatness and delicacy of the domestic woman's body.

Women made amateur crafts in order to perpetuate the values of the woman's sphere. This means that crafts had to remain personal emanations of their producer, given as sentimental tokens, irreducibly and inalienably part of the private world of the home. Susan Stewart explains:

> Thus, while the personal memento is of little material worth, often arising, for example, amid the salvage crafts such as quilt-making and embroidery, it is of great worth to its possessor. Because of its connection to biography and its place in constituting the notion of the individual life, the memento becomes emblematic of the worth of that life and of the self's capacity to generate worthiness. (139)

This was especially the case for women, whose 'self' and 'worthiness' were confirmed and publicised through the handicraft.

Because of this intimate connection with women's lives, crafts stayed firmly in the category of what Annette Weiner has called 'inalienable possessions'. In other words, they were sacred enough to be accumulated rather than traded. Their value lies in their emotional message, not their monetary worth. Nobody put it better than Elizabeth Stone, who in 1840 described crafts as:

> those numberless pretty and not unuseful tokens of remembrance, which, passing from friend to friend, soften our hearts by the intimation they convey, that we have been cared for in our absence, and that while the world looked dark and desolate about us, unforgetting hearts far, far away were holding us in remembrance, busy fingers were occupied in our behoof. Oh! a reticule, a purse, a slipper, how valueless soever in itself, is, when fraught with these home memories, worth that which the mines of Golconda could not produce. (318)

In Stone's description, domestic handicrafts are both too valuable for trade (something 'the mines of Golconda could not produce') and too worthless ('valueless in itself'), thus flying both over and under the radar of commodity culture. They thus escape commodification in the two ways Igor Kopytoff has described; they are 'sacralized' – ascribed a value beyond price and reserved for royals or priests – and they are cheap and ubiquitous enough to be virtually worthless, like a single match or a tissue (73–5). Made of worthless scraps that women salvaged and recycled, unsaleable in ordinary stores because of their amateurish construction and inadequate execution, the handicraft remained at home.

It may seem as if this amateur object, with its homemade scraps and sentimental value, was the opposite of the mass-produced commodity, but its actual relationship to the industrial economy was far more complex. By the beginning of the nineteenth century, factory production had begun to compete with manual fabrication, but as Daryl M. Hafter has pointed out, handmade work persisted alongside industrialisation, influenced it, and competed with it (ix–xii). During this period manual work was not necessarily seen as artistic; rather, it was associated with exhausting rural toil that was rapidly becoming obsolete. The condition of the workers in mills and textile factories was of course notoriously bad but hand-sewers were no better off, since they were forced to work extremely hard in unhealthy conditions to produce enough clothing to compete with cheaper machine-made wares. The plight of impoverished lace-makers was especially pitiable as they desperately tried to compete with machine-made lace (see Callen; Morris; Parker). Thus, middle-class women might well associate hand-sewn products with squalid, impoverished conditions. They might well view industrialism as the future and try to incorporate factory-made objects or use machine-influenced techniques in their own hobbies. In other words, what we have here is the amateur homemade artefact attempting to look like a mass-produced commodity. As Lara Kriegel records, 'several English commentators argued that machinery facilitated mastery and even liberation' (96). As a triumph over nature and a relief from toil, industrialism was idealised. Indeed, women's own bodies began to be in intimate contact with the triumphs of the machine age. James Laver describes the crinoline as 'the first great triumph of the machine age' – 'the application to feminine costume of all those principles of steel construction employed in the Menai Bridge and the Crystal Palace' (quoted in Briggs 26). In advances in corset design, new dyes, machine-made lace, false hair and all the other innovations of the period, the mid-Victorian beautiful body was itself a triumph of manufacturing.

The machine age, in fact, made the domestic handicraft necessary. Thad Logan explains, 'as the lives of men and women in the nineteenth century became more and more thoroughly constituted by industrial capitalism, there seems to have been a compensatory emphasis on the amateur practices of ornamental sewing and handcrafts' (164). In the late eighteenth and early nineteenth centuries, for the first time, many middle-class women were spatially separated from the site of work. The factory was located in an unsavoury locale, dependent upon advanced machinery, tied to technological and financial innovations. It was a place middle-class females were not supposed to enter.

Domestic handicraft, however, gave women an outlet for expressing their feelings about the new economy. Homemade objects were an antidote to the mass-produced commodities of the industrial era but in a complicated way, they also emulated those commodities. This was a woman's mode of production, set up as a rival to the regular industrial machinery. Domestic handicrafts proved that women, too, were capable of swift, precise, reliable production (the hallmark of industrial mass production), but also that they were able to produce objects that were far more meaningful than the generic products of the factory. In his history of hobbies, Steven Gelber astutely notes:

> hobbies developed as a category of socially valued leisure activity in the nineteenth century because they bridged the worlds of work and home. They allowed women to practice, and therefore to understand, worklike activities … As a particular form of productive leisure they expressed the deeper meaning of the work ethic and the free market. (2)

Gelber captures the way women could express their loyalty to work via what seems like its opposite, leisure. Craft allowed women to practise the same skills that the British economy was built on. Thus the crafts that emerged in the 1840s and 1850s gave middle-class women a way to assert their own economic productivity and to comment on industrialisation, as they were being reassigned to a private domestic sphere.

In the 1840s, handicraft became more fashionable than ever, after the 1837 coronation of a young queen who loved decorative arts, particularly embroidery (Hulbert 22; Lichten 7–8). New publications stressed the activity's status; several needlework books in the 1840s were either dedicated to, or edited by, princesses, viscountesses and countesses.[3] This royal imprimatur became visible at the Great Exhibition of 1851, largely organised by Prince Albert and opened by the Queen, in which handicraft played a large and visible role.

In the Great Exhibition of 1851, handicrafts received the public endorsement of representing Great Britain's manufacturing achievements. The Great Exhibition was intended to showcase industrial achievements and it only accepted art associated with mechanical processes or appliances (Steegman 221–2). Indeed, the Great Exhibition aimed to prove that industrialism was compatible with art, part of a debate that lasted from the 1830s through the *fin de siècle*, according to Patrick Brantlinger. Thus the *Official Catalogue to the Great Exhibition* called handicraft 'ornamental industry', and designated their makers either 'inventor and producer' or 'designer and manufacturer', titles that flatteringly affiliated them with industrial magnates. Indeed, Lara Kriegel points out that the ornamental arts at the Great Exhibition actually helped domesticate industrialism. They provided examples of pursuits that combined both artisanal and mechanical work, like papier mâché, ironwork and ornamental glass (96–7). Because of the double meaning of 'industry', which meant both hard work and machinery by the 1850s,

> the handicraftsman was just as much a man of industry as the operator of a machine in a textile factory, which explains why objects that were the product of exceptional craftsmanship stood side by side with objects that were the product of machines. (Auerbach 97)

Precisely at mid-century, then, 'industry' aligned handicraft with mechanical manufacture. It is worth pausing to note this fact because within 20 years William Morris and his fellow reformers would redefine craft and machine work as inherently oppositional, making it hard even to remember how allied they seemed at the Great Exhibition.

The Great Exhibition's view of 'ornamental industry' can be parsed through its physical categories. It displayed needlework and other decorative handicrafts alongside its turbines, ores and knives, glossing all these objects as equally significant components of the newly flourishing industrial economy. The organising principles of the Great Exhibition made all objects equally specular, monumental and desirable, mystifying modes of production and local differences among them. As Thomas Richards has famously explained:

> under a single ceiling, surrounded by trees and flooded with light, commodities appeared to have come out of nowhere, radiant and ordered into departments that fixed the place of each article and gave it a caption and a numbered place in the catalogue. (4)

The craft exhibitions at the Great Exhibition fell into several different groups. Some were objects remarkable for the skill of their producers. These included most of the embroidery and tapestry work; stamped-leather book covers; patriotic scenes in needlework depicting Napoleon or Mary Queen of Scots (*Official* II.564). Others were outstandingly large, like 'a hearth-rug, with the border and ends formed of upwards of 20,000 shreds of cloth, and the centre of lamb's wool', or W. Bridges's 'tapestry wool-work, "The Last Supper", after Leonardo da Vinci, containing five hundred thousand stitches' (II.573, 564). A third group consisted of objects produced, for the first time, wholly by machine, including an ivory pagoda and machine-made lace, to which the editors of the Great Exhibition catalogue could not refrain from adding the enthusiastic comment, 'The application of machinery to the production of lace is very remarkable and interesting' (II.824, 561).

This 'tapestry wool-work' was a type of needlework called Berlin-wool work. Berlin-wool work became phenomenally popular by the 1840s, although it had appeared as early as 1796, according to Leonore Davidoff and Catherine Hall (258). Traditional embroidery involves working a design on top of an opaque piece of silk or cotton. Berlin-wool work, however, offered a completely different model. A picture (often adapted from a popular painting) was divided into a grid and keyed to a piece of coarse canvas, sometimes with every tenth thread in the canvas coloured yellow to help the worker transfer each square in the grid properly. Workers used thick wools, which made it easy to fill in the picture fast. The yarn was also cheaper and easier to work than embroidery silks. Indeed, it became possible to purchase canvas with the picture printed directly upon it, obviating the need even to transfer the design. And machines that perforated paper were also used to produce cheap paper patterns with holes already punched for the needle. Such patterns could be laid over cloth and simply sewn right into the fabric (Ames 97–146). In fact it was a kind of stitch-by-numbers kit, rather like its descendant, modern needlework kits. Without needing to exercise any individual drawing skill, a worker could simply purchase and work 'The Last Supper', a Madonna and Child, a view of the Prince of Wales as a baby, a group of Royal spaniels, a basket of fruit, or a scene from Sir Walter Scott (Morris 21–3). Even a child could produce perfect replicas. This sort of work was adaptable to virtually anything – chair backs, cushion covers, even slippers and bookmarks. Aurora Leigh memorialises the range and productivity of Berlin-wool work: 'Producing what? A pair of slippers, sir, / To put on when you're weary – or a stool / To stumble over and vex you … 'curse that stool!' / Or else at best, a cushion …' (I.458–61). The slippers, stool and cushion emerge too swiftly, faster than their male recipient can learn their place.

If the Great Exhibition showcased Berlin-wool work, however, it also made a point of displaying another type of artefact: objects that pretended to be made of a material different from their actual composition. The mid-Victorians were fascinated by these 'imitative arts' (Lambert 22–3). James Howard Earle displayed a folding screen with encaustic painting 'in imitation of antique gems' beside a 'table-top imitation of buhl'. Alongside the marble statues in the sculpture galleries, the inquisitive visitor could find objects made of perforated paper, modelled in wax, cut out of cardboard, or cast in composition to resemble marble. Visitors might also spot Alexander Vischi's stall, with woollen flowers arranged on artificial pads of green turf in a porcelain basket (*Official* II.823, 826, 561). Brantlinger comments on the prevalence of imitative arts at the Great Exhibition, listing: 'furniture made from new types of fake wood (*gutta percha* and papier mâché), electroplated vases and statues, [and] painted "stained glass" windows' (92).

The imitative arts had been popular before the Great Exhibition, of course. Edward Lucie-Smith notes that 'between 1827 and 1846 thirty-five patents were taken out at the British Patent Office for processes which involved coating one substance or material so that it looked like another and (usually) more expensive one' (200). Many mid-Victorian domestic handicrafts were designed to fool the viewer by composing inexpensive matter, including household waste, into a simulacrum of a more costly consumer good. Two very popular crafts involved transferring a colourful paper print to glass and varnishing it to imitate either porcelain ('potichomanie') or stained glass ('diaphanie') respectively (see Henderson and Wilkinson 67; Dodd). Craftswomen were often exhorted to twist a rough shape out of wire or twigs, wrap it in cotton wool and slather it with molten wax to make it resemble coral (Henderson and Wilkinson 140). Even imitative arts could themselves spawn imitations. Marble might be too expensive, but 'scagliola work' was an Italian substitute made of plaster. Scagliola itself being a costly high-status object, the *Lady's Album of Fancy Work* in 1850 suggested that its readers copy the effect by using a piece of sycamore wood painted with India-ink and then varnished. The *Lady's Album* went on to point out that the sycamore itself could be imitated by a piece of cheap deal 'covered with good cream-coloured drawing-paper' (22). In this rather remarkable series, paper imitates sycamore which imitates plaster which imitates marble.

Successful imitative art testified to the thriftiness, imaginativeness and manual dexterity of the craftswoman. It also confirmed the visual sophistication of the viewer. In fact, any imitative art good enough to fool a naïve viewer would actually have failed. The viewer had to be momentarily tricked into believing the illusion, while knowing at a deeper level that it was fictional and puzzling out the method that produced it. It was precisely the successful navigation of that double perspective that made imitative art pleasurable.

The Great Exhibition provoked some anxiety about the absence of originality in imitative arts, part of a larger worry about the lack of imagination in British art generally.[4] But on the whole, imitative arts continued to signal successful manufacturing. In 1862,

> Alsagar and Neville produced papier mâché that looked like malachite. Earl Granville, speaking in a debate on paper in the House of Lords in 1860, found it a positive merit that paper could be made to look like Moroccan leather and pigskin. (Briggs 291)

When read as manufacture, 'imitative arts' were distinctly laudable. The imitative arts were the plastics of their day, promising to make heretofore forbiddingly expensive items affordable. Now working-class or middle-class consumers too could enjoy the visual pleasure and status of Moroccan leather, marble and malachite.

The crafts exhibited in 1851 fit into the machine ethos. They celebrated inexpensive materials utilised ingeniously and objects too vast for a single producer to create. The ideal craft of 1851 was made of an inexpensive, readily available material (wax, cardboard, wool), formed into the likeness of something rarer. The Great Exhibition promised magical transformations. Those vast, rough bales of raw materials, coal, cotton or iron, could go into a machine which would shape them into finished consumer items, and similarly, the detritus of Victorian life, feathers, ink, paper, wax, fabric scraps or seaweed, could be supplied to an ingenious craftsperson who would fashion them into a decorative delight.

Imitative art also satisfied the mid-Victorian fascination with ingenious ways to incorporate waste products back into an efficient economy, a fascination with recycling and salvage described perhaps most famously in Henry Mayhew's examination of how each class lived off the drippings and debris of the one above it, and in the vast dust-heaps of Dickens's *Our Mutual Friend* (1864). The imitative arts, therefore, testified that a skilful domestic manager could deliver the visual pleasure of valuable artefacts by finding novel uses for the bits of cotton, fragments of wire, scrap remnants and old candle-ends otherwise relegated to the rubbish heap. One particularly labour-intensive craft employed fish scales in lieu of sequins; the woman would scrape the scales off the fish, clean them, soak them, punch tiny holes in them, snip them into the shape of leaves and sew them to objects (Morris 161–2; Urbino and Day 302). Cucumber or melon seeds could be sewn in intricate patterns to decorate mats, bags or table ornaments (Urbino and Day 301). This craft emblematised the world in which rags became paper, textile fibres were processed into 'flock', bones turned into matches, animal and human waste could be sold for fertilizer, dead horses became glue, and coal by-products produced new dyes (Briggs 49–50). Handicrafts encapsulated a kind of progress upwards through the ranks of material objects, a material evolution, as it were, when rubbish could be reshaped into treasure, or inexpensive common things made to bear uncanny resemblances to precious materials. When the visitor to the Great Exhibition looked at imitation marble or shreds of wool, what he saw was human skill elevating waste matter to unforeseen heights.

What the visitor to the Great Exhibition also felt was the intense satisfaction of common materials representing something recognisable. The preference for careful copying dominates the history of the handicraft. While precise replication was a desideratum for all crafts, it is perhaps most often articulated in embroidery manuals because of embroidery's explicitly representational patterns. The most admired craftswoman in England from the 1790s to the 1820s was Mary Linwood, who became famous for her 'pictorial embroidery': precise replicas of famous oil paintings (by artists like Raphael and Gainsborough) done in needlework. Miss Linwood's Gallery in Leicester Square was one of the sights of London (Parker 144–6). Linwood's needlework replicas of sportive dogs, Mount Vesuvius, lobsters, pathetic nuns and King Lear were perceived as the height of skill. No wonder that in 1842 Miss Lambert wrote:

> Needlework may be regarded (if we may be allowed the expression) as the sister art of painting; the aim of the accomplished needlewoman of the present day, being to produce as true a picture of nature as possible; soaring far beyond the commonplace ideas of the ancient embroideries, which, perhaps, are more to be admired for the richness of their materials, and the labour bestowed upon them, than for any merit they possess as works of art. (20–21)

Indeed, she cautions, 'let us remember that the true intention of the art is to copy nature, not to distort her' (40). Notice that here Lambert exults in modern superiority to 'ancient embroideries'. She is dubious about medieval embroidery, so admired by Pugin and Morris, because it fails to 'produce as true a picture of nature as possible'. Similarly, Cornelia Mee, displaying her embroidery at the Great Exhibition, made a point of boasting in the catalogue that 'the needlework of most of the articles is done from flowers, minutely copied from Paxton's Magazine of Botany' (*Official* II.561). Mee, Lambert and Linwood are, in effect, reworking embroidery to resemble photography, and some of the enthusiasm for this precise replication surely comes from the enthusiasm for early photographic reproductions.

In other words, handicrafts were a local expression of the overriding mid-Victorian drive for realism. The craftswoman had to embroider what was actually there, just as authors were supposed to adhere strictly to the conventions and probabilities of real life, just as photographs were supposed to be a precise record of nature and just as applicants for the Royal Academy had to prove their drawing skill by painstakingly stippling endless copies of classical models. In Charlotte Yonge's early novel *Abbeychurch* (1844), Helen embroiders an orange rose among the more orthodox red and pink ones. Consternation ensues until it can be definitively established, by recourse to a diary entry that she had indeed witnessed an orange rose. This ocular proof makes the orange rose acceptable (230–2). No aesthetic concerns about the visual qualities of Helen's embroidery occur to the characters of *Abbeychurch*; documentary corroboration is paramount. The 'imitative arts', similarly, satisfied the shared belief that faithful mimesis of another object was the highest goal of handicraft.

Handicrafts, in fact, could even move beyond mimesis. They were a privileged locus of realism because they could be the thing, not merely represent it. In this respect, they were preferable even to photography. Craft instructions often incorporated the desirable original directly into the craft object. *Art Recreations*, a craft manual from 1861, demonstrates how to decorate already-drawn pictures or showcase existing physical objects, pasting hair, seaweed and shells onto pages and casting wax fruit from real fruit. 'Anglo-Japanese Work' consists of gluing pressed leaves directly onto the article to be ornamented and then painting and varnishing the whole product.[5] High art involved endless copying of classical models, but it was only in the realm of domestic handicrafts that one could be presented with the model itself, the actual acorn or moss, the craftsperson's only role being to fix that object in such a way as to arrest its decay. Taxidermy is perhaps the craft that most clearly expresses this naturalistic urge, since the craftsperson's entire role is simply to preserve an animal in a fit state for public display.

At mid-century, the domestic handicraft, then, expressed both modernity and tradition. Interestingly, it did each in slightly different venues. Craft items were produced according to mass-circulation magazines, utilising premade kits, often incorporating mass-produced commodities and being made to look as much like a finished, accurate, machine-made object as possible. Thus craft practice seems harmonious with mid-Victorian economic norms. Yet the craft ideal was quite different. The craft was supposed to be a uniquely personal expression of a strong domestic attachment, to bear the individual marks of the producer's particular taste, inventiveness and skill, and to be given as an inalienable testimonial to their relationship. This split between handicraft practice and handicraft rhetoric was ideologically useful; the item could secretly satisfy women's desire to emulate industrial production, hiding behind a virtuous facade of sentimental rhetoric. It was the handicraft's ability to satisfy competing imperatives simultaneously that helped make it popular.

These stresses are visible in the crafts themselves. The 'Elizabethan watch-hook' is a typical example: a large embroidered flower made of loops of decorative cord, with a mother-of-pearl watch-hook sewn in the centre (*Lady's* 10).[6] Victorians could easily buy inexpensive imitation mother-of-pearl watch-hooks (Fraser 189). So why did the women of the mid-nineteenth century feel a need to swathe this cheap disposable product in layers of decoration? The answer is that the craftswoman was literally surrounding and wrapping the bought object in the fabric which testified to her labour, skill, taste and affection. We might remember Helms's claim that craft turns dangerous 'outside' objects safely 'inside', a theory that nicely explains the motivation for this reworking. Similarly, Daniel Miller explains that purchased goods get refashioned, an act which 'may be defined as that which translates the object from an alienable to an inalienable condition: that is, from being a symbol of estrangement and price value to being an artefact invested with particular inseparable connotations' (quoted in Edwards 16). It is precisely because the artefact is purchased that it requires to be literally enwrapped in signifiers of the home.

The watch was a status symbol, an emblem of professional status, often a sign of patriarchal succession as it was inherited from a father or grandfather. It was also a personal machine that made it possible to systematise labour into mill and factory shifts, to organise railroad timetables, and to develop precise mechanisms working in concert. The man's watch signified his participation in a shared public time. But the decorative watch-hook forced him to hang up his watch, relinquishing it to his wife's or daughter's own space, making him trust this heavy valuable object to their frail container.

It is no accident that among the most popular handicrafts were men's slippers, embroidered caps and smoking accessories (tobacco pouches, cigar-cases and Orientalist smoking garb). These objects facilitated the transformation of a business-oriented man into a leisured, domestic inhabitant. When he removed his hat, shoes, watch and other appurtenances of public work, his own body would be overwritten with the work of the women of the house, from head to toe bearing the embroidered signs that he was now in a space defined by their labour and his own leisure. Thus the watch-hook, slippers and other male-intended gifts are profoundly anti-commodity; they insist on their own status as private and domestic objects.

If crafts for men emphasised male leisure in the home, then crafts for women mystified female labour in the home. One very common object was the workbasket, usually made of frail woven straw or cardboard and decorated with layers of frilled and quilted satin, studded with bows. Its fragility enforced only the most gossamer and diminutive of projects; it projected a life in which activities like the darning of men's wool socks quite literally had no place. The most popular types of handicrafts – vases, centrepieces, card-racks, picture frames and decorative stands – were meant to be shown off in the public rooms of the house. Public display confirmed that the articles were just as good as any of the professionally-made, purchased commodities around them. Such ornamental arts also confirmed that the female inhabitant had household tasks so well organised as to enjoy leisure time for delicate work.

The crafts had one disadvantage relative to mass-produced objects: they were extremely brittle. Often fastened with nothing more than weak homemade paste or bits of thread, the crafts must have fallen apart constantly. Moreover, the basic materials were not built to last. As Steven Gelber puts it, in nineteenth-century craft construction 'cardboard functioned as female wood' (169). The fragility of these objects is a fault, however, only if we assume the objects were meant to last. In the case of the domestic handicraft, however, the market preferred planned obsolescence. The craft's wobbliness was actually an advantage, because it kept women constantly employed, replacing items that were either disintegrating or outmoded. Its brittleness also guaranteed its value, paradoxically enough, for it forced its owners to treasure it, to keep it in the safest spaces of the home. And since the craft was seen as an extension of the woman herself, its bodily delicacy reinforced and guaranteed her own. Finally, there was no incentive to make permanent objects for the craft was part of the fashion system and was seen as disposable and changeable. The handicraft was closely associated with fashion: both appeared in lavish illustrations in women's magazines, both used elaborate textiles, both involved patterns and both were offered in new sets every month. Thus the craft's amateur brittleness was actually desirable. When Arts and Crafts professionalised the handicraft, they stressed that it needed to showcase strong construction and truth to materials. But these were new criteria for craft. Such professional-quality construction would have actually been counterproductive for the amateur women's craft, which wanted to showcase an attractive fragility, provide an excuse for constant alterations, and enable women to replace items with more fashionable objects.

By the 1870s, instructions for domestic handicrafts were ubiquitous but their quality had markedly declined. An 'imitation marble statuette' recommended by *Cassell's Household Guide* in 1869 reveals the deterioration of handicraft technique. This form of craft involved encasing an object in solidified wax. *Cassell's* recommended purchasing a cheap plaster cast and pouring half a pound of melted white candle wax over it until it was entirely coated. Thus the maker of the 'Wax Statuette' took a cheap commodity and expended transformative labour to render it into a sign of domestic care and an intimate denizen of a unique home. However, in this case, the transformative labour has been reduced to the merest sign. As *Cassell's* itself pointed out, 'no skill is needed; any one can do it well'. Probably, however, no one could have done it well. For even by handicraft standards, the fragility of this object is worrying. The hot wax would have probably melted the cheap plaster; even if the plaster had held its shape, the wax would have caught bits of fluff or grit, thumbprints, and smudges, it probably would have cracked as the wax cooled, and of course if displayed anywhere near the fire or candles, the whole contraption would have melted.

Part of the decay of craft quality is due, ironically, to the explosion of print venues for handicraft instructions. Technological innovations had made it possible to print patterns, colour plates and detailed illustrations better than ever before (Beetham 100–101). New Berlin-wool work designs appeared constantly; in 1876, a typical issue of the *Englishwoman's Domestic Magazine* contained 55 pages, 25 pages of which consisted of needlework and fashion engravings and patterns. With the *Englishwoman's Domestic Magazine* producing dozens of craft ideas per month; craft columns in the *Queen*, the *Girl's Own Paper* and most other women's magazines; and pamphlets and manuals constantly appearing, the competitive drive to invent new handicrafts simply outpaced any kind of quality control (Adburgham; Beetham; White). Moreover, the enormous profusion of craft articles after 1870 may not indicate that crafts had become more popular. Rather, it might actually mean that craft production had become wholly specular, that as Victorian advertising and visual culture flourished, women would rather look at engravings of crafts than actually make them (see Flint; Richards). If the pictures were the point, there was no reason to take any particular care with the instructions, which now functioned merely to make the reader feel virtuously pragmatic, to occlude her real specular hunger.

The craft had, in fact, become a residual element in Victorian culture. Just as craft technique aimed to preserve fragile natural specimens, so too did the craft genre itself sustain outmoded economic and aesthetic preferences. Craft itself became a kind of taxidermy, a stuffed relic of what had once been alive. By the 1870s, the domestic handicraft lingered on as a despised vestigial practice, becoming as a sort of underground rallying point for reactionary women who were disaffected from the new gender models, dissatisfied with the new aesthetic fashions, and distressed by the new techniques of retail trade. Identified with the early Victorian notion of domestic managerial femininity and cheerfully participating in mid-Victorian forms of mass-production, the handicraft was such a precise expression of 1840s and 1850s thought that it could not update itself. As the years marched on, anyone who made domestic handicraft was stubbornly allying herself with a mindset that was a generation or two past.

Part of the problem was that crafts came to symbolise a traditional model of womanhood. We have seen that the domestic handicraft was associated with the sentimental and industrious domestic manager, but starting in the

1860s that role competed with a range of newer identities becoming available to women. Women who wanted to affirm their fidelity to the traditional housewifely model might make handicrafts to symbolise this identification. But for women affiliating themselves with more contemporary gender models, like the emergent aesthetic or New Woman roles, the domestic handicraft symbolised a retrograde past.

Another issue was that the domestic handicraft was now seriously out of step with the artistic ideas promulgated by the Design Reform movement, the Arts and Crafts movement, and later, the aesthetes.[7] Well into the late nineteenth century, domestic handicraft retained its fidelity to mid-Victorian visual culture with bright colours, imitative arts and elaborate objects made of pasted cardboard and scraps of fabric, based on magazine illustrations or prefabricated kits. But Arts and Crafts had taught Victorians to value new standards: artistic expertise, originality, connoisseurship, tertiary colours and skilled labour. Above all, the Arts and Crafts movement introduced a new code of professionalism. Now the handicraft showcased its maker's training, its form demonstrating the craftsman's personal skill, handmade investment, historical knowledge and interest in the material. This craft was sold in stores or galleries, not exchanged as gifts or circulated in charity bazaars like its female counterpart. In this respect, the professional craft after 1860 is quite opposed to the amateur female craft.

While it is important that Aurora Leigh suffered through craft instruction in her youth, it is also important that, as an adult, she feels free to critique it. Her rejection of domestic handicraft symbolises the intellectual woman's rebellion and the decline of domestic handicraft into deep unfashionability. Aurora concludes that '… we are paid / The worth of our work, perhaps' (I.464–5). But if Aurora could not see the value of this 'work', perhaps we can. We can see how amateur handicrafts enabled women to express their ambivalence about the industrial economy, their emulation, critique and competition with the work of men. We can see how amateur handicrafts let women assert themselves as participants in mid-Victorian imitation, recycling, fashion and realism. Handicrafts articulated a specific position for women at a time of rapidly shifting values, and they achieved immense popularity because they were indeed, as Aurora noted, 'symbolical' (I.457).

## Works Cited

Adburgham, Alison. *Women in Print: Writing Women and Women's Magazines from the Restoration to the Accession of Victoria*. London: Allen & Unwin, 1972.

Ames, Kenneth L. *Death in the Dining Room and Other Tales of Victorian Culture*. Philadelphia: Temple University Press, 1992.

Auerbach, Jeffrey. *The Great Exhibition of 1851: A Nation on Display*. New Haven and London: Yale University Press, 1999.

Barrett Browning, Elizabeth. *Aurora Leigh*. Ed. Margaret Reynolds. New York: W.W. Norton and Co., 1996.

Beetham, Margaret. *A Magazine of Her Own? Domesticity and Desire in the Woman's Magazine, 1800–1914*. London and New York: Routledge, 1996.

Brantlinger, Patrick. 'Household Taste: Industrial Art, Consumerism, and Pre-Raphaelitism'. *The Journal of Pre-Raphaelite Studies* 9 (Spring 2000): 83–100.

Briggs, Asa. *Victorian Things*. Chicago: University of Chicago Press, 1988.

Callen, Anthea. *Angel in the Studio: Women in the Arts and Crafts Movement 1870–1914*. London: Astragal, 1979.

Caulfield, Sophia Frances Anne, and Blanche C. Saward. *The Dictionary of Needlework: An Encyclopaedia of Artistic, Plain, and Fancy Needlework*. New York: Arno Press, 1972.

Cohen, Deborah. *Household Gods: The British and Their Possessions*. New Haven: Yale University Press, 2006.

Davidoff, Leonore, and Catherine Hall. 'The Hidden Investment: Women and the Enterprise'. *Women's Work: The English Experience 1650–1914*. Ed. Pamela Sharpe. London: Arnold, 1998. 239–93.

Dodd, George. 'Art-Amusements for Ladies'. *St. James's Magazine* 12 (1865): 197–206.

Edwards, Clive. '"Home is Where the Art is": Women, Handicrafts and Home Improvements 1750–1900'. *Journal of Design History* 19.1 (2006): 11–21.

Flint, Kate. *The Victorians and the Visual Imagination*. Cambridge: Cambridge University Press, 2000.

Fraser, W. Hamish. *The Coming of the Mass Market, 1850–1914*. Hamden, CT: Archon Books, 1981.

Freedgood, Elaine. *The Ideas in Things: Fugitive Meaning in the Victorian Novel*. Chicago: University of Chicago Press, 2006.

Gelber, Steven M. *Hobbies: Leisure and the Culture of Work in America*. New York: Columbia University Press, 1999.

Hafter, Daryl M. *European Women and Preindustrial Craft*. Bloomington: Indiana University Press, 1995.

Hartshorne, C.H. *English Medieval Embroidery*. London: John Henry Parker, 1848.

Helms, Mary W. *Craft and the Kingly Ideal: Art, Trade, and Power*. Austin: University of Texas Press, 1993.

Henderson, Marjorie, and Elizabeth Wilkinson. *Cassell's Compendium of Victorian Crafts*. London: Cassell, 1977.

Hulbert, Anne. *Victorian Crafts Revived*. London: B.T. Batsford Ltd, 1978.

'Imitation Marble Statuette'. *Cassell's Household Guide* 1 (1869): 164–5.

Kopytoff, Igor. 'The Cultural Biography of Things: Commoditization as Process'. *The Social Life of Things: Commodities in Cultural Perspective*. Ed Arjun Appadurai. Cambridge: Cambridge University Press, 1986. 64–94.

Kriegel, Lara. *Grand Designs: Labor, Empire, and the Museum in Victorian Culture*. Durham, NC: Duke University Press, 2007.

*Lady's Album of Fancy Work*. London: Grant and Griffith, 1850.

Lambert, Miss A. *The Handbook of Needlework*. London: John Murray, 1842.

Lemire, Beverly. *Fashion's Favourite: The Cotton Trade and the Consumer in Britain, 1660–1800*. Oxford: Oxford University Press, 1991.

Lichten, Frances. *Decorative Art of Victoria's Era*. New York and London: Charles Scribner's Sons, 1950.

Logan, Thad. *The Victorian Parlour*. Cambridge: Cambridge University Press, 2001.

Lubbock, Jules. *The Tyranny of Taste: The Politics of Architecture and Design in Britain 1550–1960*. New Haven: Yale University Press, 1995.

Lucie-Smith, Edward. *The Story of Craft: The Craftsman's Role in Society*. Oxford: Phaidon, 1981.
*Miss Linwood's Gallery of Pictures, in Worsted, Leicester Square*. London: Weed and Rider, 1820.
Morris, Barbara. *Victorian Embroidery*. London: Herbert Jenkins, 1962.
*Official Descriptive and Illustrated Catalogue of the Great Exhibition*. Ed. Robert F.L.S. Ellis. 5 vols. London: Spicer Brothers, 1851.
Parker, Rozsika. *The Subversive Stitch: Embroidery and the Making of the Feminine*. London: The Women's Press Ltd, 1996.
Parkes, Mrs. William. *Domestic Duties; or, Instructions to Young Married Ladies*. London: Longman, Hurst, Rees, Orme, Brown, and Green, 1825.
Plotz, John. *Portable Property: Victorian Culture on the Move*. Princeton: Princeton University Press, 2008.
Richards, Thomas. *The Commodity Culture of Victorian England: Advertising and Spectacle, 1851–1914*. Stanford: Stanford University Press, 1990.
Ruskin, John. *Sesame and Lilies*. New York: H.M. Caldwell Company, n.d. but first published 1865.
Steegman, John. *Victorian Taste*. London: Thomas Nelson & Sons Ltd, 1970.
Stewart, Susan. *On Longing: Narratives of the Miniature, the Gigantic, the Souvenir, and the Collectible*. Baltimore: Johns Hopkins University Press, 1984.
Stone, Elizabeth. *The Art of Needle-Work from the Earliest Ages*. London: Henry Colburn, 1840.
Styles, John. 'Manufacturing, Consumption and Design in Eighteenth-Century England'. *Consumption and the World of Goods*. Ed. John Brewer and Roy Porter. London and New York: Routledge, 1993. 527–54.
Toller, Jane. *The Regency and Victorian Crafts, or, The Genteel Female – Her Arts and Pursuits*. London, Sydney: Ward Lock Ltd, 1969.
Urbino, L.B., and Henry Day. *Art Recreations*. Boston: J.E. Tilton and Company, 1861.
Weiner, Annette B. *Inalienable Possessions: The Paradox of Keeping-While-Giving*. Berkeley: University of California Press, 1992.
White, Cynthia L. *Women's Magazines, 1693–1968*. London: Joseph, 1970.
Yonge, Charlotte. *Abbeychurch*. New York: Garland, 1976.

## Notes

1 Deborah Cohen and Thad Logan are honourable exceptions. Other than those excellent recent studies, see Briggs; Lichten; Toller. Much work in allied fields sheds interesting light on handicrafts; in thing theory, for instance, see Freedgood; Plotz, and in museum studies see Kriegel; Lubbock.

2 A painted tea-tray, a Staffordshire figurine, some decorative china, were prized markers of luxury for the working poor. Hippolyte Taine's comment is revealing: 'You draw near a house, look in, and, in the half-light of a passage, see mother and grown daughter crouching, wearing little more than a chemise. What rooms! A threadbare slip of oilcloth on the floor, sometimes a big sea-shell or one or two plaster ornaments ...' (quoted in Lubbock 228–9). Here the starving women would rather have plaster ornaments than decent clothing, surely a strong testimony to the psychological appeal of such luxury items.

3 Miss Lambert dedicated *The Handbook of Needlework* (1851) to Princess Mary, while the Countess of Wilton edited E. Stone's *The Art of Needle-Work, from the Earliest Ages* (1840) and C.H. Hartshorne dedicated her *English Medieval Embroidery* (1848) to Marianne, Viscountess Alford.

4 A leader in *The Times* on July 1, 1851 complained about the 'imitative rage' among the carpets and pottery at the Great Exhibition (quoted in Briggs 71–2). Also see Kriegel's informative discussion.

5 The title alludes not to Japan, but to japanning, an effect emulated by the varnishing.

6 A similar design for a watch-pocket made of straw and ribbons appears in *The Lady's Newspaper* (later the *Queen*) 11 (5 June 1852): 342–3.

7 The Design Reform movement refers to the mid-century reformers like Sir Henry Cole, Owen Jones and Richard Redgrave who reacted to the quality of art manufactures at the Great Exhibition by vigorously championing new rules for decorative art and by setting up the South Kensington Museum to educate Britons about good design. It was strongest in the 1850s (the Great Exhibition was 1851) and its participants were prominent governmental figures. The Arts and Crafts movement got its name from the first Arts and Crafts exhibition in 1888, although its participants were, of course, active earlier. Flourishing between the 1850s and 1870s, and, obviously, overlapping with the Design Reform movement, their ranks included artists and art critics like John Ruskin, William Morris, Walter Crane and the Pre-Raphaelite painters. They rebelled vociferously against the domestic handicraft. The next generation, the aesthetes (between the 1870s and 1890s), built on their predecessors' achievements but elaborated their belief in beautiful objects into a philosophy that governed personal behaviour, morality, literature and leisure; they included Max Beerbohm, Lucas Malet, Rosamund Marriott Watson and Oscar Wilde.

2

# Light Work: Feminine Leisure and the Making of Transparencies

*John Plunkett*

> FASHIONABLE TRANSPARENCIES; – Transparent scenery – transparent pictures – transparent petticoats – transparent prisons! ('Fashionable' 2)

In *Mansfield Park* (1813), the isolated Fanny Price finds refuge in the secluded East Room at Mansfield Park, which is filled with cast-off handicrafts made by the privileged Bertram sisters:

> The room was most dear to her, and she would not have changed its furniture for the handsomest in the house, though what had been originally plain had suffered all the ill-usage of children; and its greatest elegancies and ornaments were a faded footstool of Julia's work, too ill done for the drawing-room, three transparencies, made in a rage for transparencies, for the three lower panes of one window, where Tintern Abbey held its station between a cave in Italy and a moonlit lake in Cumberland, a collection of family profiles, thought unworthy of being anywhere else … (Austen, *Mansfield* 106–7)

Embroidery, needlework and silhouettes are familiar feminine leisure activities of the early nineteenth century, yet transparencies have received surprisingly little scholarly attention in relation to their significance during the period.[1] Transparencies were one of the most important forms of popular art to emerge in the late eighteenth century; until at least the mid-nineteenth century, they were ubiquitous at pleasure gardens, balls, assemblies, hustings, dinners, astronomical lectures, theatres, fairs and – most prominently – at civic celebrations of all kinds. The most elaborate large-scale transparencies for public exhibition were usually produced by professional scene-painters, drawing-masters or even esteemed Royal Academicians, yet their prevalence stemmed from the fashionable status attached to the production of small paper and ornamental versions by amateurs. Transparencies proliferated because they could be executed in a multiplicity of formats, sizes and materials appropriate to whatever artistic or practical skill was possessed by their creator; these were then exhibited in a corresponding variety of public, civic and domestic spaces.

This chapter argues that a key element in the popularity of transparencies was their becoming part of the repertoire of refined feminine accomplishments. While they were specifically an extension of the sketching and water-colour painting that genteel women were encouraged to undertake, they formed part of the broader expansion of women's decorative and domestic handicrafts. Amelia, the heroine of an 1810 story in *The Lady's Monthly Museum* is complemented for being able to 'dash through a sonata, on the Piano Forte, very tolerably; and having naturally a taste for drawing, could sketch prettily, and even execute some transparencies in a very tasteful manner' ('Montravers' 228). Like their large-scale counterparts, the purpose of small transparencies was to be shown off, albeit as a sign of feminine creativity and sensibility rather than as a celebration of the latest military victory or royal birthday. In a letter to her sister Cassandra in October 1800, Jane Austen describes a visit to the nearby country estate of Oakley Hall where they 'admired Mr Bramston's Porter & Mrs Bramstom's Transparencies, & gained a promise from the latter of two roots of hearts-ease'(Austen, *Life* 100). Transparencies were not only to be praised and pored over in the drawing-room though; they were taken up so enthusiastically because they were used to decorate it through being incorporated in lampshades, screens and windowblinds. As Talia Schaffer and others have noted, the growth of domestic handicrafts was deeply tied to making 'women's separate-sphere virtues visible' (5). Decorative transparencies were amongst the earliest means women had to display these virtues in that they gave them the opportunity to feminise the domestic interior, making the space itself a gendered embodiment of their own decorative tastes and talents. The luminous, ethereal and translucent beauty of transparencies created a potent correspondence between their aesthetic experience and that of femininity itself.

My aim is to detail the different types of transparency, the practices involved in their domestic making and exhibition, and the way that their sensory impact was key to their appeal. Transparencies were scenes painted on paper, Irish linen, fine calico or cambric muslin that were back-lit to create an illuminated effect. One of their earliest descriptions is in Charles Taylor's drawing-manual for amateurs, *The Artist's Repository and Drawing Magazine, Exhibiting the Principles of the Polite Arts in their Various Branches* (1784):

> Transparencies, are paintings on silk, &c. with such thin and transparent colours as admit the light to pass through the picture; these are much used for decorations,

illuminations, &c. and by means of artificial and brilliant light placed behind them, they have a very gay and sprightly effect. (137)

Taylor emphasises that transparencies were an aesthetic partnership between the manipulation of the fabric or paper to create a translucent medium and the careful use of strong backlighting. With their impact dependent on the strength of their illumination, improvements in the intensity and power of artificial lighting contributed to their becoming fashionable; of particular importance is the development of the Argand oil lamp, which was patented in 1784 by Aimé Argand and was several times more powerful than existing lamps or candles. In being transformed into life when illuminated, transparencies were part site-specific art installation, part optical performance; they shared a number of features with the contemporaneous advent of the phantasmagoria, diorama and enclosed peepshow, all of which relied on different forms of backlighting. Like these optical shows, large and small transparencies provided an embodied aesthetic experience through transforming the sensory space inhabited by the audience.

The optical performance of transparencies gave them a sensual appeal that distinguished them from conventional prints and painting. Taylor tellingly praises their 'gay' and 'sprightly' effect, defining them through their phenomenological impact. With transparencies the viewer is no longer looking at painted light; s/he is actually experiencing light refracted through painted glass or translucent cloth. The heightened sensations they provided ('pleasing' was an adjective repeatedly used to describe their effect) make them an expression of the eighteenth-century taste for sensibility. Alice Barnaby has argued that they embody a broader Romantic social, perceptual and aesthetic fascination, whereby 'changes in both natural and artificial light, and therefore also darkness, became acutely palpable to the human sensorium – using, seeing, feeling and being in light became matters of intense personal and cultural concern' (16). Barnaby's work adds an extra dimension to Schaffer's claim that handicrafts express 'the dominant ways that women intersected with the material world' (25). While Schaffer focuses on how women's domestic handicraft was a rejection of the emergent industrial economy, Barnaby claims that transparencies were an aesthetic negotiation with the sensuous materiality of the world itself; they stemmed from the pleasurable manipulation of one of its primary elements – light. The making of transparencies was also part of a new focus on interior design, itself encouraged by a combination of changes in living practices, gender ideology and architectural taste, which fashioned 'subjects alert to new opportunities of sensory knowledge and sensitive to the aesthetic conditions of their surroundings' (Barnaby 30).

Transparencies became common across Europe during the 1770s and 1780s; they were employed across a range of formal and informal performance spaces, including theatres, pleasure gardens and elite social events. Philip James de Loutherbourg revolutionised theatrical scenography through his use of them during his work as a scene designer for Drury Lane in the 1770s; his *Eidophusikon,* first exhibited in 1781, was renowned for its use of coloured transparencies to create clever scenic and atmospheric effects of storms, clouds and lightning. Around the same time, they began to be used to illustrate astronomical lectures, the most prominent being Adam Walker's *Eidouranion, or Large Transparent Orrery,* which toured extensively and was still delighting audiences in the 1820s. Transparencies also became a ritual part of grand national occasions. The general illuminations celebrating the return to health of George III in April 1789 was one of the first occasions to be characterised by their widespread exhibition. Adding illuminated transparencies with patriotic and heraldic designs to major civic buildings and private residences transformed the appearance of cityscapes up and down the land: the publicness of an event was celebrated through distinct and heightened perceptual urban experience. Subsequent occasions such as the death of Nelson and the jubilee of George III were similarly marked, with newspapers publishing long lists of the allegorical transparencies exhibited in London and provincial cities. Joseph Strutt's *The Sports and Pastimes of the People of England* (1801) noted 'the profusion of transparent paintings, inscriptions, and variety of other curious and expensive devices, that seem to be almost peculiar to the present age' (295). *The Cabinet of the Arts* (1805) could similarly assert that while transparent painting was not a new invention it 'has of late years come much into vogue in this country' (Hodson and Dougall 361).

The use of large transparencies to enliven civic and elite social events overlapped with those produced by women as a means of exhibiting their own fashionable tastes. When the Countess of Buckinghamshire gave a sumptuous fete at her Chiswick villa in August 1807, a laurel bower was constructed in the centre of her garden, ornamented with a transparency traced by her own hand ('Albinia' 3). Similarly, the heroine of Mary Ann Kelty's *The Story of Isabel* (1826), bemoans her lack of artistic skill by noting that the sole products of her many drawing-lessons were 'two transparencies, which decorated the hall-windows on an illumination-night, and which I executed in one morning' (I.10–11). Paradoxically, transparencies initially became fashionable due to their being exhibited and executed by the aristocratic elite, yet their popularity stemmed from printsellers and publishers disseminating knowledge of the requisite techniques and also supplying ready-made materials and scenes. A number of dedicated manuals on how to achieve the best effects in transparent painting were published; instructions also appeared in general drawing manuals, women's periodicals and anthologies of rational recreation, handicrafts and, later in the century, hobbies; drawing-masters also began to include the teaching of transparent painting as part of their repertoire. Transparencies' assimilation into a range of artistic and decorative pursuits exemplifies their protean character, which was also part of their appeal to different social groups.

## Transparent Prints

Printsellers' principal innovation in encouraging the vogue for transparencies was the development of a format of small transparent paper prints, either for colouring, finishing or copying. I.F. Mannskirsch's, *A View on the Rhine near Bingen* (Figure 2.1), published by Ackermann on July 16, 1798, typifies the new format. Its principal feature is the play of moonlight reflecting off water; the phenomenological effect of the shadows is heightened when the print is held up to the light because, on the reverse, the principal areas of moonlight have been coloured in order to enhance the sensory impact. The effect of darkening the shadows on the reverse is conversely to prevent any light passing through the print, enhancing the way they are experienced by the viewer. The print could be viewed by fixing it against a window, holding it up to the light, or placing a candle behind it. As Barnaby has brilliantly observed, the pleasure of transparencies was bound up with a playfulness towards the materiality of light, providing 'non-narrative, open-ended and spontaneous experiences in which the role of the performer and spectator merged' (30).

*A View on the Rhine near Bingen* is typical of the way that the colouring and subject matter of transparencies worked to maximise the effect of the light coming through the print. Firelight, moonlight or stained glass windows were all common features in transparent prints as careful touching on the reverse accentuated the ethereal brilliancy of the light source in the print. The sensory impact of the print when illuminated was also strengthened by the strongest light sources in the scene being touched very carefully with spirit of turpentine on both sides to turn the paper into a more translucent medium. These areas were often also touched with varnish to make them more reflective, as described in John Imison's 1822 guide:

> When the picture is finished, and every part has got its depth of colour and brilliancy, being perfectly dry, you touch very carefully with spirits of turpentine on both sides, those parts which are to be the brightest, such as the moon and fire, and those parts requiring less brightness, only on one side. Then lay on immediately with a pencil, a varnish ... You must be careful with the varnish as it is apt to spread. When the varnish is dry you tint the flame with red-lead and gamboge, slightly tinging the smoke next to the flame: the moon must not be tinted with colour. (408)

2.1 I.F. Mannskirsch, *A View on the Rhine near Bingen*, 16 July 1798 [EXEBD70101]. Courtesy of the University of Exeter.

Ideally, light should flow through the picture and parts of the paper should appear to dissolve into light. The diaphanous quality of transparencies was also enhanced through the careful use of colour. Colours that had the most transparent qualities were recommended, particularly Prussian Blue, Burnt Sienna, Verdigris and Ivory Black. The ground colours could be mixed with mastic varnish or burnt linseed oil in order to add to their reflective qualities. Scraping or cutting away small sections of the paper could also enhance its transparency. Thus, areas depicting the sun, moon, fireworks or the illuminated windows of a building might be cut away and, where the hole was created, coloured paper soaked in varnish was added to the back of the print. This technique could be highly effective in creating an augmented experience of the luminous effect of sun and moon and was borrowed from the methods used for back-lit prints employed in optical show-boxes from at least the middle decades of the eighteenth century. William Hooper's *Rational Recreations* (1784), for instance, provides instructions on creating 'Illuminated Prospects' and 'Transparent Illuminations' using these effects (II.189–94). The various continuities in technique between transparencies and prior forms of optical exhibition highlight that what was most original about them was their status as fashionable, feminine handicrafts.

Rudolph Ackermann and Edward Orme were the two prominent London printsellers who did most to pioneer transparent prints. Both launched new series in the final two years of the eighteenth century. Ackermann had only set up a printselling business in 1795, but his *Repository of Arts* at 101, The Strand, was soon the leading supplier of prints, caricatures, colour-plate books, artists' materials and all manner of pre-fabricated items that could be used for handicrafts. Ackermann brought together the fine arts with the burgeoning world of commercialised leisure, and transparencies were one of the products that exemplified this new market for sketching, painting and handicrafts. Ackermann, for example, published a series of 109 hand-coloured aquatint transparencies over 1799 and 1800 at prices of 2*s*. plain, and 4*s*. coloured. Subjects included *The Eddystone Lighthouse* (1800), *The London Inn* (1800), and *A Moonlit Shipwreck* (1799).[2] The above were single transparencies, while others sheets sold by Ackermann, such as the Egyptian scenes in Figure 2.2, consisted of a number of smaller designs that amateurs could cut out, copy or colour.

Ackermann's chief rival in the production of transparent prints was Edward Orme, who published his own series in 1799. On January 1, Orme released the first of the individual prints that, later the same year, would be published together as *Subjects for Transparencies* (1799). Orme held the title of printseller to King George III, and his London establishment was at the corner of George and Conduit Street. *Subjects for Transparencies* consisted of black and white engravings that could be coloured and turned into transparencies. Later the same year, Thomas Rowlandson also sought to take advantage of the upsurge of interest in transparencies by publishing his own series of seven prints.[3] Paper transparencies had the obvious advantage of being produced much more readily than those painted on glass. According to Orme, a much greater effect could be achieved on paper, 'a shadow that will take you a month to work and stipple upon glass, may be produced with twice the force upon paper in the space of twenty minutes' (*Essay* 65). While Orme admitted that transparencies on silk, glass, and even paper, had been created for centuries, he ambitiously claimed to have been the first to publish transparent prints. Their invention reputedly took place in 1799, when, by accident, he dropped varnish for an oil painting onto the dark part of an engraving of *The Death of Chatterton*. The varnish made the paper transparent and simultaneously created a lacquered surface. Orme went on to produce as many as 50 subjects between 1800 and 1807; like Ackermann, they relied on striking contrasts of light and shade, including 'The Castle Spectre' (10*s*. 6*d*.), 'The Temple of the Sun, from Pizarro' (10*s*. 6*d*.), 'A Cottage on Fire' (12*s*.), and 'Large Mount Vesuvius and Companion' (3*s*. 3*d*.).

2.2 R. Ackermann, *Egyptian Transparencies* (1806) [EXEBD70407]. Courtesy of the University of Exeter.

Selling at a much higher price than Ackermann, Orme's coloured transparencies were affordable only by a wealthy few.

The new format of transparent prints was complemented by Orme's and Ackermann's instruction manuals for those desirous of making their own transparencies. Ackermann published his guide in 1799, with improved editions in 1800, 1802 and 1804. Orme published his *Instructions for Painting*

*Transparencies* in 1807, in a parallel French–English edition. In a luxury folio volume that was sumptuously illustrated with a number of transparencies, Orme provided a step-by-step visual primer on how to transform a print into a transparency. Both Orme and Ackermann's excursion into transparent prints was clearly aimed at taking advantage of the popularity of sketching and water-colour painting as genteel feminine pursuits. Ackermann specifically referred to his female readers when providing the recipe for the varnish solution used to finish transparencies (14). Orme's efforts were equally directed at a female audience in that he publicised his manual through giving away a transparent print of a cat's head with the February 1807 edition of *La Belle Assemblée*, the leading women's journal, launched in 1806, which played an important role in disseminating – both geographically and socially – the latest aristocratic fashions in dress and leisure pursuits. Unsurprisingly *La Belle Assemblée* reciprocated Orme's promotional efforts through an extensive puff for his transparencies guide, noting 'the eagerness with which they have been adopted in the realm of fashion' and that his step-by-step guide could 'render the art easily attainable even by those who have no skill in drawing' ('New' 57). This last platitude is telling in so far as Orme's and Ackermann's efforts – their manuals, prints and pre-prepared designs – extended the execution of transparencies to those women who had little or no formal artistic training.

Orme and Ackermann were far from alone in promoting the fashionable feminine status of transparencies through disseminating the necessary techniques. Drawing masters also offered tutorials as part of their range of classes. In 1799, a month's worth of 12 lessons in drawing, painting and transparencies in Windsor from Mrs A. Noel was £2 2*s*., while L. Buckley, a former pupil of Edward Orme, had graduated to offering classes in making transparencies at his Berkeley Square home in 1802 ('Windsor' 1; 'L.' 2). Instructions on transparent painting were also incorporated into a number of general drawing and watercolour manuals. When James Roberts, official portrait painter to HRH Duke of Clarence, produced his guide to water-colour painting in 1809, he added an appendix, *Instructions for Executing Transparencies in a Style Both Novel and Easy*, the reason being that 'Transparencies are becoming so extremely fashionable and popular' (35). The instructions proffered by these manuals reveal both the techniques used to maximise their sensory appeal and, more broadly, the existence of a distinct aesthetics of transparency. Roberts's method for making transparencies is similar to Orme's and Ackermann's, albeit with the additional suggestion that they could be created by washing the whole of the drawing with mastic varnish rather than simply the principal shadows and light sources.

Like all other guides, Roberts recommended subjects that made the most of the phenomenological play of light and shadow, whether fire, magma, stained glass windows or other atmospheric effects: 'Abbeys in ruin, Gothic painted windows, illuminated temples and gardens, moonlight, fires, and groups of gypsies sitting round a fire in a thick wood with the moon glimmering behind the trees' (36). John Imison's *Elements of Science and Art* (1822) provided even more detailed advice on obtaining the perfect synthesis between subject matter and sensory effect; his advice highlights the sophisticated understanding of the optical performance being created:

> Much depends upon the choice of the subject, and none is so admirably adapted to this species of effect as the gloomy Gothic ruin, whose antique towers and pointed turrets finely contrast their dark battlements with the pale, yet brilliant moon. Rays passing through the ruined windows half choaked [sic] with ivy, a fire amongst the clustering pillars and broken monuments of the choir, round which are figures of banditti, or others whose haggard faces catch the reflecting light, afford a peculiarity of effect, not to be equalled in any other species of painting. Internal views of cathedrals, also, where windows of stained glass are introduced, form beautiful subjects. (408)

Imison's ideal subjects typify the way that transparencies could literally embody the picturesque or gothic. William Gilpin believed that the variegated play of light off different surfaces was a key means of achieving a picturesque landscape, while Uvedale Price's hugely influential essays on the picturesque extended Gilpin's ideas through proclamations such as 'intricacy in the disposition, and variety in the forms and lights and shadows of objects, are the great characteristics of the picturesque in scenery' (26–7). The play of contrasting atmospheric effects that was the *raison d'etre* of the transparent print was a corporeal embodiment of the picturesque. The success of transparencies makes them part of what Ann Bermingham has labelled as the emergence of a distinct 'landscape of sensation', concerned with 'the optical features of a particular scene and their effects on the viewer's perception' (120). Bermingham argues that this aesthetic was part of the commercial appropriation of the picturesque by printsellers and publishers, citing works such as *Gilpin's Day*, which was published by Edward Orme in 1810 and which consisted of 30 monochrome aquatints showing landscapes at different times of day.

Transparent prints, *pace* Bermingham, were part of a broader perceptual, aesthetic and optical fascination with transparency and the play of light. Correspondingly, a number of different materials were used to create similar effects; these often drew upon the skills used by other feminine handicrafts, such as the production of silhouettes, embroidery and fancy paper-work. Another type of transparency, for example, was created by fastening five or six thin sheets of white paper together; the design was then marked out on the top sheet. Depending on the effect to be created, a different number of sheets was cut out. Paper crafts were a particularly admired handicraft during the late eighteenth century and its techniques could be easily redeployed for transparencies; Orme especially recommended this method to 'my fair country-women, who have a taste for cutting out figures in paper, which many ladies perform in a very astonishing manner, to make experiments in this art, and endeavour to bring it to a greater degree of perfection' (*Essay* 43).[4] Figure 2.3 is an example of this method, portraying Linlithgow Palace in Edinburgh; a comparison between Figure 2.3 and Figure 2.4, the backlit version of the transparency, demonstrates both the importance of a light source in bringing the scene alive as well as the sophisticated effects that could be achieved simply through layers of cut-out paper. The moon, sky and the light reflecting off the water are the areas where most layers of paper have been cut away, whereas the trees in the foreground are much darker and more solid, with the light having to pass through several layers of paper. Occasionally, such work reached the realm of public exhibition; in 1847, at the Cosmorama Rooms in Regent Street, there was an exhibition called *Camera Lunaris*, which consisted of 12 large paper, cut-out, back-lit transparencies, all representing the effect of moonlight on ruins, buildings and water. Their effect was created only by different layers of white paper cut out and placed over each other. The views available included Tintern Abbey and Northampton Street. *The Times* noted that they were done by a lady, although, perhaps tellingly, it did not think her deserving of name ('Camera' 5). Transparencies also appropriated the skills gained through needlework and embroidery; the Getty Research Institute holds in the Werner Nekes Collection two intricate and beautiful transparencies, produced in France, created by hundreds of tiny holes and indentations pricked with a needle; one depicts a bird on a branch and the second a bunch of flowers (see Vues d'optique and translucent prints, circa 1700–1976: Box IV, Series IB). The scenes have a wonderful delicacy that must have taken hours of precise, concentrated labour.

While Bermingham and Schaffer are right to emphasise that handicrafts and sketching channelled women's artistry through certain socially assigned modes of expression, the creativity they offered was nonetheless liberating. Cut-paper transparencies, for example, provide an inexpensive opportunity for creative fulfilment for the writer Mary Howitt who collaborated with her husband, William Howittt, on many publications from the 1820s onwards. Born in 1799 as Mary Botham, she and her sister Anna were raised in a strict Quaker household. Their home was soberly decorated, with an absence of colour; Mary's autobiography stated that 'I feel a sort of tender pity for Anna and myself when I remember how we were always seeking and struggling after the beautiful, and after artistic production, though we knew nothing of art' (I.95). When Mary was around 15, her artistic work included etching landscapes, flowers and figures on glass, as well as transparencies made out of different thicknesses of cap-paper.

2.3 Cut-out paper transparency of Linlithgow Palace, c.1820 [EXEBD69267]. Courtesy of the University of Exeter.

2.4 Back-lit version of cut-out paper transparency of Linlithgow Palace, c.1820 [EXEBD69267]. Courtesy of the University of Exeter.

Of these, the most successful was of Tintern Abbey, which, as Mary notes, survived many of their other works of art: 'The effect of light and shade was excellent; the long perspective was accurately given; there were the broken arches, the black thickness of ivy, with the loose trails hanging here and there in the light. It was about the size of a moderate pane of glass' (I.96–7). Mary Howitt's transparencies indicate how they were realisations of a pent-up desire for aesthetic pleasure using the most basic of materials, cap-paper being a particularly thin, inexpensive paper, often used for wrapping parcels or packets. The use of such readily-available material suggests that their making was taken up across the social spectrum and was not just a genteel pursuit.

Instructions on making the various types of transparency appeared regularly in books of women's recreation and women's periodicals in the first decades of the nineteenth century, ensuring their position as part of the dramatic growth of ornamental fancy work and handicrafts. *The Young Lady's Book: A Manual of Elegant Recreations, Exercises and Pursuits* (1829) is typical in that transparencies were included as part of a section on the 'Ornamental Artist'. According to the introduction to this section, decorating the domestic interior with fancy work made of 'several kinds of light materials' afforded 'graceful occupation' and provided so many 'opportunities for the display of good taste and dexterity in many interesting arts, that our work might be considered incomplete, if it did not devote a portion of its pages to some interesting subjects of this nature' (459). The production of transparencies was located alongside making models in clay, wax and pasteboard, screens, trays, baskets, and painting on glass and velvet.

The efforts of publishers and printsellers did much to further the popularity of transparencies, particularly amongst the increasing number of middle-class women. Bermingham, however, has a more critical interpretation of the promotion of drawing, water-colour painting and fancy work as genteel feminine pursuits in the period 1780–1830, claiming that they conflated femininity with amateurism as a means to remasculinise high art and disassociate it from the sphere of commerce. Bermingham has archly noted that while printsellers like Ackermann promoted feminine creativity and handicraft, thanks to their wares, 'Fancy work articles could be produced in a very short time and with a minimum of effort. Most of the decoration was prefabricated or could be produced through tracing or stencilling' (146). Transparencies were no exception in that Orme and Ackermann sold ready-made designs that only needed finishing; they also sold paper glazed on both sides that did not need to be varnished to create an effective illuminated transparency (see Ackermann, *Catalogue*). There was also a repertoire of standard subjects; Jane Austen, Mary Howitt and Mary Ann Kelty all describe transparencies of Tintern Abbey. Paradoxically, printsellers extended the popularity of transparencies at the same time as the commodification of their making hollowed out their aesthetic status – at least as judged by the fine art establishment – encouraging the perception of them as no more than feminine fancy work marked by little originality and skill.

Transparencies, as the example of Mary Howitt attests to, did provide an opportunity to express feminine artistry and taste, yet both because and in spite of this, they could be characterised as superficial, ephemeral and frivolous. Their aesthetics were conflated with their status as a feminine leisure pursuit. The *Monthly Review* dismissed them as 'merely as a toy or plaything of art; – the amusement of an idle hour, from the contemplation of more serious pursuits' ('Monthly' 316). Such overt criticism over their lack of artistic status was unusual; more common was the evoking of a potent correspondence between the aesthetics of transparencies – radiant, ethereal, passive – and the ideals of femininity. Barnaby has noted that 'The cultural construction of feminine identity as pure, pliable, transparently light (in both weight and appearance), and the aesthetic production of transparent imagery were ontologically entwined and mutually supportive' (77). Often laudatory, this figuring nonetheless worked to enforce a patriarchal construction of femininity, as evidenced in a sonnet by William Parsons, 'On Some Transparencies Done by a Lady' (1807):

> What tho' these sketches faint resemblance hold
> With the nice touch of TITIAN or LORRAINE;
> What tho' their forms, inanimate and cold,
> Unaptly plac'd, are objects of disdain:
> As spoke th'omniscient Word – 'LET THERE BE LIGHT!'
> – With sudden lustre skies, and groves, and streams,
> Start, as from Chaos old, in beauty bright,
> When new Creation felt the vital beams!
> Fain would MUSE her due applauses pay,
> The MUSE, who well each latent thought divines;
> And thus she sings: Good-Humour's genuine ray
> Thro' the transparent veil of NATURE shines;
> Thus does the mental SUN our Artist grace,
> And brighten ev'ry feature of her face!' (156)

Parsons is best-known as a member of the Della Cruscan group of late eighteenth-century sentimental poets; when not in Italy he spent his time residing in the fashionable circles of Bath. His sonnet celebrates the beauty of transparencies in a way that disavows their fine art status. Lacking the skill and quality of an Old Master, the transparencies require the external light source not only to animate them but to bring them into the realm of the aesthetic. Echoing Genesis, light rather than female artistry is made the true creative agent. The femininity of its maker is, moreover, itself like a transparency in that it is made radiant by her creativity being illuminated, albeit the transformative agency is again external, ascribed to the Muse rather than to her own talent. Repeating patriarchal norms that stress the way that handicrafts exemplify and stand in for the femininity of the user, her face is brightened and made radiant through the Muse letting forth her 'latent thought'.

Parson's correspondence between feminine beauty and transparencies was one of many; the volume of similar references underscores why they were promoted as an excellent handicraft for feminine self-expression. Isabel Sleaford in M.E. Braddon's *The Doctor's Wife* (1864) is described as having a face that 'lighted up all in a moment, and was suddenly beautiful, like a transparency which seems a dingy picture till you put some lamp behind it' (I.30). In Charles Dickens's *Hard Times* (1854), Mrs Gradgrind's passivity and lack of vitality is marked through her looking '(as she always did) like an indifferently executed transparency of a small female figure without enough light behind it' (20). Her death is similarly described as akin to a transparency going out. George Eliot's *Middlemarch* (1872) does provide one counter example to this feminised discourse with Dorothea describing Ladislaw's smile as 'a gush of inward light illuminating the transparent skin as well as the eye' (275). In the same novel, the contrast between lit and unlit transparencies is also used as a trope for an idealised, ethereal beauty, albeit one that is already gone. When Dorothea returns to Lowick Manor from her honeymoon in Rome and is beginning to realise the magnitude of her mistake in marrying Casaubon, she looks around the outmoded and faded decorations of her boudoir, formerly that of Casaubon's mother, but which she had refused to make any changes to, and realises that her youthful romantic dreams from only three months previously are memories:

> The ideas and hopes which were living in her mind when she first saw this room nearly three months before were present now only as memories: she judged them as we judge transient and departed things … Each remembered thing in the room was disenchanted, was deadened as an unlit transparency. (275)

Eliot extends transparencies' association with the domestic interior so that the lack of illumination metonymically stands for Dorothea's physical and emotional imprisonment: the boudoir is a space she refused to turn into a room of her own. More than that though, the ephemeral nature of transparencies materialises Dorothea's interiority and the process of remembrance between her current oppression and the idealism with which she had illuminated the scene only three months previously. Even so, in contrast to such lifelessness, Dorothea herself is described in the same scene in illuminated terms, as 'glowing from her morning toilet as only healthful youth can glow: there was gem-like brightness on her coiled hair and in her hazel eyes' (275). *Middlemarch* plays upon the different aesthetic properties of transparencies, alternately challenging and confirming the dominant analogies between femininity and transparency.

## Transparencies and the Domestic Interior

Large cloth transparencies were invariably exhibited at night with a number of lamps behind them; the contrast between their intense illumination and the surrounding darkness accentuated their impact. Transparent prints could be experienced simply by holding them up to natural light, but were more effective when placed against a window or, like their larger counterparts, backlit with artificial lighting. They were thus perfect for being inserted into lampshades, fans, candle shades, fire screens or window blinds. The multiple exhibition points in the domestic interior for small-scale transparencies were a crucial aspect of their success. *The Lady's Monthly Museum* of 1802 rather hyperbolically declared that when transparencies were used for 'painted lamps and lanterns that may hang in a hall, or staircase, or placed on a supper table, they surpass, for taste or elegance, everything that has yet been invented' ('Transparencies' 59). In becoming a form of interior design, the decorative use of transparencies subtlely transformed the perceptual and aesthetic environment by altering the external and artificial light illuminating the domestic space. Ackermann specifically drew attention to the heightened sensations created by their use by declaring that 'nothing can be more beautifully decorative than illuminated painted lamps or lanthorns, either suspended in halls and staircases, or fixed on supper tables, the rich variety of light affording almost fanciful effect' (*Introduction* 12).

As with transparent prints, printsellers' wares included a full range of ready-made transparent screens and shades (see Figures 2.5 and 2.6). Artistic manuals and drawing masters promoted the decorative use of transparencies; the skills required were the same as transparent prints, with their execution having the added benefit of being a practical and aesthetic enhancement of the drawing room that was simultaneously a demonstration of the host's refined taste. In 1816, the classes of Mrs Frewer's Drawing Academy in Norwich included tutorials in 'Transparent Drawing for Lamps, Windows and other Ornamental Purposes; to a View of specimens of which the Ladies are respectfully invited' ('Mrs. Frewer' 3). The centrepiece of Orme's manual is a double-page engraving showing transparencies inserted into fire screens, draught screens, window blinds, lamp shades, candle shades and fans (see Figure 2.5). Orme even suggested that a transparent print of a fire, with a light behind it, could be placed in a room in order to give the impression of warmth. The theatrical quality of these ornamental transparencies is evident in Orme's suggestion that a transparent panorama could be incorporated into a drawing-room fire screen.

2.5 Decorative transparencies from Edward Orme, *An Essay on Transparent Prints, and on Transparencies in General* (1807) [EXEBD14393].
Courtesy of the University of Exeter.

While more a set of prospects than a true panorama, they exemplify an ongoing convergence between transparencies and other forms of optical exhibition.

Orme provided instructions for creating window and decorative transparencies by a variety of methods. They could, for example, be used to create a stained glass effect; to accomplish this a paper transparency was attached to panes that were the same size as those already in place; these would then be fitted against those already installed. Plate glass could be also smeared with white putty to give it the appearance of ground glass, which was then painted upon with oil and varnish colours. The contrast of light and shade was accentuated by scraping the putty off the brightest lights so as to leave the glass clear. Isinglass size, a gelatinous semi-transparent substance, was also used for coating the surface of the glass prior to painting. All of these different methods for treating glass or paper were concerned with creating a translucent surface that allowed light to pass through the material, but did not allow the viewer to see beyond the illuminated scene. Other artists' manuals were careful to warn practitioners of the site-specific nature of their art in that transparencies for windows had to be painted differently than those screening artificial lights in order to take account of the greater intensity of illumination of the latter.

2.6 Lamp or candle-screen transparency, c.1820. Private collection.

James Roberts, for example, advised that those intended to be seen by daylight in windows 'will require less shade and more light, than those intended for candle-screens, lanterns, or fire-screens' (36).

Jane Carlyle was one genteel practitioner who was determined to use window transparencies to beautify the appearance of the Carlyles' domestic interior, in this case by replacing the much disliked exterior London view from the library window of their Chelsea home with an artificial one. The lower halves of three windows had previously been covered with 'THICK' (her capitals) short blinds because of Thomas Carlyle's 'horror of the "*Pandemonium*" without', a distaste with which Jane fully sympathised. For all the practical benefits of these blinds though, Jane found the effect rather dreary and, in 1845, perhaps judiciously waiting until Thomas was away, she was free to exercise her creative judgement without interference. Jane conceived of a plan 'for combining the Invisible with Ornamental' (Carlyle). Her long letter to her husband describing her efforts is affecting in its record of her experimentation, mistakes, changes of heart, and ultimately only partial success. Its combination of emotional frustration and artistic enthusiasm is recognisable by most who have ever attempted home improvement, and suggests that those who criticised the artistic ephemerality of transparencies missed what made it fulfilling: the process of creative experimentation mattered more than the end product. Jane first attempted to try and make the lower panes seem like ground glass by using silk paper and linseed oil, but this had the effect of giving 'the room the look of a prison – or rather of a gin-Palace' (Carlyle). Changing tack, she then sought the effect of cut-ground glass, creating a decorative pattern of a crescent moon in the middle and a star in each corner. After having done two panes in this fashion, she realised it was possible to see clearly though the moon, and was certain that her husband would be disturbed by this exterior intrusion, and thereby changed the design to one of a wreath of stars:

> *That* really looked beautiful – till the sun shone out – and then oh Heavens the brightness darting thro each of these countless stars seemed absolutely to *pierce* the whole room with little dazzling rays, which could not have failed to put out your eyesight in no time! Again I washed all off; and this time I was *almost* at the crying – but would not cry till I had made a trial of *painted* glass; since plainly *my* cut-glass would never answer – Then came forth Miss Macready's indian Taffeta and great was the clipping out of flowers – next day saw all the lower panes blooming like a flower garden – flowers, like none one had ever seen grow, on a background of snowwhite; it was "most expensive"! – upon *my* honour! – there remained only 'to oil' them – but the results of that extreme unction I had not foreseen – the *gum* and the *oil* refused to coalesce – the transparency took effect only in *patches* – thought turned into action very imperfect indeed! – And now I really *did* cry – *one* tear I think out of each eye – but tho I must give up all idea of making these confounded windows into a "work of art" – I *have* got the better of the old *dishclouts* – *have* combined invisibility with *something like* prettiness at least. (Carlyle)

Improvising with cut-out taffeta flowers, the already delicate material Jane eventually uses for her window transparencies is oiled to make it more reflective and translucent, much as large cloth transparencies were covered with size (a gelatinous solution) to create a glazed effect. Her account is striking for her awareness of the entwined social (gin palace/prison) and sensory effects (too dark/bright/clear) of the different window transparencies and how they would affect the quality of light in the library where her husband spent much of his time.

Decorative transparencies were more obviously a handicraft than transparent prints, which were closer to the fine arts. This ensured that their pleasing effects were promoted by a broader range of publications: women's journals, anthologies of handicrafts and rational recreation and manuals of interior decoration for amateurs and professionals. Their protean character equally manifested itself through a continued crossover with other forms of optical exhibition, emphasising the fluid boundaries between formal performance spaces and the domestic interior as a space for feminine display.

Amongst its various instructions for making transparencies, *The Young Lady's Book* (1829) included a technique for making double-effect transparent screens using a method akin to Daguerre's Regent's Park Diorama (first opened in 1823) and small-scale protean view prints, which became popular in the mid-1830s through Spooner's Protean Views; in both these types of diorama, changing the play of light upon the scene caused the image to transform much like a magic lantern dissolving view. Whereas most transparencies changed simply through becoming illuminated, in those described by *The Young Lady's Book* the scene itself also transformed. The effect was created using two overlaid drawings as the centrepiece of a screen or ornament. The second drawing was pasted behind the first transparency on a frame and drawn in such a way that the outlines matched as carefully as possible. When lying flat or in daylight, only the front picture was seen; when positioned in front of a lamp or fire, the second picture shone through (459). All manner of comic and dramatic metamorphoses were possible; examples given by *The Young Lady's Book* include a mouse-trap that converts into a cage, a mouse into a bird and a dog into a cat. These transparent screens fashioned an optical performance, a metamorphosis that has many similarities with the long tradition of anamorphic images.

As well as lamp shades and screens, transparencies also functioned as blinds, manipulating the natural illumination provided by windows; like other decorative transparencies, their function was to lift the domestic interior out of the everyday, making it a more pleasing aesthetic and sensory environment as well as a display of elegance and taste. The fashion for transparent painted blinds emerged at exactly the same time as that for other transparencies; in February 1801, the *Morning Post* noted that Queen Charlotte had already ordered sets for both Buckingham Palace and Windsor Castle, portraying scenes from different parts of the country, and that many other noblemen were having 'drawings taken of their country seats, and introduced in their drawing rooms and studies, in the form of spring window blinds' ('Transparent' 2). In 1808, it was reported that at the Duchess of Kent's mansion in Knightsbridge, in the grand dining parlour 'the whole of the windows are occasionally covered with painted transparencies on silk, producing the most beautiful effect imaginable' ('Description' 371). Barnaby suggests that the popularity of transparent window blinds forms part of the dynamic and complex interplay between public and private spheres. She notes that 'Rather than denying or repelling exterior light, domestic transparent imagery negotiated a perceptual dialogue between interior and exterior realms of experience' (58). Window transparencies certainly negotiated a permeable boundary between interior and exterior; however, they could also be used to transform a sense of place, replacing an external environment with an evoked virtual one. In 1812, at Mrs Dawson's grand ball and supper at her Manchester-square home just off Oxford Street, attended by '300 Fashionables', ventilation was improved when the windows were removed and replaced with transparencies painted on silk. Their effect was more than practical though, in so far as the urban scene normally glimpsed through windows was replaced by a picturesque idyll. The subjects were landscapes of 'enamelled meads, cottages, and sheep grazing; the village church in the background' as well as 'Wood and water, with Rocky cliffs and mountains, the ruins of an ancient castle, &c' ('Mrs. Dawson's' 3). John Claudius Loudon's *An Encyclopædia of Cottage, Farm, and Villa Architecture and Furniture* (1834) similarly praised painted blinds as being 'very suitable for staircase windows or the windows of cottages that have no view or one they desire to exclude' (342).

Transparent blinds were not the sole preserve of the metropolitan elite; provincial artists and drawing masters soon added them to their repertoire. In 1832, J.M. Wood's decorating business in Norwich was advertising them painted to order ('J.M. Wood' 1), while in August 1836, *Woolmer's Exeter and Plymouth Gazette* contained an advertisement from two visiting London artists, Messrs Harrison and Scott, who offered classes alongside their range of 'Transparent Paintings for Window Blinds, in imitations of Gothic and Grecian glass windows', which they would exhibit for two days in Congdon's Royal Subscription Rooms ('Messrs Harrison' 1). Individual transparencies could also be commissioned 'Painted to Ladies and Gentleman's own Designs' ('Messrs Harrison' 1). Instructions on transparent blinds were also included in Nathaniel Whittock's *The Decorative Painters' and Glaziers' Guide* (1828), an influential early guide to interior design. Whittock describes how to strain, size and then paint the cloth, as well as the colours and scenes that create the best impression. While the colours themselves were put on with the addition of mastic varnish in a fashion akin to transparent prints, blinds had their own site-specific requirements. Whittock stressed the need to take account of the distinct intensity of natural light coming in through the window in that some staple picturesque subjects, moonlit scenes, architecture, pictures of storms on sea or land 'however beautiful they may be as transparent pictures, are not suitable for use as window blinds' because they excluded too much light (200). As with other forms of transparencies, painted window blinds became part of the repertoire of feminine handicrafts. In 1857 and 1863 respectively, *The Ladies' Treasury* and *The Lady's Newspaper* published articles advising readers how to ornament white blinds with transparent pictures ('Window' 8–10; H.L.B. 449).

One of those who enjoyed the pleasure of painted transparencies as a window blind was Elizabeth Barrett; in 1844, she had one installed in her bedroom at Wimpole Street in London. It was a space to which she was frequently confined because of her poor health, making its decoration and sensory impact particularly tied to her sense of well-being:

> There is a castle in the blind, and a castle gate-way, and two walks, and several peasants, and groves of trees which rise in excellent harmony with the fall of my green damask curtains – new, since you saw me last. Papa insults me with the analogy of a back window in a confectioner's shop, but is obviously moved when the sunshine lights up the castle, notwithstanding. And Mr. Kenyon and everybody in the house grow ecstatic rather than otherwise, as they stand in contemplation before it, and tell me (what is obvious without their evidence) that the effect is beautiful, and that the whole room catches a light from it. (quoted in Lubbock 45)

Barrett's transparent blind might be typically picturesque in its scene, but the gamut of reactions she describes stresses the optical effect upon the rest of the room in that it is not only the scene that is illuminated but the room as a whole. Yet her father's dislike of diffuse, coloured light shows how such an environment risked signifying not aristocratic taste but commercial gaudiness.

## Conclusion

Transparencies were at their most fashionable in the first decades of the nineteenth century; however, books of hobbies and domestic recreation featured instructions for them until late in the century. They slowly morphed from a fashionable feminine recreation into a juvenile craft. In Frank Bellew's *The Art of Amusing. A Collection of Graceful Arts, Games, Tricks, Puzzles and Charades* (1871), he recounts finding himself in the company of a family with four daughters who are 'now enthusiastic on the subject of transparencies' (146–52). Bellew goes on to provide a number of designs for copying, consisting of landscapes created by cutting-out different layers of writing paper. With the growth of popular education, transparencies continued to be a means for realising a taste for art through even the most rudimentary knowledge of artistic techniques. In Charlotte M. Yonge's *Beechcroft at Rockstone* (1889), Kalliope, a reduced gentlewoman with artistic yearnings, makes her office at the factory her own through decorating it with window transparencies 'deliberately cut and tinted in cardboard – done, as she had told Gillian, by her little brother Theodore, who learnt to draw at the National School, and had the same turn for art as herself' (101). These transparencies use the cheapest of materials and are the product of the rudimentary training provided by one of many schools set up by the National Society for Promoting Religious Education. At the same time as transparencies were enthusiastically taken up by children, they became part of the growth of commercial handicrafts in the 1870s and 1880s. *Artistic Amusements: Being Instructions for a Variety of Art Work for Home Employment* (1880) classified them as one of the forms of glass painting that could be sold at fancy bazaars. This commercial production seems to have gone hand-in-hand with the industrialisation of its techniques.

Chromolithography, for example, meant the easy availability of pre-prepared ornate designs printed in transparent colours: the amateur creativity and freedom enjoyed by Mary Howitt and many other women was increasingly hollowed out.

During the first decades of the nineteenth century, transparencies were a fashionable and pervasive cultural presence in a new world of commercialised leisure. They deserve to be recognised as a key popular art of the period; moreover, the various descriptions of their appeal suggest that they allowed their makers to engage with the mediated world that was constitutive of nineteenth-century modernity. Paper and cloth transparencies often stood in for glass, which remained an expensive commodity. Yet this ersatz quality is crucial in that Isobel Armstrong's recent work on nineteenth-century glass has demonstrated the manifold ways its materiality expressed the modernity of the period through its mediation of subjectivity, its ability to foreground the instability and interconnectedness between seer and seen. Armstrong suggests that one feature linking a number of optical devices – the magic lantern, diorama, telescope, spectroscope and phantasmagoria – is their concern with 'managing and transforming primordial light and radiance, often forming images convergent with matter, but not *of* it (256). With their intangible, radiant beauty that transformed both light and the painted scene, transparencies need to be added to this list; yet, unlike the above devices, transparencies offered greater possibilities for active, individual, 'hands-on' engagement. The above examples of Jane Carlyle, Mary Howitt, and Elizabeth Barrett, as well as many other women, suggest they offered a way not only to pleasurably and playfully explore the creation of a mediated environment, but to do so through transforming, displaying and fashioning their feminine subjectivity.

## Works Cited

Ackermann, Rudolf. *A Catalogue of Various Prints, Adapted for Furniture, Ornaments, etc.* London: Rudolf Ackermann, 1802. Copy bound into back of Beinecke Library's copy of Rudolf Ackermann, *Introduction for Painting on Transparencies.*

——. *Introduction for Painting on Transparencies*. London: R. Ackermann, 1802.

'Albinia, Countess of Buckinghamshire'. *Morning Post,* 17 August 1807: 3.

Armstrong, Isobel. *Victorian Glassworlds: Glass Culture and the Imagination, 1830–1880.* Oxford: Oxford University Press, 2008.

*Artistic Amusements: Being Instructions for a Variety of Art Work for Home Employment and Suggestions for a Number of Novel and Saleable Articles for Fancy Bazaars*. London: The Bazaar Office, 1880.

Austen, Jane. *Her Life and Letters: A Family Record*. Ed. William Austen-Leigh and Richard Arthur Austen-Leigh. London: Echo Press, 2009.

——. *Mansfield Park*. Ed. Claudia Johnson. New York: W.W. Norton and Co., 1998.

Barnaby, Alice. 'Light Touches: Cultural Practices of Illumination, London 1780–1840'. Unpublished PhD, University of Exeter, 2010.

Bellew, Frank. *The Art of Amusing. A Collection of Graceful Arts, Games, Tricks, Puzzles and Charades*. London: John Camden Hotten, 1871.

Bermingham, Ann. *Learning to Draw. Studies in the Cultural History of a Polite and Useful Art*. New Haven: Yale University Press, 2000.

Braddon, Mary Elizabeth. *The Doctor's Wife*. 2 vols. Leipzig: Bernhard Tauchnitz, 1864.

Calloway, Anita. *Visual Ephemera: Theatrical Art in Nineteenth-Century Australia*. Sydney: University of New South Wales Press, 2000.

'Camera Lunaris'. *The Times*, 8 January 1847: 5.

Carlyle, Jane. 'To Thomas Carlyle, 10 October 1845'. *The Carlyle Letters Online* [CLO]. 2007. http://carlyleletters.org. Accessed 15 April 2012.

de Brancion, Laurence. *Carmontelle's Landscape Transparencies: Cinema of the Enlightenment*. Los Angeles: Getty Trust Publications, 2008.

'Description of the Duchess of Kent's Mansion at Knightsbridge'. *The Weekly Entertainer and West of England Miscellany*, 9 May 1808: 371.

Dickens, Charles. *Hard Times*. London: Bradbury and Evans, 1854.

Eliot, George. *Middlemarch*. Ed. Rosemary Ashton. Harmondsworth: Penguin, 2003.

'Fashionable Transparencies'. *Oxford Journal*, 6 April 1799: 2.

H.L.B. 'Ornamenting White Blinds'. *The Lady's Newspaper*, 11 April 1863: 449.

Hodson, T., and I. Dougall. *The Cabinet of the Arts: Being a New and Universal Drawing Book*. London: T. Ostell, 1805.

Hooper, William. *Rational Recreations, in which the Principles of Numbers and Natural Philosophy are Clearly and Copiously Explained*. 4 vols. London: L. Davis et al., 1787.

Howitt, Mary Botham. *An Autobiography*. 2 vols. Cambridge: Cambridge University Press, 2010.

Imison, John. *Elements of Science and Art: Being a Familiar Introduction to Natural Philosophy and Chemistry …, Considerably Enlarged and Updated by Thomas Webster*. London: F.C. and J. Rivington et al., 1822.

'J.M. Wood'. *Norfolk Chronicle and Norwich Gazette*, 21 July 1832: 1.

[Kelty, Mary Ann]. *The Story of Isabel*. 3 vols. London: Longman, Rees, Orme, Brown and Co., 1826.

'L. Buckley'. *Morning Post*, 29 March 1802: 2.

Loudon, John Claudius. *An Encyclopædia of Cottage, Farm, and Villa Architecture and Furniture*. 1834. London: Longman, Browne, Orme, Green and Longmans, 1839.

Lubbock, Percy. *Elizabeth Barrett Browning in Her Letters*. New York: AMS Press, 1972.

'Messrs Harrison and Scott'. *Woolmer's Exeter and Plymouth Gazette*, 6 August 1836: 1.

'Monthly Catalogue'. *Monthly Review* (February 1809): 316.

'Montravers and Lavinia; Or, One Winter in London'. *The Lady's Monthly Museum* 9 (October 1810): 228.

'Mrs. Dawson's Balls'. *Morning Post*, 22 June 1812: 3.

'Mrs. Frewer'. *Norfolk Chronicle*, 16 February 1816: 3.

'New Style of Transparency'. *La Belle Assemblée* 3 (February 1807): 57.

Orme, Edward. *An Essay on Transparent Prints, and on Transparencies in General*. London: Edward Orme, 1807.

——. *Subjects for Transparencies*. London: Edward Orme, 1799.

Parsons, William. 'Sonnet of Some Transparencies Done by a Lady'. *Travelling Recreations*. London: Longman, Hurst, Rees and Orme, 1807. 156.

Price, Uvedale. *An Essay on the Picturesque, as Compared with the Sublime and the Beautiful*. London: J. Robson, 1796.

Roberts, James. *Introductory Lessons, with Familiar Examples in Landscape for the Use of Those who are Desirous of Gaining Some Knowledge of the Pleasing Art of Painting in Water Colours; To which are Added, Some Clear and Simple Rules, Exemplified by Suitable Sketches and More Finished Paintings … To which are added, Instructions for Executing Transparencies in a Style Both Novel and Easy*. London: J. and W. Smith, 1809.

Rowlandson, Thomas. *Transparencies*. London: Rowlandson, 1799. Yale Center for British Art L 232 (Folio A).

Schaffer, Talia. *Novel Craft: Victorian Domestic Handicraft & Nineteenth-Century Fiction*. Oxford: Oxford University Press, 2011.

Strutt, Joseph. *The Sports and Pastimes of the People of England, Enlarged and Corrected by J. Charles Cox*. 1801. London: Methuen and Co., 1903.

Taylor, C. *The Artist's Repository and Drawing Magazine, Exhibiting the Principles of the Polite Arts in their Various Branches*. London: T. Williams, 1784.

'Transparencies'. *The Lady's Monthly Museum* 8 (July 1802): 59.

'Transparent Spring Blinds'. *Morning Post*, 9 February 1801: 2.

Verwiebe, Birgit. 'Transparent Painting and the Romantic Spirit'. *The Romantic Spirit in German Art*. Ed. Keith Hartlet, Henry Meyric Hughes, Peter-Klaus Schuster and William Vaughan. London: South Bank Centre, National Galleries of Scotland, and Oktagon Verlag, 1994. 171–7.

Whittock, Nathaniel. *The Decorative Painters' and Glaziers' Guide*. London: Isaac Taylor Hinton, 1828.

'Window Blind and Fire Screen Painting'. *The Ladies' Treasury: An Illustrated Magazine of Entertaining Literature, Education, Fine Art, Biography, Domestic Economy, Needlework, and Fashion*, 1 March 1857: 8–10.

'Windsor and the Environs'. *Reading Mercury*, 10 June 1799: 1.

Yonge, Charlotte M. *Beechcroft at Rockstone*. London: Macmillan, 1893.

*The Young Lady's Book: A Manual of Elegant Recreations, Exercises and Pursuits*. London: Vizetelly, Branston and Co., 1829.

## Notes

1 Exceptions to this are Barnaby; Bermingham; de Brancion; Calloway; Verwiebe. I am particularly grateful to Alice Barnaby for many fruitful discussions regarding transparencies, which have considerably improved this chapter.

2 These transparencies can be found in the John Johnson Collection Window Pictures and Transparencies (71–3).

3 In the copy of Rowlandson's *Transparencies* held by the Yale Center for British Art, only 'The Visit' and 'The Incantation' are signed by Rowlandson.

4 On fine paper-work, see Schaffer 69.

3

# Pertinacious Industry: The Keyboard Etude and the Female Amateur in England, 1804–20

*Elizabeth Morgan*

'Emma Woodhouse, handsome, clever, and rich, with a comfortable home and happy disposition' is in a pickle (3). The heroine of Jane Austen's 1815 novel spends most of the story making matches that have no hope of survival, ignoring the requests of her friends, and failing to understand the realities of her own heart. As much as Emma would like to shape the world into a reality that suits her by relentlessly interfering in the lives of her acquaintances, time and again, her friends prove to have minds of their own. Emma's efforts to influence her acquaintances is really only one of numerous forces that her young, female friends have to contend with, which purport to build their characters and shape them into ideal women. The whole of female education in early nineteenth-century England made such claims. This is a well-known story, documented in countless cultural histories of eighteenth- and nineteenth-century Britain (see, for example, Bermingham; Poovey). Feminine accomplishments such as drawing, dancing and music making sought to discipline and contain women under the guise of enriching and even empowering them.[1] With their schooling supervised by watchful parents and governesses, and structured by educational literature and frequent lessons with teachers, girls desiring to be accomplished simply needed to follow directions. This system of learning resonated perfectly with Jean-Jacques Rousseau's sentiments – as detailed in his influential *Émile*,[2] which was circulated widely throughout Britain – that a young lady's education should 'teach her, restrict her, form her, explain to her' (Misenheimer 3). It upheld the strictures of British society and its gender norms to a tee. End of story.

Of course, in most good stories, plots are complicated, characters are not always who they first appear to be. Like a secret engagement hidden from friends and family, or an evil disposition disguised by an amiable countenance, the truth of women's education as it was actually practised in turn-of-the-nineteenth-century Britain was neither simple nor self-evident. While Rousseau envisioned a society in which women's education was uniformly an instrument of containment, he failed to take the realities of accomplishment study – not to mention human nature – into account. The degree of agency that English women may well have claimed in their education would have made Jean-Jacques cringe.

The materials of women's schooling, from French lessons delivered by governesses to dance steps found in ladies' periodicals, were 'subject ... to a process of active consumption' by their female audience (Jones 112). So argues Vivien Jones as she examines one of the most prominent literary genres of the early nineteenth century: conduct books. Distributed by parents and teachers, these works sought to regulate every element of female education. Jones contests the modern impulse to imagine the reader peering over a conduct book as a naïve young lady, ripe and ready to submit to the advice she finds on its pages. She does not believe that these sources can be read as evidence of uniform disciplinary practice. Jones argues instead, that there were numerous readers, with different tastes, temperaments and educational goals. Embedded within the seemingly misogynistic and repressive narratives of instructional literature exists the possibility that women negotiated and questioned the often contradictory values found at large in these works, displaying what Mary Wollstonecraft aptly termed 'independence of mind' (207). Jones concludes that historical women 'read conduct books more actively and unpredictably, more resistantly, than the texts – and some modern accounts – seem to assume' (112).

The story of music making among women has long been a tale of female containment. But recently scholars have begun to identify slippage between the turn-of-the-nineteenth-century's rhetoric of discipline and music making as it was actually practised. A number of assumptions have been questioned: that women excelled in the private sphere alone; that women pianists pursued only an intermediate level of skill at the keyboard; that music making effectively enforced notions of femininity (see for example Head; Leppert). Leslie Ritchie, in particular, constructs a compelling study of music making among British women of the late eighteenth century that questions the severe distinction between public and private spheres often maintained by historians. Other musicologists, Nicholas Salwey foremost among them, have shed light on the activities of professional women musicians during this period. These historians are part of an interdisciplinary community of scholars who hesitate to enforce what Seyla Benhabib terms a 'discourse of domination that legitimises women's oppression' as they reconstruct history (93).

In this chapter, I follow the lead of scholars who have questioned musical and literary narratives of containment as I examine a genre of music that particularly resembles conduct literature: keyboard etudes. Born in the first decade of the nineteenth century, etudes were doctrines of self-improvement grounded largely in physical control and regulation. In other words, they resembled conduct literature in their disciplinary aims. Etudes were studied by a wide spectrum of keyboardists: men and women, amateurs and professionals. But their resemblance to conduct literature, a genre directed so overwhelmingly at female readers, as well as the fact that women comprised the bulk of amateur pianists in late Georgian England, is a compelling reason to look particularly at the female keyboardists who studied etudes.

In the pages that follow, I will examine keyboard etudes by way of conduct literature, comparing the disciplinary aims of both genres and considering ways in which etudes, were subject to the same processes of active consumption that Jones identifies in women's study of conduct books. In exploring keyboard etudes as a sight of contestation for young female performers, I will bring larger issues about the nature of music making among British women at the turn of the nineteenth century into focus.

## Conduct Books and Docile Bodies

Along with ladies' periodicals, conduct books educated young women of the middle and upper classes – and their mothers – on proper feminine behaviour, providing detailed advice about feminine accomplishments. Often they advocated strict systems of schooling and discipline – sometimes adopting a language to mirror their objective. In this sense, conduct materials were performative texts, in which authors enacted the schooling – and restraining – of women through meticulous instructions and a rhetoric of discipline.

One feature common to conduct books of the late eighteenth century is that they wear literary guises, designed to appeal to their intended audiences. In particular, many are works of fiction, novels that educate their readers through the moral lessons embedded within their plots. Several of the most popular novels of the Georgian period were written with moral instruction and female edification in mind.[3] *The Polite Lady*, which was first published in 1760 and then circulated for decades thereafter in numerous editions, adopts the form of an epistolary narrative, another of the most popular literary genres of its age, which, like novels, drew primarily female readers (see Whyman). The title page doesn't credit an author, except to state that the work is a series of letters from a mother to her daughter. All of the letters are fictional missives, authored not by a mother, but by a single author, and a male one at that: Charles Allen.

Assuming the persona of a mother, Portia, writing to her young daughter, Sophy, following Sophy's departure for boarding school, Allen adopts a tone intended to be both familiar and trustworthy to his young female reader. He intersperses Portia's letters with occasional responses from Sophy. Her letters are always brief, closing with valedictions such as 'Your obliged and obedient daughter' (Allen 160) and 'Your dutiful daughter' (202). Sophy's personality serves the purpose of modelling proper feminine behaviour; she is respectful towards her mother and dutiful in her studies, the perfect example of a young lady on the path to becoming an accomplished woman.

The language of Portia's letters is both kind and uncompromising; she instructs her daughter to obey her governess and teachers, to pay attention to her mother's advice as related in her letters and to apply herself to her studies with diligence. Portia assures Sophy that submission to authority is always the best course of action for a young woman. Upon receiving a letter from her daughter which requests advice about making friends, for instance, Portia exclaims:

> How shall I express the joy I received from the perusal of your last letter! How happy am I in having a daughter, who, at an age, when most young ladies imagine they can think and act for themselves, is so humble and dutiful, as to undertake nothing without the permission and advice of her mother! (48)

The extent of Sophy's submission to her mother and teachers is embodied by the infrequency of her replies. Rather than respond to Portia and remark on the events of her life at school, Sophy passively receives her education and keeps quiet.

This rhetorical framework reflects Allen's value system as it concerns women and female education; learned elders teach submissive young ladies. The subjects that Portia addresses also reflect Allen's feelings about educating women. He devotes a chapter to each of the major feminine accomplishments such as drawing, music, French and sewing, as well as one each to several other elements of female life, including friendship and conversation. Later chapters are devoted to values, such as chastity, modesty and religion. While Portia often approaches her subjects as Platonic ideals to which Sophy should aspire, she takes a pragmatic approach to elements of her daughter's education with equal frequency, imagining Sophy's concerns not as abstract ideological issues but as very real questions that she faces each day. Numerous discussions centre on her accomplishments as embodied practices. Portia praises activities first and foremost because they are useful – and she associates usefulness with beneficial employment of the body. For instance, she commends dancing for its salubrious effects on the female form in everyday life, as 'it comprehends every motion, every gesture, every attitude of the body' (26). Similarly, she praises sewing for its usefulness, but cautions Sophy that it may weaken her eyesight (41); utility cannot trump the physical hazards of pursuing an accomplishment, potentially for hours at a time. Of all her worries, Portia concerns herself most with idleness, calling it 'a most pernicious and fatal vice' (129). A life without accomplishments constitutes an idle existence; in other words, women need their accomplishments to – quite literally – keep their hands and bodies busy. As Portia's advice to her daughter suggests, well-regulated control of her body is an essential component of Sophy's education. Other conduct books strive to manage women's bodies to an even greater degree. While Allen dealt with accomplishments as embodied practices, other authors addressed such rudimentary kinds of physical activities as posture, sleeping positions, breathing and walking.

In his 1797 book, *A Plan for the Conduct of Female Education in Boarding Schools, Private Families, and Public Seminaries,* Erasmus Darwin devotes a chapter to each of the following subjects: 'Air', 'Exercise', 'Care of the Shape', 'Lisping', 'Stammering', 'Squinting' and, most amusingly, 'Involuntary Actions'. These chapters address particular ailments common in young people, offering practical advice. For instance, he recommends that the lisping girl place a finger inside her mouth to force her tongue into the correct position for pronouncing the letter *s*. He advises the stuttering child to practise pronouncing words that give her trouble and to seek more experience in the company of strangers, so that she can build confidence in front of people she doesn't know.

Informed by his medical and scientific training, Darwin also argues that education in the accomplishments renders women 'too sedentary; which impairs their strength, makes their countenances pale and bloated, and lays the foundation of many diseases' (97). Thus he advocates numerous athletic activities, such as playing shuttlecock and dancing, to give women relief from the physical detriment caused by their sedentary lifestyles. With his detailed advice, Darwin promises to improve the overall health and physical appearance of young women. Rather than balance the rigidity of women's education with physical activities that encourage freedom, however, Darwin takes pains to establish meticulous regulations for the exercises and pursuits he recommends. His suggestions cater to society's standards for female beauty and propriety. Darwin advocates pastimes and exercises which 'produce activity' and 'promote the growth of the person', not those that are 'robust and muscular' (97). He safeguards against anyone misinterpreting his recommendations by providing extraordinary detail. Addressing posture, for instance, Darwin devotes several pages to sleeping positions, baths, homeopathic oral remedies, and stocks and backboards, giving precise instructions as he discusses each topic, and requiring women to pursue his suggestions with 'pertinacious industry' (137). With this abundance of detail, Darwin recommends activities to counterbalance elegant accomplishments that strive towards a similar degree of control over women's minds and bodies.

Through his efforts to manage women's corporeal movements and activities, Darwin sometimes advocates almost severe physical discipline. For instance, in his chapter on 'Involuntary Actions', which addresses tics and twitching in young people, Darwin recommends applying a bandage or adhesive plaster tightly over the spastic muscle in question, so that the girl feels pain when the movement occurs. Most of his recommendations treat the body gently but, like his pain-inducing cure for tics, they are hands-on, uncompromising efforts at moulding their subjects into women of ideal shapes and perfect temperaments.

Darwin's *Plan for the Conduct of Female Education* illustrates the extent to which the English system of female instruction sought physical and psychological control over young women. British education aimed to render its female pupils what Michel Foucault would one day call 'docile bodies' (138), objects of a system in which they were 'subjected and practiced' (138). Foucault argues that many social institutions, such as schools in late eighteenth-century France, enclose and partition the space in which their subjects live and work, and that they embrace a strict system of time management. Unlike institutions of earlier centuries, which made their subjects feel that a precise time regimen was imposed upon them, by the seventeenth century, institutions had begun to give their subjects the sense that they had the good fortune to use and exhaust each hour in the day. Foucault goes on to discuss systems of command, focussing on the relationship between teacher and student in France in the latter years of the 1700s. In Foucault's fictional classroom, the teacher gives instructions that are brief and clear and which do not need interpretation (166). He also uses signals such as bells and clapped hands to elicit certain behaviours. School children respond to instructions and signals with appropriate physical actions. Their movements and gestures are controlled by commands.

Many aspects of Foucault's discussion aptly describe British female education as idealised by conduct books, as does one of the underlying messages of his volume: that social institutions such as schools and hospitals operate with the same principle of controlling bodies as prisons do. Such a comparison casts those institutions – and women's education in early nineteenth-century Britain – as organisations that rigidly restrain their subjects. In paying meticulous attention to topics like improving posture and correcting speech impediments, Darwin's *Plan for the Conduct of Female Education* demonstrates a desire to participate in that kind of female containment, endeavouring to control even the most basic and seemingly self-evident actions of the female body. The abundance of accomplishments that conduct books like Darwin's encouraged women to study echoes Foucault's description of institutions of the eighteenth century that instructed their subjects to indulge and exhaust the expanses of time before them; conduct literature, teachers and parents certainly sold accomplishments as useful and enjoyable activities for which there were sadly too few hours in the day. Portia's letters to Sophy mimic this aspect of women's education exactly; she commends her daughter for acknowledging the 'inestimable worth and value' of her time, which 'is the most precious treasure [you] can possess, as it is the foundation and ground-work of every other blessing' (Allen 127). In other words, the hours that comprise her daughter's days are invaluable because they allow her to pursue accomplishments and activities that enrich and interest her. Like Foucault's students, obediently responding to the commands of their teacher, young women like Sophy receive instructions from literature and mentors that demand little interpretation. In following these directives, they submit to a regimented system of education that controls even their most minute gestures.

Foucault's framework is extremely useful for understanding how conduct books sought control over their subjects. Yet the philosopher largely ignores the subjects themselves and their reactions to the disciplinary forces around them. Clearly, the disciplinary function of piano etudes, like that of conduct literature, played directly into the world of female containment. Etudes, like conduct books, had physical control at the top of their lists of objectives. But rather than read these sources as evidence of disciplinary practice, we need to ask ourselves what women themselves made of them. Studying etudes gave women an opportunity to resist containment, claiming agency in their musical studies. Unlike applying a bandage to a spastic muscle or pursuing exercises to cure the tendency to lisp, studying etudes could lead to newfound power in the form of increased pianistic prowess. In fact, while keyboard etudes, like conduct literature, sought physical control of their subjects, they were also developed with the express purpose of increasing a pianist's technical skill.

## Independence of Mind

Music making, particularly singing and playing the pianoforte, was one of the most popular feminine activities in early nineteenth-century England. It mirrored the values of the emerging middle class, which prized the possession of leisure as a sign of social status, and thus it flourished in late Georgian society, receiving particular attention from the authors of conduct books as they assessed its worth. Numerous writers took up their pens to recommend the activity but they circumscribed its practice within limits, cautioning girls against studying overly complex works as well as physically demanding ones. In fact, they tended to equate compositional complexity with virtuosity, advocating, instead, repertoire that was easy to understand and easy to play. A conduct book entitled *The Young Lady's Book*, for instance, condemned keyboard virtuosity, rallying against the 'parade pieces, of which the music-shops are so prolific' and favouring 'beautiful and intelligible compositions of Dussek, Cramer, and Hummel, or of Mozart and Beethoven' in their place (368). Meanwhile, composer W.T. Parke praised the compositions of J.C. Bach, who, after injuring his hand, had begun to compose works that were not too difficult technically. 'In general', noted Parke, 'his compositions for the piano-forte are such as ladies can execute with little trouble' (348).

While British society held fast to the ideals of amateurism and easiness in music where women were concerned, in practice, drawing room pianists shared a great deal of repertoire with virtuosos on the public stage. Jane Austen's collection of sheet music, for instance, includes pieces like Steibelt's Grande Concerto, Opus 33, a work made famous by the composer's own performances of it on major European stages. Similarly, in her popular conduct book, *Private Education* (1815), Elizabeth Appleton provided a list of keyboard repertoire suitable for the female amateur. She praised Clementi's Opus 12, a work Clementi most likely had performed in public concerts in London in 1784, and noted by Leon Plantinga for its 'impressive bursts of virtuosity' (95).

The overlapping musical repertoires of amateurs and those of professionals pose the problem of how a single piece of music could belong at once to the virtuosic, public, professional and masculine sphere of music making and to the *easy*, private, amateur and feminine sphere. The circumstances of a work's presentation – such as venue, identity of the pianist (gender, background, class, nationality), technical proficiency and chosen tempo, audience expectations and the pianist's physical demeanour were all factors which determined whether or not a performance was received as virtuosic. As musicologist Matthew Head notes in a study of music making among eighteenth-century German women, *easiness* was not grounded in the musical and physical substance of the works that performers studied so much as it was rooted in the purpose of those pieces, whether the works were designed for amateur or professional use. What mattered for women musicians – especially in the eyes of the men who sanctioned their musical educations – was how the works that they studied *seemed* (Head 214). Thus professionals and amateurs shared repertoire but the culture of virtuosity belonged demonstrably to the public, professional world alone. Perhaps the assumption that virtuosity was, by definition, public, actually granted women some leeway in determining what repertoire they would study at home. This certainly seems to be the case in their study of piano etudes. Etudes were composed with the amateur in mind, but they were written by many of the most famous concert pianists of the late Georgian era; while these pedagogical works weren't intended for public performance, they share many bravura physical demands with the repertoire made famous on the public stage.

While there were comparatively few concerts in London during the first decade of the nineteenth century, in part because of the economic strains caused by the wars between England and France, enthusiasm for the pianoforte was growing rapidly (Weber 4). This zeal for piano performance yielded a large number of treatises and method books in England and continental Europe on playing the instrument. Perhaps the most famous of these, which remains in use today, was Muzio Clementi's *Introduction to the Art of Playing on the Piano Forte*, published in London by the expatriate Italian in 1801. It was popular throughout England, prompting Elizabeth Appleton to declare: 'Of all introductions … that of Clementi is best' (137).

Clementi's *Introduction* was designed for use in conjunction with lessons from a music master or governess, but could also take the place of a teacher. It opens, for instance, with a section entitled 'Preliminaries', which provides the beginning pupil with instructions on reading notation, fingering for scales, and exercises to build strength and agility, as well as her very first pieces for study. With Clementi's guide, the beginning pianist, confronting a piece for the first time, can deduce the best fingering for that work. In other words, by practising Clementi's exercises, her hand learns the principles of good fingering and is shaped into the best positions for executing passages frequently found in keyboard compositions. She is, in essence, moulded into the capable pianist; Clementi's exercises discipline her body.

In addition to method books like Clementi's, a new kind of keyboard composition was on the rise in the early years of the 1800s, a genre that came to fruition with a collection by one of Clementi's former students, John Baptiste Cramer. Cramer's *Studio per il Piano Forte,* the first volume of which was published in 1804, inaugurated the piano etude as a viable genre of composition.[4] Like conduct books disguised as epistolary narratives and novels, these works cloaked the technique-building aim of exercises in more musically inviting wear; while Cramer wrote them for pedagogical purposes, many of them looked and sounded like performance pieces.

The influence of Cramer's *Studio* was phenomenal; the 84 works contained within the first two volumes (1804, 1809) would transform piano composition and technique in the years following their publication. As soon as Cramer's opus appeared on the market, Clementi claimed publicly that Cramer had stolen the idea for the collection from his former teacher. Clementi had reason to be jealous. The collection was Cramer's most famous work, and it inspired almost every other major London composer to write his own volume of piano etudes in the coming years. Joseph Woelfl and Daniel Steibelt, two piano virtuosi living in London, each released a collection entitled *Methode de Pianoforte* within five years. Even Clementi jumped on board; in 1817, he published the first volume of his *Gradus ad Parnassum,* a work that remains a cornerstone of piano pedagogy to this day. Later collections would include Ignaz Moscheles's *Studien* Opus 70 and the numerous volumes of studies by Carl Czerny. Even the concert etudes of the next generation, by continental composers such as Liszt and Chopin, would grow from the compositional strides made in Cramer's volumes. But while the keyboard studies of the first two decades of the nineteenth century may have set a precedent for the concert etude, these pieces never made it to the public stage. They were pedagogical tools, securely ensconced in the drawing room.[5] And, like so many genres of keyboard works at the turn of the nineteenth century, etudes were marketed to women. As Nicholas Temperley tells us, 'Cramer's *Studio per il piano forte* (1804, 1809) is the work that set the pattern for the piano étude, turning technical exercises into acceptable music in a way that catered precisely for the (predominantly female) amateurs who formed the principal market for published piano music' ('London' 291).

Despite the likely influence of method books on Cramer's innovation, the composer did not organise the pieces in his *Studio* from easiest to hardest. In the 1835 edition, in which he increased the total number of etudes from 84 to 100, Cramer specified that the pianist should study the first 10 chronologically, but that the order of subsequent pieces was arbitrary. He also mentioned which technical challenges were addressed by particular etudes. In other words, he designed his opus as a collection of pieces useful for the developing pianist, who could approach them with her own taste and discretion as her guide.

Each study in Cramer's collection addresses a specific technical challenge, often repeating a melodic pattern over and over again throughout the work. But Cramer cleverly mediates between repetition and variation to keep his etudes interesting. If he repeats a melodic and rhythmic pattern over and over, he compensates for the lack of melodic variation with shifts in harmony and colour. In his third Etude in D Major, for instance, the right hand executes intricate four-note configurations from start to finish. The etude works all five fingers in the right hand, concentrating on building their autonomy and independence from each other. In particular, it demands stretching between the second and fourth fingers. These stretches occur again and again, physical analogues to musical repetition. Meanwhile, the left hand performs sequences of descending eighth notes. It provides the musical meat of the work, creating shifts in harmony and its own melodic contour beneath the fast-paced right hand. Figure 3.1 is the score of the entire etude; the element of repetition is not difficult to spot, even from a cursory glance at the page.

By using melodic and rhythmic repetition to generate his D Major etude, Cramer inevitably embraces a third kind of repetition throughout the piece: physical. He calls on the pianist to perform the same bodily gestures again and again as she covers the expanse of the keyboard with sequencing four-note configurations. In doing so, Cramer creates a microcosm of the practice of female accomplishments; the piece both requires and develops physical discipline, addressing even the smallest movements of the female body. Moreover, the practitioner learns to perform the etude much as she pursues her other skills, by rote. We can't know how the typical young woman practised, whether or not repetition was her choice method of learning, but we do know that in playing Cramer's etude even a single time – as well as the countless works modelled after it – the young female pianist repeated the same corporeal motions again and again. Physical repetition is innate to the genre.

3.1 John Baptiste Cramer, Etude in D Major.

While at first glance the D Major etude appears to address technical obstacles in the right hand alone, at closer inspection the pianist realises that it challenges the left hand as well, even though the fancy finger work above masks those challenges. The left-hand line is songful and melodic and therefore necessitates legato (or connected) execution. But the chords on the first beat of each measure make that impossible without awkward finger crossings. For instance, to play the second and third measures without breaking the legato, the pianist must twist her hand at least once, crossing a left-hand '3' over '4' (most likely on the second beat of Measure 3). Cramer doesn't provide any hints as to how the pianist ought to capture a seamless legato; the entire left-hand staff is bereft of fingerings. (Figure 3.2 shows the left-hand legato line.) By giving the left hand what is essentially the melody of the piece, the etude asks it to perform a right-hand function. In this sense, Etude No. 3 is a study for both left and right hands.

Cramer's manner of exercising left and right hands equally, which broadcasts the difficulty of the right-hand material and masks that of the left hand, makes for a provocative musical sensibility; the affect of the etude is at odds with its level of difficulty. The work is hard to execute but sounds melodious and pleasant.

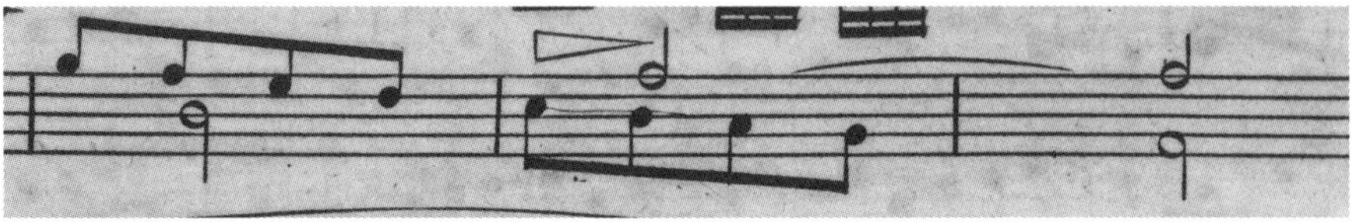

3.2 John Baptiste Cramer, Detail from Etude in D Major.

Interestingly, the emotional sensibility corresponds exactly with the personality of the performer who, according to the dictates of conduct books, ought to be pleasant and agreeable herself, possessing a pliant disposition. Cramer has chosen a musical style for this piece to reflect the one who plays it.

Many of the other studies in Cramer's collection resemble the Etude in D Major in their pleasant, songful style. Not only did this compositional approach appeal to the tastes of Cramer's potential performers, but it was very likely also an effort to make this new genre of keyboard composition palatable to British culture at large. In light of the cultural stipulations against female virtuosity, Cramer needed to give his etudes – which are, by definition, virtuosity-building pieces – some other reason for being. He had to prove that the technical elements of his studies were not gratuitous and consequently inappropriate for the female amateur. In his Etude in D Major, Cramer catered to the woman pianist – and society's expectations of her – by cloaking the study in the rhetoric of female music making, just as conduct books enticed their readers by assuming the forms of novels and women's correspondences.

In his seminal volume of 1817, *Gradus ad Parnassum,* Clementi took Cramer's idea to the next level; he adapted the etudes within the volume to fit the model of female education but simultaneously challenged that paradigm with his pieces, potentially transforming musical education forever. *Gradus ad Parnassum,* certainly made a splash when it arrived on the scene. Published in three volumes (1817, 1819, 1826), the collection was a musical memoir of Clementi's career, which included pieces that he had written as early as 1780 (Plantinga 270). While each of Clementi's 100 pieces bears the title 'exercise', not all of the works within the three volumes are technical studies like those written by Cramer. Instead, Clementi addresses a broader kind of musicianship with his opus, requiring such varied keyboard skills as contrapuntal playing, expressive execution and, of course, virtuoso technical prowess. *Gradus ad Parnassum* explores pianistic and general musical skills, and it showcases the varied compositional abilities of its composer. It is host to an array of genres: fugues, canons, scherzi, character pieces, sonata-like works and etudes. It is, in essence, a summary of Clementi's compositional career.

Like Cramer, Clementi sought ways to make *Gradus ad Parnassum* acceptable to teachers and parents who oversaw the purchase of sheet music for young ladies. Cramer masked pieces of virtuosic content with a charming, feminine sensibility, and Clementi utilised techniques of disguise as well. From its very first page (see Figure 3.3), *Gradus ad Parnassum* wooed female consumers. Its title page informed the prospective buyer that the work was 'Composed and Dedicated to Her Excellency the Princess Sophia Wolkonsky'. Wolkonsky, who was a member of the Russian aristocracy and a patroness of the arts, exemplified elegance and refinement in her noble title. Her patronage was a desirable endorsement of Clementi's collection, and may well have given the volume a kind of legitimacy in the eyes of wary mothers and teachers.

The second page worked in Clementi's favour as well. He kicked off the first volume with a single page entitled 'Preliminary Observations on Fingering', which provided rudimentary advice on fingering, using the C Major and Minor scales as examples. But the second page also provides clues to the seriousness of his volume. In mentioning that scales 'Are often to be played with great swiftness' and scolding 'some eminent performers' for neglecting to practice chromatic scales in contrary motion, Clementi addresses himself to the serious-minded pianists among his buyers. In short, the work promises to satisfy consumers with a variety of objectives.

Of the compositions in *Gradus ad Parnassum* whose uniform melody, rhythm and repeated physical patterns make them studies in the same sense as Cramer's, several adumbrated the concert etudes that would flourish on European stages only a few years later. These resemble works of Chopin and Liszt because of their wide emotional spectrums and varied palettes of colours; despite their dependence on repetition, they embraced the emotional and intellectual range of concert works. My discussion will centre on Clementi's Exercise in G Minor from Volume 2 of *Gradus ad Parnassum*, but there are numerous works in his magnum opus that display equal levels of musical interest. What concerns me most is how the Etude in G Minor, in all its virtuosic brilliance and contrapuntal complexity, caters to the female market.

The Etude in G Minor is a perpetual motion-type piece, which addresses finger stretching and agility. The work opens with a tune that will return in numerous keys and guises over the course of the six pages that make up the etude. By requiring the lower fingers in the right hand to sustain notes while the upper fingers execute intricate patterns above, the study builds nimbleness and independence in the fingers that are typically the weakest, four and five. Often the pianist has to stretch her hand, particularly between her second and fourth or third and fourth fingers. Many of these stretches aggressively push the fingers apart. On the second and third beats of the second measure, for instance, the pianist must sustain her thumb on a D while stretching up to E-flat with her fifth finger.

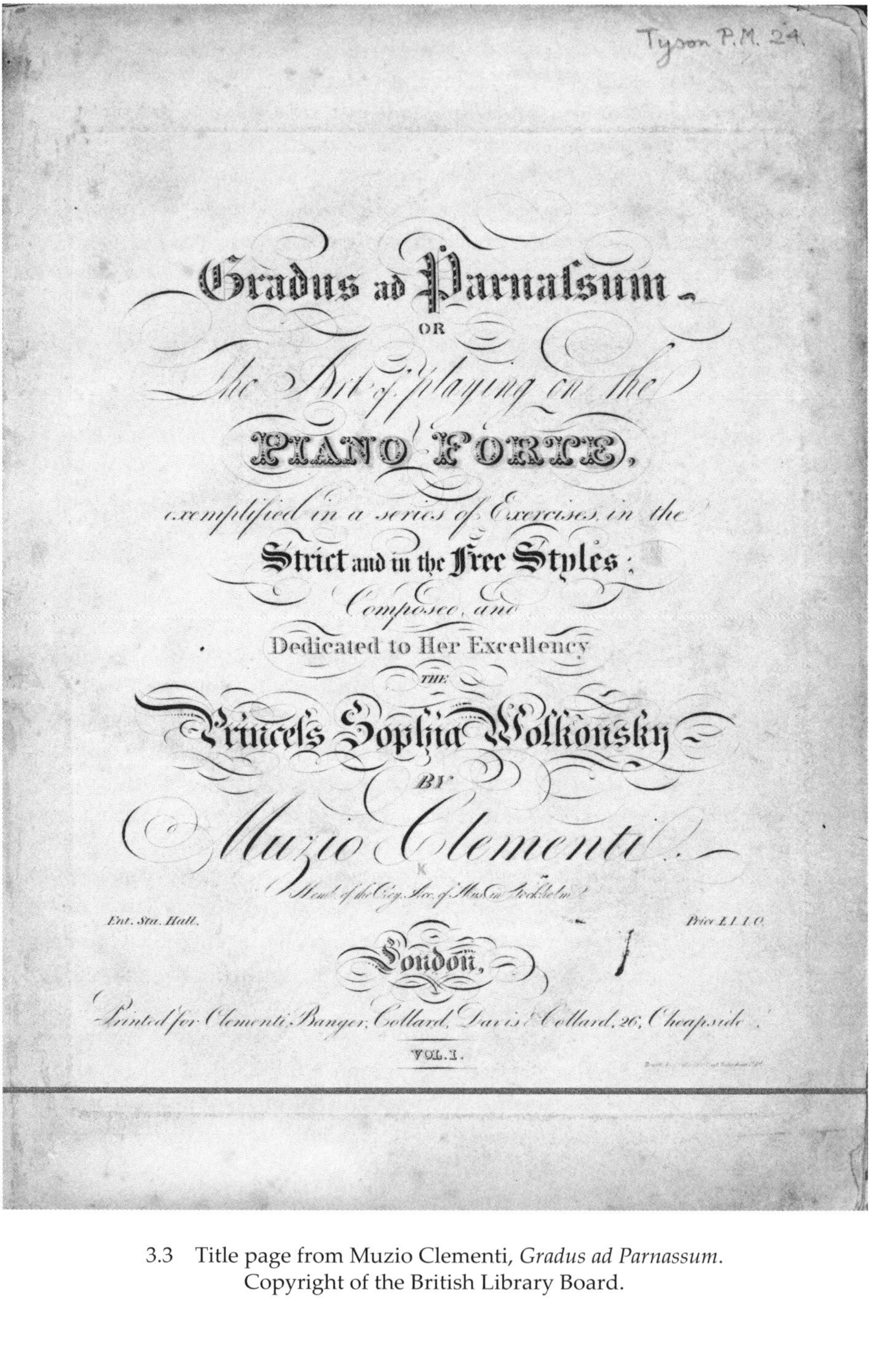

Tyson P.M. 24

Gradus ad Parnassum

OR

The Art of playing on the

PIANO FORTE,

exemplified in a series of Exercises, in the

Strict and in the Free Styles;

Composed and

Dedicated to Her Excellency

THE

Princess Sophia Wolkonsky

BY

Muzio Clementi.

Mem. of the Roy. Acc. of Mus. in Stockholm.

Ent. Sta. Hall.

Price L. 1. 1. 0.

London,

Printed for Clementi, Banger, Collard, Davis & Collard, 26, Cheapside.

VOL. I.

3.3 Title page from Muzio Clementi, *Gradus ad Parnassum*.

In addition to right-hand agility, the etude addresses leaping and twisting in the left hand, as well as crossing left over right hand. Much like the right-hand material, the left sometimes has to stretch or even contort itself to execute Clementi's demands. For instance, after marking the left-hand material *sempre legato* in Measure 9, Clementi provides a series of octaves descending the keyboard (see Figure 3.4). To perform these *legato* as indicated, the pianist must reach an octave between her thumb and fourth finger and use a silent finger switch from '2' to '1' on the first and third beats of each measure. (The first page of the etude is displayed in Figure 3.4. Much like the score to Cramer's third etude, it is not difficult to see repeated patterns on the page reproduced here.)

The G Minor etude is lengthy, taking four or five minutes to perform at a reasonably brisk tempo. It is propelled by incessantly repeating patterns which modulate rapidly from key to key. In fact, on the first page alone, Clementi presents the main theme in five keys. The affect produced by this unyielding sequencing is one of obsession; it almost seems as though, with each modulation, or key change, the pattern is trying to rescue itself from the throes of repetition. Unlike Cramer in his Etude in D Major, Clementi makes no effort to mask his study as a character piece evocative of proper feminine repertoire.

In addition to its gripping affect, other musical features contribute to the etude's compelling narrative. It bursts with chiaroscuro shifts from minor to major, which further its sense of endless and tormented searching. The etude is also alive with contrapuntal, or independent, voices. Inner melodies adorn an otherwise repetitive texture, providing rich variety to the repeating motives and rhythms. This marriage of surface repetition and endless inner variety reflects the dual roles that the etude must play; just as the work is at once for an amateur and designed to build a virtuoso's technique, the etude is seemingly repetitive and, at the same time, infinitely varied. Perhaps its perpetual repetition helped to grant the work a place in the musical notebooks of female amateurs. In a culture that disapproved of women performing works of noticeable musical complexity, this piece masks its musical worth, embedding its contrapuntal lines – its most interesting musical feature – within a busy texture. Much as Cramer's etude disguised the degree to which it called for virtuosic abilities, Clementi's study masquerades as mindlessly repetitive.

Methods of disguise secured a spot for the etude in the musical libraries of amateurs but it is the physical demands of the G Minor Etude that gave the work its legacy. Like corporeal exercises found in conduct literature, and piano exercises in the pages of method books, the choreography of the etude calls for rigorous physical control. It stretches, shapes, moulds and contorts the pianist's hand. And like those other genres, it does so with the promise of cultivating an improved version of the pianist at the bench – who, in my story, is a young lady. But etudes like Clementi's also offer the pianist a resource, which, guided by her own agenda, she can pursue to an unlimited and self-determined end.

3.4 Muzio Clementi, Exercise in G Minor from *Gradus ad Parnassum*. Copyright of the British Library Board.

Should she excel at the keyboard to the point that playing the G Minor Etude becomes second nature to her, the young pianist will have reached far beyond the confines of intermediate-level parlour pianism. She will be a consummate virtuoso. In other words, the physical discipline required and cultivated by Clementi's volume does not control and restrain its subjects as conduct books seek to do; instead, as she acquires more skill and control, the pianist gains increased power with which to further her education at the piano and shape her musical world.

## Returning the Gaze

Conduct books, piano etudes, teachers, parents and even – in the case of Jane Austen's *Emma* – young women's friends, purported to enrich the lives of young British women, but they also served a disciplinary function. In Foucault's paradigm, they resembled the Panopticon, designed by Jeremy Bentham in 1785. The Panopticon permitted officials to observe prisoners without their knowing that they were being seen; Foucault argued that other hierarchical structures also permitted what he calls an 'unequal gaze' through similar one-sided observation. Useful as the theory of the 'unequal gaze' is, theory and practice are very different realities. In the case of the keyboard etude, the embodied act of study and performance turned its disciplinary function on its head, allowing pianists the opportunity to be agents in their own musical destinies. Keyboard etudes permitted transgression without revealing that deviance. These works were so successful at disguise that many historical narratives have continued to assume that the disciplinary methods functioned as they were supposed to, that music did, indeed, act as an effective instrument of containment.

In other words, history has typically viewed female education through a lens that renders women objects of an effective system of discipline. But some scholars have revealed the possibility for counter-narratives to a history comprised of female oppression and submission. Jacques Lacan criticised Foucault's notions of the unequal gaze, arguing that the object herself claims agency with a gaze of her own which shifts the balance of power in a hegemonic structure. In turn, Vivien Jones revealed the way in which readers of conduct literature gazed back at the disciplinary forces around them. In doing so, she gave voice to women whom history had long neglected. Looking at music making among British women of the late eighteenth century, Leslie Ritchie argued that 'musical women were sometimes able to manipulate the ideas of disciplined musical practice meant to control them to their own advantage' (56). Studying etudes allowed women to build the kind of keyboard technique suited to the public practice of music making, that of a virtuoso performer. In doing so, they sounded a critique of their culture's desire to exclude them from that virtuosic world. Their critique echoes about us now, as we examine the world in which British women lived 200 years ago. Rather than retelling a one-sided narrative of containment perpetuated in conduct literature, we should welcome the opportunity to imagine, recreate and study the story returned from the piano bench.

## Works Cited

Allen, Charles. *The Polite Lady; or, a Course of Female Education in a Series of Letters, from a Mother to her Daughter.* 1760. Philadelphia: Printed for Matthew Carey, 1798.

Appleton, Elizabeth. *Private Education or a Practical Plan for the Studies of Young Ladies.* London: Henry Colburn, 1815.

Austen, Jane. *Emma.* Oxford: Oxford University Press, 1991.

Benhabib, Seyla. 'Models of Public Space: Hannah Arendt, the Liberal Tradition, and Jürgen Habermas'. *Habermas and the Public Sphere.* Ed. Craig Calhoun Cambridge: MIT, 1992. 73–98.

Bermingham, Ann. *Learning to Draw: Studies in the Cultural History of a Polite and Useful Art.* New Haven: Yale University Press, 2000.

Darwin, Erasmus. *A Plan for the Conduct of Female Education in Boarding Schools.* Derby: Printed by J. Drewry for J. Johnson, London, 1797.

Foucault, Michel. *Discipline and Punish: The Birth of the Prison.* 1975. New York: Vintage Books, 1995.

Head, Matthew. 'If the Pretty Little Hand Won't Stretch: Music for the Fair Sex in Eighteenth-Century Germany'. *Journal of the American Musicological Society* 52.2 (1999): 203–54.

Jones, Vivien. 'The Seductions of Conduct: Pleasure and Conduct Literature'. *Pleasure in the Eighteenth Century.* Ed. Roy Porter and Marie Mulvey Roberts. Houndmills: Macmillan, 1996. 108–32.

Lacan, Jacques. *The Seminar, Book 1, Freud's Papers on Technique, 1953–1954.* Trans. J. Forrester. New York: W. W. Norton & Co., 1988.

Leppert, Richard. *Music and Image: Domesticity, Ideology and Socio-Cultural Formation in Eighteenth-Century England.* Cambridge: Cambridge University Press, 1993.

Loesser, Arthur. *Men, Women, and Pianos: A Social History.* New York: Dover Publications, 1990.

Misenheimer, Helen. *Rousseau on the Education of Women.* Washington: University Press of America, 1981.

Parke, W.T. *Musical Memoirs: Volume 1.* London: Henry Colburn and Richard Bentley, 1830.

Piggot, Patrick. *The Innocent Diversion: Music in the Life and Writings of Jane Austen.* London: Douglas Cleverdon, 1979.

Plantinga, Leon. *Clementi: His Life and Music.* London: Oxford University Press, 1977.

Poovey, Mary. *The Proper Lady and the Woman Writer.* Chicago: University of Chicago Press, 1984.

Ritchie, Leslie. *Women Writing Music in Late Eighteenth-Century England: Social Harmony in Literature and Performance, 1740–1800.* Aldershot: Ashgate, 2008.

Salwey, Nicholas. 'Women Pianists in Late Eighteenth-Century London'. *Concert Life in Eighteenth-Century Britain.* Ed. Susan Wollenberg and Simon McVeigh. Aldershot: Ashgate, 2004. 273–90.

Temperley, Nicholas. 'Domestic Music in England 1800–1860'. *Proceedings of the Royal Musical Association,* 85th Sess., 1958–59.

—. 'London and the Piano'. *The Musical Times* 129.1744 (1988): 289–93.

—. *The London Pianoforte School: 1766–1860.* 9 vols. New York: Garland Publishing, 1985.

*The Young Lady's Book: A Manual of Elegant Recreations, Exercises, and Pursuits.* London: Vizetelly, Branston and Co., 1829.

Weber, William. *Music and the Middle Class: The Social Structure of Concert Life in London, Paris, and Vienna.* New York: Holmes and Meier, 1975.

Whyman, Susan H. 'Letter Writing and the Rise of the Novel: The Epistolary Literacy of Jane Johnson and Samuel Richardson'. *Huntington Library Quarterly* 70.4 (2007): 577–606.

Wollstonecraft, Mary. *A Vindication of the Rights of Woman: With Strictures on Political and Moral Subjects*. London: Printed for J. Johnson, 1796.

## Notes

1 For music as a feminine accomplishment in late eighteenth- and early nineteenth-century Britain, see Loesser; Piggot; and Temperley, 'Domestic'.

2 Rousseau's famous *Émile*, written in 1762, was translated into English immediately and widely circulated throughout Britain.

3 Samuel Richardson first fashioned his most famous work, *Pamela*, as a conduct book. Other works that were part-novel and part-conduct book included Hannah More's *Coelebs in Search of a Wife* (1809), Frances Burney's *Evelina* (1778) and Maria Edgeworth's *Belinda* (1796).

4 Nicholas Temperley recognises Anton Reicha's *Etudes ou Exercises*, Opus 30, which was published in Paris in 1801, as the first volume of keyboard studies. Cramer's etudes, as Temperley points out, were much more influential as a model and prototype for the many collections by numerous European composers that would follow (*London* IX.xvi).

5 Cramer is the only composer of Classical repertoire mentioned by name in Jane Austen's novel *Emma*.

# 4

# Dresses and Drapery: Female Self-Fashioning in Muslin, 1800–1850

*Alice Barnaby*

This chapter discusses practices of designing and making dresses and drapery by genteel and middle-class women in the first half of the nineteenth century. Particular attention is drawn to the cultural significance of the textile muslin and its dual status as a fashionable, luxury material for female clothing and its use as a central element in interior design, specifically in the area of window drapery. The chapter establishes that muslin's double role as domestic and feminine decoration was the result of particular aesthetic effects engendered by the fabric's unique interaction with ambient light. Its capacity to surround both the animate and inanimate in a cloud-like aura of weightless, pure, transparent evanescence appealed to the period's Romantic sensibilities and in so doing provided daily opportunities to make personal visual statements which keyed into wider debates about class, taste and gendered identity. Therefore it is the cultural meanings of the material and the associations of femininity and domestication conferred upon muslin that forms the principle subject of this chapter. What is particularly noteworthy about the aesthetic collaboration between dress, drapery, light and muslin is the extent to which it was driven by a predominantly amateur and female desire to self-fashion through acts of domestic design. By looking at sources such as fashionable periodicals, etiquette manuals and literary and visual representations of the fabric I offer an analysis that suggests that between 1800 and 1850 a historically specific ontological continuum existed between dress, drapery and female identity. The investigation into the genteel crafting of muslin begins by taking into consideration its status as a fashionable textile and its use in female clothing. The second half of the chapter moves away from the intimate relationship between muslin and women's attire to consider how female pre-professional designs extended into drapery in the gendered space of the middle-class drawing room.

A considerable body of work exists which charts the history of design through an interpretation of the material artefacts of domestic life in relation to the formation of female identity in the nineteenth century (see for example Cohen; Logan; Ponsonby). However, the time frame under investigation in these studies tends to concentrate exclusively on the second half of the century. Recently the history of design has received critical attention from scholars interested in the subject of gender and the process of professionalisation in the design industry; indeed, the present collection of chapters directly contributes to this area of enquiry. Previously Emma Ferry has considered the work of the decorators Rhoda and Agnes Garrett, and Grace Lees-Maffei made an important contribution to the field with her introductory essay to the 2008 special issue 'Professionalizing Interior Design 1870–1970' in the *Journal of Design History*. The general consensus of this scholarship identifies the last three decades of the nineteenth century as the period in which professional female design activity began to establish itself. What had begun as semi-private, non-commercial craft activities had by the end of the century been transformed into a wide-scale and nationally significant industry of interior design coupled with the professionalisation of female design practitioners such as the Garrett cousins (see Ferry).[1] By contrast my chapter is concerned with the time before these efforts to standardise and institutionalise had been asserted, the pre-professional era when the status of amateurism had not yet come to denote a lack of quality, but rather a plenitude of it in the possession and expression of personal, polite accomplishments.

Since the seventeenth century, muslin had been brought to English markets via the trading activities of the East India Company (Riello and Parthasarathi; Lemire). It proved to be a highly successful commodity drawing together the increasingly powerful threads of empire, national industry and feminine fashionability. The initially scarce supply of this imported material meant that demand was high and prices were set at a premium, thereby conferring a luxury status on the fabric and limiting its consumption to elite quarters of society. In the penultimate decade of the eighteenth century, imported products were substituted for domestically manufactured textiles, making muslin more affordable and dramatically increasing availability and consumer demand (Berg; Harley 67–8; Riello; Styles 'Product'). Yet the shift from scarcity to accessibility did not dampen the public's desire for the material, as evidenced by a writer from 1788 who commented upon the industrial improvements of 'British Callicoes and Muslins, printed and plain' which he claimed had 'become the dress of the lower ranks all over Great Britain' (Colquhoun 12). As John Styles explains the evidence does not actually bear out this commentator's belief in the fabric's total cross-class penetration; nevertheless, the comment does reveal key aspects of the fabric's desirability. Styles's nuanced analysis of the situation states that '[t]he spectacular early triumph of cotton depended most of all on its visual, decorative, fashionable qualities. Where appearance was crucial cotton succeeded. Where utilitarian durability counted, cotton sometimes lagged behind' ('What' 326). A chillingly brutal piece of evidence from 1790 supports Styles's assertion of the fabric's fashionable appeal when on April 7 that year a woman called Sophia Jones was caught shoplifting 100 yards of muslin from a shop in Oxford Street, London. This sizable quantity of muslin was valued at £20. Seventeen days later Sophia Jones appeared at the Old Bailey, was found guilty and sentenced to death ('Trial').

By the first decade of the nineteenth century muslin was still a predominantly middle-class commodity and was regularly advertised with other luxury commodities in etiquette manuals, encyclopaedias of domestic economy and fashionable periodicals such as Rudolf Ackermann's *Repository of Arts, Literature, Commerce, Manufactures, Fashions and Politics,* itself a new fashionable commodity published in monthly instalments between 1809 and 1829. Ackermann's *Repository* and other similar publications such as *La Belle Assemblée* (1806–32) and *The Lady's Monthly Museum* (1798–1832) provided a fresh discursive space that sought to nurture and exploit a polite, amateur and creative interest in matters of personal and household design.

In both the *Repository* and *La Belle Assemblée* content was directed towards a predominantly genteel and female audience with articles ranging from theatre reviews, to society news and polite artistic pursuits. A key part of each periodical's appeal was the inclusion of fashion plates, which accompanied copy detailing and judging the season's latest fashions. A short piece on 'Kensington Garden Dresses' from *La Belle Assemblée*'s August edition for 1807 typifies the periodical's attention to style. This excerpt meticulously describes a '[r]ound train dress of India muslin, with short sleeves, ornamented round the bottom and sleeves with a rich border of needlework' (53). The degree of visual and textual detail was more than just aesthetically motivated for it allowed readers to accurately reproduce clothing for themselves. The reference to the muslin's place of origin denotes a belief in the higher quality of the more expensive import, as opposed to domestically produced muslin. Ackermann's *Repository* went one better than *La Belle Assemblée,* for in addition to the standard theatre reviews, and society and fashion news, it also frequently provided needlework patterns and featured advertisements where actual samples of muslin or lace were included so that readers could physically judge quality for themselves. The arrangements of the periodical's content page is particularly revealing in that it suggests that readers' *savoir faire* was built upon a combination of urbane social skills, such as familiarity with the latest styles from Paris, and an ability to set about reproducing those impressions in their own homes, with their own hands. It is perhaps worth remembering that today such a combination would not prove to be a winning formula for a luxury magazine – after all *Vanity Fair* does not include sewing patterns alongside its articles on Hollywood stars and high-profile news reportage; making and consuming are now separate acts in the high-end luxury market. Yet at the beginning of the nineteenth century Ackermann's content page announced at one glance the rich and diverse relationship between women, craft and culture during this period.

In addition to fashion periodicals, etiquette manuals were also equally important for the acquisition and circulation of knowledge relating to female self-fashioning. In keeping with the period's popular style of neoclassical dress, the writer of *The Mirror of Graces; or, the English Lady's Costume* (1811) drew upon Greek mythology for inspiration when recommending muslin:

> In the spring of youth, when all is lovely and gay, then, as the soft green, sparkling in freshness, bedecks the earth; so, light and transparent robes, of tender colours, should adorn the limbs of the young beauty. If she be of the Hebe form, warm weather should find her veiled in fine muslin, lawn, gauzes and other lucid materials. (71)

Similar stylistic advice was offered in the *Repository* for January 1813 which illustrated and described a '[m]orning Walking Dress' as '[a] round robe of Cambric muslin, with long full sleeves, and simple short collar, confined in the center of the throat with a stud or broach' ('Ladies'' 55). These elements of soft, transparent female fashion located in an outdoor landscaped setting very much played into a wider visual language that treated both nature and femininity with the same light, fresh and idealised representational strategies. The dress of the female promenaders depicted in J.M.W. Turner's *Richmond Hill on the Prince Regent's Birthday* (Tate Britain) from 1819 may very well have been taken from Ackermann's fashion plates, and the aesthetic blurring of arboreal foliage with the clouds of muslin surrounding the women indicates a deeper desire to blur ontological boundaries between women, dress and environment (Ribeiro 67). This issue of blurring boundaries is significant because it occurred on a number of levels. For the moment we will leave the aspect of aesthetic blurring between muslin and women, and concentrate instead on middle-class women's level of creative amateur involvement with their dress, in which we see a functional overlap between maker and wearer.

In Beverly Lemire's study of the British Cotton trade from 1600–1800 she notes that at the end of the eighteenth century '[m]ore than in any previous time, this period saw fashion step down from the pinnacle to become a shared attraction for much of society' and that changes in styles were beginning to occur on a monthly basis (173–4). Inevitably this monthly cycle was fuelled by the rise of early nineteenth-century fashion journalism in periodicals such as the *Repository*. However, it is also important to remember that with this new rapid change in fashion there was still only a limited availability of ready-made shop-bought items. As a result maintaining a fashionable appearance required both more time commitment and greater skills in the production of bespoke garments. Rather than purchasing new expensive items owners frequently developed ingenious techniques of adaptation and modification which demanded either developing one's own textile skills or nurturing even closer relationships with professional, often female, artisans from the clothing trade, be it milliners, seamstresses or dressmakers who needed to be equally attentive readers of the fashionable press if they were to satisfy their customers (Ribeiro 76). Even when commissioning a new garment, a considerable degree of creative flexibility existed in the client's involvements with the fabrication of her own clothing either through consultations in shops or via home visits from professionals.

In a tightly focused study of skilled craftswomen in Boston, USA, Marla Miller comments upon this very process of collaboration between amateur and professional. Miller writes that '[a]s genteel women traveled, they learned of emerging trends and communicated them to their friends at home in person or through the mail, who in turn conveyed these new preferences to local craftswomen' (385). Miller identifies the 1790s trend for empire-line muslin dresses as a particularly interesting instance of the dynamic between client and dressmaker when she notes that '[f]ar from a style imposed by clothing producers, garments with waistlines just under the arms were imposed on producers by consumers, which forced artisans to devise and cultivate new abilities' (385). At times the creativity of the artisan was removed from the process altogether; Miller notes that:

> At least one mother deprived a Boston craftswoman of income when she instructed her daughter, 'I think you had better make a light pink [illegible] of [sarcenet] or very mean silk instead of your beautiful lutestring – and should think you could do it yourself as it is only to wear under muslin, but do as you please'. (386)

The combined acts of crafting, collaborating and adapting associated with the new fashion for muslin shows that early nineteenth-century clothing still possessed a quality of self-expression which was lost when later in the century producer and consumer were separated through the proliferation of machine-made and shop-bought clothing.

The overlap between professional and amateur dressmakers was particularly pronounced at the level of decoration, where the articulation of personal taste and artistry was most visible. Skilled execution of decorative needlework, particularly embroidery on muslin, was considered to be both a useful and improving pastime for genteel ladies. This type of ornamental work, frequently undertaken in the social space of the drawing room, was considered to be an activity of accomplishment, a cultivating and improving process rather than a primary act of economic labour. An idealised and aestheticised example of this type of activity and the women who performed it can be seen in Joshua Reynolds's 1781 portrait *The Ladies Waldegrave* (National Gallery of Scotland). Aileen Ribeiro meticulously identifies the figures, their apparel and their equipment stating that the women are:

> Dressed in white silk *polonaise* dresses over muslin skirts, with lace trimmed fichus over their shoulders, the filmy costumes echo the pale grey of their powdered hair. From left to right, Maria holds a skein of silk, which Laura winds on to a card, and Horatia embroiders muslin on her tambour frame. The embroidered bag on the table would have contained sewing impedimenta (silks, cards, needles, scissors, etc.) and was to become a fashion accessory in its own right at the very end of the century, the forerunner of the handbag. (70)

These acts of needlework were not simply concerned with the production of fashionable clothing, but also directly contributed to the creation of female identity. The significance of proving one's female worth through the dexterous handling of clothing, accessories and its equipment is playfully extrapolated in a scene from Jane Austen's *Northanger Abbey* (1817). During the section of the novel set in the fashionable city of Bath, Catherine Morland converses with her chaperone Mrs Allen and the object of her affections Henry Tilney. In response to Tilney's unusually (for a man) knowledgeable observations about the price of muslin, Mrs Allen exclaims, 'Do you understand muslins sir?' (28). Further demonstrating his ability, Tilney explains how he bought a muslin for his sister's gown and proudly claims that 'it was pronounced to be a prodigious bargain by every lady who saw it. I gave but five shillings a yard for it, and a true Indian muslin' (28). The dialogue continues with Tilney reassuring Mrs Allen that Catherine's recent purchase of muslin, whilst not necessarily appropriate for a gown, could nevertheless be creatively re-purposed. He says, 'Muslin always turns to some account or other; Miss Morland will get enough out of it for a handkerchief, or a cap, or a cloak. Muslin can never be said to be wasted' (28). Of course by using the romantic hero as an unfamiliar mouthpiece for feminine topics of conversation, Austen is humourously drawing attention to readers' highly gendered expectations of characters and their traditionally generic limitations. But Austen is also simultaneously emphasising (albeit in a mocking tone) the central role that muslin played in the lives of many women during this period.

By the middle of the nineteenth century the appetite for and accessibility of aristocratic and genteel female fashions had expanded to include a middle-class market. Etiquette manuals and needlework handbooks complemented the periodical press's interest in the latest styles, fabrics and dressmaking techniques. *The Drawing Room Magazine: or, Ladies' Book of Fancy Needlework and Choice Literature* (1848) announces by its title alone that the act of needlework was in part performative and suitable for the polite social space of the drawing room. A slightly earlier publication from H.G. Clarke entitled *The Ladies' Hand-Book of Embroidery on Muslin and Lacework* (1843), describes the occupation of needlework as a kind of task which 'shed a calm, and diffused a radiant sunshine over their leisure hours' (vi). Such a statement reveals that physical contact with muslin sensorily affected the quality of female experience and the atmosphere of the immediate environment; by wearing and working in muslin the light-diffusing properties of the fabric created an impression of the pure radiance of womanhood. Muslin's material qualities were encouraged to exercise a mode of aesthetic agency upon states of feminine embodied consciousness. The act of touching, making and projecting a form of creative vision in needlework onto muslin had the effect of transforming not only the muslin but also the woman into a refined artefact. The author of the handbook continues with the conviction that by representing nature in needlework a woman's corporeality would favourably dematerialise, appearing as merely a miraculous illuminated essence of femininity:

> And she, whose deep sensibilities, and nicely-judging skill, are elicited by the effort to rival nature in the production of a mimic flower, will be very likely to conceive some nobler aim, and to become an orb of brightness, diffusing comfort, happiness and joy, through the whole circle in which providence has appointed her to move. (47)

Through the act of making, the woman was improved and her 'orb' or aura of brightness and comfort reached out beyond her physical boundaries to influence and improve others in her sphere. The processing of raw material into a refined and ornamented material refers equally to both the woman and the muslin; both were rendered culturally eloquent through the woman's handling of muslin. As she sat in the drawing room and worked upon the muslin, it also worked upon her in a reciprocal act of improvement.

*The Ladies' Work-Table Book* of 1844 was explicit in this agenda of improvement with regard to muslin embroidery when, in the introduction, the author stressed that '[w]e are anxious to render elegant amusements conducive to the attainment of moral ends; and to lay that foundation of intellectual superiority, and affectionate regard, for the comfort and happiness of others, which can alone give light and animation, sweetness and blooming freshness, to the interesting scenes of future life' (xv). The author concluded this prescriptive sentiment by explaining that '[o]ur aim in this work has been, while seeking to promote the purposes of genuine education, to raise high the moral sentiments, and cultivate to an eminent, degree the best sensibilities of the soul' (xvi). Small daily activities such as these demonstrated that a carefully constructed ideological relationship of aesthetic and ontological mutuality existed between how both women and muslin were valued and judged. The qualities of refinement, subtlety and pliability associated with muslin and the skills necessary to work it were equally valued as attributes of feminine identity. To a certain extent then muslin created constructions of femininity rather than female identity defining the cultural meaning of muslin. Moreover this type of work actually succeeded in creating amateur communities of female needlecraft, binding together and reinforcing identities through shared activities and shared objects. In her notably erudite publication *Needlework as Art* (1884) Marian Margaret Alford describes how 'English ladies' in the first half of the century 'designed and collected patterns from each other, and gave the produce of their industry as gifts to their friends for collars, cuffs, and trimmings' (348). Unlike the professionalisation of textile and interior design practices in the second half of the century, this type of amateur industry was valued for reasons of sentiment rather than profit (Schaffer).

## Drapery in the Drawing Room

The second half of this chapter continues to think about amateur creativity and the nature of the mutually constituting relationship of muslin and women, but moves away from a focus on the immediate and intimate sphere of female bodily adornment to consider instead women's role in the aesthetic management of the middle-class household. On the subject of decorative arrangements in mid- to late eighteenth-century genteel dwellings, Amanda Vickery sums up the domestic dynamic accordingly, '[H]onourable men, ripe for domestication, were ready with the sample book and their credit, but ladies' preferences carried the day' (88). By the 1830s and 1840s this gendered division of household responsibilities had been consolidated. Elizabeth Langland emphasises that 'the house and its mistress served as a significant adjunct to a man's commercial endeavours. Whereas men earned the money, women had the important task of managing those funds towards the acquisition of social and political status' (8). Household responsibilities such as these are depicted in Mary Howitt's domestic novel, *Strive and Thrive* (1840). In the chapter entitled 'New Home' the protagonist Margaret and her husband are obliged to move to less expensive accommodation due to the couple's financial difficulties. In the new residence, Margaret takes charge of her new domain, and Howitt details her creative efforts to adequately decorate and furnish the home with greatly reduced means. Arbiters of taste referred to this type of design activity as 'household art', 'household taste', 'household beauty' and 'domestic decoration', which aimed towards the creation of appropriate environments for middle-class family life. Martha Crabill McClaugherty claims that these practices only emerged as a distinct discourse in the last third of the nineteenth century, as evidenced by a wave of prescriptive household guides such as texts by Charles Eastlake and Lady Orrinsmith. However, it is misleading to conclude that those discourses alone mark the birth of a nineteenth-century aesthetic relationship to the home. Manuals of domestic economy, etiquette guides and craft handbooks from the first half of the century gave voice to an active culture of female design activity and frequently dedicated chapters to appropriate decoration and decorum. In particular these texts all focus on the importance of the drawing room.[2]

Above all other communal areas of the house, the drawing room was associated with discourses of female identity, and, like female identity, the drawing room was also defined and regulated by a set of idealised aesthetic qualities. Its primary function in the household was to provide a semi-private space for polite socialising. Receiving visitors, displaying cultural status and forming beneficial family alliances (such as marriage) were all regularly enacted in the drawing room. The writers of *Domestic Duties*, a guide from 1825 on matters of etiquette and household practicalities for middle-class women, were all too aware of the drama of the drawing room. They reminded their readers that it was in this very setting 'that the graces of social intercourse are chiefly displayed' (Parkes 49). But the drawing room was also a platform for the middle-class woman to gain a perspective on and interact with the wider world of commerce, industry, engineering, politics and culture, partly through her judgement, acquisition and display of luxury geo-political commodities such as muslin. Successful choreography of material objects and performances in sociability required the presence of a refined and harmonious atmosphere and it was a woman's responsibility to skilfully conjure up an appropriate ambience using a subtle blend of material and immaterial properties; the crafting and filtering of natural and artificial light through fabrics such as muslin was integral to the success of this atmospheric concoction. Towards the end of the eighteenth century certain developments in architectural styles, exemplified by architects such as Humphrey Repton, directly affected a room's atmospheric conditions due to a new preference for larger, often floor to ceiling-sized windows (see Figure 4.1). This had a knock-on effect on the look and feel of interior spaces and new techniques of interior design evolved to accommodate these visual changes. The soft furnishings of window curtains and drapery were particularly important as they provided a frame and filter for the new drama of light and glass, the generous prospect beyond the house, and the associated statement of affluence.

It is no coincidence that the increasingly rapid cycle of fashions using muslin in clothing was accompanied by a similarly new range of styles in soft furnishings for drawing-room decorations. Curtains and drapery were at the forefront of this fad due to their ability to enhance and emphasise the spectacle of fashionably larger windows. Many of the styles and skills associated with female dress were seamlessly transferred to dressing windows, and an intentional co-ordination emerged between the way women dressed themselves and the way they dressed their windows. The aim of this unified treatment was to create a continuous impression of sophisticated and cultured femininity originating in the woman's personal aura and radiating out into her daily habitat. The soft, transparent fabric of muslin was highly adaptable and ideally suited for both window and clothing decoration. The dual uses of muslin meant that, in addition to the precise and delicate skills demanded by needlework and dressmaking, women were also developing accomplished practices of interior design long in advance of the discipline's professional recognition later in the nineteenth century.

4.1 *The Old Cedar Parlour and Modern Living Room*, colour lithograph of interiors from Humphry Repton, *Fragments on the Theory and Practice of Landscape Gardening* (1816). Private collection/The Stapleton Collection/The Bridgeman Art Library.

In spite of this significant shift in architectural and interior design, scholarship dedicated to the history of windows and curtains is limited. Samuel J. Dornsife's article, 'Design Sources for Nineteenth-Century Window Hangings' and Clare Jameson's book *The Potterton Pictorial Treasury of Drapery and Curtain Designs, 1750–1950,* both chart stylistic and technical developments but no sustained or detailed work into the cultural significance of early nineteenth-century window drapery exists. The work of Penny Sparke, Wolfgang Schivelbusch and Beverly Gordon makes passing references to window curtains and is primarily concerned with the later cultural history of interior design. Further fleeting reference to the use of curtains is made by Peter Thornton who merely notes that 'many windows did not have curtains at all until well into the eighteenth century' (23). The art historian Anne Hollander provides some additional clarification about the emergence of the window curtain in the nineteenth century when she suggests that:

> [W]indow curtains … had never been a feature of earlier luxurious dwellings. They tended to be functional extensions of wall hangings if they existed at all, and their decorative draping was not thoroughly explored until the Neo-Classic taste began to celebrate the catenary. (67)

Whilst secondary sources concerned with the impact of curtains are scarce, primary sources describing the new fashion for window curtains and the popularity of muslin are numerous. Trade and consumer publications of the period, such as the aforementioned Ackermann's *Repository,* consistently featured articles and illustrations about the newest style of drapery and advertisements for textiles in addition to and alongside the season's most desirable outfits for men and women. As early as 1809, in the regular slot entitled 'Fashionable Furniture' it was declared that 'in no department of furnishing has the inventive power of fancy been more assiduously employed, than in the disposition of draperies for windows, beds, alcoves and other suitable objects. It is the elegance and lightness of drapery that have given reputation to the most famous sculptors' (255). The aesthetic status of drapery, and more generally artistry of the home, is at stake here; the reference to sculpture attempts to ally newer practices of interior design with older, elite traditions of fine art as opposed to the lower status of more recent artisanal trades such as upholstery.

In 1823 Ackermann's articles relating to window drapery and furniture design from the *Repository* were considered sufficiently à la mode to appear in a single volume work entitled *A Series, Containing Forty-Four Engravings in Colours, of Fashionable Furnitures.* The range of styles such as Gothic demonstrates the degree to which the practice of window drapery absorbed and adapted the popularity of wider stylistic trends which were also articulated in ladies' clothing fashions. Illustrations were accompanied by a textual interpretation of the design, detailing specific 'light and elegant' fabrics and colours, stating that the sub-curtains should be of 'transparent materials richly embroidered' (14) (descriptions which could just as easily be applied to women's luxury clothing). The presence of Repton's influence is evident through the high windows framed first by the clear muslin which hangs in a gathered vertical swag from cornice to floor, followed by subsequent additional and ornamental layers of cloth. The formulaic view is extended and moves from the interior through to a typically picturesque landscape beyond, depicting water, figures, hills and distant habitation. Given that the drawing room was the site of precisely performed social rituals, it is no coincidence that such a stylised representation of the home gave the appearance of a theatrical set, particularly if we take into consideration the fact that muslin was also frequently used for set designs in theatres.[3] Therefore, on both the public stage and in the domestic drama of the drawing room, muslin was used to create atmospheric transformations for purposes of performance by controlling lighting levels and framing the act of viewing.[4]

The decorative and performative nature of muslin as costume applied to both rooms and their occupants. The highly influential early nineteenth-century French interior designers Charles Percier and Pierre Fontaine neatly articulated the correlation between designing drapery for the home and dressing the person: '[D]ecoration and furniture become for homes what clothes are to people' (quoted in Dornsife 69). Such a view was echoed by Mrs L. in Parkes's *The Domestic Duties* (1825) who observed, '[T]he style of drawing-room furniture is almost as changeable in fashion as female dress; sometimes it is Grecian, then Egyptian, and now Turkish' (193). Towards the middle of the century, publications such as this and Ackermann's *Repository* were accompanied by less high-end, more practically oriented texts for women like *The Workwoman's Guide, containing instructions in cutting out and completing articles of wearing apparel, etc. which are usually made at home; also, explanations on upholstery, straw-platting, bonnet-making, knitting, etc.* (1838). Such was the aesthetic affinity between dress and drapery that creative (or possibly prescriptive) guidance for women's personal and household appearance was now routinely packaged together between the covers of one book handling both topics.

In Elizabeth Gaskell's novel *Cranford,* published as a serial in *Household Words* from 1851, we can imagine perhaps that some of her female characters benefited from the advice offered by *The Workwoman's Guide* when in a recalled conversation the narrator Mary Smith turns a reference to a far-flung family member seamlessly into the topic of household management:

> The only fact I gained from this conversation was that certainly Peter had last been heard of in India, 'or that neighbourhood'; and that this scanty intelligence of his whereabouts had reached Cranford in the year when Miss Pole had brought her Indian muslin gown, long since worn out (we washed it and mended it, and traced its decline and fall into a window-blind before we could go on). (133)

Following Elaine Freedgood's literary strategy of reading materials' meanings through their metonymic associations, we can interpret the reference to 'Peter' and 'India' as suggestive of the British Empire, trade and masculinity which, through muslin and its commercial trajectory, is then yoked to realms of the domestic, local and feminine. Attention is then drawn to the shared attire of women and windows when the clothing cast-offs of Miss Pole are frugally and resourcefully re-purposed into household equipment. These representations of quotidian events are significant for the manner in which they unquestioningly position women, muslin and windows in a seemingly natural and harmonious continuum, but also highlight a sense of women's skills of creative adaptation. Moreover skills such as these were evidently embedded in communities of shared physical and emotional memories, note the plural in 'we washed it and mended it'.

Although the scope of this chapter is concerned with the period 1800 to 1850, it is worth briefly looking ahead by a few decades because the historically specific amateur status of female design practices in muslin is brought into sharper focus by subsequent developments. By the 1870s and 1880s craft-based communities of sewing expertise were beginning to receive official recognition. In 1872 the Royal School of Art Needlework (RSN) was established. Its role in the development of professional female textile designers was significant both in the UK and abroad; the American textile and interior designer Candace Wheeler was particularly influenced by the work of the RSN which she saw exhibited in 1876 at America's first World's Fair Exposition in Philadelphia. Yet while the status of female designers was moving from private to public practice in the second-half of the century, muslin, and cotton in general, was not such a popular choice for women's clothing styles or soft furnishings. Bolder, shinier fabrics such as silk and satin that reflected light and reliably held a range of stridently coloured new synthetic aniline dyes, such as mauveine invented by Sir William Henry Perkin in 1856, were increasingly favoured above muslin's delicate transparent appearance of 'woven air' (Birdwood 343).[5] The domestic and daily affinity between women and muslin was becoming a thing of the past; former handmade practices were increasingly eclipsed by innovations in machine-made techniques of sewing, and the wider availability of ready-to-wear items.[6] These changes in the conditions of production and consumption of clothing and soft furnishings were accompanied by new pressures and possibilities associated with shifts in the political and intellectual formation of female identity.[7] The polite pastime of delicately embroidering muslin in the privacy of the drawing room had ceased to be an adequately imaginative activity of self-fashioning by the 1870s and 1880s. Muslin's aesthetic effects of transparency, insubstantiality and ephemerality no longer creatively merged with newer ideological conceptions of womanhood.

## Works Cited

Ackermann, Rudolf. *A Series, Containing Forty-Four Engravings in Colours, of Fashionable Furnitures*. London: Ackermann, 1823.

Alford, Lady Marian. *Needlework as Art*. London: Sampson Low, Marston, Searle, and Rivington, 1886.

Austen, Jane. *Northanger Abbey*. London: Penguin, 1995.

Baugh, Christopher. 'Philippe James de Loutherbourg and the Early Pictorial Theatre: Some Aspects of its Cultural Context'. *The Theatrical Space*. Ed. James Redmond. Cambridge: Cambridge University Press, 1987. 99–128.

Berg, Maxine. 'In Pursuit of Luxury: Global History and British Consumer Goods in the Eighteenth Century'. *Past and Present* 182 (2004): 85–142.

Birdwood, George. *The Industrial Arts of India*. 2 vols. London: Chapman & Hall, 1880.

Cohen, Deborah. *Household Gods: The British and Their Possessions*. New Haven: Yale University Press, 2006.

Colquhoun, Patrick. *Observations on the Means of Extending the Consumption of British Callicoes, Muslins, and Other Cotton Goods, and of Giving Pecuniary Aids to the Manufacturers, under Circumstances of the Highest Respectability and Advantage*. London, 1788.

Dornsife, Samuel J. 'Design Sources for Nineteenth-Century Window Hangings'. *Winterthur Portfolio* 10 (1975): 69–99.

*The Drawing Room Magazine: or, Ladies' Book of Fancy Needle-work and Choice Literature*. London: Houlston and Stoneman, 1848.

Eastlake, Charles. *Hints on Household Taste in Furniture, Upholstery and Other Details*. London: Longmans, Green, 1868.

'Fashionable Furniture'. *Repository of Arts, Literature, Commerce, Manufactures, Fashions and Politics* 1 (1809): 255.

Ferry, Emma. '"Decorators May Be Compared to Doctors": An Analysis of Rhoda and Agnes Garrett's *Suggestions for House Decoration in Painting, Woodwork and Furniture*'. *Journal of Design History* 16.1 (2003): 15–33.

Freedgood, Elaine. *The Idea in Things: Fugitive Meaning in the Victorian Novel*. Chicago: University of Chicago Press, 2006.

Garrett, Agnes, and Rhoda Garrett. *Suggestions for House Decoration in Painting, Woodwork and Furniture*. London: Macmillan, 1876.

Gaskell, Elizabeth. *Cranford*. London: Penguin, 2006.

Gilman, Caroline. *The Lady's Annual Register and Housewife's Memorandum-Book*. Boston: T.H. Carter, 1838.

Godley, Andrew. 'The Development of the UK Clothing Industry, 1850–1950: Output and Productivity Growth'. *Business History* 37.4 (1995): 46–63.

Gordon, Beverly. 'Woman's Domestic Body: The Conceptual Conflation of Women and Interiors in the Industrial Age'. *Winterthur Portfolio* 31.4 (1996): 281–301.

Harley, C. Knick. 'Cotton Textile Prices and the Industrial Revolution'. *Economic History Review* 51.1 (1998): 49–83.

Haweis, Mary Eliza. *The Art of Decoration*. London: Chatto & Windus, 1881.

Hollander, Anne. *Seeing Through Clothes*. Berkeley: University of California Press, 1993.

Howitt, Mary. *Strive and Thrive*. London: Thomas Tegg, 1840.

Jameson, Clare. *The Potterton Pictorial Treasury of Drapery and Curtain Designs, 1750–1950*. Thirsk: Potterton Books, 1987.

'Kensington Garden Dresses'. *La Belle Assemblée* 2 (1807): 53.

'Ladies' Fashion' *Repository of Arts, Literature, Commerce, Manufactures, Fashions and Politics* 1 (1813): 55

*The Ladies' Hand-book of Embroidery on Muslin, and Lacework*. London: H.G. Clarke, 1843.
*The Ladies' Work-Table Book*. London: T.B. Peterson, 1844.
Landon, Letitia Elizabeth. *Fisher's Drawing Room Scrap Book*. London: Fisher, Son, and Jackson, 1832.
Langland, Elizabeth. *Nobody's Angels: Middle-Class Women and Domestic Ideology in Victorian Culture*. Ithaca, NY: Cornell University Press, 1995.
Lees-Maffei, Grace. 'Introduction: Professionalization as a Focus in Interior Design History'. *Journal of Design History* 21.1 (2008): 1–18.
Lemire, Beverly. *Fashion's Favourite: The Cotton Trade and the Consumer in Britain, 1600–1800*. Oxford: Oxford University Press, 1991.
Logan, Thad. *The Victorian Parlour: A Cultural Study*. Cambridge: Cambridge University Press, 2001.
McClaugherty, Martha Crabill. 'Household Art: Creating the Artistic Home, 1868–1893'. *Winterthur Portfolio* 18.1 (1983): 1–26.
Miller, Marla. 'The Last Mantuamaker: Craft Tradition and Commercial Change in Boston, 1760–1840'. *Early American Studies: An Interdisciplinary Journal* 4.2 (2006): 372–424.
*The Mirror of the Graces: or, the English Lady's Costume ... With Useful Advice on Female Accomplishments, Politeness, and Manners ... By a Lady of Distinction*. London: B. Crosby & Co., 1811.
Orrinsmith, Lucy. *The Drawing-Room: Its Decorations and Furniture*. London: Macmillan, 1878.
Panton, Jane Ellen. *Homes of Taste: Economical Hints*. London: S. Low, Marston, Searle and Rivington, 1890.
Parkes, Mrs William. *Domestic Duties: or, Instructions to Young Married Ladies, on the Management of Their Households, and the Regulation of Their Conduct in the Various Relations and Duties of Married Life*. London: Longman, Hurst, Rees, Orme, Brown, and Green, 1825.
Ponsonby, Margaret. *Stories from Home: English Domestic Interiors, 1750–1850*. Aldershot: Ashgate, 2007.
Ribeiro, Aileen. *The Art of Dress: Fashion in England and France, 1750–1820*. New Haven: Yale University Press, 1995.
Riello, Giorgio, and Prasannan Parthasarathi, eds. *The Spinning World: A Global History of Cotton Textiles, 1200–1850*. Oxford: Oxford University Press, 2009.
Schaffer, Talia. *Novel Craft: Victorian Domestic Handicraft & Nineteenth-Century Fiction*. Oxford: Oxford University Press, 2011.
Schivelbusch, Wolfgang. *Disenchanted Night: The Industrialization of Light in the Nineteenth Century*. Berkeley: University of California Press, 1995.
Sparke, Penny. *As Long as It's Pink: The Sexual Politics of Taste*. London: Pandora, 1995.
Styles, John. 'Product Innovation in Early Modern London'. *Past and Present* 168 (2000): 124–69.
——. 'What Were Cottons for in the Early Industrial Revolution?' *The Spinning World: A Global History of Cotton Textiles, 1200–1850*. Ed. Giorgio Riello and Prasannan Parthasarathi. Oxford: Oxford University Press, 2009. 307–26.
Thornton, Peter. *Authentic Decor: The Domestic Interior, 1620–1920*. London: Weidenfeld and Nicolson, 1984.
'Trial of Sophia (wife of John) Jones, 24 April 1790'. Ref. t17900424-4. *Old Bailey Proceedings Online*. www.oldbaileyonline.org. Accessed 1 August 2011.

Vickery, Amanda. *Behind Closed Doors: At Home in Georgian England*. New Haven: Yale University Press, 2009.

*The Workwoman's Guide, Containing Instructions in Cutting Out and Completing Articles of Wearing Apparel, etc. Which are Usually Made at Home; also, Explanations on Upholstery, Straw-platting, Bonnet-making, Knitting etc.* London: Simpkin, Marshall, 1838.

## Notes

1 Other publications include Mary Eliza Haweis, *The Art of Decoration* (1881) and Jane Ellen Panton, *Homes of Taste* (1890). American female counter-parts to decorators such as the Garretts included Candace Wheeler, Edith Wharton and Elsie de Wolfe.

2 For example see L.E.L., *Fisher's Drawing Room Scrap Book* (1832); Caroline Gilman, *The Lady's Annual Register and Housewife's Memorandum Book* (1838).

3 The best known and innovative theatrical effects produced with muslin were executed by Philippe de Loutherbourg, the artist and theatrical scenographer, who, by experimenting with the angle of light projected through or onto painted muslin scrims, was able to produce smooth scene changes and atmospheric effects such as representations of moonlight or firelight (see Baugh).

4 Muslin's relationship to the ambient light surrounding women and drawing rooms is discussed in greater detail in my forthcoming monograph *Light Touches: Cultural Practices of Illumination, London 1800–1900* (Routledge 2015).

5 A fine example of a British-made silk mauveine coloured dress from 1873 can be found in the Victoria and Albert Museum, catalogue number: T.51&A-1922.

6 Although the sewing-machine was exhibited at Crystal Palace in 1851, sales only really began to gather momentum in the 1860s (Godley 56).

7 A number of significant political landmarks included the 1857 Matrimonial Clauses Act, which allowed divorce through the courts rather than through private bill, and the 1870 and 1882 Married Women's Property Acts provided women with greater financial independence.

# PART II

# The Artistic Career

# 5

# Contrary to the Habits of Their Sex? Women Drawing on Wood and the Careers of Florence and Adelaide Claxton

*Catherine Flood*

When Florence Claxton executed her first drawing for the *Illustrated Times* in 1858, she

> had done what no female artist in all the world had attempted before – made a drawing on wood for an illustrated weekly paper … which involves a very unpleasant amount of hurry, bother, downright drudgery and night-work. (Clayton 44–5)

Ellen Clayton's claim in *English Female Artists* is true in spirit. A few illustrations attributed to women had already appeared in the pages of the illustrated press, but Florence Claxton, her sister Adelaide and their contemporary Mary Ellen Edwards were the first women to forge careers and establish names in the field. Women were already book illustrators, but drawing for the periodical press suggested a more overtly commercial and professional transaction. Less prestigious and more ephemeral than book illustration, the periodical press offered a steadier flow of income and constituted the bread and butter work for the illustrators of the 1860s. Significantly, the best known female book illustrators of the 1850s, Eleanor Vere Boyle and Jemima Blackburn, were well-off women who, although proficient and widely published, styled themselves as amateurs, the former donating the proceeds of her work to charitable causes. Ellen Clayton's description of the pressure, hard graft and daring of Florence Claxton's work, on the other hand, is firmly removed from any idea of drawing for the sake of it or as an elegant pastime. While female periodical illustrators were few in number at the beginning of the 1860s, they were squarely in the public eye. Their work by its very nature achieved a wide distribution and the signatures of Florence and Adelaide Claxton had extraordinary visibility.

This chapter examines how the new figure of the female periodical illustrator intersected with mid-century debates over the lack of employment for middle-class women, the nature of the female artist and the hierarchies of an industrialising image trade. The 1860s illustrator was regarded as akin to the fine artist in requiring a high level of artistic ability and 'imaginative power', and illustrators of this period were often also exhibiting painters. The Claxtons and Mary Ellen Edwards are a case in point, and both their painting and illustration would have been subject to many of the same broad prejudices that framed the female artist. However drawing on wood was a materially distinct form of image making requiring a particular mode of draughtsmanship and the production of wood-engraved illustration attracted specific signification in terms of the perceived masculine and feminine qualities of the technique. It was a collaborative medium circumscribed by the text, the technique of the wood engraver, and the commercial vision of the publisher. By this date the illustrator was usually commissioned to make a drawing on the block, which was then passed to the engraver for cutting. The illustrator might be classified as a creative artist, but he or she was also one part in an industrial process and limited by how the drawn line could be drawn, engraved and mass printed. Illustration therefore bordered the realms of both the academic artist and the mechanical artisan. The first part of this chapter looks at how the illustrator's cultural status in relation to these other practitioners was frequently articulated in reference to sexual politics in ways that both opposed and enabled the idea of women drawing on wood.

I then take Florence and Adelaide Claxton as a case study, looking at the significance of graphic illustration in their careers and the niche they established within the periodical press for humorous social scenes. As commercial artists and humorists they posed a double challenge to expectations of female art and feminine behaviour. Humour, often associated with the qualities of vulgarity and aggression, was deeply problematic territory for women, to the extent that some commentators denied or obscured the existence of female humorists and caricaturists (Kunzle 26–31; Spielmann 529). I suggest that the Claxtons' social satires were accepted in reference to concepts of 'amiable humour' and drawing-room sociability and provided a medium for social comment on the condition of the middle-class woman.

The idea of a woman drawing professionally for wood-engraving surfaces in Wilkie Collins's 1859–60 novel, *The Woman in White*, only to be refused in a way that exemplifies how publishable illustration was ascribed masculine values and agency. Drawing forms a thread through the book, and the heroine Laura Fairlie is introduced to readers as a lady sketcher. Towards the end of the novel she is rescued by her former drawing master, Walter Hartwright, from the asylum where her husband has imprisoned her. Walter then supports Laura and her sister while they are in hiding in London by earning money drawing on wood for an engraving firm. To aid her rehabilitation from trauma and smooth over the fact that he has no claim to be supporting her, Walter encourages Laura to draw and creates the 'innocent deception' that he is selling her drawings along with his own. In reality they are 'poor, faint valueless sketches' (433) that Walter squirrels away for sentimental reasons. The scenario gives a nod to the fact that women were drawing professionally for publishers at the time the book was written, but retreats into the ideal of the supported, dependent female. Throughout the novel, Laura is characterised as desirably fragile and vulnerable and her slight drawings that have no commercial value contribute to this vision of femininity, which is set apart from the sphere of work. Drawing for a publisher also signifies an important juncture in Walter's development as the assertive hero, shifting his relationship to Laura from drawing master and paid servant to provider and putative husband. The opening line of the novel declares that '[t]his is a story about what a woman's patience can endure and what a man's resolution can achieve' (1), and Collins uses stereotypes of different drawing practices to help pinpoint the contrast, juxtaposing the 'poor faint' lady sketcher with professional male draughtsman who is described working with 'steadfastness and facility' (389).

Drawing on wood was a physically different process to sketching on paper, employing different equipment. A 3H plus pencil or ink pen was used to firmly mark an end grain boxwood block. It was the ability to draw directly on the wood block, rather than submitting a sketch on paper to be transferred that distinguished the professional periodical illustrator from the occasional or amateur contributor. A particular approach to composition was also necessary since the final image would be printed in binary black and white lines, prohibiting tonal effects created by a pencil and, of course, excluding the use of colour. John Jackson set out the demands of this exposed technique in his treatise on wood engraving, stressing the discipline of clear accurate lines: if the draughtsman 'is incorrect and feeble in his drawing he will not be able to produce a really good design for the wood engraver … [h]e cannot resort, as in painting, to the trick of colour to conceal the defects of his outlines' (591). His reasoning reflects academic art tradition which prioritised line over colour, regarding line as rigorous, rational and masculine while colour was designated sensuous and feminine. Praise for Victorian draughtsmen frequently interprets the physical precision and firmness of line required by drawing on wood in terms of male decisiveness and vigour. Describing Charles Keene, George du Maurier writes that 'he had a physical gift of inestimable value for work such as ours – namely a splendid hand – a large, muscular, well shaped, and most workman like hand' that gave him an 'unerring precision of touch' (*Social* 82–3). Similarly, John Leech worked in the 'quickest, simplest, down-rightest pencil strokes' (du Maurier, *Social* 34). In an illustrated letter, du Maurier caricatured himself lifting weights, explaining his labour as an illustrator and the courage needed by an aspiring draughtsman as a triumph of healthy masculine energy (*Young* 40).

In 1882 comic writer Charles Ross satirised the young woman of the period who makes herself ridiculous by her attempt at virile execution in the implicitly unfeminine fields of history painting and drawing on wood. Painting classical figures, she 'seemed to throw their arms and legs at them, leaving it to chance where they stuck, so rapidly did she work'. Confronted with her first woodblock she 'straightaway dipped a pen in ink and dashed down a lopsided man toppling over into space'. Her illustration is, predictably, commercially useless: the editor describes it as a 'dead weight dangling in my coat-tail pocket' (109–10). In reality Charles Ross was known to employ a number of female illustrators in his capacity as editor of *Judy* (including Adelaide Claxton and his own wife, Marie Duval), but the masculine nature of drawing on wood was a strong enough trope to be invoked regardless, and the confident girl who mistakenly assumes she can draw on wood remained good for a laugh.

The 'redundant woman question' and the issue of female employment had become urgent topics of social debate after the 1851 census revealed a surplus of middle-class women who could not aspire to financial support through marriage. Commentators advocating an expanded field of women's work hailed the periodical press as an opening arena of opportunity for women as editors, writers, artists and engravers. An article on female labour in the *Liverpool Mercury* in 1863 pointed to an illustration in *London Society* drawn by Florence Claxton and engraved by Mary Ann Williams as 'a great step in the progress of woman's mission' ('Female Labour' 7). However, in most instances when the illustrated press is cited as an opportunity for women's work, noticeably more attention and enthusiasm is given to wood engraving than drawing on wood. The division of the two operations, when performed by separate individuals, matched the familiar premise that women were physically and mentally better suited to dextrous and repetitive crafts than expressive art. The same requirement for disciplined printable lines could be used to justify a large, muscular hand for the creative act of drawing the image, but 'the patient habits and delicate manipulations' ('Female Designers' 4) of female hands in following and cutting it. The facsimile function of engraving was the stage of production where female labour could most readily be imagined and Henry Cole promoted it as 'every way becoming to their sex and habits' (278). When the wives of draughtsmen Edward Burne-Jones and George du Maurier took up wood engraving as a hobby in the early 1860s, Ruskin wrote to Georgiana Jones with high praise, savouring the symbolic implications of the scenario:

> I am delighted to hear of the woodcutting. It will not I believe interfere with any motherly care or duty, and is far more useful and noble work than any other of which feminine fingers are capable without too much disturbance of feminine thought and nature. I can't imagine anything prettier or more wifely than cutting one's husband's drawings on the woodblock: there is just the proper quality of echo in it and you may

put the spirit and affection and fidelity into it which no other person could. (quoted in Flanders 83–4)

The vision of a wife sympathetically and faithfully cutting her husband's drawings on wood enshrined the idea of wood engraving as women's natural function within the processes of illustration. As a model, the artistic collaboration of husband and wife guaranteed what Ruskin would have regarded as the proper hierarchy of draughtsman and engraver, seeming to clarify (and de-industrialise) a relationship that was difficult in practice: draughtsmen were often frustrated that their authorship of the image was compromised by the interpretation of the engraver who translated their lines from one medium into another and usually added a second signature to the block.

The association of women with the amateur rather than the professional, the artisan rather than the artist, resisted the idea of women drawing on wood. It is when illustration is measured against painting that the most positive construction of the professional draughtswoman emerges. George du Maurier had trained as a painter and saw illustration as a compromise of his ambition, describing his profession as 'not the highest unfortunately, but a paying one I suppose' (*Young* 264). However his letters of the early 1860s show that he also regarded his work as a wholesome discipline and derived satisfaction from being able to support himself, marry and establish a domestic life through the regular exercise of his pencil. In this light he compared himself favourably with the more self-indulgent painting of his friend Tom Armstrong, who, he complains, 'seems to lack some kind of practical energy; what I am learning and find it so hard to learn. What a lesson it is to have to depend upon yourself!' (*Young* 149).

In *Daniel Deronda* (1876), George Eliot transposes the same merits of professional illustration onto the character Kate Meyrick, who helps support her widowed mother and siblings by drawing for a publisher. It is an affirmative depiction of female labour that works in counterpoint to the vocation-less and financially cornered heroine Gwendolen Harleth. The description of Kate working at her drawing by candle-light, surrounded by her family 'united by a triple bond – family love; admiration for the finest work, the best action; and habitual industry' (163) is an image of domesticity that absorbs Kate's professionalism. Far from contaminating the haven of home, Kate's work secures it. The passage echoes an article on artistic work for women in *Once A Week* which imagined a family of daughters all pursuing different artistic professions within the home, arguing that such a family circle, underwritten by the earning potential of its members will not be broken up if disaster strikes the head of the household ('Women's' 372–4). It is an argument that stretches the conventional rationale that women's pursuit of amateur artistic accomplishments 'tends to keep a household together' because they are practiced at home (*Elegant* iv).

Kate compares favourably with her brother Hans who irresponsibly, yet romantically, yields to 'his yearning for art over the attractions of secured income' (Eliot 163) and pursues studies in fine art. In terms of duty, Kate is morally the worthier sibling but is valued less as an artist: when their mother consults Hans's artistic opinion, Kate reminds her that she too is an artist, observing, '[Y]ou don't consult me … I notice mothers are like the people I deal with – the girls' doings are always priced low' (405). In comparison to painting, Kate's illustration work signifies the conventional feminine role – sacrificing herself to the needs of the family and demonstrating an abnegation of ambition that society approved in a woman. Eliot does not obscure the problematic nature of the compromise but, at the same time, she suggests that society could most positively embrace the female illustrator as a modest and limited figure, rising stoically to the unavoidable necessity of female labour.

Not unlike the fictional character of Kate Meyrick, the careers of Florence and Adelaide Claxton seem to suggest a guiding principle of economic realism. They were the daughters of the painter Marshall Claxton,[1] and their approach to the art world may have been coloured by the disappointments of their father's career which had not fulfilled its early promise in terms of recognition and remuneration. In 1850 Marshall Claxton took his family to Sydney in search of new outlets for his work, but, failing in this enterprise, he moved the family on to Calcutta before returning to Britain via Sri Lanka and Egypt around 1857. At this point Clayton tells us that it was 'a matter of necessity' for Florence and Adelaide Claxton to work for an income (II.44). Florence Claxton's first gallery exhibit was a series of sketches that humorously catalogued the trials of a female artist, demonstrating her keen awareness of the additional obstacles that faced a woman aspiring to success as a painter.[2] By 1858 Florence Claxton was also contributing sketches to the illustrated press,[3] and it is very possible that her exhibited work was intended to generate interest in her potential as a humorous illustrator rather than launch a career as a painter. From what we know of her early exhibition pieces, their style and subject matter had a greater affinity with graphic satire than academic art, a fact noted by contemporaries: an exhibition review in the *Athenaeum* suggested that 'Miss Claxton would be an auxiliary to any book illustrating firm. She sketches with grace, humour and originality' ('Society' 258). The strategy seems to have paid off as it was apparently Florence Claxton's satire on the Pre-Raphaelites, *The Choice of Paris: An Idyll*, exhibited at the Portland Gallery in 1860 and reproduced in the *Illustrated London News*, that made her name famous ('Female Labour' 7).

The sisters may have gained a vital introduction to editors such as Henry Vizetelly through their father, who occasionally provided illustrations for the *Illustrated Times*, while their visual knowledge of social life abroad gave them an additional lever in the market: they interested Vizetelly as '[t]wo very smart young ladies … who had been around the world in their teens' and 'cleverly satirised the social follies of both hemispheres' (389). Collaborating closely with each other, Florence and Adelaide Claxton established a niche for humorous social subjects working principally in the early 1860s for the *Illustrated London News, Illustrated Times, London Society, Churchman's Family Magazine* and the women's magazines the *Queen* and the *English Woman's Domestic Magazine*. Their style of drawing was pitched for this smart social end of the periodical market and differed from the more self-consciously artistic 'sixties school' approach to illustration based on Ruskinian principles of careful drawing from nature. Their work had its roots in the older humorous tradition of Richard Doyle, 'Phiz' and John Leech, animated by caricature, pronounced gestures and imaginative drawing.

The tendency for art historians to concentrate on 'sixties school' illustration has eclipsed the contemporary popularity and currency of Florence and Adelaide Claxton's work. During the 1860s their illustrations appeared prolifically in print; reviews of the illustrated press noticed their work enthusiastically, and their names were quoted in press advertisements and even on bill posters to help sell the publications they drew for. George du Maurier admitted that while the illustrator of the 1860s was increasingly subject to the scrutiny of the art critic, '[F]irst there is the wide public for whom we work and by whom we are paid', and the public, he claimed, were more alive to the social detail of an illustration than the manner of its drawing (*Social* 10–12). It was on exactly these grounds that the Claxtons delighted the periodical buying public. The illustration 'The Constitutional' by Adelaide Claxton appeared in *London Society* in 1863 (432); it was praised in the *Belfast News-Letter* because 'it photographs to the life a London fashionable boarding school en promenade. The faces of the young ladies are such as we have all recognised in our park walks' ('Literary' 4). In this illustration, there is in fact little attempt at formal realism; its 'photographic' quality refers to a mine of visual information about the characters delivered through physiological and satirical types, specific fashion references and gestures quoted from figures in fashion plates to suggest the girls' affectations of style.

Popular as it was, the Claxtons' mode of illustration contradicted expectations of female art. While Mary Ellen Edwards drew and painted in a style of refined naturalism and was understood as producing femininity through figures that 'set a high standard of winsome, dainty girlhood' ('Art' 98), the Claxtons often found their effect in the unbeautiful. 'Clever' and 'inventive' were the adjectives most often applied to their work, which appealed to the intellect (however playfully) rather than the eye and was undeniably vocal: In 'The Third Annual Exhibition of the Society of Female Artists' (1859) the *English Woman's Journal* singled Florence Claxton out as '[t]he one female exhibitor who means something, and says what she means … whose every stroke is instinct with thought' (54). In particular their 'satirical view of life' was surprising and considered 'contrary to the habits of their sex'

('Standard' 188). This view is substantiated by an article in the conservative *Saturday Review* on 'Feminine Humour' (1871) which opens with the flat prescription that '[t]he humour of women it is said resembles the snakes in Iceland. In other words it does not exist', and bases its argument on humour's apparently unavoidable tendencies to vulgarity and cynicism – qualities that the author will not countenance in women of the middle classes (759).

Since the 1840s, however, *Punch* had been practising a model of domesticated humorous journalism that eschewed vulgarity and took pride in its suitability for the drawing room and the boudoir. *Punch*'s approach was predicated on the Enlightenment theory of amiable humour as a desirable human quality founded on social sympathies and separate from forms of antagonistic comedy motivated by passion and aggression (such as satire and irony). This division was crucial in sanctioning both women's consumption and production of humour and is evoked in Ellen Clayton's short section on 'Humorous Designers' in *English Female Artists* (in which she included herself, Georgina Bowers, Adelaide Claxton and Marie Duval). Taking 'wit' as her term for an amiable 'genteel' humour, Clayton contends that:

> [W]oman may be allowed to possess Wit, but … she is denied any perception of Humour … a quality scarcely coveted by Ladies … Wit is fine and elegant, wit shines and scintillates in drawing rooms and boudoirs, but Humour may run the risk of stepping over the boundaries of vulgarity. (319)

She goes to lengths to present Georgina Bowers and Adelaide Claxton on the right side of the divide, downplaying the direct humour in their work and stressing ordinary un-bohemian private lives. She is less defensive over Marie Duval who she admits as one of the few living comic artists 'who can be called really a humorous designer' (332–3). As a foreigner, former actress and illustrator of the low-class, grotesquely-drawn cartoon character Ally Sloper,[4] both Duval's own persona and her work seem to have been more loosely moored to the middle-class ideal, and her difference suggests something of what determined vulgarity in the female illustrator. There is a sense in which formal coarseness of drawing was a type of vulgarity in itself, and distorting or caricaturing a figure an act of cruelty. Clayton insists that Adelaide Claxton's 'figures are always more or less graceful and elegant' (330), but this is partly obfuscation, for while Florence and Adelaide Claxton's style was never iconoclastic to the extent of Duval's, they mixed straight drawing with varying measures of exaggeration and caricature. Perhaps more important was the female illustrator's social relationship to her subject matter.

The Claxtons principally drew social scenes of contemporary life where their own physical presence as middle-class women could be respectably imagined, alongside that of the journal's target demographic. This helped maintain the crucial principle of shared social sympathy and positioned humorous illustration as an extension of the artist's supposed participation in polite society. Ellen Clayton could therefore claim that Adelaide Claxton 'seeks her groups in the salon and boudoir' (330), or that Georgina Bowers lingers 'in the salon, the boudoir, the garden and the hunting field … always in the best of good company' (320). Polite humour was conceptualised as a social exchange and therefore the responsibility for generating it lay partly with the recipient. *The Gentleman and Lady's Book of Politeness* advised that 'mild, kind, harmless pleasantry should be taken in good part, even by those who are the subjects of it; it is a friendly and sportive contest' (Celnart 380). In several instances, critics used their own response to the Claxtons' work to collude in heightening the flavour of genteel humour. A reviewer of Florence Claxton's 'Scenes from the Life of an Old Maid' and 'Scenes from the Life of an Old Bachelor' wrote that '[t]hese sketches evince so much raciness and good humour that some young gentlemen of our acquaintance would willingly compete to be laughed out of countenance by her' ('The Society' 380). Another reviewer in the *Sporting Times* praising Adelaide Claxton declared that:

> If I intended starting a 'comic journal' I should make a point of securing her services; that is, if she would let me, for, after all, women are perverse creatures, and have to be delicately managed. They may treat us to vinegar, but we must always repay them with honey; the cruel exacting dears!' ('About Town' 100).

He imagines dealing with Adelaide Claxton, not as a business transaction, but as a form of 'friendly sportive contest' between the sexes during which he will indulgently counteract her with the 'honey' of his own good humour. Both examples speculate a social encounter with the artist and project the milieu of drawing-room politeness onto her work. The link between illustration and the social manners of the artist meant that male humorists such as Charles Keene could feel restrained by chivalry in depicting and caricaturing women (Spielmann 141), and, on this count, Florence and Adelaide Claxton perhaps had the greater license as female illustrators. While in some eyes the Claxtons' humour was 'contrary to the habits of their sex', there was equally a mode of discourse that assimilated their professional humour with women's sociable duties in entering into company and maintaining 'that ritual exchange of courtesies' that defined middle class social life (Beetham 98).

Within the body of the Claxtons' illustration work, the problem of the 'redundant woman' is a signature theme and one they approached from many humorous angles – including a projection of the year 1960 when men are exhibited in the British Museum as an extinct species. It was a live topic of social debate for the periodical reading public, and an issue close to the Claxton's own experience as professional women. In 1861 Florence Claxton exhibited a satirical oil painting that constituted a biting attack on the lack of professional opportunity for women. *Women's Work, A Medley*, exhibited at the Portland Gallery in 1861, was, in the words of one contemporary summary, designed to 'symbolise in one group the tyrannical repression by which Man keeps back the energies of Woman' ('Fine' 187), and it troubled audiences on a number of levels (Cherry 33–47). With this painting Florence Claxton had transgressed the boundaries of amiable, genteel humour and was attacked by one contemporary reviewer for her 'superabundant flow of misanthropy' ('Institution' 332). At least part of the problem was her use of the serious medium of oil paint and the forceful and prescriptive nature of the imagery (backed by a lengthy explanation in the catalogue) which a reviewer in the *Spectator* compared to the vulgarity of advertising, declaring in disgust that the painting bore 'little more affinity to true art than the collection of sign boards at the corner of New Oxford Street' (332). Next to the campaigning mood of *Women's Work, A Medley*, Florence Claxton's light-hearted periodical work on the redundant woman has disappointed modern commentators who have interpreted her illustrations as conservative, quick to reproduce popular stereotypes of women, and compromised by the demands of the market (Cherry 48; Gaze I.405). An analysis of one of Florence Claxton's stand-alone illustrations in the *Queen*, published a few months after the exhibition of *Women's Work, A Medley*, suggests that this view of her graphic work may be reductive and underestimate the multivalent potential of amiable humour.

*Study, South Kensington*[5] (Figure 5.1) depicts a mix of male and female art students copying in the recently extended modern paintings galleries at the South Kensington Museum. The humorous inversion is that most of the students are flirting, studying each other rather than the paintings, and the issues framed by the illustration are the proper use of the space and women's claim to be or become artists (given that copying in public galleries was one of the few training opportunities that women had at this date). Claxton shows the women's presence to be disruptive, possibly even sexually disruptive; they turn a space set up for the study of art into a social scene and the illustration can be read as an ironic negation of the female artist in which the viewer is invited to identify with the annoyance of the man in the foreground. A quota of dismissive female stereotypes supports this reading: the mannish strong-minded woman, the feeble painter who needs male assistance and the fashionable dilettantes. However the woman sitting at the centre of the image potentially redirects the humour; she is focussed on her painting, unassumingly dressed, neither fashionable nor unfeminine, and quietly set apart from the crush of other characters. If this unobjectionable figure is understood as a form of reality check, then the stereotypes become not so much embodiments of truth about the female artist as parodies of the ideological nonsense surrounding her. *Queen* readers may well have identified with the fashionable pair in the foreground, suggesting an additional, possibly empowering, context for the scene.

5.1 Florence Claxton, *Study, South Kensington* (1861), original design in pen and watercolour for a wood-engraved illustration. Courtesy of the Victoria and Albert Museum.

New cultural venues such as the galleries at South Kensington represented an expansion of the urban locations that *Queen* readers could legitimately enjoy, and the women in this illustration have taken possession; their body language expresses perfect ease in the space while the male painter looks hunched and embattled. It is also possible that the women have discovered him misusing the gallery and not the other way around. The previous year there had been a scandal over students copying modern paintings at South Kensington and selling them as originals. The *Athenaeum's* exposé on the affair had begun with a description of students flirting in the gallery ('Copying' 756). One further version of the female artist is implied in the scene – the illustrator, Florence Claxton herself. The tension in the image between the artistic and the social captures something of her own status: as a humorous illustrator she is present in the space as a practicing artist, but, like the subjects of her illustration, her interest is in the people not the paintings. *Study, South Kensington* does not simply re-inscribe or subvert a dominant cultural position. It addresses divided sympathies and offers multiple points of identification, demonstrating what Gregg Camfield describes as humour's 'potential to address and manage ambiguity, to step outside binary opposition' (6). Where *Women's Work, A Medley* had alienated its audience, a tone of amiable humour and the ephemeral pages of the periodical press gave Florence Claxton a mode of engaging the public in contentious subject matter.

Both sisters' artistic practice evolved in the decades following the 1860s. Adelaide Claxton continued to draw for the illustrated press during the 1870s and 1880s, particularly in association with the comic paper *Judy*, which aimed at an expanding lower-middle-class readership. She continued to exhibit paintings and specialised in watercolour ghost scenes which she would repeat several times to satisfy demand, approaching painting like a form of mechanical reproduction. Fragments of evidence suggest she was also involved in a wide range of design activities including wallpaper, theatre programme covers, fashion illustration and advertisements, so that her drawing permeated throughout the pages of the periodicals into the advertising sections.[6] In the 1890s she patented several devices for correcting different body parts, and at least one, the 'Claxton Ear-cap', was manufactured and sold.[7] Adelaide Claxton used the recognition her name had as an artist to promote her inventions and drew the advertisements for them herself. In 1874 she married the younger son of a clergyman who describes himself on one census return as managing his wife's business, and Adelaide's artistic production seems to have supported her husband and child. By 1923 she was a resident at 'The Artists' General Benevolent Fund' home where she was photographed at her easel for an article of February 7, 1923 in the *Daily Graphic* 'aged 81, still painting' ('Home' 16).

By contrast Ellen Clayton records that Florence Claxton withdrew from professional art on her marriage in 1868 'though occasionally exhibiting' (II.45). Her last traceable published work is a satirical picture book *The Adventures of a Woman in Search Her Rights* drawn for the Graphotype Company in 1871. She married in Paris, and her married life was probably based abroad. She re-emerges around 1880 as a painter on china at the height of the craze for china painting, entering the Howell & James competitions in the amateur category, although the categories had little bearing on whether entrants earned money from their practice, and Florence Claxton stated 'artist china painter' as her occupation in the 1881 census. China painting at this date could be as lucrative as painting on canvas, but there was a degree of subterfuge surrounding commercial transactions, which were conducted under the atmosphere of a social bazaar through competitions or philanthropic exhibitions. According to Anne Anderson's chapter in this volume, the hazy line between amateurism and professionalism and china painting's association with beautifying the home gave the genre a very feminine profile. Florence Claxton's china painting may simultaneously represent the economic exploitation of the latest popular art trend and the repositioning of her career after marriage in a more acceptably feminine and 'amateur' genre. It is not certain whether Florence Claxton needed remunerative work during her marriage, but financial necessity continued to be a theme in her later life. In a final act of unorthodoxy she committed suicide in 1920 aged 82; according to a local newspaper report, she was not willing to compromise her strong sense of independence in the face of a dwindling income and poor health ('Aged' 5).

Illustration could mean both opportunity and limitation for the female artist. For Helen Allingham, who began working a decade after the Claxtons, it held out an alternative to her future of teaching, while Georgina Bowers found 'herself a sketcher when she desired earnestly to take rank in a far higher line of art' (Clayton II.323). Florence and Adelaide Claxton's profiles as popular illustrators of social subjects in the 1860s positioned them on the ephemeral margins of the fine art establishment. While the 1860s witnessed a new artistic impulse in wood engraved illustration and the young men of the 'sixties school' used illustration as a rung on the ladder to academic success, the Claxtons' paintings were usually 'out of the common beat' (Atkinson 370) and suggest their approach to the image market as a whole was little concerned with high art. Seen within the overall shape of their careers, wood-engraved illustration is one instance of the Claxtons' engagement with the popular medium of the moment. This pragmatism did not, however, preclude an impulse for social comment on the themes that touched their lives and those of their, often female, audience.

Like the character of Kate Meyrick within *Daniel Deronda*, the Claxtons' significance for their contemporaries was not their cultural status as artists, but the example they pioneered of female professionalism. Their names crop up regularly within the discourse on women's work, and often it is their industry rather than their artistry that is noted. Frances Hays in *Women of the Day* (1885) summarised Adelaide Claxton in the following terms: '[S]he worked in watercolour and designed on wood as a means of support, and is one of the most hard-working of lady artists' (199). Commentators found ways to rationalise the Claxtons' identity as middle-class female illustrators, but drawing on wood and drawing humour were essentially classed as masculine practices. The ambivalence of their position and the conflict of economic opportunities and social pressures they negotiated may be reflected in the divergence of the sisters' profiles once they married. Florence Claxton's apparent reinvention of herself in the feminine field of china painting suggests, perhaps, how far working in graphic satire had carried her from the ideal of middle-class womanhood. Adelaide Claxton on the other hand capitalised on her experience as an illustrator to build a portfolio as a commercial artist and woman of business.

## Works Cited


'About Town'. *Sporting Times,* 29 March 1873: 100–101.

'Aged Widow's Suicide'. *Isle of Wight Chronicle,* 6 May 1920: 5.

'The Art Life of M. Ellen Edwards'. *Girl's Own Paper,* 16 November 1907: 98.

Atkinson, J. Beavington. 'Exhibitions of the Year'. *Fine Arts Quarterly Review* 1 (1866): 343–74.

Beetham, Margaret. *A Magazine of Her Own. Domesticity and Desire in the Woman's Magazine, 1800–1914.* London: Routledge, 1996.

Camfield, Gregg. *Necessary Madness. The Humour of Domesticity in Nineteenth-Century American Literature.* Oxford: Oxford University Press, 1997.

Celnart, Mme. *The Gentleman and Lady's Book of Politeness.* Boston, MA: Allen and Ticknor, 1833.

Cherry, Deborah. *Beyond the Frame: Feminism and Visual Culture, Britain 1850–1900.* London: Routledge, 2000.

Clayton, Ellen. *English Female Artists.* 2 vols. London: Tinsley Brothers, 1876.

Claxton, Adelaide. *Brainy Odds and Ends.* London: A. Claxton, 1899.

Cole, Henry. 'Modern Wood Engraving'. *The London and Westminster Review* 31 (1839): 265–80.

Collins, Wilkie. *The Woman in White.* London: Penguin Popular Classics, 1994.

'Copying Modern Pictures'. *Athenaeum,* 1 December 1860: 756.

du Maurier, George. *Social Pictorial Satire.* London: Harper and Brothers, 1898.

——. *The Young George du Maurier: A Selection of his Letters, 1860–67.* Ed. Daphne du Maurier. London: Peter Davies, 1951.

*Elegant Arts for Ladies.* London: Ward and Lock, 1856.

Eliot, George. *Daniel Deronda.* Chatham, Kent: Wordsworth Editions, 2003.

'Female Designers'. *New York Times,* 26 December 1855: 4.

'Female Labour'. *Liverpool Mercury,* 21 October 1863: 7.

'Feminine Humour'. *Saturday Review,* 14 July 1871: 75–6.

'Fine Arts'. *John Bull,* 23 March 1861: 187.

Flanders, Judith. *A Circle of Sisters: Alice Kipling, Georgiana Burne-Jones, Agnes Poynter and Louisa Baldwin.* London: Viking, 2001.

Gaze, Delia, ed. *Dictionary of Women Artists.* 2 vols. London and Chicago: Fitzroy Dearborn, 1997.

Hays, Frances. *Women of the Day, a Biographical Dictionary of Notable Contemporaries.* London: Chatto & Windus, 1885.

'The Home of Art and Age'. *Daily Graphic,* 7 February 1923: 16.

'Institution of Fine Arts'. *Spectator,* 30 March 1861: 332.

Jackson, John. *A Treatise on Wood Engraving.* London: H.G. Bohn, 1861.

Kunzle, David. 'Marie Duval: A Caricaturist Rediscovered'. *Woman's Art Journal* 7 (Spring, Summer 1986): 26–31.

'Literary Notices'. *Belfast News-Letter,* 5 November 1863: 4.

Ross, Charles, and Dawer Wilson. *Flirting Made Easy.* London: Judy Office, 1882.

'Society of Female Artists'. *Athenaeum,* 19 February 1859: 257–8.

'The Society of Female Artists'. *Spectator,* 3 April 1858: 379–80.

Spielmann, M.H. *The History of Punch.* London: Cassell, 1895.

'The Standard Bearer'. *Illustrated Times,* 19 March 1859: 188.

'The Third Annual Exhibition of the Society of Female Artists'. *English Woman's Journal* 3 (1859): 53–5.

Vizetelly, Henry. *Glances Back Through Seventy Years. Autobiographical and Other Reminiscences.* London: Kegan Paul & Co., 1893.
'Women's Work'. *Once a Week* 2 (1860): 372–4.

## Notes

1 Florence Anne Claxton (1838–1920) and Adelaide Sophia Claxton (1841–1927) were the daughters of Marshall Claxton and his wife Sophia Hargrave.

2 *Scenes from the Life of a Female Artist* was exhibited at the Society of Female Artists second annual exhibition. Florence and Adelaide Claxton also put their names to the 1859 letter petitioning for the Royal Academy schools to admit women as students.

3 Clayton states that Florence Claxton's first illustration 'Miserable Sinners' was published in the *Illustrated Times* in 1859. It actually appeared in the *Illustrated Times*, 18 December 1858: 408.

4 On Marie Duval's authorship of Ally Sloper, see Kunzle.

5 The illustration 'Study, South Kensington' was published in the *Queen*, 26 October 1861. The Victoria and Albert Museum has an original sketch for this illustration [E.3613–2004].

6 Her advertisements can be found on the back page of the *Queen* from 1879 onwards.

7 There is an example of the Claxton Ear-cap in the Science Museum. An advertisement of the back cover of Adelaide Claxton's *Brainy Odds and Ends* (1899) reads 'Claxton Patents, Ear-caps for outstanding ears, Stooping Braces for round shoulders. Classical corset for comfort and looks. Mask veil for cycling, motoring and driving'.

6

# The China Painter: Amateur Celebrities and Professional Stars at Howell and James's 'Royal Academy of China Painting'

*Anne Anderson*

A Sewell and Cross young man
A Howell and James young man,
A pushing young particle – what's the next article –
Waterloo house young man! (Gilbert and Sullivan 45)

James McNeill Whistler's *Purple and Rose: The Lange Leizen of the Six Marks* (1864) ostensibly shows a lady china painter 'brush in hand'; but this is a ruse, simply a pose, as the pot she is holding is clearly finished and fired. This kimono-clad painter may be drawing inspiration from a Chinese Kang Hsi (1662–1722) porcelain vase, but she cannot be painting it. Yet this female figure has consistently been read as a 'china painter': 'to place *The Lange Lijzen* [sic] in the tradition of paintings of artist's studios is to take this china painter in fancy dress seriously as an artist and to grant porcelain, one of the decorative arts, a status reserved in the West for easel paintings' (Merrill 54–5).[1] *The Lange Leizen* draws our attention both to the high esteem in which Whistler held his Old Blue and the emerging role of women as china painters.[2]

This chapter considers the repositioning of china painting as a suitable occupation for both amateur and professional women; it could be a productive hobby, contributing to the ornamentation of the House Beautiful,[3] or offered a means of income if faced with the prospect of finding a 'lady-like' profession. The raised status of china painting led to its commodification, with retailers Howell and James of Regent Street offering annual exhibitions and prizes. At the 'Royal Academy of China Painting' female amateurs and professionals competed alongside each other; they even rose to the challenge of competing with their male rivals. This in turn stimulated the demand, as women were provided with a vehicle that allowed them to express their artistic potential as well as offering remunerative rewards.

The 'mania' for china painting also highlights the enhanced status of the decorative arts within the context of the Aesthetic Movement or Cult of Beauty (c.1860–90). Repositioned within the artistic canon and linked to the demand for *objet d'art* in décor, artists were encouraged to forsake canvas and paper for ceramic surfaces. Women participated as both producers and consumers, as china painting provided both domestic entertainment and encouraged new forms of consumption; women even entered the fray as interior decorators.

## Painting on China

Howell and James's 'Royal Academy of China Painting' may have elevated the status of china painting, but it still held a lowly position in the hierarchy of the fine and decorative arts. Deemed decorative or ornamental, it was positioned as 'feminine'. 'The Career Path of the Artistic Girl' (Figure 6.1) tracks an evolution from painting the drawing room door panels through pots, furniture and menu cards before ascending to the easel, on which the lady artist will 'libel' her friends in rendering their portraits.[4] If the Artistic Girl is a 'pretty little duffer', this progression may be halted by wedded bliss; the talented or serious practitioner will not arouse enthusiasm in the breast of the male student.

'The Career Path', while humorous, still holds women's art in contempt as amateur and frivolous; she is 'great on decoration' but here 'most families draw the line'. But under the auspices of the Aesthetic Movement, which pursued Beauty in art and design, the status of the decorative arts was raised. *The Lange Leizen* suggests that the House Beautiful can be achieved through judicious consumerism, notably collecting *objet d'art*; the objects depicted functioned both as 'properties' in Whistler's studio and as decorative elements in 'our withdrawing room' (Anna Whistler, quoted in Spencer 72). The House Beautiful demanded artistic commodities, furniture, textiles, ceramics and glass, which prompted a burgeoning of art industries: 'the direction which it [painting on china] has taken in England amongst amateurs has been decorative in the sense of providing effective bits of decoration for a room' (Monkhouse, '"Royal"' 247). New roles emerged for women as amateur and professional decorators, their mission to beautify the home for the benefit of their husbands and children; art was now lauded as a refining influence. Positioned as art, china painting was deemed a proper activity for the Lady of the House or Lady Artist; such work did not erode her feminine status even when a pastime was transformed into remunerative employment, as seen in William Powell Frith's *The Road to Ruin: Struggles* (1877–78, Museum of London).

6.1 'The Career Path of the Artistic Girl' from *Hearth and Home* (1895): 631 [N.2288 b.22]. Courtesy of the Bodleian Library, University of Oxford.

Contemporary accounts stress the importance of china painting as a suitable occupation for young ladies who found themselves in 'distress', affording 'a profitable resource for those whose circumstances necessitate their making some contribution to the household expenses' (Hancock 6). China painting, which had hitherto been confined to commercial factories and seen as the 'employment of men', the subject of 'selfish and cruel trade laws' which denied women access to all but the 'commonest' pieces, was repositioned as 'more especially suited to women' (Hancock frontispiece; Callen 52). At a time when the employment of gentlewomen was a serious social problem, china painting offered an ideal solution. Appropriate occupations had to be identified that would not erode their class status or impair their chances of marriage. China painting was not physically demanding and it could be conducted within the privacy of the home. 'Colourman' and art supplier Campbell Hancock, who had a vested interest in promoting the art, opined 'works above mediocrity will attract and charm, and employment be assured of a large or lesser recompense; while as employment merely it is pleasant as well as profitable'

(Hancock frontispiece). Art critic Cosmo Monkhouse considered the new art 'harmless and charming' and being 'pleasant and profitable' it 'opened out a congenial career to hundreds of women' ('"Royal"' 246). As Monkhouse pointed out on June 22, 1878:

> It is a benefit to the whole sex by revealing its capacity to produce original and beautiful work of a class which was formerly thought to be outside, not only their province, but their power. It is also of much benefit to the cause of art itself in encouraging original design and in extending the sphere of ornamental painting in a new direction with unexpected and delightful results. ('Paintings' 565)

For many women china painting was simply a welcome distraction, combating ennui: '[Women] sit idle at home, envying the activity which is denied to them' ('Art-Work' 66).

Paintings on china were essentially for display, often taking the form of plaques or plates to be hung on the wall: 'The flowers of art, intended to brighten the atmosphere of ordinary life with the perpetual presence of grace and colour' (Monkhouse, '"Royal"' 247), although ladies were also encouraged to apply their energies to useful articles. However, for some the results were too 'young-ladyish' and 'prettiness' was too prevalent ('The Exhibition' 177). Many examples were nothing less than pictures on plates, whose subjects and treatment would have been just as suitable for water-colours or even paintings in oil: 'Some may be inclined to quarrel with this movement as the invasion of one branch of art into the provinces of others', but Monkhouse concluded that 'the experiments are justified by their success' ('Paintings' 1878: 565). Indeed the special character of the ceramic medium offered artists' great potential: 'Lucidity of ground and limpidity of glaze may enable artists to realise certain qualities of light and air to which the opacity of paper or the best-grounded canvas and the inferior transparency of varnish oppose obstacles' ('Paintings' 1878: 565). But its defects were also obvious, namely extreme brilliancy, the difficulty of obtaining variety in colour and gradation of tint, and spurious finish. This was balanced by the permanence of the ceramic process and the comparatively modest outlay required to procure a fine example. Prices in 1878 averaged little more than two guineas, 'or about the amount we should have to pay for a good specimen of an old blue and white Oriental plate' ('The Exhibition' 176). However, professional artists could be highly rewarded, while china painting's raised status, and the promise of financial gains, inevitably enticed male artists into the fray.[5]

As well as being 'fit work for ladies', women's practice as china painters was also legitimised by the ideology of the House Beautiful, as promoted by Oscar Wilde: 'Nothing looks better on the walls than a well decorated plate or plaque' ('The Exhibition' 177). Paintings on china fuelled the craze for china collecting, dubbed *Chinamania* by the *Punch* cartoonist George du Maurier; sixteenth-century Italian Maiolica, which provided a model for china painting, was to become a millionaire's 'collectable', alongside Sevres, Chelsea, Meissen and all forms of old blue-and-white porcelain and pottery. Antique specimens were soon beyond the reach of the average collector, but substitutes were at hand; the burgeoning art pottery industry was led by large commercial concerns, namely Doulton and Minton, with William de Morgan and the Martin brothers catering for a more rarefied audience.[6] The '"mysteries" of the craft' ('Fifth' 392), revealed through numerous practical manuals,[7] enabled women to create (or purchase) unique, handcrafted ceramics as a means of enhancing their domestic interior. Hancock noted amateur china painters had the 'opportunity of decorating their houses in a manner which would be impossible had the works to be purchased'; rather than resembling 'specimen drawing-rooms' as 'set out in the upholsterers' windows', homes would now bear traces of the 'special tastes of its members':

> As we enter such a house, our eye catches a tasteful little design on the drawing-room door-plate, instead of a mere slab of white china with the conventional gilt wreath … A decorative cabinet, which the next-door neighbour would not venture to buy, because of the cost of its inlaid china tablets, has been readily procured here because the daughters of the house have painted the tablets themselves. On the shelf is a dainty time-piece, inlaid still with 'the girl's work' … pretty little indications of good taste. (Hancock 4)

Thus the visitor was met 'at every turn with the individualised and highly finished work, which … is the true sphere of the amateur, who should be as readily recognised by his painting as by his handwriting' (Hancock 5). Art in the Home enabled the demonstration of personal tastes, underpinning the cult of individuality, as promoted in contemporary manuals on home décor from Charles Locke Eastlake's *Hints on Household* Taste (1868) to Mrs H.R. Haweis's *The Art of Decoration* (1881).[8] But in addition to revealing one's personality, the domestic interior was also to offer solace, an oasis of calm in a hectic and competitive world:

> Cannot the daughters of England help their fathers in their too often exhausting labours by such means? And what payment so sweet as the quiet smile with which the over-wrought merchant or professional man greets his daughter as he returns from his day of worry, and finds her busy fingers have been thus ministering to his comfort! (Hancock 6)

Paintings on china were invested with a sentimental value, as mementoes and relics: 'Will not the memory of such a daughter be sweet to the father after she has left his roof – as he gazes fondly upon the results of her forethought and skill?' (Hancock 6). Paintings on china did not obey the economic premise of supply and demand but entered the world of the 'one-off', the unique and the rare; imbued with sentimental value, they operated as collectables and 'memorabilia'.

China painting's potential, as a decorative art product, a genteel hobby and a valuable asset to be sold for commercial and charitable purposes, was soon realised. Howell and James's annual china painting exhibition, dubbed 'The Royal Academy of China Painting', spurred a 'mania'; here art and society coalesced: '[The exhibition] has already become quite an institution, and all the world that pretends to be of the world – all at least of those who move with the stream of fashion – must sooner or later drift thither' ('Fifth' 392). Initiated in 1876 these annual exhibitions continued into the 1890s, when china painting was ousted by the more robust art forms associated with the Arts and Crafts Movement, namely metalworking and jewellery.

However, voices were raised against the Cult of Beauty and its consequences – the production of inferior work in the name of art. The craze for painting everything (Figure 6.2), a manifestation of the female passion for ornamentation, was according to Rosamund Marriott Watson, author of *The Art of the House* (1897), out of control:

> Once allow an unoccupied woman (and her name is legion) to suppose that she is imbued with artistic ideas, give her her head and some painting materials, and she will run amuck amid the simplest principles of taste, breathing destruction as she goes to all that crosses her path. It is but the first hand-painted article that costs, be it stool or cupboard or table; she will have tasted blood, as it were, and the craving grows with indulgence. From that moment whatever germ of an aesthetic conscience that may have lain dormant in her being is wiped out at once and forever. (Watson 151)

For such an innocent past-time Watson's language is highly charged. Women are running 'amuck', 'breathing destruction' and tasting 'blood'. An unstoppable vandal, devoid of aesthetic conscience, she paints everything in sight. Art was supposed to be morally improving but now the feminine desire for decoration was beyond control. Caught up in 'the rabble rout of all manner of ugly and foolish fads and fancies', women had become deranged monsters (152). Watson concludes, 'There's no help for it, unless perchance the hand-painting habit comes to be recognised at last as one of the dire diseases of the day, and a Home be instituted for the restraint and special treatment of its victims and the general good of the community at large' (152). As Schaffer observes, here the passion for ornamentation is condemned as 'one of the neurotic diseases of the century's end, fit to be catalogued with egomania and graphomania in Max Nordau's *Degeneration*' (90); Nordau, writing in the context of Art Nouveau, saw excessive ornamentation as reflecting a degenerate, effeminate state of mind. Female taste comes under scrutiny and, as in the eighteenth century (see Clunas; Kowaleski-Wallace), denounced as grotesque; domestic harmony was ruined by 'plaque disfigured walls' (Watson 150) and a surfeit of clutter loaded with sentimental values. Offering an antidote, Watson advised the 'pure' domestic lady to practise housewifery, by arranging flowers, selecting menu cards and purchasing antiques.

6.2 Walter Satterlee, 'The Craze for Painting Everything' from Josephine Pollard, *The Decorative Sisters, a Modern Ballad* (1881). Courtesy of Anne Anderson.

Yet the *Spectator* hoped that pottery painting would instill some knowledge of the first principles of design. It was easy to laugh at an amateur's first blundering attempts at high art, but any attempt was commendable:

> [M]any a one who paints execrably badly upon china and pottery, to her own despair and her friend's annoyance, may be gaining unsuspected and unsought power of appreciation of good pictures or good designs. It is, we think, a great thing that an exhibition like this at Messers Howell and James can be held at all – a very great thing that it can be supported by so numerous a body of contributors. ('Amateur Pottery' 912)

Amusingly, the *Spectator* likened the fad for china painting with the popularity of Lawn Tennis:

> Two occupations which have become fashionable for young ladies deserve to be set a little above the usual level of elegant trifling, which is usually attained by fashionable pursuits. These – 'Lawn Tennis' and 'Pottery Painting' – seem to be each, in its own way, as if some real good might be got out of them. ('Amateur Pottery' 912)

Both helped to overcome ennui and foster a healthy body and mind.

## The Royal Academy of China Painting

Liberty of Regent Street is undoubtedly the best-known retailer associated with supplying the products necessary for cultivating 'life-style' Aestheticism. The House Beautiful required large quantities of peacock feathers, sunflowers and lilies, as well as sage green hangings and blue and white china. However, Liberty was not the only concern to offer the 'populuxe' commodities that signalled the *haute-bourgeois* desire to be considered artistic. Responding to popular demand, Howell and James, a prestigious London retailer since 1819, also offered artistic products, especially ceramics.[9] Their purpose-built Art Pottery Galleries at 5–9 Regent Street were opened in 1876 to showcase the annual exhibition of *Painting on Pottery and Porcelain*, which became a social and artistic event that rivalled the Summer Show of the Royal Academy. Apparently the educated classes, their art instincts aroused, jumped at the idea of china painting

> when they discovered that these could find adequate expression in more tangible and concrete form than on paper and canvas, that prizes were offered to encourage their efforts, and a ready market for whatever they might do almost assured to them, the enthusiasm for ceramic Art, whether in modelling or painting, reached such a pitch that Messers. Howell and James had to build new galleries, and the works now on show equal in number those of the kindred arts exhibited at the Royal Academy. ('Painting on China by Lady' 164)

The *Magazine of Art* commented both on the success of the annual event and on the suitability of china painting for lady artists:

> The reason of the favour which has been accorded these gatherings is not far to seek; for, while an evident want has been supplied in the provision of a suitable gallery for the display of the china painter's art, a real benefit has been bestowed on numerous lady artists seeking a channel for remunerative and suitable occupation for their leisure. ('The Exhibition' 176)

The company claimed that the exhibition of 1878 contained upwards of 1,000 original works, mostly by ladies, and was frequented during its two-month duration by nearly 10,000 visitors. Queen Victoria's artistically inclined daughters, Princess Louise and Princess Alice, the Grand Duchess of Hesse, were amongst the throng ('Messers.' 178). Over 10 royal prizes would be bestowed, for both professional and amateur painting on china, transforming the exhibition into a prestigious annual event. Art critic Cosmo Monkhouse dubbed it the 'Royal Academy of China Painting' in 1884, as the annual exhibition had secured recognition through royal patronage and prizes awarded by respected academicians. Monkhouse's title was far from fanciful, as Howell and James had exerted a 'long and powerful influence in developing the art of painting on china, both by amateurs and professionals' (Monkhouse, '"Royal"' 246). In a review of the eighth exhibition, Mr Buxton Morrish, who initiated the Howell and James china painting exhibitions, was praised for his achievement:

> Through his exertions china painting has become in England a favourite artistic occupation as well as a remunerative industry for lady artists, amateur and professional. The studios the firm established and the facilities it afforded to ceramic artists to bring their work before the public, spread the taste for this fascinating pursuit all over the United Kingdom and similar undertakings abroad, especially in America and Germany, took their origin and strength from the parent institution in London.[10] ('Prize' 537)

Those with artistic pretentions gathered at Howell and James, which rivalled the Grosvenor Gallery (1877–90), founded by Sir Coutts Lindsay and his wife, Blanche, to showcase avant-garde contemporary art, as the place to be seen; as Whistler astutely observed 'Art is upon the Town' (Staley 59; see also Denney). At Howell and James the 'pushing' classes hoped to gain access to the private domains of the elite. This much resented socio-economic group was of course caricatured by *Punch*, shortly after its founding in 1841, in a monthly series called 'The Side Scenes of Society', which chronicled the social advances of an unattractively nouveau riche family, the Spangle Lacquers:

> You will always be certain to meet at the Lacquers' a great many persons with whom you are perfectly well acquainted by sight, but to whom you can assign no fixed position in society, having generally met them in places where distinction was

> acquired by paying for it. You will see them sailing up the avenues of a morning concert – they cross your pathway in going to their carriages from Howell and James's; they brush against you at the conclusion of the performances at the opera. ('Side' 59)

As a retailer of luxury goods, Howell and James assumed the same standing as Harrods of Knightsbridge,[11] coming to denote not only quality but also social pretensions. Its annual china-painting exhibition took the retailers into a new league. Lady amateurs showed their work alongside both male and female professionals, with some lady amateurs moving into the professional category of 'artist'. Royal and aristocratic amateurs were not motivated by economic concerns. Rather they wished to demonstrate their talent and ability, which, in some cases, vied with professional standards. For such women china painting remained a pleasurable hobby conducted in privacy, but the fruits of their labours could now be shown at a public venue. Hitherto craftswomen were isolated in the home and constrained, by the need to maintain propriety, from the spectacle of exhibiting. Showing at Howell and James offered entree to fashionable society as well as showcasing 'feminine' artistic skills; conversely patronising the Royal Academy of China Painting allowed a demonstration of superior taste, as well as providing a means of beautifying the home. Social cachet legitimised this spectacle, as practitioners moved in the upper echelons of society. Adverts and editorial comment on Howell and James's annual show constantly refer to the 'season', the period from April to July when fashionable society took up residence in London, stressing the social milieu being cultivated. At the same time, Howell and James were 'advancing the interest of needy women' with prizes 'awarded to lady amateurs, as well as to those who are "professionals"' ('Painting' 1876: 255); as Anthea Callen notes the quotation marks indicate awkwardness in referring to women as professionals (55):

> While varied in merit, there were many that indicated great ability, giving assurance of that which is so greatly needed – a remunerative market for the sale of ladies' work, and, moreover, a safe and dignified depot in which their productions may be placed to be seen and disposed of … This long established firm is doing much to advance the interest of Ceramic art. ('Painting' 1876: 255)

March 1878 saw a special display of Howell and James's exhibits for the Paris Exhibition. The collection comprised 114 specimens representing the work of 32 amateur and 36 professional artists, by far the greater part of them ladies. These were selected from approximately 300 works submitted and had been judged to be worthy of representing the art of china painting in England. In the amateur class Mrs A.H. Lee received the first prize, Mrs George Stapleton the second and Miss Budgett the third. In the professional class Mrs John Sparkes carried off the first prize with two figure subjects, *Cowslip Balls* and *Blackberrying* (Figure 6.3). The second went to Charlotte Spiers for a female head. Also commended were Mrs Mallam, Miss Ellen Welby and Miss Edith Cowper.

During their visit to the Paris Exhibition, the Prince and Princess of Wales purchased five paintings on pottery from the Howell and James display, two heads of *Isabel* and *Babille* by Mrs Mallam, the prize plaques of Mrs Sparkes and a specimen of Miss Welby's work. The company's achievement was duly acknowledged, with a prize medal awarded by the international jury, 'in recognition of their successful efforts in developing the Art of Ceramic Painting, and in originating a movement that has already done much to supply a greatly needed employment to cultivated women' (Advert np).[12]

## Amateur Celebrities and Professional Stars

Reviewing the third exhibition, the *Magazine of Art* stressed:

> China-painting has for far too long a time been neglected, and while to artists of every degree have been accorded numerous facilities for displaying their works to the public, painters on china have hitherto found really no opportunity of bringing their productions into notice. Now, however, all this is changed, for there is at present a great 'rage' for ceramic art; and Messers Howell and James can complain of no lack of 'Royal and distinguished patronage', while members of the Royal Academy come forward to act as judges. ('The Exhibition' 176)

Adjudicating was always of a high standard, all the judges being Academicians who had 'the confidence of the public' (Monkhouse, '"Royal"' 246). Initially this duty went to Edward Poynter, later President of the Royal Academy, and E.W. Cooke. Frederick Goodall succeeded Poynter, supported by Richard Norman Shaw and Stacy Marks. The event attracted a large number of entries, from which the judges selected those for exhibition: in 1876 547, in 1878 941, in 1879 more than 1,500, in 1880 1,641, in 1881 2,062 and in 1883 1,691 ('Fourth Annual Exhibition of Paintings on China by Lady' 504; 'Paintings' 1880: 409; Monkhouse, '"Royal"' 246). This decrease was due, according to Monkhouse, to the increased rigour of the judges as china painting was not only flourishing but also improving in standard, with the distinction between amateur and professional work diminishing: 'The judges since 1881 considerably raised their standard and the diplomas, which reached 243 in that year, sank to about 90 in 1882' (Monkhouse, '"Royal"' 246). The craze appears to have peaked by 1884, for in 1886 the number of exhibits had dropped to 949 and newspaper coverage had lessened considerably; repoussé metalwork in brass and copper, the latest artistic fad, challenged painting on china, or as the *Queen* mused, 'The weaker members of the craft seem to have taken to ornamenting drain pipes, milking stools, slop-pails, and other oddities, while ladies of culture and taste persevered in their long-continued and successful efforts of perpetuating the traditions of true ceramic art in England and abroad' ('Exhibition' 613).

6.3 Catherine Sparkes, 'Blackberrying' from *Magazine of Art* 1 (1878): 176. Courtesy of Anne Anderson.

Despite competition from new novelties, the annual exhibitions continued into the 1890s. As the fashion for china painting waned, Howell and James experimented with exhibitions of painting on tapestry and pastels.

The support of the Prince and Princess of Wales was granted in 1878, while full recognition was accorded the following year when the Queen asked for a selection of the best specimens to be submitted for her inspection. Many members of the Royal family both patronised the event and presented prizes: the Duke and Duchess of Edinburgh; the Duke and Duchess of Connaught; Victoria, Princess Royal and Crown Princess of Germany; Alice, Grand Duchess of Hesse-Darmstadt;[13] Helena, Princess Christian of Schleswig-Holstein;[14] Princess Louise, Marchioness of Lorne, and Prince Leopold. In 1877 the Crown Princess initiated a gold medal for the best work by a lady amateur, which remained the most coveted prize. To this she added a silver medal for professionals in 1879. Princess Alice instituted an amateur and a professional prize (silver enamelled badges), continued after her death by the Grand Duke of Hesse. In 1879 the Princess Alice prize was awarded to Miss Edith S. Hall, for her *Lilies* and *Daffodils* and *Rose Elves*, which displayed 'great decorative skill'; the silver badge designed and given by Princess Christian was awarded to Miss Ada Beard, an amateur, for her 'charming lily tiles' ('Paintings' 1879: 485). HRH Prince Leopold; the Grand Duchess of Mecklenburg Strelitz; Princess Mary Adelaide, Duchess of Teck, and the Countess of Flanders added their support in 1880 (see Figure 6.4). By 1885 there were no less than 12 royal patrons and 10 royal prizes in addition to those granted by notable society ladies. The Countess of Warwick prize for 1879 was awarded to Lady Rawlinson for a portrait of her husband, Sir Henry, while the Lady Olive Guinness Prize went to Miss Everett Green ('Paintings' 1879: 485).

Alongside royal and aristocratic prizes many more were given annually or occasionally by the proprietors of magazines, by the judges and the founders, Howell and James (see Figure 6.5). From its inception the exhibition was supported by the *Queen*, which gave a prize and always devoted several pages to illustrating the prize works. The *Magazine of Art* and Messers Hancock of Worcester, ceramic colourmen, also initiated prizes. There was even a Howell and James Studio Prize, won in 1881 by a Miss F.M. Minns (Monkhouse, 'Paintings' 401). Between 1880 and 1884 the average number of prizes exceeded 20, in addition to diplomas of merit in three classes.

6.4 Viscountess Hood, 'The Hon. Mabel Hood' from *Magazine of Art* 3 (1880): 395. Courtesy of Anne Anderson.

6.5 Charlotte H. Spiers, 'Poppies and Tiger Lilies' from *Magazine of Art* 3 (1880): 392. Courtesy of Anne Anderson.

Works were graded Very Highly Commended, Highly Commended and Commended.[15]

Amateurs rivalled the professionals, even though they were awarded prizes in different categories. A review of the 1876 exhibition noted that the two chief prizes, in both the professional and amateur classes, were awarded to women. The reviewer, however, was not impressed by the work of Miss Linnie Watt, who won the professional category, with a landscape with figures, as neither in style or design nor in execution did it match *The Arts, Poetry, Painting, Architecture, Sculpture and Music* of Mr Holiday ('Pleasant' 21). The ladies were now either enjoying positive discrimination or the idea that a professional female could outclass a highly trained male artist disturbed the status quo. Linnie Watt became one of the stars of the annual show, winning the Crown Princess's silver medal for professionals in 1879. Monkhouse likened Miss Watt's work to that of Helen Allingham, who made her name painting watercolours of Surrey cottages. Her 'dainty pictures of English country' (see Figure 6.6) were enlivened with 'not less charming or less English figures of girls and children'. Indeed Monkhouse considered that the work of Linnie Watt expressed the true spirit of painting on china:

6.6 Linne Watt, 'The Bird's Nest' from *Magazine of Art* 7 (1884): 249.
Courtesy of Anne Anderson.

> Taken altogether, the decorative pictures of Miss Linnie Watt are perhaps the most novel and satisfactory product of the taste for paintings on china in England. They are specially fitted for daily companionship, eloquent of grace and beauty when appealed to, and at other moments silently adding by their light and colour to the general cheerfulness of the room. ('"Royal"' 249).

Linnie Watt's English idylls consistently won approval; *Primrosing* and *The Little Fisherman* took the Princess Alice prize in 1880. Her subjects were fitted 'for daily companionship' and brought 'cheerfulness' to a room, while the more academic pieces which professional artists, such as Henry Holiday, perhaps felt duty bound to submit were not as 'homely'.

Linnie Watt's work was compared with that of Catherine Sparkes (see Figure 6.3), wife of the progressive head of the Lambeth School of Art and head of the National Art Training Schools at South Kensington from 1876. Monkhouse considered her 1878 submission *Do you like Butter?* to be the most 'forcible' in the exhibition but it arrived too late to be entered into the competition ('Paintings' 1878: 565). John Sparkes, described by Monkhouse as 'the man who has perhaps done more than any other artist or teacher in England to develop the art of painting on china' ('"Royal"' 247), was committed to the development of art pottery and persuaded Henry Doulton to open workshops for the production of stoneware. Catherine Sparkes, who trained at Lambeth, worked freelance for Doulton's in the 1870s and possibly later. She assisted her husband in the development of painted faience, producing an enormous tile panel that was exhibited by Doulton's at the International Exhibition at Philadelphia in 1876. Callen describes her as 'a talented, all round artist' (53).

Miss Charlotte H. Spiers, Miss Rebecca Coleman and Miss Ellen Welby all specialised in heads and often carried off prizes. Monkhouse commended Spiers for her healthy, handsome, natural faces, both gentle and refined; although her designs were considered to be on the severe side, her subjects occupied in thought, she produced work 'thoroughly English, and pure, and masterly also, if such an epithet can be applied to designs which are feminine in the best sense of the word' ('"Royal"' 249). Monkhouse considered Miss Welby's treatment of 'girlish beauties in graceful attitudes and charming draperies' to be 'more ideal and more purely decorative. She has a light and gentle fancy, and stands almost alone among her sister artists' ('"Royal"' 249).

Rebecca Coleman was the sister of W.S. Coleman, the first director of Minton's Art Pottery Studio, and her sister Helen Cordelia (Mrs Angell) was also a respected china painter. Both sisters may have worked at Minton's, but, certainly after its closure, Rebecca worked freelance and established her reputation through Howell and James; her patrons included the Prince of Wales. In 1881 she was awarded the *Queen* prize for a female head (see Figure 6.7). Her last works were entered posthumously in the 1884 ninth exhibition, and Monkhouse commented: 'The loss which this branch of china-painting has sustained with the death of the latter is not easily overestimated. In the skill of handling, in the bright purity of her tints, she was unequalled. The last work of hers which I have seen was like a rainbow' ('"Royal"' 247).

Miss Florence Lewis was another talented professional, rewarded with the Princess Alice Prize in 1879 for her 'superb arrangement of chrysanthemums' ('Paintings' 1879: 485). For this she adopted the technique of impasto or barbotine painting evidently with great success. In 1881 Lewis was accorded the highest honour, the Crown Princess's silver medal, for her exquisite flower painting. Lewis became one of Doulton's most distinguished artists, her manual on *China Painting* becoming a best seller.

Watt, Sparkes, Spiers, Welby, Coleman and Lewis were established professionals but Miss Scott Smith, who took the Crown Princess's Gold medal for amateurs in 1882, was awarded the Silver medal for professionals the following year, achieving the transition from 'Lady Amateur' to 'Artist'. Monkhouse was impressed by the amateur work, especially as it suffered a serious technical disadvantage:

> The amateur work, though not generally so complete in its technical proficiency as the professional, yet holds its own well, especially when it is considered that it starts

> with the great disadvantage of being painted over instead of under the glaze. Some of the amateur-work is of its kind unrivalled, and this in qualities where it might have been expected to be least successful. In, for instance, the special ceramic quality of pure and lustrous ground-colour there is nothing in the professional work to excel the turquoise blue behind Miss L.H. Busby's *Daises* or the green which sets off Miss A. Gresley's *Marguerites*, while these specimens are equally remarkable for the drawing of flowers treated decoratively without conventionality. ('Paintings' 1878: 565)

In 1878 amateur artists contributed 650 specimens, mostly the work of ladies, compared to 250 by professionals. The Crown Princess's Gold medal for work by a lady amateur was awarded to the Countess of Warwick, for a profile study of *Lady Eva Greville*, her daughter, against a background of sky-blue and apple blossom. By 1879 the amateurs were gaining in strength and confidence, producing works that often exceeded in originality their 'friendly rivals' ('Paintings' 1879: 485). The Crown Princess's Gold medal for amateur work was again awarded to a lady of high rank, Viscountess Hood. Her two portrait-plaques, full-length figures of the *Hon. Mable Hood* and the *Hon. Neville Hood*, were 'equal in execution to those of the other amateur prize-takers', especially given the greater difficulty of the subject matter. In 1879 all the major prizes, except one to Mr Percy Anderson, were awarded to ladies and 142 amateurs (male and female) were honourably noticed.

Lady amateurs were spurred into action by the plethora of charity bazaars and exhibitions, which necessitated a constant stream of fancy goods to sell. Exhibitions such as those held annually by the Amateur Art Society[16] provided another showcase for their industry, an outlet at which artistic goods were invariably sold at inflated prices in the name of a good cause. Such events traded on the celebrity or notoriety of the participants:

> For a small entrance fee the public has the privilege of enjoying and scrutinising the productions of unprofessional artists in different branches of art work, not a few of considerable merit, and all testifying to the great improvement which has taken place of late in the artistic skill and taste of the higher classes. ('Amateur Art' 399)

Contributors included Victoria, Princess Royal, H.I.H. the Crown Princess of Germany; HRH Princess Louise; Louisa, Marchioness of Waterford; Lady Dorothy Neville; and Lady Marian Alford, one of the founders of the Royal School of Needlework.[17] Embroidery, lace, woodcarving and china painting were regularly shown (Bradley 495). Lady amateurs were often praised for their labour and devotion rather than talent, their work invariably categorised as 'imitative' rather than original. For example, the Countess of Warwick's portrait plaque of *Mrs Bromley Davenport* was said to equal the works of the most celebrated maiolica painters of ancient Italy (Bradley 495). Such 'not-for-personal-profit' exhibitions opened up new possibilities for the lady amateur; by supporting worthy causes her artistic ambitions could no longer be condemned as selfish.

6.7 Rebecca Coleman, 'Dora: A Round' from *Magazine of Art* 7 (1884): 248. Courtesy of Anne Anderson.

## Conclusion

China painting can be located within the wider context of *Chinamania* and the construction of the House Beautiful; paintings on ceramics were positioned as art, becoming collectables that rivalled or even surpassed those of the past. Seen as 'art', china painting achieved an elevated status; production reached unprecedented levels, spurred on by royal and aristocratic support and 'not-for-profit' exhibitions. The annual exhibition of china painting at Howell and James encouraged women to compete for prestigious royal awards. Here middle-class amateurs and professionals competed against aristocratic dilettantes, moving in the same social circles. For those with talent, a professional career, or at least serious recognition, was possible.

It can be argued that the vogue for 'hand-decorated' work underpinned the growth of the commercial and studio Art Pottery industry, which promoted decorating ceramics as 'fit work for women' while simultaneously satisfying the demand for artistic goods. Women decorators played a vital role at Doulton and Linthorpe (Callen 59–77).[18] The art industries opened up new opportunities for the female practitioner, while, as consumers, women were encouraged to utilise such artwork for its ornamental effect.

Yet although a 'useful art', china painting was primarily ornamental, with chargers and tiles framed like oil paintings or plaques fitted into tables and mirror frames. Ceramic art may have enhanced the House Beautiful but it was seen to encourage clutter, was often of a poor standard and had little functionality. The Arts and Crafts Movement would valorise 'beautiful objects of everyday use', but china painting was decried as 'all surface and no substance', undermining dictums such as 'form must follow function' and 'honesty of construction'. Emerging at the beginning of the 1880s, the Arts and Crafts Movement reclaimed the decorative arts for the male sphere, emphasising professional craftsmanship and co-operative production based on guilds:

> Morris praised the everyday crafts of exotic men – a fourteenth-century peasant, a Kurdish shepherd, and an 'oppressed Indian ryot' – rather than domestic women, while Crane's examples of good embroidery come from Japanese, Persian, and Renaissance textiles, rather than from modern English upholstery. (Schaffer 75)

Schaffer suggests that 'the men who made crafts famous, William Morris and Walter Crane, placed the craft tradition firmly in the Middle Ages and regretted the decline of women's tapestries without seriously considering the popularity of women's decorative arts in their own period' (75). But Morris knew all too well the popularity of art in the home and even catered for the domestic needlewoman; his company supplied completely finished embroideries or the materials for working them at home. He had encouraged women into the decorative arts so effectively that they now endangered the livelihoods of his workmen.[19] Morris saw craft as a means of reforming industry and the workplace for men. He did not anticipate the prospect of 'not-for-profit' amateur work ousting the products of professional men. The brotherhood inherent within the Guild system frequently excluded woman from the creative and manufacturing process. Women retaliated by forming their own single-sex groups or sisterhoods. But lady-like delicate arts, such as china painting, tapestry painting and fan painting, were replaced with the more masculine and strenuous pursuits of woodworking and metal beating. Although women made a significant contribution, through such institutions as the Home Arts and Industries Association founded in 1884, they were all too often assigned the role of teacher rather than designer or maker. Women excelled in the founding of such educational or 'improving' societies, which relied on the traditional female skills of nurturing and instructing, deemed more wholesome and altruistic than the selfish desires and personal ambitions of the independent artist. In this way the excesses of the female artist were to be curbed, as well as the clutter in her drawing room, and she was brought back into the fold as dutiful teacher and devoted supporter of her pupils.

## Works Cited

Advert for 'The Exhibition of Paintings on China by Lady Amateurs and Artists'. E. Campbell Hancock. *The Amateur Pottery and Glass Painter*. London: Chapman & Hall, c.1879, np.

'Amateur Art Exhibition at Lowther Lodge'. *Queen*, 1 June 1878: 399.

'Amateur Pottery Painting at Messers. Howell and James's Galleries'. *Spectator*, 17 July 1880: 912.

Anderson, Anne. '"Doing As We Like": Grant Allen, Harry Quilter and Aesthetic Dogma'. *Journal of Design History* 18.4 (2005): 335–55.

'Art-Work for Women I'. *Art Journal* 11 (1872): 65–6.

Aslin, Elizabeth. *The Aesthetic Movement: Prelude to Art Nouveau*. London: Elek, 1969.

Bradley, J.W. 'The Exhibition of Amateur Art at Lowther Lodge'. *Academy*, 1 June 1878: 495.

Callen, Anthea. *Women in the Arts and Crafts Movement*. London: Astragal, 1979.

Clunas, Craig. 'Oriental Antiquities/Far Eastern Art'. *Positions: East Asian Cultures Critique* 2.2 (1994): 318–55.

Denney, Colleen. 'Acts of Worship at the Temple of Art: the Grosvenor Gallery and the Second-Generation of Pre-Raphaelites'. *Collecting the Pre-Raphaelites: The Anglo-American Enchantment*. Ed. Margaretta Frederick Watson. Aldershot: Ashgate, 1997: 65–75.

Eastlake, Charles Locke. *Hints on Household Taste in Furniture, Upholstery and Other Details*. London: Longman, Green, and Co., 1868.

'The Exhibition of Paintings on China'. *Magazine of Art* 1 (1878): 176–9.

'Exhibition of Paintings on China at Messers Howell and James's Art Galleries'. *Queen*, 19 May 1888: 613–15.

'The Fifth Annual Exhibition of Paintings on China'. *Magazine of Art* 3 (1880): 392–5.

'The Fourth Annual Exhibition of Paintings on China'. *Magazine of Art* 2 (1879): 269–72.

'The Fourth Annual Exhibition of Paintings on China by Lady Amateurs and Artists'. *Queen*, 31 May 1879: 504–5.

Gilbert, W.S., and Arthur Sullivan. *Patience, or Bunthorne's Bride*. Woodford Green: International Music Publications, 1988.

Hancock, E. Campbell. *The Amateur Pottery and Glass Painter*. London: Chapman & Hall Co., c.1879.

Haweis, Mrs H.R. *The Art of Decoration*. London: Chatto & Windus, 1881.

Kowaleski-Wallace, Elizabeth. *Consuming Subjects: Women, Shopping and Business in the 18th Century*. New York: Columbia University Press, 1997.

Lewis, Florence. *China Painting*. London: Cassell, 1884.

Merrill, Linda. *The Peacock Room: A Cultural Biography*. Washington: Freer Gallery of Art and Yale University Press, 1998.

'Messers. Howell and James: The Exhibition of Painting on China'. *Pottery and Glass Trades' Journal* 1.12 (1878): 178.

Monkhouse, Cosmo. 'Paintings on China'. *Academy*, 22 June 1878: 565–6.

—. 'Paintings on China'. *Academy*, 28 May 1881: 401.

—. 'The "Royal Academy" of China Painting'. *Magazine of Art* 7 (1884): 245–50.

Neiswander, Judith A. *The Cosmopolitan Interior: Liberalism and the British Interior 1870–1914*. New Haven and London: Yale University Press, 2008.

'Painting on China'. *Art Journal* 15 (1876): 255.

'Paintings on China'. *Academy*, 29 May 1880: 409–10.

'Painting on China by Lady Amateurs and Artists'. *Art Journal* 18 (1879): 164–5.

'Paintings on Porcelain'. *Academy*, 31 May 1879: 485.

'A Pleasant "Exhibition of Paintings on China, Plates and Plaques"'. *Academy*, 1 July 1876: 21.

'Prize Works at Messers. Howell and James's Eighth Exhibition of Paintings on China'. *Queen*, 9 June 1883: 537.

'Side Scenes of Society'. *Punch* 5 (1843): 59.

Schaffer, Talia. *Forgotten Female Aesthetes: Literary Culture in Late Victorian Britain.* Charlottesville and London: University of Virginia Press, 2000.

Spencer, Robin, ed. *Whistler: A Retrospective.* New York: Hugh Lauter Levin Associates, 1989.

Staley, Allen, '"Art Is upon the Town!" The Grosvenor Gallery Winter Exhibitions'. *The Grosvenor Gallery: A Palace of Art in Victorian England.* Ed. Susan P. Casteras and Colleen Denney. New Haven: Yale University Press, 1996. 59–74.

Watson, Rosamund Marriott. *The Art of the House.* London: G. Bell, 1897.

Whiteford, Sydney T. *A Guide to Porcelain Painting.* London: George Rowney, 1873.

## Notes

1 Anna Whistler suggests that the model only appears 'as if intent upon painting a beautiful jar which rests upon her lap', an allegorical reading which implies the artist is inspired by the colour and form of the porcelain (Spencer 72). This reconfigures the scene as an artist's studio, although Whistler told Fantin-Latour he had portrayed 'une Marchande de porcelaine' and his mother noted the 'several pieces of china and a pretty fan … arranged as if for purchasers' (Spencer 72).

2 *The Observer* remarked, 'the name given to it [the painting] has puzzled a good many people; but it is explained as having a technical reference to the painting of blue china – the picture itself is less capable of explanation' (Merrill 53). As Merrill points out, the title of the picture suggests the provenance of Whistler's collection, for the phrase *lange lijzen* is Dutch for the 'lanky people' or 'dawdlers' found on Chinese porcelain of the K'ang Hsi era. In England, the term was corrupted into 'Long Elizas': 'Virtually every critic [at the 1864 Royal Academy exhibition] began the discussion of Whistler's work with a go at the title, which evidently remained in the recondite language of connoisseurship' (Merrill 53).

3 The phrase, originally Bunyan's, was taken by Clarence Cook as the title of his book (1878) and purloined by Oscar Wilde for his American lecture.

4 *Hearth and Home* was founded by Mrs Charlotte Talbot Coke, who won the special prize, in the amateur class, at Howell and James's 'Royal Academy of China Painting' in 1878.

5 In 1876 the top professional prize at Howell and James was £15 15/-. Male practitioners numbered Lewis F. Day and Henry Holiday.

6 Minton's Art Pottery Studio at Kensington Gore was founded in 1871 with the specific intention of providing occupations for the female students of the South Kensington Schools. Due to a variety of problems the venture was not a great success and following a fire in 1875 the studio was closed. However, many of the artists found employment at Doulton's Lambeth works or carved out independent careers.

7 These manuals include Sydney T. Whiteford's *A Guide to Porcelain Painting* (George Rowney 1873), Campbell Hancock's *Amateur Pottery and Glass Painter* (Chapman & Hall 1879); Florence Lewis, *China Painting* (Cassell 1883). George Rowney, like Hancock, was another colourmen and art supplier, while Lewis was a professional china painter.

8 See Anderson; Neiswander. Mrs Haweis was especially prolific with *The Art of Beauty* (1878), *The Art of Dress* (1879), *The Art of Decoration* (1881) and *Beautiful Houses* (1882).

9 The company closed in 1922.

10 The American contingent played a significant role in furthering the development of amateur under-glaze painting on china. In 1883 the Cincinnati Pottery Club sent a selection of its pottery to the exhibition which, as Monkhouse noted, could teach the English lady amateur china painter

much about china decoration. The president of the club, Miss Louise McLaughlin, published a book on the subject.

11 Harrods can be traced back to 1834, while the current store on Brompton Road, a site acquired in 1849, was constructed 1894–1905.

12 Howell and James were not the only retailers to realise the potential of china painting. John Mortlock's, a well- established firm with their Old Pottery Galleries and Pottery Studio situated on Oxford Street, offered daily lessons either at the studio or in the privacy of one's home. Colours, bisque and glazed pottery, paint boxes and all necessary materials could be supplied and the paintings fired twice weekly. The principal artist was Miss A.E. Black, formerly a pupil at the South Kensington Schools and Minton's Art Pottery Studios, Kensington Gore, who specialised in female heads. Mortlock's, like Howell and James, sold art pottery, including the work of Emile Lessore and W.S. Coleman, previously head of Minton's Art Pottery Studio, and boasted an unrivalled collection of Marc Louis Solon's *pâte-sur-pâte*. They also carried a selection of antiques pieces of Serves, Worcester, Chelsea and Dresden, as well as reproductions of old Serves from Mintons. In 1879 Mortlock's advertised their Art Studio for Painting on Pottery. All materials were supplied at cost price. Designs were lent free and the paintings fired hourly. *The New Treatise,* giving full particulars and instructions, was available at 1*s*. In 1879 Mortlock's also opened an Art Studio for painting on glass, with daily lessons given in every description of glass painting and decoration. Howell and James also sold blanks and colours for both under-glaze and over-glaze painting for amateurs; Hancock & Sons Worcester Ceramic Colours were the main suppliers. They also offered suggestions for subject matter, such as the copying of Walter Crane's picture books. An art-pottery studio was opened in c.1880, with instruction provided by Miss Florence Judd, previously at Minton's Art Pottery Studio: 'Messers Howell and James Art Pottery Classes … [They] have opened a studio at their Art-galleries where classes are held daily, Saturdays excluded' (quoted in Callen 54). Classes were from 11am to 1pm and 3pm to 5pm, a course of 10 lessons of two hours each costing £3.3.0*d*., six lessons £2.0.0*d*., and three lessons £1.0.0*d*. By 1887 the principal of the school was, according to the *Queen,* Miss Mary Salisbury.

13 Princess Alice, Queen Victoria's second daughter, died in December 1878. She passed her love of art to her son, Ernst-Ludwig, who founded an artist's colony in Darmstadt based on Arts and Crafts principles.

14 Helena, Princess Christian of Schleswig-Holstein, known as Lenchen by the family, was the third daughter of Queen Victoria. She was, according to her daughter, very talented: she played the piano and had a distinct gift for drawing and painting in watercolours. She opened the retrospective exhibition of the works of the Marchioness of Waterford in 1891.

15 In 1880 25 were VHC, 54 HC and 61 C.

16 This exhibition and sale of amateur work was in aid of the Parochial Mission Women's Society. The Annual Amateur Art Exhibition evolved into the Royal Amateur Art Society, which was still holding annual shows until 1909.

17 Lady Dorothy Neville excelled at china painting, winning prizes at Howell and James's annual exhibition.

18 Both Doulton, Lambeth, and Linthorpe, Middlesborough, made a point of employing women; this may have been partly for economic reasons, but it was also used as a promotional ploy, being seen as mark of social responsibility.

19 Morris's wife and sister-in-law produced most of the textiles for Red House. Women manufactured all the embroidery made by Morris & Co.; his daughter, May, managed the workshops from the age of 23.

# 7

## Creative Industry:
## Design, Art Education and the Woman Professional

*Patricia Zakreski*

Charlotte Perkins Gilman's well-known story 'The Yellow Wall-paper' (1892) is perhaps the most famous ever written about the horrors of bad interior design choices. In this story, the narrator is famously driven mad by the yellow wallpaper's grotesque colour and poorly conceived pattern, which is described as committing 'every artistic sin' (648). Commenting on the confusion and disturbance created by the pattern, the narrator notes:

> I know a little of the principle of design, and I know this thing was not arranged on any laws of radiation, or alternation, or repetition, or symmetry, or anything else that I ever heard of.
>
> It is repeated, of course, by the breadths, but not otherwise.
>
> Looked at in one way each breadth stands alone, the bloated curves and flourishes – a kind of 'debased Romanesque' with *delirium tremens* – go waddling up and down in isolated columns of fatuity.
>
> But on the other hand, they connect diagonally, and the sprawling outlines run off in great slanting waves of optic horror … (651)

Critics have offered a variety of explanations for the narrator's horror of the yellow wallpaper; some have attributed it to the woman's reaction against her confinement within various patriarchal structures such as normative domesticity (Gilbert and Gubar) or medical discourse (Thrailkill). Others have suggested that, through the late nineteenth-century associations with the colour yellow, the paper encodes anxieties about the degenerate and contaminating effects of decadent aesthetics (Heilmann) or the 'yellow peril' of the racial other (Lanser). These, and many other such readings of the yellow wallpaper, offer convincing and nuanced analyses of the symbolic weight that the wallpaper carries in this story. In the pursuit of the symbolic, however, it is important not to lose sight of the literal: the wallpaper is simply very ugly. Having been for a time a student at the Rhode Island School of Design, Gilman herself, like her narrator, would have known something of the principle of design. Heather Kirk Thomas has described in detail how in this story Gilman draws on her design education to discuss women as consumers of household decoration. But the narrator also possesses the detailed technical knowledge of a producer of wallpaper designs that she uses to identify the paper as horrific. The narrator's problem with the paper is not just that the colour is a putrid, sickly sulphur ('not beautiful … like buttercups' (653)) or that it contains shapes that resemble eyes which seem to follow her around the room; she is also disgusted by the technical flaws of the pattern – that it is simultaneously distributed along horizontal, vertical and diagonal lines; that the pattern does not continue across the individual breadths of the paper which are created by the width of the printing block or roller; and that it is not arranged according to any of the necessary 'laws' of pattern designing such as radiation, alternation, symmetry, or repetition. Whereas the narrator knows a little of the principle of design, the designer of this paper was obviously unaware of the technical requirements of how to design a pattern for mechanical reproduction.

Throughout the second half of the nineteenth century, horror stories abounded of patterns that, once printed, got lost or confused in the folds of a fabric, made walls appear as if they were slanted, or made floors seem as if they were not flat. In a description of one such pattern that closely resembles that of Gilman's narrator, a writer for *Once a Week* remembered a pattern that represented a little vase of flowers:

> most exquisite in itself [but] … [t]here was a slight want of balance in the group of flowers, which, when they were regularly repeated, and seen from a little distance as a whole, gave them the appearance of slanting not quite diagonally; and this … had in a dress the effect of making the figure looked crooked. In the same manner we have all, no doubt, detected in the papering of a room some one-sided cast of this kind in flowers, leaves, or any other figures, making the paper look as if not placed straight upon the wall, or making even the wall itself appear slanting, so that the eye becomes continually puzzled, and painfully occupied in tracing out lines which have no agreement either with the horizontal or the perpendicular. (S.S. 125)

In this example it is not the drafting skills of the artist that are at fault; the drawing of the little vase of flowers is 'most exquisite in itself'. The problem occurs when the individual object is repeated – multiplied and expanded over a large surface area, where a slight want of balance, which might be charming in the individual picture, is ruinous when repeated. As this example makes clear, the skills and techniques needed to design a successful ornamental pattern for use in the manufacture of textiles or wallpapers were distinct from those needed to paint a beautiful picture. It was these skills and the aesthetic theories behind them that in the nineteenth century were known as the principles of design.

These principles, which are so familiar to Gilman's narrator, were disseminated widely in the nineteenth century, both in the US and UK, through a national system of art training schools that were developed by what has become known as the design reform movement. The first Government School of Design was opened in 1837 in London's Somerset House and, over the course of the century, the number of schools grew to over 150 across the UK (Kriegel 20). Beginning in the 1830s, this movement aimed at improving the artistic design of industrially manufactured goods; it rapidly expanded after the Great Exhibition, when Henry Cole and Richard Redgrave were placed in charge of the Department of Practical Art and the Schools of Design. Redgrave worked to establish a curriculum in teaching art and design that included a highly systematised programme of lessons in geometrical, perspectival and model drawing.[1] Under Redgrave's direction, the schools also added what he described as the 'simple and elementary *principles*, which may place the student in a position to cultivate afterwards, by his own exertions, a more matured acquaintance with those particular branches of Science or Art which may be more immediately related to his especial avocations' (*Necessity* 10–11; emphasis in original). It was not the job of the art schools, Redgrave argued, to teach an artisan how to make knives, or textile, or plates, or wallpaper. Instead, Redgrave advocated theoretical training in design principles alongside practical lessons in drawing that would improve not just students' artistic skill but also their ability to create and to recognise 'correctly' ornamented commercial goods.

The plan of design reform was for the widespread aesthetic development of society, both producers and consumers, where a broad understanding of the principles of good design could improve the taste, and by extension, the morality of the nation.[2] Redgrave's educational system was an attempt to define a set of rules that could be taught to anyone and everyone regardless of the reason they attended art classes. Some came for training to work in industry or in the decorative arts, whereas others may simply have wanted to extend their artistic accomplishments or improve their aesthetic judgment. As a place where one could gain affordable and 'proper' artistic instruction, the schools and their principled curriculum, Redgrave argued, which were 'not alone for the upper and middle classes, but for all, even the poorest, must tell upon the rising generation' (*Manual* 16–17). Design reform, therefore, included both the improvement of the design capability of individual producers and manufactories and the belief in good design as a force that could reform the nation.

Redgrave's principles of design focussed around debates such as the purpose of ornament, the connection between the decorative surface and the interior depths of an object, and the correct way of seeing and representing nature, issues that contributed an important perspective to the central tension between imitation and expression that has characterised aesthetics since the late eighteenth century. This chapter explores how design negotiated this tension, focussing on the relationship between creativity and structure that is exemplified by two of Redgrave's most famous principles: that (1) 'ornament does not consist in the mere imitation of natural objects, but rather in the adaptation of their peculiar beauties of form or colour to decorative purposes', and (2) 'ornament requires a specific adaptation to the material in which it is to be wrought, or to which it is to be applied' (*Necessity* 12). While the first principle grants the designer a degree of freedom, arguing for a conventionalised rather than imitative rendering of nature, the second highlights the limitations within which the designer must work; both, however, suggest the ways in which the designer adapts existing material to ornamental ends. The limitations within which designers worked were described by the decorative artist and industrial designer Lewis F. Day in his educational textbook, *The Anatomy of Pattern* (1887), when he writes:

> The popular idea of the process of ornamental design is, that the artist has only to sit down before a piece of paper, and, like a spider, spin out the fancies that may crowd his fertile imagination. Indeed, there is scope in design for all his fancy; but he is no Zeus that ornament should spring, Athena-like, full-grown from his brain. (3)

Discourses of design like Redgrave's and Day's constructed a model of creativity that had to exist within and develop out of the theoretical constraints of design aesthetics and the technical limitations of industrial production – the exquisite vase that survives repetition and expansion or the wallpaper that is arranged upon the rational laws of pattern construction. The chapter argues that the tension between freedom and constraint that design epitomised carried a particular resonance for professional creative women who sought to strike a balance between the expectations of gender ideology and their own professional and artistic aspirations. For women writers, like Gilman, who knew something of the principles of design, the ability to design a wallpaper or textile that was both beautiful and technically proficient was a compelling paradigm for the meaning and value of female creative work more generally.

## Ways of Seeing

By adding theory to practice, the purpose of the schools, Redgrave argued, was 'to teach the *right* mode of seeing and making use of nature' (*Manual* 18; emphasis in original). For Redgrave, Day and other industrial designers, this right mode of seeing involved looking beyond the specifics of the visual world and discerning the patterns that structured and determined the individual experience. In a series of important volumes on ornament and design that he published in the 1880s, Day describes how the method through which the designer can hone his ability to look beyond the decorative surface of an object to discern the deep structures that served as the constructive framework. 'Ornament is constructed', Day argued, 'patiently (I will not say laboriously, for the artist loves the labour), patiently built up on lines inevitable to its consistency' (*Anatomy* 3). Day differentiates between the work of the industrial designer and the god-like qualities of the fine artist. Rather than having a white canvas or a blank piece of paper upon which his powers of invention could work freely, the decorative artist works upon certain 'lines', certain pre-existing structures out of which the designer builds a harmonious and integrated whole. For Day, these lines are 'few and simple' (*Planning* 2), a basic set of shapes that are common to all patterns whatever their decorative style. Drawing out the metaphor of the anatomy of pattern that forms the title of his first volume, Day describes these basic shapes as the 'skeleton' of a pattern, arguing,

> [J]ust as the physiologist divides the animal world, according to anatomy, into families and classes, so the ornamentist is able to classify all pattern-work according to its structure. Like the scientist, he is able even to show the affinity between groups to all appearances dissimilar; and, indeed, to point out how few are the varieties of skeleton upon which all this variety of effect is framed. (*Anatomy* 3–4)

In Day's metaphor, the designer works like the scientist, looking beyond the varieties of style to observe, to categorise, and to rationalise the essential properties of the object to be decorated. Design thus seems to become a process of arrangement and management rather than creation and invention. As Day argues, 'A design is in harmony, not when it is strictly according to Greek or Gothic precedent, but when the parts all fit' (*Planning* 34). The designer's success exists not in the imitation or the slavish repetition of the forms of any one particular decorative style, or even in the invention of new ones, but, as the title of Day's second volume of design textbooks, *The Planning of Ornament* (1887), suggests, in good planning. A good illustration of this process is given in the frontispiece that accompanied the volume (see Figure 7.1). In this collection of patterns, the surface ornament is partially stripped away to reveal the skeleton underneath. But Day's anatomical metaphor expresses more than a logic of pattern. This collection of shapes illustrates the two levels of design that Day describes, stylised surface ornamentation and the deep structure of geometric lines. Day makes sense of the programme of lessons in geometric drawing that featured as part of the debated curriculum of the schools of design by illustrating the organic connection that existed between form and content, one of the most basic principles of design reform. The designer, like the physiologist, looks beyond the surface of an object and discerns the shapes beneath, which are already naturally present in it.

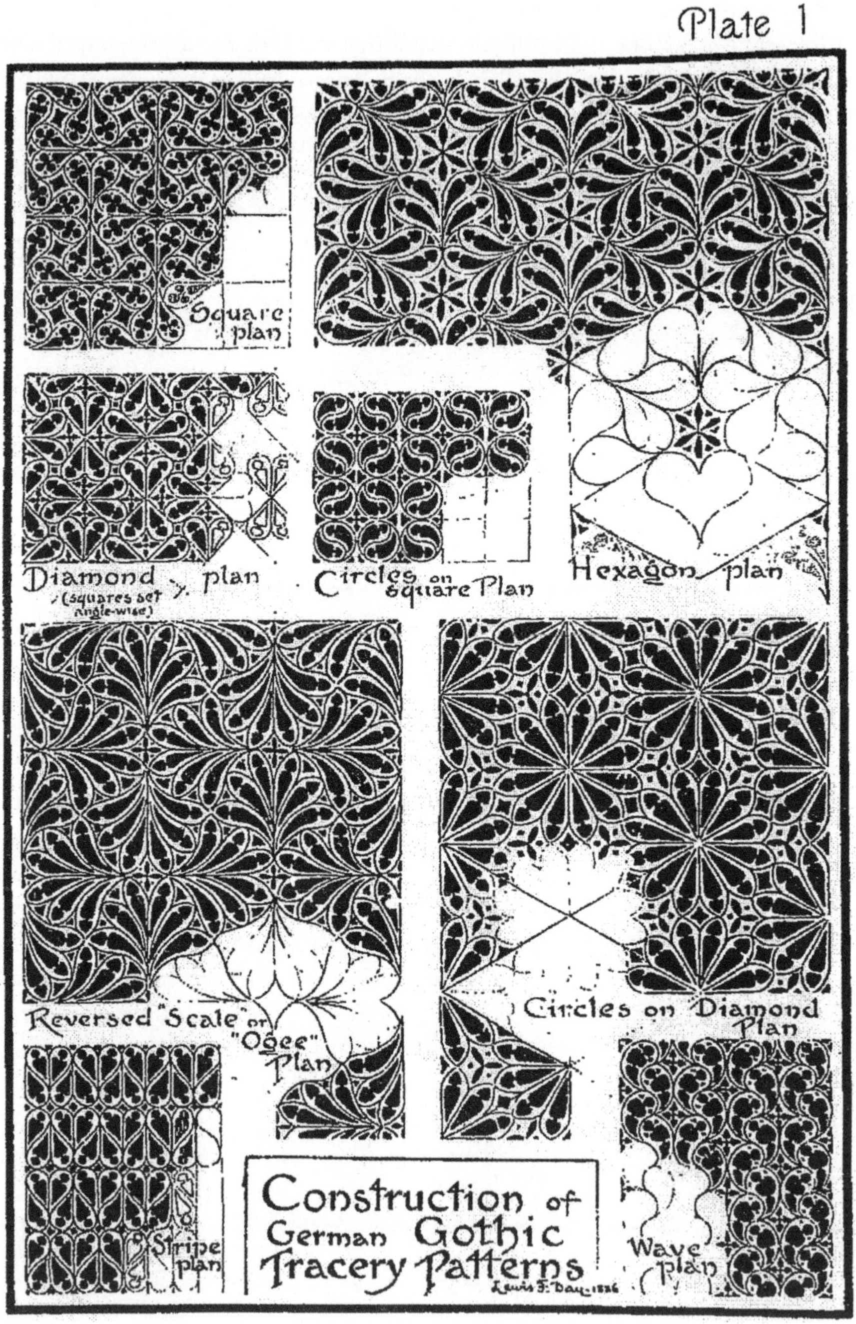


7.1 Lewis Day, 'Construction of German Gothic Tracery Patterns' from *Anatomy of Pattern* (1887).

The organic connection between form and content and surface and depth was repeatedly made in discourses of design, most strongly when nature itself was the subject of representation. Like Day, Redgrave argued that the right mode of seeing nature was to look beneath the 'accidents and disturbances of growth' and to discern the 'strict geometrical and numerical rhythm' that determines the laws of natural growth (*Manual* 18). Considering, for instance, the way that leaves and flowers are distributed by the laws of nature, Redgrave explains, that 'three, corresponding with the triangle, is the law of inflorescence of all endogenous vegetation, whilst the flowers of exogens are developed numerically as five, corresponding with the pentagon, … thus contributing to the greatest amount of symmetry consistent with variety' (*Manual* 19). It is phrases like 'the greatest amount of symmetry consistent with variety' that represent how design discourses theorised in aesthetic terms the relationship between freedom and constraint. The connection between geometry and creativity in design is certainly apparent here as what may seem to be random natural growth is reduced to the stark terms of the triangle and the pentagon. Though the growth of leaves on a tree or the shape of different flowers may seem random to the untrained observer, they are in fact controlled by very specific botanical laws.

To the correctly trained observer, these laws not only become apparent, but they also become the basis for representing that natural object. Rather than looking at a bunch of flowers and just copying what one sees, the designer needs to conventionalise the natural object, to represent it according to the natural laws which determine its growth rather than the random instance of the individual plant. This type of conventionalised treatment and Redgrave's law of 3*s*. and 5*s*. is evident in Figure 7.2, an illustration from fellow design reformer Owen Jones's *The Grammar of Ornament* (1856), in which Jones attempts to 'awaken a recognition of the natural laws which prevail in the distribution of form', including the radiation of the leaves from the parent stem, the alternation with which the leaves and stems are placed on the parent stem, and the repetition of the qualities of the individual leaf in the assemblage of leaves so that harmony is produced (Jones 156–7). Following these laws of radiation, alternation, repetition, and symmetry, which Gilman's narrator had searched for in the yellow wallpaper, would constitute, in Redgrave's terms, the '*right* mode of seeing and making use of nature' (*Manual* 18; emphasis in original). The instruction students of design received was therefore in large part an optical education, the honing of a fundamental ability to negotiate visually between structure and ornament, which in turn generated the designer's ability to structure and create.

7.2 Plate XCVI, 'Leaves from Nature No. 6' from Owen Jones, *The Grammar of Ornament* (1856).

The theory of design was that, within reason, such analytical vision could be liberating, but only within reason. Once the designer can recognise the lines upon which he must work, Day argues, 'there is scope in design for all his [the designer's] fancy' (*Anatomy* 3). In this way certain freedoms are possible within certain constraints, or variety is possible within certain symmetries. Day's Gothic tracery patterns illustrate this dual nature of design clearly. The designer is forced to work within the constraints of a few simple geometric shapes, such as the diamond, square and circle that in the illustration assert themselves through the surface ornamentation, because Day argues, they are naturally present in all objects and 'if you don't arrange for them they arrange themselves' (*Anatomy* 6). However, once the structure is identified, the designer is free to place upon this structure any style and pattern of ornament that fits. In this way, the designer creatively transforms the structure and asserts mastery over it. But, lest one thinks that Day is advocating too much freedom, he reminds his reader that one must not get too carried away. Even 'at his very freest he [the designer] is limited ... to certain methods of procedure' (*Planning* 2):

> It is refreshing to see that a man is not afraid of infringing occasionally upon the margin – on sufficient grounds; but the licence needs always to be justified by some excuse other than the artist's impatience of order. We have to be on our guard against a certain spirit of anarchy which appears to have taken possession of so many a modern artist ... Urgent need there may be of reform in our ideas of art, perhaps even of revolution; but sobriety recognises in the artistic anarchist only the enemy of art. (*Planning* 10)

As a way of seeing and understanding the deep structures that defined and determined the material world, discourses of design provided a method for imagining a process of incremental change, pushing gently at the margins and the boundaries of structure. If one didn't get too carried away, reform could be quietly achieved.

## Reform or Revolution? Women and Design

Although both Day and Redgrave speak of the designer as 'he', throughout the 1850s and 1860s, the art schools and the principles of design they promoted became increasingly associated with female labour as the art-industries came to be seen by many as a perfect solution to the problem of the redundant woman. While most forms of factory work were considered too physically and socially degrading for the middle-class woman, the growth in the market for industrial and decorative art objects offered what seemed to be a particularly useful form of employment for which the middle-class woman was well suited. As Ann Bermingham notes, 'Art work was something women could do and still remain feminine and polite, for design was neither physical labour nor commercial trade' (226). Some recent critical attention has been given to the work of women as designers in the second half of the nineteenth century. This work has tended to treat design in relation to specific industries, such as china painting, fashion or domestic decoration (see, for example, Burkhauser; Ferry; Helland; Helland and Alfoldy; Lees-Maffei). However, though undoubtedly linked to particular industries and arts, design was conceptualised as a discipline with its own laws and discourses whose methods might be universally applied across these industries. As such, design could be seen as a mediating discourse, combining knowledge of industrial processes, and sometimes even the physical presence within the factory setting, with a certain 'natural' artistic sensibility. Neither a physical labour nor exclusively an artistic occupation, design could therefore be recommended as suitable work for middle-class women, negotiating in a subtle but simple way between art and the market.

The particular middle-ground that design occupied was drawn out by Leader Scott [Lucy Baxter] in an article about the suitability of decorative art as a career for women. Scott differentiates between genius, talent and dexterity in art work, associating these distinctions with qualities of soul, mind and body: 'The corporeal part of art is technicality, requiring only hand and eye; the intellectual is composition, requiring thought and reason; the spiritual, the inner and higher meaning which soul alone has the power of expressing' (98). Those with genius, Scott argues, may pursue the 'highest forms' (98) of art, namely watercolours and oils; those with dexterity can be 'the handmaid to other minds' (99). But for those with talent, who are 'endowed with a correct eye and clever hand' and can 'readily adapt forms to their uses and give a certain intellectual value to composition', there was an opportunity for work throughout the decorative industries: 'To her the many branches of decorative art are open' (98):

> She may etch, and draw on wood. She may design chintzes and wallpapers for the manufacturers; paint on china in a porcelain manufactory; paint tapestries for hangings, portières, and screens, and also paint on silk dresses. (99)

It was the capacity of the intellect, as opposed to soul or the hand, that the principles of design and art education worked to foster, and training the mind as well as the hand seemed to offer, for Scott, the 'possibility of independence' (99).

What Scott meant by independence in this context is perhaps debatable. While she specifically mentions independence from the necessity of marriage and the less appealing types of 'drudgery' available to women such as teaching (99), education in design principles could also be seen to offer women professional independence, the capacity for self-determination, flexibility and choice in the workplace. This narrative of independence had been illustrated in an 1860 article on 'Woman's Work' for *Once a Week*, which drew on the exemplary story of three young ladies who, after receiving training at a school of design, began work engraving the backs of watches. Within six months, the article asserts, 'they became as practised artists as a mere apprentice would have been in six years' (A.W. 373). The suggestion here is that the education available in the schools was superior to that offered by the more traditional system of apprenticeship, allowing the student to progress more quickly. The fact that such an assertion needed to be made attests to the controversies that surrounded art education, particularly after 1850. In his 1857 report to the National Association for the Promotion of Social Sciences on the Schools of Art, George Wallis, the superintendent of the Birmingham School of Art, described the disappointment experienced by manufacturers when they realised that the schools, to which they had subscribed money, would not teach designing for particular trades, but would instead teach what Wallis describes as 'the merest elements of art, and systematically develop the art-power of the country in the direction of industry' (vii). Wallis describes opponents of the schools' educational programme as short-sighted. While the manufacturers, in their instrumentalist mind-set, might view education in design principles as superfluous, Wallis contended that they are in fact elementary, like learning an alphabet before trying to learn a new language. While the student of a language might be able to memorise vocabulary or reproduce the sounds of another language, without an understanding of grammar, the student would never be able to be creative with that language. The same principle applied to the grammar of ornament.

The anecdote of the three young watch engravers stands as a testament to training in the grammar – rather than the reproduction – of ornament. Pushed out of the watch engraving profession by jealous male colleagues, these girls, the author tells us, 'were not to be beaten; they immediately turned their attention to engraving on glass, and are now employed at this delicate employment, and earn as much thereat as they did before at watch engraving' (A.W. 373). 'The secret of their success', the author asserts, 'is, that they have adopted drawing as a profession' (A.W. 373). Rather than learning a particular craft or trade, art education provided these women with a professional flexibility that prepared them to work in the range of art-industry occupations. For the correctly educated woman: 'the whole world of design is opened to her, and the field of her labour is almost boundless' (A.W. 374).

## Freedom within Constraint

While the estimation of the woman's field of labour as boundless is perhaps an exaggeration, the belief in the freedoms and opportunities that art education could afford for women persisted throughout the second half of the century. In describing how the principles of design could afford women a new kind of opportunity, the anecdote of the three young watch engravers also exemplified the social and professional obstacles women faced in their quest for employment. Branded 'foreigners' by the male colleagues who feel this industry belongs to them, scorned by polite society for their turn to trade, and ill-prepared by ignorant and imprudent parents, these girls provide an indictment of the society that had placed them in need and then obstructed their efforts to help themselves. In these circumstances, the education offered by the art schools stands out in stark contrast to these oppressive forces, providing a stirring, emotional narrative in which the genteel woman in reduced circumstances could learn not just a skill or an industry, but could get the basic tools she needed to sustain herself regardless of local circumstances. It was argued by supporters of design reform that an understanding of the principles of design rather than the mechanical processes involved in training for a specific industry would make it possible not only for women to find suitable remunerative work, but also to move fluently between occupations, bringing their knowledge as well as their skills with them. As a more general field of study, then, design seemed to promise increasing independence, self-sufficiency, intellectual development and creative opportunity. In her study of art education in nineteenth-century America, for instance, April Masten explains how 'midcentury women artists seized in the economic realm what had been denied them politically – their independence' (6). The field in which this freedom operated was primarily ideological, a relaxation of the boundaries of femininity and an expansion of woman's sphere to include notions of paid work and public life.

But the freedoms afforded by art education had a physical dimension as well, which gave rise to both anxieties, on the one hand, and idealistic plans on the other. One of the fears of the physical freedoms facilitated by art education is nicely illustrated by the image discussed in this volume by Catherine Flood in her chapter 'Women Drawing on Wood and the Careers of Florence and Adelaide Claxton'. Florence Claxton's *Study, South Kensington* (see Figure 5.1) presents a scene in which male and female art students mingle closely and perhaps flirt unchaperoned under the guise of study. Mary Bramston also dramatises these fears in her 1885 novel *A Woman of Business* when Muriel, a very pretty 19-year-old student at a London art school, allows a male student to buy her Bath buns on her lunch break. Bramston was generally a conservative writer, who was a friend of Charlotte Yonge; she contributed regularly to *The Monthly Packet* and published many novels, including this one, with the Society for Promoting Christian Knowledge. It is telling, then, that Bramston does not blame the system of co-education for placing women in such unsavoury situations. The school, the narrator explains, was arranged so that the male and female pupils did not have to meet each other. There was, however, a set of 'loud and fast young ladies, among whom Muriel seemed to be intimate; but they were a very small number out of the whole set, and the only ones whom the independence of modern London seemed not to suit' (50–51). Bramston accepts a young girl's independence as a fact of modernity, and though she has no interest in pushing her female characters back into private domesticity, the heroine of her novel, the eponymous 'woman of business', Nettie Raymond, understands that independence must be constrained by 'discretion':

> At first, like most young things, Nettie thought that this freedom was simply delightful ... But there came a time when she began to perceive that there were two sides to the question, and that the responsibility of independence meant the risk of serious difficulties in the case of a 'fair' girl without sufficient 'discretion'. (32)

Bramston suggests that independence comes with responsibility and that women's social emancipation must therefore be accompanied by a self-imposed restraint. Unlike the domestic angel, who never sinned because never challenged, the modern woman must learn how to be morally self-reliant.

Nettie's movement from a quiet, privileged and sheltered life in the country to the activity and dangers of a life in the business world of London functions as a parable of female development that places design and paid labour at the centre of woman's moral and social progression. When Nettie discovers that her family's toyshop is failing, potentially leaving the family destitute, she rescues its fortunes by designing, manufacturing and selling her own series of dolls' rooms. Working in her own drawing room, Nettie produces tidy and tasteful domestic scenes, such as 'The Nursery' or 'The Schoolroom', for the amusement and edification of children but nothing more. Bramston is careful to emphasise that there is nothing extraordinary or ideologically threatening about Nettie: 'though not gifted with genius, nor exactly given to profound thought or lofty imagination, Nettie was helpful, kind-hearted, and thoroughly efficient in the ordinary work of life' (3). Nettie's design ability accords almost exactly with Scott's notion of talent in art work. Combining 'clever fingers' (56) with a modest skill for 'invention' (9), Nettie creates her rooms from a blend of homemade and mass-produced material, decorating the schoolroom with artfully constructed 'paper simulacra of books' and an already existing doll's piano found at the back of the toyshop (56).

But Nettie's true talent is in design. Sourcing out the constructive work to a local artisan, Nettie concentrates on creating new designs for her workman to realise. With a growing number of employees, a detailed register of designs, including highly accurate costings and modest financial success,

Nettie begins to enjoy being a 'woman of business', revelling in the idea that, 'No one can say I have done this in an amateur or young-lady way' (107). The sense of mastery and independence that comes from her freedom to walk alone through London, to make business deals with workmen and to act as the saviour of her family suggests how design could be a largely positive force for women within modern society. Indeed, within the novel, working in the profession of design can lift a woman out of her narrow, sheltered existence and teach her to look beyond the surface of life, 'to break down the limitations of her nature' (187).

While Bramston explores how design can break down the limitations of gender, she also critiques what she sees as another powerful, limiting discourse – that of business. As the novel proceeds, Bramston demonstrates through Nettie's treatment of her workman the negative effect on all members of society of relationships based only on business. Though Nettie is proud of her business acumen, other characters worry that her focus on work has become a 'business plague' which, they warn her, will 'spoil all that's good and tender and womanly in you till you get to be just a hard shell for money-making like the rest of 'em ...' (130). As a friend cautions, 'If you don't look out, you will become frightfully limited ... Limited in your sympathies, and in your power of entering into other people's feelings' (166). In a perhaps unsurprising opposition, Bramston juxtaposes femininity and business but, as the title of the novel makes clear, this story is about reconciling these discourses and finding not just a conception of femininity that can exist within a business world but a notion of business that can incorporate the conventionally feminine quality of sympathy. As a theoretical concept, the 'woman of business' offers an alternative to the prevailing discourses of political economy in which self-interest formed the key motivating factor of the market and production. Bramston's woman of business thus becomes exemplary of a feminine restructuring of social relationships in the business world, calling for a balance between self-interest and sympathy. Bramston's perspective is a far-reaching one, extending the insights of a domestic or familial economy into the industrial sphere. Extending Redgrave's assertion that the principles of good design might improve the morality of the nation, Nettie's significance is doubled within the terms of this debate. As a talented designer, whose genius was for the exercise of limited creative freedom within formal constraint, she presents a model for female intellectual engagement within the creative industries. As a modern female entrepreneur, Nettie embodies an immanent critique of unrestrained economic self-interest. In both cases, she exemplifies the apparently contradictory formula promoted widely within principles of design, embodying the vision of freedom within constraint as the correct way of interacting with the modern world.

## Design in the 1890s

By the 1890s, such idealistic rhetoric of design reform, particularly in relation to the opportunities it could offer women, was routinely called into question, and the bitterness expressed by some about art education, such as that discerned by Valerie Sanders in her chapter in this volume, perhaps points out a growing sense that the ideals of art culture had failed to deliver on their promises to revolutionise women's lives. However, even in some of the most critical works, traces of the earlier idealism about art education's revolutionary potential remain. The representation of art education in Ella Hepworth Dixon's *The Story of a Modern Woman* (1894), for instance, seems to construct a critique of the schools' ambitious project. The description the narrator gives of the school supports such a reading:

> The Central London School of Art, though backed by all the majesty of state support, was, at the first blush, a somewhat disillusioning place to the youthful aspirant for fame. To the over-nice, to be sure, it lacked an art 'atmosphere', except such a material one as is generated by ancient paint-tubes, oily rags, furtively munched sandwiches, and the presence of a preponderance of people to whom the daily tub is possibly not of vital importance. (83–4)

With greying blinds, dirt-covered windows, and equally dirty students, the state-run school seems to represent the faded ideals of what, by the 1890s, had come to be known as the South Kensington system. The education Dixon's heroine, Mary Erle, receives in the school adds further to this critique, where students who hope to transfer from the government school to the Royal Academy spend months in the repetitive and painstaking process of stippling an outline drawing of the classical statue *The Lacoön* to make it appear like a dotted engraving. Having already spent six months on this picture, it began 'to dawn on Mary that the whole thing was a foolish pretence at work' (88).

While it may seem as if the whole system of art education is coming under attack here, the specific target of Dixon's critique is the 'over-nice' Royal Academy aspirant who attends the school more for its atmosphere than the practical lessons it can teach. It is the unrealisitic heights of Mary's artistic ambition rather than art education in itself that Dixon criticises. Rather than attending the school in order to train for a remunerative career and learning something of the commercial side of art work, Mary begins her art education as an amateur pursuit and continues to follow her idealistic vision 'to paint' even when, after her father's death, she must find a way to support herself and her brother. Though the lustre is certainly taken off the schools, as well as the idealism that lauded art education as the panacea to the Woman Question, Dixon's reproach is more directly targeted at the class and gender-based structures that encouraged middle-class women to aim for careers in the high rather than popular arts and failed to give them the technical training needed to succeed in the commercial world.

In the same year Dixon's novel was published, a similar critique was levelled at the contemporary world of design education by Alice Gordon. In an article in the *Fortnightly Review* entitled 'Women as Students in Design', Gordon argues that the art of design requires that its student understand a broader range of concerns than the practitioner of the fine arts. Both must have training in technique; an understanding of materials and form; knowledge of historical style; and a proper sense of harmony, perspective and proportion. But the student of design also requires a special course of study concerning the business and mechanical elements of industry. Gordon, however, sees this type of training as something beyond what was currently available in the government-run schools. Referring to a letter from a correspondent who has just completed such a course, she quotes:

> South Kensington teaching, so far as it goes, is excellent, but after passing through a course of training there the designer wants further instruction, more practical, technical, up-to-date. She also wants to be put into communication with the manufacturer, and through the criticism of able working designers learn the technical requirements of the market, in fact, having been shown the theories of her *Art* she wants to master her *Craft*. (523; emphasis in original)

The implication here is that the education offered by the schools of design was too rarefied and too lacking in the practical knowledge that the women designer needed in order to understand the business procedures of the manufactories for which they designed. These business issues included technical knowledge such as how a small design would translate to a large area, what would be the difference in tone when colour was applied to different material, and what materials were available as a result of international trade. Designers also needed to know the limitations of machinery in reproducing the patterns created. Designers for textiles and paper hangings, for instance, were generally advised to keep in mind the size of the blocks which were used to print the material in order to ensure that their design was repeatable according to this mechanical requirement. It is this type of knowledge, Gordon argues, that the current system of art education fails to give to women.

Gordon calls for more technical training for women. As she argues, this is because:

> [T]hey will have not merely the manual and mental dexterity required to design a pattern for a wall-paper or a cretonne, but they will have the great advantage of learning something of the business side of their calling, for they will be brought into contact with manufacturers and employers of labour, so that when they leave the School (whatever department of designing they may elect to make their profession) they will have learnt something of simple business ways and customs, which knowledge should prove an invaluable training to women. (527)

In denying women the technical knowledge more common to men, the system of art teaching that was lauded by Redgrave in the 1850s as education for 'all' is shown by Gordon to have a strong gender bias. Describing the plight of 'outside designers', those not employed directly in a factory but working, as most women did, on a freelance basis, she notes,

> [O]utside designers are, in most cases, unpractical people, who do not understand trade requirements, and the 'amateur's' design often causes the British (or other) workman to scratch his head, and wonder why designers were created for the apparent purpose of setting him problems which he can never solve. (522)

To deny women technical knowledge, Gordon argues, keeps them outsiders – outside the structures of industry and thus outside the profession. It is not that amateurs could not produce beautiful designs, but that they had more trouble producing workable ones. It is these outside designers who would be more likely to make the kind of mistakes described at the beginning of this chapter: to produce exquisite vases that lack harmony when repeated or even to create yellow wallpapers that aren't arranged according to any laws of radiation, alternation, repetition, or symmetry. In breaking the fundamental rules of good design, Gilman's yellow wallpaper points to a lack of proper training on the part of its designer. The pattern offends because it is too amateur, too unlearned, and too much a reminder of institutional and social limits that are placed on women's creative aspirations. The woman that peeks out of the paper, who also represents 'a great many women' (654), can be seen as the amateur female artist who is trapped, like the narrator, by the ideological and institutional forces that keep creative women locked in domestic and amateur frameworks. By inscribing the horrific pattern over the figure of the confined woman, Gilman maps the principles of the design reform movement onto the debates about the limitations of women's creative work. In this story, the creative woman is locked in the structures of domestic femininity – the nursery, wifely obedience, inactivity and dependence. But, as demonstrated by the wallpaper, she is also confined creatively within the terms of amateurism, primarily through a lack of proper training.

The class and gender biases that limited the commercial training of women in design are echoed in the aura of vulgarity, the patina of dirt, and the sense of disillusionment that infect Mary's feeling about the Central London School of Art. These feelings come from the perspective of the daughter of a famous scientist rather than the reduced gentlewoman, and as Mary gets more used to her new social position, her attitude towards commerical artwork also begins to change. When her fellow student, Perry Jackson, suggests that she write a story for a popular magazine to accompany an illustration he has already drawn, Mary 'who had never heard of this primitive method of producing imaginative literature' (103), begins a career as a professional journalist, writing little romantic stories for illustrated journals, reviewing art exhibitions, and trading on her father's famous name to earn a living.

While these journalistic productions are not the artistic masterpieces Mary had hoped to create, they do allow her to survive the mundane problems of life (such as how to pay the bootmaker's bill) and to live an independent existence. But, though this work is perhaps not Mary's ideal, there are moments in which the art education Mary has had enables her creative vision to flourish. In descriptions reminiscent of Day's, Redgrave's and other design reformers' claims that design education teaches the student the correct way of seeing nature, Mary, after her time at the Central London School, comes to see the world around her through the eyes of her training:

> Underfoot was a layer of greasy mud. In the little shops a bleared gaslight made an orange patch in the all-pervading greyness. At the fruiterers' the mounds of golden oranges, crimson apples, and scarlet tomatoes flamed with startling assurance against the blurred, brownish-grey of the houses, the pavement, the very atmosphere. She was curiously alive, now, to the effects of colour, to 'values'; everywhere the girl saw a possible picture. (101)

The narrator's use of the technical term 'values', or tone, is a reference to the interplay of light and shade that is repeatedly explicated in artistic teaching manuals, such as John Collier's (husband of Marian Huxley Collier) *A Primer of Art* (1882), which he addresses 'to all those who are endeavouring to learn the Arts of Design, in the hope that it may remove some practical difficulties from their path, and at the same time give them some insight into the principles that underlie these difficulties' (Preface). The reference to this term suggests that Mary's ability to see pictures everywhere is not the result of an innate artistic sensibility or a general class-based refinement – reasons that were often given for art as a suitable employment for middle-class women. Mary's creative vision is directly attributable to her education in art. Her training does not prepare her for entrance to the Royal Academy or for work in industry, but it does change the way she sees the world. Looking beyond the greasy greyness that pervades the dreary London cityscape, she can find in this bleak scene moments of beauty and creative potential.

Though Mary's creative vision is only a potential – the ability to see 'possible' pictures – Day's argument that once the designer can see the principles that structure something, he is able to creatively transform the structure and assert mastery over it, lurks in the background. Dixon extends the social implications of Mary's creative re-visioning in the final moments of the novel when Mary stands on the top of a hill looking out over London. In an ekphrastic description of the city reminiscent of a painting by Monet or Whistler, London becomes a place of beauty rather than pain:

> All around her was the joyous activity of springtime. Nature, who never ceases, who never rests, was once again at her work of re-creation. Once again the lilac trees were burgeoning with waxen blossoms. Once again a thrush, somewhere among that great city of sleepers was swelling its brown throat with an amorous song. The sunset touched her face, her hand, the flush of hawthorn above her head. At her feet, beyond the foreground of spreading trees, lay stretched out a vase ocean of houses, softened, made vague with a silvery veil of smoke, and pricked by endless spires. Here and there a blurred block, a monster hotel, a railway station, rose out of the great sea of dwellings. It was London that lay stretched out at her feet; majestic, awe-inspiring, inexorable, triumphant London. (191–2)

Although the novel ultimately ends with a futile gesture, as Mary stretches out her hand 'as if to grasp the city spread out before her', but withdraws it only to 'plod homeward' (192), her creative vision has provided her with at least a moment of sublime mastery.

In her chapter in this volume, Pamela Nunn describes the continuing association of women with amateurism, the domestic, and 'lower' genres of art even after the supposed 'watershed' moment in 1894 (the year Dixon's novel was published) when the Royal Academy allowed its female students to attend life study classes. Despite growing evidence for women's equality in the arts, Nunn argues, such 'ideological clutching at straws' shows the continuing institutional entrenchment of gender hierarchies that were at odds with and misrepresented women's progress in the professional art world. Also, the intellectual and artistic reputation of the types of art generally associated with women, namely the practical arts, suffered as a result of their association with both female labour and with industry, but I have argued that design offered creative women a different, more productive, positive model of professional work. Discourses of design instigated debates not just about the fundamental notion of women's right and ability to work, but also about their capacity to choose which professional spheres they wished to enter. Principles of design, because regarded as generic and basic within several branches of industry, offered not only a possible career for women but promised an unprecedented capacity for professional self-determination. Optimistic accounts of the design reform movement suggested that the creative vision generated by education in the principles of design could also produce alternative ways of seeing and making use of the world. And the actual education women undertook and the work they did expanded and normalised their presence in public, industrial and commercial spaces as producers as well as consumers. Discourses of design therefore gave space for female writers to imagine how a different kind of society could be designed. Such idealism was also critiqued with increasing frequency towards the end of the century, but even when confronted with the failure of art schools to create professional spaces of female self-expression, design remained a vital locus for discussion of what self-determination, professional mastery, social equality and freedom (within constraint) might actually look like if it could be achieved.

## Works Cited

A.W. 'Woman's Work'. *Once a Week* 2.43 (1860): 372–4.

Bermingham, Ann. *Learning to Draw: Studies in the Cultural History of a Polite and Useful Art*. New Haven: Yale University Press, 2000.

Bramston, Mary. *A Woman of Business*. London: Society for Promoting Christian Knowledge, 1885.

Burkhauser, Jude. *Glasgow Girls: Women in Art and Design, 1880–1920*. Edinburgh: Canongate, 1990.

Collier, John. *A Primer of Art*. London: Macmillan, 1882.

Day, Lewis F. *Anatomy of Pattern*. London: B.T. Batsford, 1887.

——. *Planning of Ornament*. London: B.T. Batsford, 1887.

Dixon, Ella Hepworth. *The Story of a Modern Woman*. Ed. Steve Farmer. Ontario: Broadview, 2004.

Ferry, Emma. '"Decorators May be Compared to Doctors": An Analysis of Rhoda and Agnes Garrett's *Suggestions for House Decoration in Painting, Woodwork and Furniture*'. *Journal of Design History* 16.1 (2003): 15–33.

Garson, Marjorie. *Moral Taste: Aesthetics, Subjectivity and Social Power in the Nineteenth-Century Novel*. Toronto: University of Toronto Press, 2007.

Gilbert, Sandra M., and Susan Gubar. *The Madwoman in the Attic: The Woman Writer and the Nineteenth-century Literary Imagination*. New Haven: Yale University Press, 1979.

Gilman, Charlotte Perkins. 'The Yellow Wall-paper'. *New England Magazine* 5 (1892): 647–56.

Gordon, Alice. 'Women as Students in Design'. *Fortnightly Review* 55.328 (1894): 521–7.

Heilmann. Ann. 'Overwriting Decadence: Charlotte Perkins Gilman, Oscar Wilde, and the Feminization of Art in "The Yellow Wall-Paper"'. *The Mixed Legacy of Charlotte Perkins Gilman*. Ed. Catherine J. Golden and Joanna Schneider Zangrando. Newark: University of Delaware Press, 2000. 175–88.

Helland, Janice. *British and Irish Home Arts and Industries, 1880–1914: Marketing Craft, Making Fashion*. Dublin: Irish Academic Press, 2007.

Helland, Janice, and Sandra Alfoldy, eds. *Craft, Space and Interior Design, 1855–2005*. Aldershot: Ashgate, 2008.

Jones, Owen. *The Grammar of Ornament*. London: Day and Son, 1856.

Kriegel, Lara. *Grand Designs: Labor, Empire, and the Museum in Victorian Culture*. Durham: Duke University Press, 2007.

Lanser, Susan, 'Feminist Criticism, "The Yellow Wallpaper", and the Politics of Color in America'. *Feminist Studies* 15.3 (1989): 415–41.

Lees-Maffei, Grace. 'Introduction: Professionalization as a Focus in Interior Design History'. Special Issue: Professionalizing Interior Design 1870–1970. *Journal of Design History* 21.1 (2008): 1–18.

Masten, April F. *Art Work: Women Artists and Democracy in Mid-Nineteenth-Century New York*. Philadelphia: University of Pennsylvania Press, 2008.

Redgrave, Richard. *Manual of Design*. London: Chapman & Hall, 1882.

——. *On the Necessity of Principles in Teaching Design*. London: Chapman & Hall, 1853.

Schor, Naomi. *Reading in Detail: Aesthetics and the Feminine*. New York: Methuen, 1987.

Scott, Leader [Lucy Baxter]. 'Women at Work: Their Functions in Art'. *Magazine of Art* 7 (January 1884): 98–9.
S.S. 'Women's Work: Designing Patterns'. *Once a Week* 4.83 (1861): 124–5.
Thomas, Heather Kirk. '"[A] kind of 'debased Romanesque' with *delirium tremens*": Late-Victorian Wall Coverings and Charlotte Perkins Gilman's "The Yellow Wallpaper"'. *The Mixed Legacy of Charlotte Perkins Gilman*. Ed. Catherine J. Golden and Joanna Schneider Zangrando. Newark: University of Delaware Press, 2000. 189–206.
Thrailkill, Jane F. 'Doctoring "The Yellow Wallpaper"'. *ELH: English Literary History* 69.2 (2002): 525–66.
Wallis, George. *Schools of Art: Their Constitution and Management, Comprising a Statement of the Present Position and Working of the Birmingham Central and Branch Schools*. London: Simpkin, Marshall & Co., 1857.

## Notes

1 For a full discussion of the curriculum debates in the early years of the school's history, see Kriegel, chap. 1.

2 For a discussion of the relationship between taste and morality, see Garson.

# 8

## Dorothy's Career and Other Cautionary Tales

*Pamela Gerrish Nunn*

That the formulation of a history (or, it now seems more apt to say, histories) of women artists and their works has been driven by the self-consciously feminist energy of the women's liberation movement that emerged in the late 1970s is very clear. The governing belief in late twentieth-century western feminism was in the possibility of progress towards an ideal that, while it may never yet have been manifested, might be attained by the recruitment of enough adherents to form a critical mass; they needed to be persuaded by the exposure of past wrongs and the vision of a better world, which it could be shown women themselves had periodically attempted to envisage and articulate. This project thus tended to the search for signs of progress upon which a journey of improvement from the (bad) long-distant past to a (better) more recent past and eventually to the (vigorously reformed) present could be built. These signs of progress towards the desired ideal might be actions that dismantled or events that diluted the male privilege of defining and producing art; women's resistance to the thrall of misogynistic culture; or the ceding of contested ground by men (as the possessors of privilege and the gatekeepers of the territories women wished to enter); with a particular occasion for celebration being revelations of the achievement of a body of work or key works by women despite the force of law, usage and opinion. The body of knowledge about women artists, their works and their experiences has grown immeasurably during the course of this endeavour, which is now successful and sophisticated enough for some of its premises and holy cows to be revisited and in some cases superseded by ideas and habits that seem more useful or accurate in the early twenty-first century.

One site examined for such signs of progress has been the academy, which was a crystallisation of the will to keep the practice of fine art in men's hands and the identity of artist as a male monopoly. Academies of art were established during the eighteenth and nineteenth centuries throughout Europe, modelled on that which had been founded in France in 1648; the Royal Academy in London was set up in 1768. Although two female artists of the time, Angelika Kauffmann and Mary Moser, were amongst its founding members, it developed like all other European academies of art as an institution explicitly devoted to the promotion of the artistic profession as a career for men (see Gaze). Early in 1894 the Royal Academy Schools gave its female students the life study that had traditionally been the lynchpin of an academic training and taken for granted by male artists as an essential element of training, a move attributed in the art press to '[t]he appeal of the lady students in favour of the use of the semi-nude model – a privilege [which], with more prudence than sense, has hitherto been denied them' (Spielman 218). This came after years of the Academy's wrangling over women's ambition to participate in its career trajectory on equal terms with men, shifting reluctantly in the early 1860s from its long-standing habit of denying women entry at all to the conditional admission of a quota, the results of which were themselves then the subject of internal complaint from aggrieved Academicians. This move, which the writer cited above framed as 'the singular disposition towards progress which the Academy has evinced of late – a tendency to reform which will mark the year 1893 as a red-letter epoch in its calendar' (Spielman 218), has been taken in feminist art history as a sign of progress, a marker on the journey mooted above from a situation of actual marginalisation and ideological manipulation to one of equality with men in the exercise of talent. This capitulation of the patriarchal establishment, as it has been characterised, has traditionally been identified as an event of 1893, following Sidney Hutchison's authoritative history of the Royal Academy, but it in fact occurred early in 1894. It would indeed seem to signify some abandonment of historic resistance to the professionalisation of female artistry, some acquiescence in the fundamental idea of the professional female artist: one of the signs that feminist art history can identify as proving progress. However, an examination of the culture of the years 1893 and 1894 reveals, contradictorily, vigorous promotion of the creative female as an amateur who must ever struggle to realise her talent, who would always feature naturally in the domestic or personal sphere but awkwardly or unconvincingly beyond the home. The Royal Academy exhibitions themselves demonstrated this insistence on women's necessary amateurism as an ideological clutching at straws, as an increasing number of exhibits in the 'higher' genres by women were selected for show and acknowledged in the press by comment and reproduction. This conflict of fact and opinion on territory habitually designated as key to a history of women artists is the focus of this chapter.

8.1 Margaret Dicksee, 'Miss Angel' (1892; engraved 1897), engraving from *Art Journal* (March 1897): 83. Courtesy of the University of Exeter.

Amongst representations of the female artist generated earlier in the period, Anne Thackeray Ritchie's historical novel *Miss Angel* played a key part in the moment I am concerned with. It appeared in 1875, first running as a serial in the *Cornhill Magazine*, and yet still had currency enough nearly 20 years later for Margaret Dicksee's painting of that title (see Figure 8.1) to be selected for the 1892 Royal Academy exhibition. Indeed, when in September that year Frances Gerard's biography of the eighteenth-century artist came out, more than one review attributed public interest in its subject to Ritchie's more than 20-year-old novel ('Books' 4; 'Angelica' 26). This painting began a series of works that Dicksee exhibited at the Academy over the next decade which took for its subjects well-known artists whose biographies were familiar to the general public, primed since the 1840s to relish the formative years of individuals who as adults made their mark in Britain's cultural life. The next year it was *The Child Handel*, with Oliver Goldsmith, Jonathan Swift, Walter Scott, Thomas Lawrence and Richard Brinsley Sheridan following yearly until 1901 (Dicksee died in 1903): Kauffmann was the only female protagonist.

Though Thackeray Ritchie's narrative has Kauffmann introduced to Reynolds as a colleague, Dicksee shows her rather as an admirer of the older painter's work, which stands before her on the easel with its back turned towards the viewer, whose gaze then rests rather on the youthful beauty of Kauffmann's face and figure. This attractive woman is not represented as an artist herself but within that visual tradition of the studio scene in which a female visitor appraises the work made by the studio's occupant, traditionally male. This reluctance to identify Kauffmann as an executive character is there in Dicksee's source: Thackeray Ritchie presents her as an inveterate naif, the adjective 'poor' being most often attached to her name. 'Poor little Angelica!', she writes in the first several pages:

> Over-praised, over-loved, deceived … She was no great genius, as people once thought, no inspired painter of gods and men. Her heroes stand in satin pumps and feathered toques; her nymphs are futile and somewhat dislocated beings; one laughs at them, but one loves them too. … She never thought about herself, but gratefully accepted kindness, hoped, loved, believed, was happy, was miserable, without much method, innocent and unresenting. (5, 84)

Repeatedly characterised as a spoilt child – 'a princess in her own little kingdom' (10), who grows without maturing – 'this careless and lighthearted girl' (72), 'this little impulsive, well-meaning, foolish creature, who had, by sheer hard work and spirited determination, earned a right to this panelled nest' (139) – she produces 'poor little flimsy fancies – cut paper flowers upon the altars of art' (42).

Few individual or specific works by her are identified, and the only analytical discussion about art involving Kauffmann occurs in a scene shared with Anne Damer, who became known for her sculpture, and Sir Joshua Reynolds, whose views on the topic, being wise, judicious and sound, outclass both Damer's vehemently argued misconceptions and Kauffmann's demure acquiescence: 'Do you know', says this latter in support of her mentor's disagreement with Damer, 'I seem sometimes to have found out of late that obedience is best? Now as I am painting, the more completely I can obey the colour of your beautiful brown hair, the better my likeness will be' (296–7). No wonder that the author sums up her protagonist quite late in the book by saying, 'Angelica Kauffmann was a woman born to be a slave, easily influenced by stronger wills, but still more by her stubborn ideas of sentiment' (287). She is a Dora, a pretty little thing who delights while exasperating the men who must take responsibility for her errors and the women who know better their place in society.

This characterisation of the female artist was neither invented by Thackeray Ritchie nor revived by Dicksee, but was the latest reiteration of the established deployment of femininity by those resisting the professionalisation of women artists. Interestingly, Dicksee herself was complimented at the 1894 Academy for painting 'with the modesty becoming a lady' ('Royal' 715). One might expect this hostility to women's artistic ambitions on what had been by habit and usage if not by law men's territory, but it was just as frequent within what looked like 'women's culture', which assumed to speak for women as well as to them. Thus for instance, in the *Girl's Own Paper*, whose project was firmly to encourage female ambition only in ways which supported marriage, the family and Christian belief, artistic activity often occurred in stories, poems and illustrations (see Figure 8.2). The trend of these representations, whether free-standing images or illustrated stories, is to show women's artistry being corralled within the domestic sphere, and controlled even when remunerative by a marital or familial economy. As Terri Doughty observes, 'Without exception in these stories, wilfulness, ambition and "unwomanliness" are punished' (8). This is exemplified in the story 'Dorothy's Career', which ran in the immediate wake of the Royal Academy reform, March 1894. The tone is set in the opening passage by the man whom Dorothy declines to marry because 'she wants to have a career; she wants to be famous; she wants to go to London and have a studio of her own, and become a Miss Raphael or a Miss Michael-Angelo' (344). 'It is all the fault of this over-education, Mrs Bruce', he tells the heroine's mother; 'Dorothy's head has been full of all this rubbish about a career, and the higher life, and self-culture, and the position of women ever since she left college'. The complete theme of the story is indeed there in the first scene, as he goes on to complain that, though admittedly 'a very clever artist', Dorothy only has talent like 'hundreds of girls' but not genius, and so 'She will never be a great artist; no woman ever was in my opinion, and I'm sure Dorothy won't be'.

8.2 Isabel Brittain, 'Amateur Artists' from *Girl's Own Paper*, 1 July 1893: 640.

He is of course proven right – men are usually right, in the *Girl's Own Paper* – but before that conclusion is reached, Dorothy's ambition is contrasted explicitly with the proposition of her mother that, between an artistic career and marriage and motherhood, 'The highest life for a woman is to be a good wife and a good mother' although 'we live in a highly unfilial age, in which it is the fashion to sneer at home-life with its many trials and many blessings' (345), and with the stance of her friend and flatmate modest, virtuous Mabel Fox, who 'had no aspirations after immortal fame, no particular desire to have a career, no wish to immolate herself on the altar of art' (362). The working out of the plot has the typical element of the unfeminine woman's come-uppance being delivered by the previously spurned suitor – men usually being given the role of humbling not to say humiliating the ambitious woman, not as woman's enemy and oppressor, but as her teacher and protector into whose care/control she is lucky and grateful to be admitted by the close of the story.

The issue is never, in this discourse, whether or not women exercise their creativity – there is no wish to ban it – but always the issue is its character and its standing: its currency, one could say. Thus when in October 1894 the *Girl's Own Paper* changed its banner image (see Figure 8.3) from a bland female messenger from the classical repertoire to a much more specific, decorative and up-to-date image of two girls actively writing and drawing, this implied no encouragement of the professionalisation of women's art. This but prettied up the amateur tradition, wherein girls' talent and sensibility are harnessed for the consummation of true womanhood – detailed, for those needing to be schooled in it, in the package called femininity. The figures were editorially defined as 'two maidens artistically attired in white sitting in graceful ease' (Doughty 17), which expresses well the comfort that the *Girl's Own Paper* editors promised women would enjoy if they were but content with amateurism, its separate arena, and its junior cultural rank.

A more celebrated proponent of the theme pursued by these *Girl's Own Paper* contributors – though his celebrity has tended to overlook this aspect of his activities – was George Moore, whose contribution had appeared some months earlier. His collection of essays *Modern Painting,* appearing in May 1893, included the grotesquely misogynistic piece 'Sex in Art', written some months earlier for *The Speaker*. Moore's was the pugnacious face of the sector of society that believed, along with the writer of the *Illustrated London News* column 'Art Notes' in March 1893, that '[t]he mere man is having a bad time just now' (376). Moore also cited the figure of Kauffmann, but as a model of female artistry:

> [T]hough her work is individually feeble, it is stamped with the charm of the tradition out of which it grew and was fashioned. Moreover, she was content to remain a woman in her art. She imitated Sir Joshua Reynolds to the best of her ability, and did all in her power to induce him to marry her. How she could have shown more wisdom it is difficult to see. (224)

8.3 Henry Ryland, Banner image from *Girl's Own Paper*, 6 October 1894. Courtesy of the University of Exeter.

In a sustained attack on the woman artist, Moore's contention is that the only woman in the history of art with any credibility is Elisabeth Vigée-Lebrun ('among these well-intentioned ladies … one artist of rare excellence') (225), of whose work he has, however, seen only two examples. As it happened, one, a portrait of Marie-Antoinette, was illustrated in the *Art Journal* a few months later to accompany the review of a French publication *La femme dans l'art* by Marius Vachon ('Recent' 273–4). Amongst his contemporaries, Moore approved the Canadian painter (resident in England) Elizabeth Armstrong Forbes and the French Impressionist Berthe Morisot. Other current figures he named only to ridicule were Elizabeth Thompson Butler, who had risen to fame as a battle painter in the 1870s; Rosa Bonheur, the leading female artist in France and internationally famous for her animal painting; Annie Swynnerton, an independent painter of allegory, classical subjects and portraits; and Louisa Lady Waterford, a prominent watercolourist recently dead.

The last of these had provoked considerable discussion not long before, when a huge (300–400 works) memorial show in London in June 1892, and then an extensive appearance in the Old Masters exhibition at the Royal Academy in January 1893 (74 works) drew prolonged comment in the art press on the nature of amateurism and the importance of distinguishing between talent or gift (which it was not denied Waterford possessed) and true artistry (which was deprecated by many, in contradiction of Ruskin's widely reported praise of Waterford's genius) (see Editor, 'Old'). Many of those offering their six-penny-worth on Lady Waterford, like George Moore, posited the sex of the artist as essential to the evaluation and function of art – when the artist was a woman. In Waterford's case, the artist was also a member of that other sector traditionally required to content itself with amateur status, the aristocracy. Moore was emphatic that, whatever her class standing, the creative woman must conceive of herself as essentially gendered, exhibiting femininity in her own conduct as well as in her own work's subject-matter, style and sentiment. This includes, fundamentally, the awareness that she will never achieve the same standard as a man (though he avoids drawing out the logic of his own prejudice so far as to declare whether *any* female artist's work would always fall short of *any* male artist's work). Should she not, her efforts will be ridiculous, even monstrous, and no tolerance will be accorded to such wrong-headed efforts.

There was more latitude offered the would-be professional woman artist in a book of essays published in October 1893 under the title *Ladies at Work*, an anthology of articles collected from *The Monthly Packet* which included in its survey of possible paid work for women a chapter entitled 'Art'. The editor, liberal feminist Mary Lady Jeune, began by talking up the recent improvements in women's position, doubting that 'the franchise' was needed for

> [I]t can hardly be said that a woman's position is a hard one because that privilege [sic] is withheld, for in the most important matters affecting education, training, and choice of professions a woman's field of choice is hardly less limited than that of a man. Medicine, science, teaching, literature, and art are all open to her, in all of which she has won laurels, while even that most conservative and exclusive of careers, the law, is now being invaded by her … (1)

The note on which her introduction concluded is then predictable:

> To the majority of women the profession ordained by Nature will be the one open to them, and in no other is their influence more potent or wide-spreading; but every woman cannot be a wife and mother, and it is to such women that all the questions with which this volume deals are so important. (13)

To become, say, a professional artist, then, is to gain only second prize – the consolation prize, one might say.

The chapter on art, written by Florence Reason, a little known painter and illustrator, proposed art as something that women may work in professionally. However, this proposition resonated with the *Girl's Own Paper*'s parables on the vanity of ambition and the folly of individual rebellion against convention. Her opening passage is worth quoting in its entirety for the clever way in which it uses a humorous version of the typical *Girl's Own Paper* narrative to blandish its readers into assuming the author's own viewpoint:

> Many are the tales in which the heroine, in difficulties of one sort or another, turns to painting, and so finds a way out of them in a very short time. Have we not all read stories in which the heroine's sweet girlish figure – she's only seventeen – and the rapid touches of her brush – which she wields with the skill of a master who has been at work for forty years – fill the hero with amazement and admiration, as he suddenly comes upon this charming figure … he gazes at the picture and exclaims, 'This is a masterpiece! From whom did you learn this manner of painting, combining the sweetness of Raphael with the majesty of Michael Angelo?' To which she replies, 'Oh I am so glad you like my little effort; I taught myself!' Then the plot thickens; he goes away, she loses her friends, her money, everything, except her paints and brushes. With these she rapidly covers a large canvas, painting some easy little

> subject such as … Joan of Arc leading her troops to Victory … sends the picture to the Academy, where the hanging Committee exclaim as one man, 'This is a work of genius …' and when the heroine wakes on the first Monday in May, she finds herself famous … [T]he hero, just returned from visiting the Grand Llama of Tibet … purchases the picture which he recognises as the handiwork of the very young genius [he had once met] … He finds her as sweetly modest as ever, although all England is ringing with her praises. They are married in due course, and henceforth she devotes herself to painting only for the delight of her husband and friends, although the dealers go on their knees to her for examples of her work. (44–5)

'This sort of tale belongs, of course', Reason says, 'to the past; no-one would now think of writing or reading such a story, so I need not warn girls with artistic inclinations that such things are impossible. The hero and the girl of seventeen may exist, but not the pictures' (45). She makes the familiar point that training is necessary for the professional, and identifies perseverance, originality, good workmanship and a good eye as the qualities necessary for success. In implied accusation of unfounded ambition, she asks of the would-be art student, whether she

> has she an intense desire to learn to paint or to model? Without that strong desire she will fail, even if her talent be great, for the power of doing good work can only be obtained at the price of more patient drudgery than is needed for most other occupations. (46)

This echoes also the leitmotif of mainstream reviews of the annual exhibitions of the Society of Female/Lady Artists, which had over the years belittled or denied the value of the organisation by condemning its shows as 'dreary array of amateurish efforts' ('Recent Exhibitions' xxxv), despite claiming a year later in July 1894 that they gave 'a depressing and unjust idea of the standard of women's work' ('Exhibitions' xxxviii). This reproach, that women could not or did not bother to distinguish between amateur and professional standards of achievement, was a frequent element of this discourse of complaint. It was still possible to blame women's failure to meet alleged professional standards on a lack of training as in the 1850s, but some preferred to blame women's own laziness and naivety. Reason's reader is told that anyway 'most young artists' earn their living not by fine art but by illustrating and teaching, and other 'bye-ways' which are recommended are chromo-lithographic work, designing Christmas cards, painting panels, screens and fans, and drawing costumes for the press. In this view of the world, women's creativity is more readily allowed to be remunerative if it is artisanal rather than if it is professional, despite the fact that the women envisaged by this book are 'ladies'. One of the ideological reasons for this is surely that applied art carried no intellectual cachet.

Contradicting this emphasis on the difficulties of woman becoming an artist and the unacceptability to mainstream opinion of this aspiration is a variety of evidence that would have come to the notice of any desultory visitor to the 1893 and 1894 exhibitions and any cursory reader of the art press in those same two years. Firstly, the 1891 census statistics, published in 1893, reported 3,032 women identifying as painters, engravers or sculptors, alongside 9,250 men: this ratio, of female practitioners numbering one third of the number of male, was substantially higher than had ever been recorded before, suggesting that the reforming Academy was only catching up with an already established trend. Then, the Royal Society of Watercolourists, another of the artist associations which had lived with the issue of women artists since it arose in the 1850s, boosted its female membership markedly in the first few years of the decade: the popular and highly visible Helen Allingham was made a member in 1890, having been an associate since 1875; the Venetian viewpainter Clara Montalba was made a member in 1892, having been an associate since 1874; and the Irish artist Rose Barton was made an associate in 1893.

Secondly, individual cases of women whose production and conduct were consistent with the traditional definition of professional art were more and more visible in London, if not nationally. At the same time, reviewers often still noticed female exhibitors' work together, as if it constituted a class of its own – a practice established in the 1850s, when, against a backdrop of the Woman Question, female artists first began to be seen in the annual exhibitions in sufficient number and variety to attract comment. While these artists' professionalism could not be denied, it often provoked derogatory remarks about women as a class. This indicated resentment at the fact that these women were performing as professionals, reproducing the ideology described above. Greeted by one critic at the Royal Academy of 1893 as 'a thoroughly well trained painter who, unlike most lady artists does not take things easily nor fail in thinking out her subject' ('Royal' 542), Marianne Stokes is one woman who operated at the top of the hierarchy of genres. After a great success with *Hail Mary* at the Academy of 1891, it was her *Angels Entertaining the Holy Child* that attracted attention on this occasion. Already represented in the Liverpool public collection, and seen at the progressive New English Art Club, the liberal New Gallery and in the commercial sector as well as the mainstream Academy, Stokes – in fact an Austrian, born Marianne Preindlsburger – was most associated with the French-influenced, progressive Newlyn School of painting and was based in Cornwall with her husband painter Adrian. Indicating the versatility which marked these professional women artists of the *fin de siècle,* in April 1894 she was also noticed in a key show at the Grafton Galleries showcasing contemporary practices. Also attracting attention at the well-established exhibitions of 1893 was the aforementioned Elizabeth Armstrong (Mrs Stanhope Forbes), who figured amongst 'some rising artists' profiled in the *Magazine of Art* a few months later. Her Academy exhibit, *Moorland Princesses,* and her exhibit at the New Gallery, a costume piece called *The New Song*, could easily be seen as supporting George Moore's approval of Forbes, in their use of female figures and pleasant colouration, though they attested equally to a self-confidence unknown to the minor or junior artist that he insisted women must inevitably be. Moreover, Forbes's 1894 Academy exhibit *At the Edge of the Wood* revealed the Newlyn School's French roots, and a long article in *The Studio* that year recognised her as a printmaker. Another female Academy exhibitor recognised in both column inches and reproduction in 1893 and 1894 was Jessie MacGregor, producing imaginative historical figures *News from Trafalgar* in 1893 and *Arrested* in 1894. An erstwhile student of the Academy Schools, she was another female artist whose work had been bought for the Liverpool public collection not many years before.

These artists all figured in the Chicago World's Fair, the latest in the tradition of international expositions which had been started in 1851 with the Great Exhibition in London. Running from May to October 1893, it was an event widely reported in the English press. An attention-getting feature of it was the Woman's Building, whose Fine Art section boasted an international selection of female artists' work including pieces by two generations of British painters, the most reported of which in Britain were Henrietta Ward (*Mrs Fry Visiting Newgate* 1876), Elizabeth Thompson Butler (*The Roll Call* 1874; *To the Front* 1888–89), Marianne Stokes (*Hail Mary* 1891; and others), Henrietta Rae (*Eurydice caught back to Hades* 1887; *La Cigale* 1891; *Doubts* 1886), Louise Jopling (*An English Maiden* date unknown), Elizabeth Armstrong Forbes (*The Witch* 1893), Annie Swynnerton (*Mater Triumphalis* 1892), Jessie MacGregor (*In the Reign of Terror* 1891), Helen Allingham (*The Sick Duckling* 1893; and others) and Clara Montalba (various Venetian scenes). Adding to the impact of this event for the issue under discussion here was the fact that fine art was noticed at far greater length by English reviewers than forms such as lace-work, leather-work and carving, which also featured in the Woman's Building displays.

One of the female artists representing Britain at the Chicago Fair, Henrietta Montalba, sister of Clara, who had been practising since the mid-1870s, died in September 1893. The conflict of opinion provoked by the visible professionalisation of the female artist was reflected in the comment with which Marion Hepworth Dixon opened the reminiscence of Montalba that he wrote for the *Art Journal*, saying:

> I do believe, one of the canons of the 'new' criticism – or at least the chief creed of one of its more truculent mouthpieces – is that women have been tried and found finally wanting, as original artistic exponents. This is neither the time nor the place to enter into the vexed question of sex in art, but were the question at issue, it is obvious that a pretty argument for the defence might be raised by the mention of the names of a dozen women who have of late gained little short of universal recognition. (215–17)

Not coincidentally, he was the brother of Ella Hepworth Dixon, one of the New Women novelists, whose *The Story of a Modern Woman,* with its failed artist heroine, came out in the same year that his article appeared: that is, in 1894.

The female artist was also conspicuous by this time in the expanding commercial sector of the British art world, indicating that she commanded considerable market value (although she was typically seen as a watercolourist and thus skirting amateur territory, according to the logic of gendered thinking). From Rose Barton at the Japanese Gallery in March 1893 to Kate Greenaway and Helen Allingham, at the Fine Art Society in January and March 1894, there was a procession of women through the dealer galleries of London. Indeed, these latter two must be reckoned amongst the best known artists of the day at this point in time. This implied a business-like acceptance among women of the commodification of art and the ability to produce for the open market in a timely and consistent manner. Though those who wished to elevate art above other bread-winning practices might disdain such proofs of professionalism, this trend demonstrated that women's artistry could hold its own in the multi-faceted profession that art making was in the late nineteenth-century city.

That the female artist had by no means yet, however, been given a future-proofed imprimatur is indicated by the development of the Tate Gallery of modern art, another prime event of the 1893–94 art scene (detailed for the *Art Journal* by Walter Armstrong). The nation already owned one piece of contemporary art by a woman, the Chantrey Bequest purchase of 1891, Anna Lea Merritt's child nude *Love Locked Out.* This had provoked the comment from the then President of the Royal Society of British Artists (Wyke Bayliss) that 'One of the loveliest of the Landmarks in the realms of Art has been discovered within the lifetimes of most of us. I mean the formal, authoritative recognition of the fact that women can paint pictures' (quoted in Treble 59). However, the immediate results of this alleged revelation were hardly positive, with only one woman's work offered by Henry Tate for this extension of the national art collection. This work – Elizabeth Lady Butler's *Remnant of an Army* – was given short shrift by some commentators, who generally preferred her *Scotland for Ever,* which was seen at the Guildhall loan exhibition of contemporary art in spring 1894. Furthermore, only three more women's works were added to the pool for the new gallery in the next few years (Lucy Kemp-Welch 1897; Mildred Butler 1896; Dorothy Stanley 1896) (Foster 7).

The contingent nature of the acceptance of the professional female artist is epitomized by the exhibition at the 1894 Royal Academy of Henrietta Rae's *Psyche before the Throne of Venus* (see Figure 8.4), an ambitious piece which may have been spurred by her ground-breaking inclusion in 1893 on the Hanging Committee of the Liverpool Autumn Exhibition, one of the most important annual shows of contemporary art outside London and a consistent showcase for women artists.

76 x 120

PSYCHE AT THE THRONE OF VENUS.

HENRIETTA RAE.

8.4 Henrietta Rae, 'Psyche before the Throne of Venus' from *Royal Academy Pictures* (1894). Supplement to *Magazine of Art* (1894): 13.

Though Neo-classicism had already been shown to be Rae's chosen mode, M.H. Spielmann, who reckoned himself a supporter of women artists, called it in a tone of affront 'a work we hardly expected from a woman' (Editor 'Royal' 274). The reviewer for *The Times* – by contrast, no friend to women's emancipation – suggested, however, that Rae's huge painting (6'4" x 12'), which was hung in a central and advantageous position, would be the one of its class not only 'most discussed' but 'probably most admired' ('Royal' 16). Certainly some in the Academy must have believed that the professional female artist's time had come, or were attempting to test whether or not that was so by its selection and placement. Opinion was vociferously divided over the work, and it is surely significant that the chief reproach made of Rae's *machine* was 'prettiness', an allegation not only of the inevitability of sexual difference but of a fundamental mismatch between femininity and the requirements of the classical tradition. That femininity was not, however, natural or inevitable to the female artist but was rather the socialised form of the female required by the belief in women's otherness could be seen from the recent exhibits in the neo-classical vein by Annie Swynnerton, *Cupid and Psyche* (Royal Academy 1891) and *Mater Triumphalis* (Royal Academy 1892). These had received from the same sector of opinion that poured scorn on Rae's magnum opus a shudder of disgust and revulsion. Those few who endorsed Swynnerton's advances into the highest realms of painting's tradition and those who supported Rae's were not identical: Swynnerton's *Mater Triumphalis* was purchased by Aestheticist Edmund Davies and Rae's *Psyche* by the mainstream George McCulloch. But those who rejected both women's forays into the Academy's topmost genre were surely united in their realisation that the professional woman artist was not necessarily going to perform in accordance with the precedents set by her male colleagues. While the scale and aim of Rae's work implied professionalism in its widely accepted sense, the negative responses to its assertiveness suggest that for proponents of the doctrine of sexual difference, Rae, like girly Angelica Kauffmann, had mistaken her talent for genius and, like deluded Dorothy, needed to be corrected for her own good; equally, for supporters of women's emancipation, Rae's feminine language gave in to men's traditional authority over classicism.

In sum, on re-examination the Royal Academy's concession in its Schools seems to have been more a symptom than a watershed. It was contemporaneous with other indicators of women's continuing move beyond the home and family into the wider world of citizenship and humanity: the revolt of the daughters, the battle for female suffrage, and the rise of the New Woman. An example of the fine-art dimension of this general trend is found in the Bible of popular culture, *Punch*, when George du Maurier suggested in 'Social Agonies' (9 June 1894) that by the mid-1890s women had taken over the guardianship of art, exposing men's habitual assumption of ownership thereof as a glib sham (see Figure 8.5). The stage presented further visions of women taking over from men: the figure of Vesta Tilley expressed, with her song 'Sisters', a solidarity amongst women that threatened to squeeze men out, while the latest production at the Court Theatre in the spring of 1893, A.W. Pinero's *The Amazons*, had female characters in knickerbockers prone to take the lead when dancing, handy with a rifle, and given to standing legs firmly planted apart and arms akimbo.

But the Royal Academy's liberalisation of women's participation did not change the terms of the insistent debate around women artists, rather merely modified them. The tools to explain away women's claim on art with a capital A were still ready to hand, with misogynists, recalcitrants and conservatives characterising the rising evidence of the female artist who saw herself as simply and unconditionally an artist as illustrating the lamentable fact that contemporary women were stupidly trying to imitate men and overturn the natural hierarchy of the sexes. Preaching the inherent superiority of domestic, marital and familial life over any other choice a woman might make, such reactionaries celebrated femininity as the antithesis of the qualities that make the respected artist, their discourse exposing femininity as the force which limits a talent to the ante-room of hobby and accomplishment. These voices were insistently audible in the years of the Academy's concession.

8.5 George du Maurier, 'Social Agonies' from *Punch*, 9 June 1894: 270.

In 1895 music critic Ernest Newman felt obliged to castigate those who 'have started out with the theory of the natural inferiority of women, have assumed – like Rousseau in the previous century, because it suited them to do so – that her "true" sphere was the home and her "true" function maternity, and then persuaded themselves that they had biological reasons for keeping her out of the universities and for denying her a vote' (Newman np).

It could be argued that by 1893 women such as Stokes, Forbes, MacGregor, Swynnerton, Allingham, Rae and the Montalba sisters had shown themselves capable of achieving professionalism without the Royal Academy's support – through its rivals the Slade School and the government-run South Kensington School, and the expansion of exhibition alternatives in the diversifying London art scene of the *fin de siècle*. Thus perhaps the Academy thought it could ill afford to look so comparatively *retardataire* as to keep its female students contained at mid-century levels. It can also be surmised that, with many male artists choosing to sidestep the Academy in their pursuit of professional success, it was bound to shore up its constituency however it could. But its deep-seated resistance to sharing with women the professional identity which its formation in 1768 was designed to establish is shown by the fact that membership of the institution itself, still a badge of a certain standard of achievement despite the mainstream's fading authority, was doggedly withheld from women for a further 30 years. Thus the Academy still invested in male privilege as a defining sign in the achievement of professionalism, even though it might have appeared in 1894 to be encouraging women to participate in the aspiration towards professional status. To believers, membership of the Academy marked the artist as not only a professional but a gentleman: it wasn't until the gentleman himself had become passé that the artist could incontrovertibly and uncontroversially be a woman.

## Works Cited

'Angelica Kauffmann'. *Art Journal,* 1 January 1893: 26.

Armstrong, Walter. 'The Henry Tate Collection'. *Art Journal,* 1 March 1893: 65–71; 1 April 1893: 121–6; 1 May 1893: 129–34; 1 July 1893: 193–8; 1 October 1893: 299–301; 1 June 1894: 177–80; 1 July 1894: 193–6.

'Art Notes'. *Illustrated London News,* 25 March 1893: 376.

'Art Notes'. *Illustrated London News,* 20 May 1893: 612.

'Books of the Week'. *The Times,* 29 September 1892: 4.

'Dorothy's Career'. *Girl's Own Paper* 15 (3 March 1894): 344–5; 10 March 1894: 362–3; 17 March 1894: 376–9.

Doughty, Terri. *Selections from* The Girl's Own Paper, *1880–1914*. Peterborough: Broadview, 2004.

EBS [Eve Blantyre Simpson]. 'The Paintings and Etchings of Elizabeth Stanhope Forbes'. *The Studio* 4 ([date uncertain] 1894): 186–92.

Editor. 'The Old Masters Exhibition'. *Magazine of Art* 15 (1 January 1893): 113–14.

——. 'The Royal Academy 1894. I'. *Magazine of Art* 16 (1 April 1894): 218.

——. 'The Royal Academy, 1894. II'. *Magazine of Art* 16 (1 May 1894): 269–74.

'Elections at the Royal Academy of Arts'. *Art Journal,* 1 December 1893: 361–2.

'Exhibitions'. *Magazine of Art* 16 (1 July 1894): xxxviii.

Foster, Alicia. *Tate Women*. London: Tate Gallery Publications, 2004.

Gaze, Delia, ed. *Dictionary of Women Artists*. 2 vols. London and Chicago: Fitzroy Dearborn Publishers, 1997.

Hepworth Dixon, Marion. 'Henrietta Montalba, a Reminiscence'. *Art Journal,* 1 July 1894: 215–17.

Hutchison, Sidney. *The History of the Royal Academy*. London: Chapman & Hall, 1968.

'Illustrated Review'. *Illustrated London News,* 11 March 1893: 296.

Jeune, Mary, ed. *Ladies at Work*. London: A.D. Innes and Co., 1893.

'Lady Waterford's Painting'. *Saturday Review* 74 (28 May 1892): 627.

'Lady Waterford's Sketches'. *Pall Mall Budget* no. 1237 (9 June 1892): 834.

Moore, George. *Modern Painting*. London: Walter Scott, 1893.

Newman, Ernest. 'Women and Music'. *Free Review* 4 (1895): np.

Postlethwaite, Helen. 'Some Rising Artists'. *Magazine of Art* 16 (1 January 1894): 114.

Reason, Florence. 'Art'. *Ladies at Work*. Ed. Mary Jeune. London: A.D. Innes and Co., 1893. 44–51.

'Recent Exhibitions'. *Magazine of Art* 15 (1 June 1893): xxxv.

'Recent Illustrated Books'. *Art Journal,* 1 September 1893: 273–4.

'Royal Academy'. *Athenaeum,* 29 April 1893: 542.

'Royal Academy'. *Athenaeum*, 2 June 1894: 715.
'Royal Academy'. *The Times*, 5 May 1894: 16.
Spielmann, M[arion] H[arry]. 'The Noble Amateur'. *Magazine of Art* 16 (1 December 1892): 62–4.
Thackeray, Miss [Anne]. *Miss Angel*. London: Smith, Elder & Co., 1875, 1884.
Treble, Rosemary. *Great Victorian Pictures*. London: ACGB, 1978.

# PART III

## The Craft of Self-Fashioning

# 9

## Negotiating Fame: Mid-Victorian Women Writers and the Romantic Myth of the Gentlemanly Reviewer

*Kyriaki Hadjiafxendi*

The feeling which lies at the bottom of our great admiration for old books, and which causes us to exaggerate their merits, has yet to be analysed. (Lewes 145)

George Eliot did not see herself as occupying the same position as popular women authors. George Henry Lewes's practical note of 1877 to John Blackwood communicates, perhaps with a degree of envy, Eliot's anxiety about her potentially declining readership: 'While Mrs. Henry Wood, Miss Braddon, Wilkie Collins etc. sell their novels at 6/- surely G.E. may expect a public?' (Eliot, *Letters* VI.345). Braddon and Eliot embodied rival models of authorship, as professional women writers; yet, they were affected by the same pressures about respectability, fame and notoriety. Like Eliot, who supported Lewes and his legal family, Braddon used the earnings from her serial fiction to provide for her partner, the publisher John Maxwell (whom she finally married in 1874 after the death of his estranged and institutionalised wife), their five illegitimate children and the children of his legal marriage. A comparison between Eliot's and Braddon's engagement with the difficulties of public renown reveals its destabilising effect upon mid-Victorian women's authorial identities, and can help us rethink how the process of female professionalisation was shaped in response to, and through, the intense personalisation of the figure of the author.

Contemporary scholarship on Eliot (Tush), Braddon (Gilbert; Palmer; Tomaiulo) as well as Victorian popular fiction (Cvetkovich; King; Tromp), has demonstrated that popular and elite literary cultures were not hermetically sealed from each other. A comparative examination of Eliot's and Braddon's negotiations with literary fame demonstrates that not only were they unable to police their reputation, but they were also subjected to the conflation of their lives with their work. Despite the growth of recent studies on celebrity culture in the long nineteenth century (see Mole; Salmon), there is still a paucity of scholarship on women writers and the different, sometimes contrary, ways they were both subjects and objects of celebrity (see Hawkins and Ives). This chapter argues that, when dealing with literary renown, Braddon and Eliot appropriated the critical models of the late Romantic period to meet their own creative needs. For all their differences, it is notable that when responding to the commercial dynamic of the mid-Victorian literary market-place, both Eliot and Braddon turned to the past and deployed the notion of 'gentlemanly' reviewing as a way of managing their authorial identities. This type of appropriation accords with what Ann Rigney calls 'procreativity' (12); that is, the capacity of the past to generate new models of authorship in the form of other texts and media. Eliot's and Braddon's appropriation of Romantic print culture is an index to their self-fashioning in the 1850s and 1860s. The fact that these two women writers felt the need to deploy the model of the 'gentlemanly' reviewer (and the patriarchal structures embedded in its mythology) manifests the still inchoate nature of their professionalism.

In explaining how Romantic print culture became an all-pervasive point of reference, this chapter argues that Eliot's and Braddon's engagement was with an invented tradition of 'gentlemanly' publishing. As David Stewart has pointed out, periodical literature in the Romantic period was part of the 'commercial culture which it denounced' (2); the '*Edinburgh Review* wholly changed the perception of the republic of letters as a genteel space occupied by men of leisure' with its ruthless reviewing style (25). Romantic magazines and metropolitan literary culture provided Eliot and Braddon a model for analysing their own authorship in relation to the expectations of the reading public and conceptualising how their editorial and literary careers, including adopting and maintaining their pseudonyms, were influenced by the shifting character of the publishing industry. But what is revealing in their invocations of 'Romanticism and its legacies'[1] is that whereas Eliot claimed to be genuinely interested in the more conservative model of the 'gentlemanly' reviewer, Braddon deployed it as a much more nuanced performance in defence of her reputation. Instead of creating shared narratives and hence collectivising a memory of the past, Eliot and Braddon used Romantic print culture as a template to articulate seemingly contrasting values and to define conflicting identities for their authorships.

In her first novel *Adam Bede* (1859), for example, Eliot conservatively compared the progressive character of the mid-Victorian period to the Romantic past, when the man of letters used to make sense of himself through a slower, more solitary contemplation. Eliot's lament over the bygone age of 'Old Leisure' can be read as a critique of the age of sensation, in which the self dispersed under the sway of a constant procession of amusements. It anticipates the way in which her literary work was distinguished from sensation fiction not because of the absence of sensation but because of the alternative type of feeling she aimed at evoking: 'Only in sympathy', claims Ludwig Feuerbach, whom she translated in 1854, 'does sensation rise into feeling' (283). In the following extract Eliot's reimagining of the 'gentlemanly' figure of 'Old Leisure' includes an unhurried simpler world of print media, characterised by the solitary newspaper rather than the succession of periodicals and 'exciting novels':

> Ingenious philosophers tell you, perhaps, that the great work of the steam-engine is to create leisure for mankind. Do not believe them: it only creates a vacuum for eager thought to rush in. Even idleness is eager now – eager for amusement: prone to excursion-trains, art-museums, periodical literature, and exciting novels: prone even to scientific theorizing, and cursory peeps through microscopes. Old Leisure was quite a different personage: he only read one newspaper, innocent of leaders, and was free from that periodicity of sensations which we call post-time. He was a contemplative, rather stout gentleman, of excellent digestion, – of quiet perceptions undiseased by hypothesis: happy in his inability to know the causes of things, preferring the things themselves. He lived chiefly in the country, among pleasant seats and homesteads, and was fond of sauntering by the fruit-tree wall, and scenting the apricots when they were warmed by the morning sunshine, … (*Adam Bede* 559– 60)

Although aware of its own nostalgia, this extract's looking backwards to the standards of a 'gentlemanly' past is key to understanding Eliot's response to literary fame and more particularly what she called the 'disagreables of reputation' (*Letters* II.292). In *The Spanish Gypsy* (1868), which marks her poetic debut, Eliot finds another way to reconstitute Romanticism through the Byronic hero of Don Juan. Though a fifteenth-century character, Eliot's Juan still embodies the Romantic ideal of the solitary poet who lives free from market saturation. Eliot's dialectical response to Byron's poem, and Romantic print culture more generally, comes to affirm her idealistic desire for artistic freedom, truthfulness and experimentation against the grain of the commercial popularity of her work. As Eliot put it in a letter of July 1862 to Sara Sophia Hennel about her writing of her novel *Romola* that was serialised in the *Cornhill Magazine* from July 1862 to August 1863:

> Of necessity, the book is addressed to fewer readers than my previous works, and I myself have never expected – I might rather say *intended* – that the book should be as 'popular' in the same sense as the others. If one is to have freedom to write out one's own varying unfolding self, and not be a machine always grinding out the same material or spinning the same sort of web, one cannot always write for the same public. (*Letters* IV.49)

Linda Peterson has recently explored the question of how Victorian women who entered the profession of letters 'articulated their role as authors, negotiated the material conditions of authorship, and constructed myths of the woman author, often against the material realities' (5–6). This mythological construction was self-conscious and performative in that it offered women writers a set of strategies that they could use to define their roles. Thinking about female authorship in these terms can help to explain why both Eliot and Braddon turned back to a masculine mode of gentlemanly authorship to defend themselves against the demands of literary renown in the mid-Victorian literary market-place. The boom of the shilling monthlies in the 1860s was accompanied by a more aggressive style of publishing, not of the gentlemanly sort, which catered for the reading public's craving for biographical detail. The issue was no longer whether the 'inconvenience of celebrity' was, in Elizabeth Barrett's (later Browning) words, 'a noble tax to pay' in exchange of the love they incited in their audience (II.375). Rather it was more about the management of the structures of feeling generated by a publicity-hungry culture.

It is within this context that Eliot's and Braddon's adoption of masculine personae and the rhetorical discourse of 'gentlemanliness' needs to be seen. In 1859, the well-known critic E.S. Dallas would also bemoan the way in which authors and editors encouraged the personalising of their relationship with the reader through photographs, engravings and biographies as well as literary tourism:

> Think of the rage for biographical incidents, and personal details, and private diaries, which has been developed of late years – think of all the biographical dictionaries and portrait galleries that have been sold – and observe how vigorously the photograph and the etching have ministered to this craving for personal acquaintance, how the cheapness of travelling has brought a legion of visitors to the door of every celebrity, … (188–9)

What Dallas had in mind were publications like *The Annual Gift Book: A Drawing-Room Portrait Gallery of Eminent Personages* (1859), which claimed to be mediating what was seen as the reading public's natural and healthy desire to have personal intercourse with literary celebrities by offering up their photographic likeness together with their authorised biographies ('Preface' iii).

Eliot and Braddon had a similar yet antithetical response to the type of public intimacy and immediacy described by Dallas's critique. Whereas Braddon manipulated her reputation to police what she saw as the public's natural desire to have personal intercourse with popular authors, a mortified George Eliot encouraged her middle-class readership, after the example of Sir Walter Scott, to develop a sympathetic relationship with her characters rather than an intimate one with herself. While there has been much work on the scope and limitations of sympathetic feeling in Eliot's work (see Ablow), little reflection has been conducted on how it was informed by her experience of lionised fame and, more particularly, of the fraught dynamics between literary celebrity and female authorship in the mid-Victorian period.

Deriving from the Greek words συν (with) and πάθος (feeling), which means 'with emotion', rather than being 'in an emotional state', sympathy is the imaginative ability to understand otherness in its difference. Eliot's privileging of sympathetic feeling over intimacy is crucial to her efforts to empower herself – to legitimate her own difference[2] – as an elite author within a publicity-hungry culture. Whereas her publisher John Blackwood kept congratulating her on being 'a *popular* as well as a great author', Eliot was still haunted by the dread of 'the large section of Novel readers who have little or no mind to give' (*Letters* III.33). In her letter of 25 November 1859 to Charles Bray, Eliot tried to imagine for herself how it would feel to yield to the temptations of financial success to which popular serial novelists succumbed. Her imagining consolidated rather than eradicated her feeling of otherness within the literary market-place:

> Do you see how the publishing world is going mad on periodicals? If I could be seduced by such offers, I might have written three poor novels and made my fortune in one year. Happily I have no need to exert myself when I say, 'Avoid thee Satan!' Satan, in the form of bad writing and good pay is not seductive to me. (*Letters* III.214)

Eliot's narrative of temptation and deception communicates her anxiety about the exploitation of her literary success by unscrupulous publishers. When one publisher, T.C. Newby, attempted to produce the false impression that *Adam Bede, Junior* was a sequel to *Adam Bede*, Eliot was highly concerned that this piracy would contribute to her growing reputation as a 'popular author' (*Letters* III.211–13). What made the 'Newby affair' particularly upsetting to her is that it followed the false attribution of the authorship of *Adam Bede* to Joseph Liggins of Nuneaton. In 'Leaves from a Note-Book' (1884), Eliot makes the point that, it is 'lawful' for an author to want to sell one's work at a good price, but inexcusable 'to force or hurry his production' for the sake of 'bringing up his income to the fancy pitch' (*Essays* 359). Castigating anybody who carried on authorship with what she called 'the principle of the gin-palace', she argues that when a writer's interest in the economics of publishing dominated over one's artistic vocation, the author is 'on the level with the manufacturer who gets rich by fancy-wares coloured with arsenic green' (359). In the same volume, Eliot also tellingly declares that 'Sympathetic people are often incommunicative about themselves: they give back reflected images which hide their own depths' (377). Her self-fashioned image as the 'Great Unknown', as she put it, was one of these images behind which she hid in order to empty out her name from her personality and separate her life from work.

By focussing on the controversy around Eliot's and Braddon's use of pseudonyms in 1859 and 1867 respectively, I will now compare and contrast their manipulation of masculine authorial personae and the discourse of 'gentlemanly' criticism and reviewing. In a letter to John Blackwood on

December 1, 1858, George Eliot noted that, if there were rumours concerning her authorship, they could be contradicted after the example of Sir Walter Scott who was well-known for taking serious precautions to maintain his secrecy. Alluding to Scott's 'General Preface' to the *Waverley Novels*, in which he explained the reasons behind his anonymous authorship, Eliot declared that, like Scott, she preferred to deny the rumour rather than give an equivocal answer or surrender her identity:

> If it [the rumour of the authorship of 'George Eliot'] reach us in the way of question, it will be met with direct contradiction, for I am of Scott's opinion on that point. An incognito can be maintained on no other condition, and in such a case one ought to say "No" to an impertinent querist as one would decline to open one's iron chest to a burglar. (*Letters* II.505)

Eliot's description of the impertinent reader as a burglar reveals how strongly she felt about her right to anonymity. What exactly was such a burglar stealing though? A name? An identity? A mask? Ever since the publication of her first collection of short stories *Scenes of Clerical Life* (1858), followed by that of her first novel *Adam Bede*, there were widespread rumours about the identity of 'George Eliot'. These were fuelled when one Reverend Anders of Kirby wrote to *The Times* to assert that Joseph Liggins of Nuneaton was indeed George Eliot. The more Eliot insisted on keeping her identity secret, the more her readers looked to locate 'George Eliot' and the originals of her literary characters in real life. Eliot initially found the rumours about 'Mr. Liggins or some other "Mr." who knows Coton stories' amusing, and went along with John Blackwood's and Lewes's exploitation of the rumour to increase the sales of her work. It was only when the rumour was stated in *The Times* that, for her, 'lionised' fame became synonymous with the abuse of literary integrity.

What Eliot disliked about the 'Liggins affair' was not simply the false attribution of her books to somebody else but the type of biographical reader that Anders and his champions represented. Eliot's anxiety about the unwanted attention she received was stimulated by her resistance to the commodification of her authorial figure. In her letter of February 24, 1859, to her publisher John Blackwood, Eliot adopted a Romantic persona by imagining herself as a solitary writer, living 'apart from the world, with no opportunity of observing the effect of books' (*Letters* III.23). Eliot's experience of fame after the publication of *Adam Bede* made her see her readers' affection as an attempt to turn her into a spectacle of personality. Eliot demanded that both Blackwood and Lewes mediate her relationship with readers and critics against whom she felt that she needed to be safeguarded.

Significantly, when Lewes wrote as 'George Eliot' in a rejoinder to *The Times*, he publicly defended her right to anonymity in the name of the bygone 'gentlemanly standards' of reviewing:

> Allow me to ask whether the act of publishing a book deprives a man of all claim to the courtesies usual among gentlemen? If not, the attempt to pry into what is obviously meant to be withheld – my name – and to publish the rumours which such prying may give rise to, seems to me quite indefensible, still more so to state these rumours as ascertained truths. (Eliot, *Letters* III.50)

The revelation of Eliot's identity as Marian Evans Lewes coincided with the advent of signed publication in highbrow journals such as *Macmillan's Magazine* (1859), followed by *Cornhill Magazine* (1860) and *Fortnightly Review* (1865). In cross-dressing as George Eliot, Lewes connects the erosion of the publishing policy of anonymity with that of the gentlemanly standards of reviewing. For him, this phenomenon seems to imply that readers' and critics' speculations over the author's life take over the contemplation of the literary work. Following Anders's assertions in *The Times*, the 'Literary Chronicle of the Week' of the *Leader* and the weekly gossip column of the *Athenaeum* used the vexing question about the author of *Adam Bede* as an excuse to launch a more general attack against the convention of anonymity. A comparative reading of these two responses to Lewes's letter to the editor of *The Times*, signed 'George Eliot', demonstrates the way that Eliot's appropriation of Scott's 'gentlemanly' model of authorship simply did not get any cultural traction in the literary market-place of the 1850s, and was actually misunderstood and misinterpreted by contemporary reviewers.

Comparing the 'Liggins affair' to a similar controversy over the authorship of Robert Chambers's anonymously published *Vestiges of the Natural History of Creation* (1844), the reviewer in the *Leader* drew attention to the way Eliot constructed her authorial figure after Scott's reputation as the 'Great Unknown'. As is well known, Scott initially published his *Waverley Novels* anonymously, not revealing his identity in print until 1827. Although Scott stayed anonymous in part because he was a social climber and the novel was a low form, in his 1829 'General Preface', he claimed that his decision to maintain his anonymity stemmed partly from his inherent personal character and inclination and partly from the fact that he had already enjoyed a considerable amount of literary success. The following quotation from the *Leader*'s article of April 23, 1859, is interesting in that, while invoking Scott, it suggests that his model was no longer tenable in the late 1850s in the face of the commercialism that Eliot so disliked:

> Scarcely has the *vexata quaestio* about the authorship of the 'Vestiges' died away, when a sort of minor squabble about who wrote a moderately successful novel, called 'Adam Bede' follows in its wake. From some cause or causes unexplained, the author of this ephemeral trifle chooses to conceal his name, and affect the airs of a 'Great Unknown'. … To mystify the matter still more, it is now said that Eliot is not Eliot, but merely a *nom de plume*. Now, what nonsense this is! What right has Mr. Eliot, or Mr. Blank, *alias* Eliot, to assume that there is any courtesy to prevent the discovery of his identity? … let us hear no more of Mr. Eliot's interpretation of the 'courtesies

usual among gentlemen'. Let him tell the truth as to his name, and shame Mr. Anders. ('Literary' 524)

More precisely, the *Athenaeum* accused Eliot of manufacturing the Liggins affair as a stage-managed diversion from her own authorship, with the ultimate aim of calling greater attention to her personality in order to artificially encourage public discussion of *Adam Bede*. As it was argued in 'Our Weekly Gossip' of July 2, 1859, 'George Eliot' was nothing but a commodity, a label that was being strategically manipulated and puffed in order to enhance the celebrity of both fiction and author:

> It is time to end this pother about the authorship of 'Adam Bede'. The writer is in no sense a 'great unknown'; the tale, if bright in parts, and such as a clever woman with an observant eye and unschooled moral nature might have written, has no great quality of any kind. Long ago we hinted our impression that Mr. Liggins, with his poverty and his pretensions, was a mystification, got up by George Eliot, – as the showman in a country fair sets up a second learned pig to create a division among the penny paying rustics. … The elaborate attempt to mystify the reading public, pursued in many articles and letters at the same time, but with the same Roman hand observable in all, is itself decisive of the writer's power. No woman of genius ever condescended to such a *ruse*, – no book was ever permanently helped by such a trick. (20)

What makes the critique in this letter so strident is that it followed the rumours, let out by Herbert Spencer and John Chapman, suggesting that the author of *Adam Bede* was Marian Evans Lewes, a woman in partnership with a married man. While the *Leader* saw Eliot's following in the path of Scott as an authentic attempt to maintain her distance from her readership, the *Athenaeum* saw it as a commercial ruse from a 'fallen woman' with an abundance of 'showy sentiment' ('Our' 20). It interpreted the manipulation of Eliot's readership as a proof that the moral sentiments of her literary work were not underwritten by the personal character of the author. 'George Eliot' was accused of being merely a manufactured performance, a type of popular show.

The *Athenaeum*'s stinging attack against 'George Eliot' illustrates the problematic nature of anonymous/pseudonymous authorship in the context of the changing dynamics of the literary market-place. Tellingly, the *Athenaeum* was not alone in its suspicions; a critic in *The Era* similarly remarked of the public mystery and that 'In America we should know that the whole squabble was got up to increase the notoriety of the book, but both ADAM BEDE and Messrs. BLACKWOOD are far above any such unworthy devices' ('Topics' 9). The adoption of 'George Eliot' could not express the author's dislike of being turned into a spectacle of personality because, in these more commercial times, the pseudonym risked being sceptically seen as a ploy to enhance the interest in her identity. It seems that it was primarily Blackwood's carefully nurtured reputation and traditions, which, as David Finkelstein has shown, were founded on a paternalistic regard for its 'family' of authors as well its appreciation for literary taste, that helped to validate its assertions over the identity of 'George Eliot' (21–48). Even the *Illustrated Times* questioned the veracity of the letter from 'George Eliot' of *The Times* denying the authorship of Liggins, noting that it 'need not have much weight, as it bore no address, and if false, could not easily have been detected' ('Author' 7). In fact, it was argued, in a fashion akin to *The Era*, that 'Messrs. Blackwood were the proper persons to move in this matter' (7), as their established reputation carried far more weight than a pseudonymous author. Revealingly, one of the reasons why John Blackwood did not write to *The Times* to counter the 'Liggins business' in the way that Eliot desired was that 'we thought our doing so might be interpreted as a publishing dodge to reraise the discussion and stimulate curiosity' (Eliot, *Letters* III.58). It was only when Charles Bracebridge of Atherstone accused him of not paying Liggins for *Adam Bede* that Blackwood recognised the seriousness of the situation and saw the need to put an end to Liggins's hustling for money from the reading public.

Blackwood's judgment of the publishing industry was probably more accurate than that of Lewes's and Eliot's nostalgic reimagining of Romantic models of gentlemanly authorship. He feared that, given that 'some of the myrmidons of the press do not seem disposed to admit an author's right to privacy', a protest from his firm might encourage those supporting the removal of anonymity to turn the case of 'George Eliot' into a *cause célèbre* (Eliot, *Letters* III.58). His caution illustrates the difficulties of maintaining Eliot's pseudonym at a time when the mood towards anonymity was undergoing a significant shift: it had become a mask that invited further attention rather than deflecting it. The fact that Blackwood made a public statement only after the reputation of his firm was at stake was a sign, in the eyes of Eliot, that the 'gentlemanly standards', to which she adhered and she thought that the House of Blackwood represented (at least ideologically), were of a bygone age.

The performativity that the *Athenaeum* detected in Eliot's reliance on Scott's model of anonymous authorship intriguingly corresponds to Braddon's astute yet defensive deployment of a similar discourse of gentlemanly publishing in response to a literary controversy she became embroiled in during 1867 over the authorship of *Circe*, a novel then being serialised in *Belgravia*. It was a furore that the *London Review* compared to one of her own sensational plots, 'a delicious mystery which only wants a murder, a bigamy, and a fair-haired tigress to make it complete' ('Miss' 372). Whereas the 'Liggins affair' made evident to Eliot that she was as much in need of sympathy from her readers as she was incapable of bending herself to their tastes, Braddon moved and manoeuvred between different authorial personae and roles, deploying each like a performance for a specific audience. Such multiple identities were, in part, the product of her various activities as writer and editor, as well as the publication of her first serial fiction in a variety of cheap periodicals. 'The Black Band; Or, The Mysteries of Midnight', for example, was initially published under the pseudonym of 'Lady Caroline Lascelles' in the *Halfpenny Journal* from July 1861 to July 1862. Yet despite these pseudonyms, as the above comment from the *London Review* suggests, her celebrity meant that there was a countervailing desire to conflate her life with the sensationalism of her fiction. Such conflation could accentuate Braddon's notoriety, but could equally damage her professional status. As Patricia Zakreski has argued,

> The belief in literature as a revelation of personality was repeatedly denied by writers throughout the second half of the nineteenth century not only because it destabilised private respectability; it also undermined the perception of literature as a professional occupation for both men and women. (138)

Like Eliot and the 'Liggins' affair, the *Circe* controversy demonstrates how Braddon negotiated issues of status, professional hierarchy and authorial identity within a heterogeneous literary market-place; like Eliot, when most under critical pressure, she returned to models of gentlemanly publishing to defend herself.

The way Braddon tried to control the making of her own reputation is often linked to her early career as an actress. Acting as a profession invited a more intimate relationship with the body of the female performer, which contrasts with the mediation that comes with print. More generally, Beth Palmer has argued that in the case of sensationalist women in the 1860s, particularly Braddon, Ellen Wood and Florence Marryat, the press functioned as 'their stage, and imagining it as such allowed them to exert authority in a male-dominated magazine market' (1). Braddon's *Circe* spat is an example of the performative character of her authorship and her ability to turn the patriarchal values of the periodical press against itself, but it is equally a cautionary tale of how such performativity could undermine her authorial reputation.

The nature of Braddon's success was shaped by the growing dominance of literary celebrity. One of the mechanisms that made this possible was serial publication in that its sustained regularity made writers and their work part of their readers' everyday, affective lives (see Hughes and Lund; Turner). Braddon's work exhibits a knowing attitude towards the reading public's biographical approach to authorship, which was one by-product of the increasing transformation of writers into celebrities. In *The Doctor's Wife* (1864), first serialised in the shilling monthly *Temple Bar* (of which John Maxwell was the publisher), Braddon pokes fun at the naivety with which readers built up authorial personalities. She does this through the character of the sensation novelist, Sigismund Smith – a celebrity of penny serial fiction whose readers desire him to resemble the Byronic heroes of his fiction:

People who were impressed by his fictions, and were curious to see him, generally left him with a strong sense of disappointment, if not indignation. [They had their own idea of what the author of the *Smuggler's Bride* and *Lilia the Deserted* ought to be, and Mr Smith did not at all come up to the popular standard; so the enthusiastic admirers of his romances were apt to complain of him as an impostor when they beheld him in private life.]

Was this meek young man the Byronic hero they had pictured? Was this the author of *Colonel Montefiasco, or the Brand upon the Shoulder-blade?* They had imagined a splendid creature, half magician, half brigand, with a pale face and fierce black eyes, a tumbled mass of raven hair, a bare white throat, a long black-velvet dressing-gown, and thin tapering hands with queer agate and onyx rings coiling up the flexible fingers. (13)

On the one hand, Braddon sympathetically depicts the demands placed upon authors by the desires readers invested in them (although a more sceptical interpretation of this episode might be that it conveniently pushes responsibility for celebrity onto readers and thereby downplays the agency of writers in creating their own sensational reputations). Conversely, Sigismund Smith seems to be a kind of playful mask, inviting the reader to discern in him her own experience even as she displaces it onto one of her characters.

Braddon enjoyed a position of prominence, security and status when she became the editor of *Belgravia*, a role she occupied from November 1866 to February 1876. She was the leading light of the journal; the frontispiece declared that it was 'Conducted by M.E. Braddon', and, as Palmer notes, she 'performed varying voices in all of its genres', writing 'articles on French novels, on the position of women in contemporary society, on periodical literature, and on numerous other subjects' (58). In contrast to Eliot who relied on the silence of friends and the support of publisher and partner, Braddon used her editorial power and the patriarchal standards of criticism to defend her work and, as importantly, her right to have multiple authorial identities. In 1867, the *Pall Mall Gazette* justly made accusations of plagiarism against her story *Circe*, which was serialised in *Belgravia* under the male pseudonym Babington White, claiming that it was largely modelled on Octave Fuillet's *Dahlia* (1857), and reproduced virtually verbatim a number of scenes and incidents. The *Pall Mall Gazette* then published a purported response from Braddon – in her role as editor – in which she proclaimed to have been wronged by the plagiarism:

Let me at once assure your readers, those who are subscribers to *Belgravia*, that I was unconscious of Mr. Babington White's deception, he having undertaken to contribute an original novel. As the worker of precious metals will never refuse for his honour's sake to take back the base stuff he may have sold, unconsciously, for gold, so I should wish at once to publish my willingness to return the amounts paid by my subscribers for those numbers of *Belgravia* in which 'Circe' has usurped a place. (Braddon, 'Mr.' 3)

Such a penitent offer to refund subscribers was munificent; however, it was indeed too good to be true in that the letter was seemingly forged, and the exaggerated concern expressed with literary quality, authenticity and integrity was itself an ironic hit at Braddon. In response, she published an outraged letter offering 100 guineas reward for discovery of the imposter ('Metropolitan' 6). The *Pall Mall Gazette* then published an anonymous letter commenting that no 'professional *litterateur*' had ever met Babington White; most suspected that no such figure existed and that *Circe* had been written 'by a certain lady novelist of considerable popularity' (Mag's Man 4). (*The Doctor's Wife* had similarly been a loose translation of Gustave Flaubert's *Madame Bovary* (1856) so Braddon had a track record of liberal borrowing.)

In this spat of presumed and assumed identities, Braddon's pseudonymous identity as 'Babington White' was widely commented upon. The *Saturday Review* noted that no sensation in her novels could match that aroused by the controversy over her supposed pseudonym and related plagiarism ('Romance' 399). It is also important to note that it was part of an ongoing critical effort to fix, perhaps restrict, the performativity of Braddon's multiple literary activities; only four months previously in March 1867, there had been a dispute between Hugh Morgan of the *Athenaeum* and John Maxwell regarding her use of pseudonyms in her early work, and her concomitant unwillingness to subsequently take responsibility for them:

> As Miss Braddon does not seem inclined to 'give her explanation' as to whether she is or is not the author of 'The Black Band' ('Diavola', I believe, is not denied) but is content that Lady Caroline Lascelles (whoever she may be) should have the credit of it, I think, on looking at the facts, there will be no difficulty in setting this vexed question at rest. … Surely all this would lead to the fact that the Lady Caroline Lascelles of the *Halfpenny Journal* is the Miss Braddon of *Belgravia*; and surely in the interests of literature it behoves Mr. Maxwell that he should lose no time in giving his explanation of this scandal, which may be used to Miss Braddon's disadvantage. (Morgan 290)

Maxwell indignantly refused to confirm or deny Morgan's accusation, and the affair rumbled on for several months, segueing into the *Circe* controversy. As Jennifer Hedgecock has noted, Braddon's authorship of her early work was relatively obvious, but what was at stake in the public accusations of disguise and deception was the insinuation 'that the subversive nature of her fiction exposed something about *her* character, *her* past' (100).

Unsurprisingly, criticism of the *Circe* plagiarism often honed in upon the loss of Braddon's professional status and reputation; her pseudonym as 'Babington White' was tied into a belief that she was using it as a disguise to treat literature as a commodity. The *Kentish Gazette* bemoaned that this was another episode that would make it more difficult for writers to claim the status of authorship as a profession, noting that 'Literature in this country is struggling to be accepted as a profession, and to have its members accepted into that brotherhood which men belonging to the learned professions maintain' ('New' 2). The gendered 'brotherhood' of this prospective community only accentuates Braddon's crime: for the *Kentish Gazette*, cuckoos in the nest like Braddon needed to be expelled from the 'brotherhood' of literature in order for professional status and homosocial fraternity to be achieved. Again, as with George Eliot and *Adam Bede*, the *Kentish Gazette* wondered whether the whole furore might have been an 'advertising "dodge" were it not so clumsy and ineffective' ('New' 2). The *Saturday Review* similarly believed that the affair marked Braddon's forfeiture of her claim to literary and professional respectability; rather than her pseudonym functioning as a desire for anonymity, it was another example of her unchecked desire for popular adulation and celebrity:

> If, wearied with the glitter of fame and name, she chooses to mix with the crowd in disguise, why should she not? The Caliph used to mix with his subjects in the humble apparel of a porter. On the same principle, Miss Braddon is, without any breach of moral or literary law, perfectly free to descend from her lofty throne, and take her place in the rank of magazine-writers, just like any common unqueenly person. … Perhaps she was tormented with a conquerer's craving for new realms to conquer. … She had covered the name of Braddon with immortal glory. But this may have palled on a nature of sublime capacity. So she created Babington White somewhat in her own image, and him too she resolved to crown with laurels. ('Romance' 399)

Such a narrative highlights how Braddon's authorial performativity could be turned against her; whereas other women writers might adopt pseudonyms as a sign of their demure respectability, the *Saturday Review* turned this narrative inside out. Not satisfied with her own fame, Braddon needed the alter ego of Babington White to confirm her adulation.

Braddon's most significant response to the '*Circe* affair' was 'A Remonstrance', an article published in *Belgravia* in November 1867 in which she attacked the irresponsible power of the critic, and in particular the *Pall Mall Gazette*'s focus on her biographical identity. This piece was only possible due to the platform given to her as editor, and Palmer has correspondingly noted that it was 'her author-editorship that allowed Braddon most control over the performative display of her celebrity persona and of the genre for which she was famous' (15). Fascinatingly though, given that the whole furore concerned the adoption of unacknowledged pseudonyms, and just as Braddon previously depicted the pressures of celebrity through the male writer Sigismund Smith, in 'A Remonstrance' (1867), she adopts the voice of Captain Shandon, the original founder of the fictional *Pall Mall Gazette* in W.M. Thackeray's *The History of Pendennis* (1850). Thackeray's Captain Shandon prepares the prospectus of 'The Pall Mall Gazette' in the Marshalsea as 'written by gentlemen for gentlemen'. Braddon plays upon the 'gentlemanly' standards adopted by the *Pall Mall Gazette* under Shandon's imaginary stewardship, which themselves derived from the well-established Reviews of the Regency period such as the *Edinburgh Review* and *Quarterly Review*:

> By what right, sir, do you ask to know more of any author than the book which it is your pleasure to review, and the name on the title-page of that book? … [I]t can be no more necessary for you to know what manner of man he is than it is necessary for him to discover the name of that accomplished critic who, in truculence of temper and choice of diction, resembles rather the Jeffreys of the Bloody Assize than the caustic chief of the *Edinburgh Review*. (Shandon 82)

Braddon as Shandon judges the criticism she received as a failed attempt to reproduce not so much the famous slashing style of the reviewer Francis Jeffreys, but the Judge Jeffreys who was famous for presiding over the Bloody Assizes in 1685, ordering large numbers of public executions for treason.

Even though there was a world of difference between the old quarterlies and the new shilling monthlies, Braddon argues that, in contrast to other famous examples of personal criticism given to such as 'Mr. Wordsworth' and 'Mr. Tennyson', the attack against her was not legitimate because it was 'not against the writer of the work you dislike, but against the Lady who conducts the Magazine in which the work appeared' (Shandon 81). The critic had no right to know the identity or personality of the author beyond the name that appeared on the title page, because he himself published anonymously. In the following extract, Braddon emphasises how far removed the editor of the *Pall Mall Gazette* – a journal supposedly written by gentlemen for gentlemen – is from the standards of 'gentlemanly' reviewing set by Joseph Addison and Richard Steele, and continued by the *Edinburgh Review* and *Quarterly Review*:

> Go to school, Mr. Editor, and learn what it is to be a gentleman. Learn of Addison and Steele, whose papers are models of all that is gentle and gentlemanly in literature. … Learn of Jeffrey and of Brougham, those masters of critical sword-play, who had no need to fall to fisticuffs, like dirty little boys in the gutter, in order to belabour the object of their antipathy. Those gentlemen, sir, were the high-priests of literature: they offered up their victim with something of the solemnity attending a pious sacrifice; and, as the leper-priest of the mediæval legend felt his leprosy leave him at the moment when he offered the supreme sacrifice, so these masters of the art of criticism banished from their minds all party spirit and all personal feeling while engaged in the performance of their self-assumed function. …
>
> The English mind, sir, is quick to resent anything that savours of persecution; and if you have the interests of your paper at heart, you will do well in future to refrain from these noisy onslaughts upon popular female novelists; which are more characteristic of the disappointed author of two or three unprecedented novels than of the gentleman editor who writes for gentlemen readers. (Shandon 85–6)

Her accusations against the 'ungentlemanly' standards of the *Pall Mall Gazette* here take on an added charge because Braddon recognises and exploits the patriarchal bias of the critical landscape. Assuming the role of the 'decentred, 'disoriginated', 'de-institutionalised' female subject, to use Nancy K. Miller's words, Braddon capitalises on her position as a female novelist in a male-dominated literary market-place to criticise the masculine standards of reviewing. It ties with the ideological construction of *Belgravia* as a periodical that tried to create a new democratic and united community of equal buyers (Gabriele xvi).

Braddon's adoption of the persona of Captain Shandon is no less manipulative of the existing structures of power than Eliot's self-fashioning as 'the Great Unknown'. Ironically, Braddon admired the way in which Eliot created her own network of support through the imaginary community of the House of Blackwood and her reliance on the secrecy of friends she had worked with at the *Westminster Review*. As Braddon told Edmund Yates in a letter written around 1859, but not published before February 11, 1885, in *The World*, Charles Bray, one of Eliot's close friends, had had long conversations with Braddon and her mother about phrenology and natural religion which opened new worlds to her,

> but not a word was ever said of *Adam Bede*, although the literary world was just at that time alive with criticism and discussion about that great book. The Brays respected the author's *nom de plume*, and there were no hints or head-shakings, no 'we could an if we would' from any member of that happy trio. (rpt. in Humberstone 5)

Bray's silence complies with the gentlemanly standards of reviewing, the loss of which Eliot lamented. On the contrary, Braddon strategically appropriated these old and venerated networks in order to empower her position within the literary market-place. Shandon's proclamation of 'gentlemanly' values sits rather uneasily against Braddon's commercial acumen. The complaint against the anonymity of the critic is even more problematic given that Shandon was itself obviously a pseudonym. Robert Lee Wolff has identified 'F.G.' – the critic with whom Braddon had the spat over *Circe* – as the journalist Frederick Greenwood, who had been a contributor, together with his brother, to Maxwell's *Welcome Guest* in the late 1850s. Jennifer Carnell has pointed out that the *Pall Mall Gazette* attacks on Braddon might have been motivated by a possible grudge with Maxwell, who was well-known for his sharp practices.

There is, moreover, one last twist in the tale to the literary spat between Braddon and the *Pall Mall Gazette* in terms of the performance of different authorial identities. Braddon was widely assumed to be behind the Captain Shandon riposte, but in the rather unlikely pages of the *Leamington Spa Courier*, an alternative emerges. In response to this newspaper's presumption that the piece in *Belgravia* was Braddon's response, a fact that the reviewer for the *Leamington Spa Courier* notes was 'current gossip' and which had 'appeared in a score of uncontradicted forms' ('Belgravia' 8), John Maxwell personally wrote to the proprietor of the paper to refute this presumption:

> Permit me to say, Sir, that the wrong done by this guess-work kind of criticism is most grievous; and that it is a perversion of the worst kind for critics to assume and assert that Miss Braddon is the author of any piece which she does not avow as her own production. In the case in question I must request you to state that the well-deserved castigation administered in the current number of *Belgravia* to the editor of the *Pall Mall Gazette* is not the production of Miss Braddon's pen. (quoted in 'Belgravia' 8)

Maxwell's assertion seems to have made little public impact, probably due to the fact it was not published until November 23, 1867, in a provincial newspaper (and not republished by other newspapers), by which time the spat had exhausted its ability to generate debate. Nonetheless, it adds another layer of intrigue. Was 'A Remonstrance' in fact written by Maxwell? Was it, in fact, a double performance of 'gentlemanly' values by a man protecting his partner? Did, however, Braddon's propensity for authorial performance mean that, whoever was responsible for this piece, it was always likely to be ascribed to her in a way beyond the control of either her or Maxwell? This was the sceptical response of the *Leamington Spa Courier* which rather pointedly noted that, while Maxwell claimed that Braddon always put her name to whatever she authored, the evidence of the *Circe* scandal rather proved the contrary.

Eliot's and Braddon's invocation of the 'gentlemanly standards of reviewing is another example of the Romantic afterlives that continued to haunt and inspire the Victorians. This chapter as a whole demonstrates the intriguing ways in which two female authors, who appear to occupy opposite ends of the market, handled the legacy of required female respectability in the Victorian culture of literary celebrity, fuelled by the very print culture in which these authors made their living as professional writers. Yet while most recent criticism of Victorian print culture has stressed its novelty and modernity, this chapter suggests that such newness could equally prompt traditional, perhaps conservative reinventions of Romantic models of authorship. That it was two ground-breaking women writers who invoked such models is testimony to the patriarchal values still underpinning the practice and discourse of criticism; yet such invocation in support of their professional authorial identities was not without its hazards. In the cases of both Eliot and Braddon, the reception of their deployment of models of 'gentlemanly' authorship and reviewing was out of step with the publishing dynamics of the 1850s and 1860s, provoking scepticism rather than understanding. The protective roles of Lewes and Maxwell in both controversies also raises questions concerning the way the professional identity of women writers was still mediated through their partners.

Equally important is the contrary aims of Braddon and Eliot in the way they appropriated Romantic print culture. While Eliot consciously tried to place herself outside those publishing practices that, for her, were redolent of popular literature and mass readership as she joined the imaginary community of Blackwood authors, Braddon capitalised on the opportunities that the periodical press offered for different authorial personae and tried to maintain her 'lead' as a sensation fiction writer. (Carnell suggests that some of the contributors at *Belgravia* complained that Braddon ran the periodical as a theatrical company within which there could be only one leading performer – a role that she only temporarily held on the stage in the provinces but did not manage to sustain.) Unlike Eliot who took book publication as a marker of professional status, Braddon, as if still in the theatre, judged her success on her ability to maintain her role as a Leading Lady in metropolitan London – a position that only popularity rather than literary distinction without fame could guarantee.

## Works Cited

Ablow, Rachel. *The Marriage of Minds: Reading Sympathy in the Victorian Marriage Plot*. Stanford: Stanford University Press, 2007.

'The Author of "Adam Bede"'. *Lincolnshire Chronicle*, 6 May 1859: 7.

'Belgravia and its Critics'. *Leamington Spa Courier*, 23 November 1867: 8.

Braddon, M.E. *The Doctor's Wife*. Oxford: Oxford World's Classics, 1998.

Braddon, M.E. 'Mr. Babington White's New Novel'. *Pall Mall Gazette*, 17 September 1867: 3.

Browning, Elizabeth Barrett. *The Letters of Elizabeth Barrett Browning to Mary Russell Mitford*. Ed. Meredith B. Raymond and Mary Rose Sullivan. 2 vols. Waco: Armstrong Browning Library of Baylor University, The Browning Institute and Wellesley College, 1983.

Carnell, Jennifer. *The Literary Lives of Mary Elizabeth Braddon: A Study of Her Life and Work*. Hastings: The Sensation Press, 2000.

Casaliggi, Carmen, and Paul March-Russell, eds. *Legacies of Romanticism: Literature, Culture, Aesthetics*. London and New York: Routledge, 2012.

Cvetkovich, Ann. *Mixed Feelings: Feminism, Mass Culture and Victorian Sensationalism*. New York: Rutgers University Press, 1992.

Dallas. E.S. 'Popular Literature. – The Periodical Press'. *Blackwood's Edinburgh Magazine* 85.520 (1859): 180–95.

Eliot, George. *Adam Bede*. London: Penguin, 2008.

——. *Essays and Leaves from a Note-Book*. Edinburgh and London: William Blackwood & Sons, 1884.

——. *The George Eliot Letters*. Ed. Gordon S. Haight. 9 vols. London and New Haven: Yale University Press, 1954–78.

Feuerbach, Ludwig. *The Essence of Christianity*. Trans. George Eliot. New York: Harper and Row, 1957.

Finkelstein, David. *The House of Blackwood: Author-Publisher Relations in the Victorian Era*. University Park, PA: Penn State University Press, 2002.

Gabriele, Alberto. *Reading Popular Culture in Victorian Print:* Belgravia *and Sensationalism*. Basingstoke: Palgrave, 2009.

Gilbert, Pamela. *Disease, Desire, and the Body in Victorian Women's Popular Novels*. Cambridge: Cambridge University Press, 1997.

Hawkins, Ann R., and Maura Ives, eds. *Women Writers and the Artifacts of Celebrity in the Long Nineteenth Century*. Farnham: Ashgate, 2012.

Hedgecock, Jennifer. *The Femme Fatale in Victorian Literature: The Danger and the Sexual Threat*. New York: Cambria Press, 2008.

Hughes, Linda K., and Michael Lund. *The Victorian Serial*. Charlottesville: University of Virginia Press, 1991.

Humberstone, F.W. 'Miss Braddon and Coventry'. *Coventry Herald*, 12 February 1915: 5.

King, Andrew. *The London Journal, 1845–83: Periodicals, Production, and Gender*. Aldershot: Ashgate, 2004.

Lewes, George Henry. 'Charles Lamb: His Genius and His Writings (May 1848)'. *Versatile Victorian: Selected Writings of George Henry Lewes*. Ed. Rosemary Ashton. London: Bristol Press, 1992. 139–55.

'Literary Chronicle of the Week'. *Leader* 10.474 (23 April 1859): 524.

A Mag's Man. 'Who is Mr. Babington White?' *Pall Mall Gazette*, 18 September 1867: 4.

'Metropolitan Gossip'. *Sheffield Independent*, 28 September 1867: 6.

Miller, Nancy K. *Subject to Change: Reading Feminist Writing*. New York: Columbia University Press, 1988.

'Miss Babington White'. *London Review*, 5 October 1867: 372.

Mole, Tom. *Byron's Romantic Celebrity: Industrial Culture and the Hermeneutic of Intimacy*. New York: Palgrave, 2007.

——., ed. *Romanticism and Celebrity Culture, 1750–1850*. Cambridge: Cambridge University Press, 2009.

Morgan, Hugh. 'Manufacture of Novels'. *Athenaeum*, 2 March 1867: 290.

'A New Literary Scandal'. *Kentish Gazette*, 8 October 1867: 2.

'Our Weekly Gossip'. *Athenaeum*, 2 July 1859: 20–21.

Palmer, Beth. *Women's Authorship and Editorship on Victorian Culture: Sensational Strategies*. Oxford: Oxford University Press, 2011.

Peterson, Linda. *Becoming a Woman of Letters: Myths of Authorship and Facts of the Victorian Market*. Princeton: Princeton University Press, 2009.

'Preface'. *The Annual Gift Book: A Drawing-Room Portrait Gallery of Eminent Personages. From Photography by Mayall, and Other Eminent Photographers. Engraved on Steel by D. J. Pound with Memoirs by the Most Able Authors*. London: The London Joint Stock Newspaper, 1859. iii–iv.

Rigney, Ann. *The Afterlives of Walter Scott: Memory on the Move*. Oxford: Oxford University Press, 2012.

'The Romance of Babington White'. *Saturday Review*, 28 September 1867: 399–400.

Salmon, Richard. 'Signs of Intimacy: The Literary Celebrity in the "Age of Interviewing"'. *Victorian Literature and Culture* 25.1 (1997): 159–77.

Shandon, Charles [M.E. Braddon]. 'A Remonstrance'. *Belgravia* 4 (November 1867): 80–86.

Stewart, David. *Romantic Magazines and Metropolitan Literary Culture*. Basingstoke: Palgrave, 2011.

Tomaiulo, Saverio. *In Lady Audley's Shadow: Mary Elizabeth Braddon and Victorian Literary Genres*. Edinburgh: Edinburgh University Press, 2010.

'Topics of the Week'. *The Era*, 12 June 1859: 9.

Tromp, Marlene, Pamela Gilbert, and Aeron Haynie, eds. *Beyond Sensation. Mary Elizabeth Braddon in Context*. Albany: State University of New York, 2000.

Turner, Mark W. '"Telling of My Weekly Doings": The Material Culture of the Victorian Novel'. *A Concise Companion to the Victorian Novel*. Ed. Francis O'Gorman. Oxford: Blackwell, 2005. 113–33.

Tush, Susan Rowland. *George Eliot and the Conventions of Popular Women's Fiction: A Serious Literary Response to the* 'Silly Novels by Lady Novelists'. New York: Peter Lang, 1993.

Zakreski, Patricia, *Representing Female Artistic Labour, 1848–1890: Refining Work for the Middle-Class Woman*. Aldershot: Ashgate, 2006.

## Notes

1 For the changing notion of Romanticism, the applicability of the term, and the ways in which it has been reconstituted from the 1830s onwards, see Casaliggi and March-Russell.

2 Eliot's encouragement of her readers to develop a sympathetic relationship with her characters rather than an intimate relationship with her as the author legitimates her difference not only from some of her contemporaries but more importantly from her Romantic predecessors. There are ample examples of the way in which Romantic poets (for example, Charlotte Smith) pressed sympathy into intimacy, or the way in which reviewers (for example John Wilson) read with the illusion of intimate access to the Byronic turmoil of heart and soul.

10

# Crafting the Woman Artist: Ouida and *Ariadnê*

*Andrew King*

'Look', she said, and led me in and let me stand before the statue she had made, and which she had herself cut out from the block, and shaped in every line, till it stood there, a white and wondrous thing, erect in the sunlight shining from the skies, and seemed to live, nay, to leap forth to life as the Apollo does in the Belvedere.

It was the same form that she had made in the clay at Venice and at Paris; that is, it was Hilarion: the man made god, by the deifying power of the passion which thus beheld him. Every curve of the slender and symmetrical limbs was his, every line of the harmonious and Greek-like features his also; but it was no longer a mortal, it was a divinity; and about his feet played an ape and an asp, and in his hand he held a dead bird, and he looked at the bird in weariness and doubt.

That was all.

There was no other allegory. She knew that marble must speak in the simplest words, as poets spake of old, or not at all. (Ouida, *Ariadnê* 323)[1]

[R]eflect but a moment upon all the divers and numerous qualities which are of necessity existent in the creator of a fine novel before it can be produced; not only imagination but wit, not only wit but scholarship, not only scholarship but fancy, not only fancy but discrimination, observation, knowledge of the passions, sympathy with the most opposite temperaments, the power to call up character from the void, as the sculptor creates figures from the clay, and, for amalgamating, condensing, and vivifying all these talents, the mastery of an exquisite subtlety, force, and eloquence in language. All these various gifts must be united in one writer before a fine novel can be produced; and when it is produced it requires (to be duly estimated) as cultured and as respectful a study of it as an educated traveller would take to the Vatican or to the Uffizi. (Ouida, 'Secret' 115)

When we use the phrase 'crafting the woman artist', what is it that we are referring to? Most obviously, we refer to depictions of women artists in texts, such as (to use an anachronism) the performance artist heroine of Madame de Staël's *Corinne, ou l'Italie* (1807) or, indeed, the sculptor heroine in Ouida's *Ariadnê: The Story of a Dream* (1877). Yet my juxtaposition of the two quotations above suggests that we cannot think of depictions of artists without thinking of the artists who created those depictions: Ouida indeed seems to be recalling *Ariadnê* in her 1893 *Fortnightly* essay, and in a letter to Frederic Harrison from seven years later she makes the connection between her own artistic practices and those of *Ariadnê*'s heroine by stating how she treated proofs 'as the wet clay to the sculptor' (Lee, Elisabeth 96). In the epigraph from *Ariadnê,* when the sculptor shows her statue of a man to the narrator she is also displaying herself and her passion: the artist is an inseparable part of the message being sent. How an artist (or indeed any figure) is portrayed in a text, then, necessarily has some elements of a self-portrait. This chapter, focussed on Ouida as a woman artist, accordingly has a double aim: to think about how a new portrait of Ouida herself might be crafted and how one of her novels where a woman artist is the protagonist might be understood.

'Ouida' was a name that sold enormously well from the early 1860s until the early twentieth century. She was often belittled by the literary cultural police and, echoing that, the four book-length biographies that have been written about her are all patronising in one way or another, either censoring letters, perhaps to avoid offence to those still living (as in the first biography) or carelessly translating and altering evidence for comic effect (as in the last) (see Bigland; ffrench; Lee, Elisabeth; Stirling). Ouida is frequently mentioned in surveys of Victorian print culture as an abstract reputation based mainly on vaguely high sales figures, on references to a very small selection of work and on a handful of supposedly representative anecdotes culled from doubtful sources.[2] As Carol Poster put it, Ouida tends to be treated as 'a non-literary author … not a legitimate subject for scholarly articles, books or dissertations, except within the extremely limited confines of "women's studies" or "popular culture"' (293–4). Ouida is not helped by her opposition to feminism. Pamela Gilbert, in an exceptionally perceptive essay, remarked that Ouida's hostility to the New Woman, 'combined with stylistic extravagance, has contributed to render Ouida invisible within today's canon, in which she can be classified neither as canonical nor as a feminist foremother' (170). Ouida has not usually been granted (to use her words) 'as cultured and as respectful a study … as an educated traveller would take to the Vatican or to the Uffizi' (170). Amongst the few exceptions to take Ouida seriously, besides Gilbert and Poster, Natalie Schroeder, Jane Jordan and Talia Schaffer figure prominently. Schroeder and Jordan, like Gilbert, present Ouida principally as subversive of conventional sexual mores, though Jordan also details Ouida's financial dealings with her publishers.[3] Schaffer argues, importantly for literary history, that Ouida is a forgotten mother of male aestheticism. (This is a point G.S. Street, unremarked by Schaffer, had made as far back as 1895.)

The picture of Ouida I offer seeks to continue the political work of scholars keen to think about how power and knowledge were and continue to be interlinked in gendered terms. I aim to treat this 'non-literary' writer with the seriousness usually reserved for the 'Vatican and Uffizi' by offering a reading of *Ariadnê: The Story of a Dream*, through whose eponymous heroine Ouida explores the status of the woman artist and of art more intensively than in any other of her works. I also want to show how she engages with and critiques high-status writers. Previous studies of Ouida have silently assumed her ignorant of high-status culture, as though the mass market were sealed off from the exclusive. Instead, I wish to demonstrate that Ouida was very concerned with contemporary aesthetic discussions and more especially with the role artists played in society. I have explored elsewhere Ouida's initial encounter with Italy, her late essays on Italian or British politics and Italian, French and British literature (see King, 'Origins'; King, 'Ouida'; King, 'Sympathetic'; Ouida, *Massarenes*). My contention throughout is that Ouida gradually moved from a commercial conception and practice of art, which disavowed its commercial nature, to a political, altruistic, view and practice where the artwork's impact upon society was more important than personal financial gain. This is a journey – by no means unchallenged or linear – from art considered for its exchange value to art as ethical utility. In short it is a transformation from art as trade to art as profession, where the latter concept is defined by a core of what came in the twentieth century to be called the impersonal 'public service ideal'.[4] In constructing this narrative I do not wish to contradict the unassailable evidence adduced by Jordan and Weedon that Ouida was intensely interested in the financial value of her writing. The professions have never done that and neither did Ouida. However, both the professions and Ouida offer alternatives to commercial priorities even while operating within them.

As part of this trajectory I am concentrating here on the two qualities in Ouida's work that G.S. Street saw as important in 1895: politics and beauty. I am also continuing Schaffer's discussion of aesthetics and filiation, though suggesting a very different organisation and set of priorities. Rather than promoting Ouida as a forgotten mother of men – in other words, reading her teleologically with men as her endpoint – I want to deepen our understanding of the aesthetic values of Ouida's works by linking them to contemporary high-status writers, mainly here Nathaniel Hawthorne, George Eliot and Walter Pater. The image of Ouida I am presenting is, then, of an argumentative sister professing her own identity, a subject in her own right, rather than of a literary mother defined by her feeding into now more famous men.

The image of Ouida that most insistently represents her as an artist is not one of the very few portraits of her that survive but the pseudonym with which she identified herself. 'Say Ouida alone please', she wrote to Wilfred Scawen Blunt when he asked how to address her. Associated mainly – but by no means exclusively – with male-centred stories in *Bentley's Miscellany*, the *New Monthly Magazine* and from 1864, the *British Army & Navy Review*, the name 'Ouida' was originally thought a masculine pseudonym despite its feminine-sounding final -a.[5] Only towards the end of the 1860s did critics start acknowledging that 'Ouida' concealed a female body. If the gendering of 'Ouida' vacillated, then what of its sound? Is it the disyllabic *ui:də*, as *Punch* suggests in the 18-part '*Strapmore. A Romance* by Weeder' that it ran in 1878 by its then editor, Francis Burnand, or the trisyllabic ōi*:da* I have heard many academics say, or perhaps *u:i:da*? Ouida herself claimed it was her own childhood pronunciation of her second name. 'Louisa' was an Anglicisation and feminisation of her father's name 'Louis' (Lee, Elisabeth 17). If this still leaves the pronunciation in doubt, perhaps we might anchor it by other means. Jane Jordan (*Writings* 198–9) suggested that we might lock it down psychoanalytically as 'Oui-da', 'yes daddy'. Since it omits the author's first name on her birth certificate 'Maria' which derived from a dead aunt and her mother's friend, her godmother Mary Ann Lockwood, should we decode the name as a sign of obedience to the Father and scotomisation of female lineage?[6] Or perhaps, since Ouida is an orthography the author adopted at the suggestion of a female cousin and there is no patronymic, we might unpick it as 'où-i-da?': 'where (is) daddy?', a technically hysterical question that would fit better Ouida's obsession with father figures who are again and again lost and found, always *fort und da*. Ouida's self-portrait in this understanding becomes a fetish both denying and signifying the loss of the father.

In her volume-form publications from 1873 and in cobalt blue on her headed letter-paper from Italy, Ouida offered a visual representation of her pseudonym by recomposing its letters into an aristocratic escutcheon after the fashion of the *scuderi* added to Florentine palaces in the 1860s and 1870s.[7] This is the visual portrait of Ouida as artist that she presented to society, its very icon (see Figure 10.1).

What stories can we craft from this knotted signature, with its hints of the *fleur-de-lys* and seemingly metallic clasps that hold the O and U together on either side? Extending the emphasis on patriarchy, it might be read as an obedient incorporation of aristocratic modes of self-representation and the (Lacanian) Law. The aristocratic association of the escutcheon becomes a defensive acknowledgement of lack; that is, the fullness of rank an escutcheon implies covers up the lack of a social position that a constant father-figure might have conferred. (Ouida, by the way, was certainly not the aristocratic-sounding 'Louise de la Ramée' she later claimed and was mistakenly named by many critics and reference texts.) Although this way of crafting 'Ouida' is not a pathway to later male writers, she is nonetheless still missing a man who leaves a hole in her life, still being granted meaning through a dependent

10.1 Ouida escutcheon taken from the title page of *Pascarèl* (1873).

relationship to men. We seem determined to separate her from the idea of the independent, impersonal professional dedicated to public service.

In 1876 Ouida publically declared her identity and at the same time the origin of her pseudonym in an interview she part wrote for Edmund Yates's series 'Celebrities at Home' in *The World*. Her assertion did not stop later wags interpreting 'Ouida' as a colloquial French expression of amazement, 'Oui-dà!' (see [Burnand] 117ft; 'Concerning'): clearly Ouida's attempt to control the meaning of her pseudonym was not altogether successful, though she could have tried harder to assert it had she really wanted to. Fundamentally, 'Ouida' did not wish to be known: in Bacon's three degrees of 'hiding and veiling of a man's self', 'Ouida' preferred 'closeness, reservation and secrecy' rather than simulation or dissimulation (cf. Bacon 77). In this she was a typical woman writer. The question is what form this secrecy took. Returning to the materiality of the escutcheon, one notes that unless one already knows what the name is, one simply cannot read it. The escutcheon seems designed solipsistically to confirm one's pre-existent knowledge of it, whatever that knowledge is. The point is surely that 'Ouida', both name and escutcheon, is a self-portrait by an active subject that calls attention to its mirror-like unknowability, an inscrutable armour and device welded together from letters. Certainly, like 'Phiz' or 'Boz' or 'A.L.O.E.', its initial function was as an intriguing marketing device for the short stories and romances from 1859 on that were a 'gold mine' for Ainsworth, for Chapman & Hall, and for Chatto & Windus after them.[8] The signal peculiarity and association with the commercial of this pseudo-armorial plate seems to have blinded us to the intellectual and political content and context of the words associated with it, and it is to these that I now turn.

Her novels of Italian peasant life constitute Ouida's most direct attempts to struggle with questions of the use and exchange values of art, and of the function of the artist's labour in the economy more generally. They were not as commercially successful as her scandalous novels of High Society which combined sensation and silver-fork fiction. As a result, Ouida was forced to return again and again to the society novel to generate income. It is a pity indeed that much recent criticism has taken these latter as a metonym for her entire *oeuvre*, ignoring what some early readers saw as her best writing: that on Italy (see ffrench 83; Lee, Elisabeth 247–68; Lee, Vernon 2). In 1873, the

*Athenaeum* noted *Pascarèl*'s difference from her previous work, praising it as 'of rich nature, but highly wrought art, with art itself, and genius and Italy for its themes … far in advance of [her] earlier novels' ('Novels' 405). Her following novels, *Signa, In a Winter City, Ariadnê,* and finally and most disastrously for Ouida's social life, the *roman à clef, Friendship,* all engage in explicit debate over forms of art – the theatre, music, painting, writing and sculpture – and their production, consumption and falsification. Unlike her earlier work, all of them, to varying degrees, concern the relation of art to the market and more generally the place and function of art in society. In *Friendship* Ouida offers a portrait of herself as the writer Étoile, but the novel as a whole treats art as a subsidiary to the triangular affair between Étoile, Joan Challoner and Ioris. *Friendship* is more of a chronicle of betrayal, misunderstanding and social hypocrisy than a portrait of the artist as a woman: Étoile is not significantly transformed *as an artist* over the course of the novel and her work remains loftily detached. In *Ariadnê,* on the other hand, Ouida offers a proper *Künstlerroman,* placing a woman artist at the centre of her narrative for the first time, debating art at greatest length and with greatest intensity, and tracing the effects of the social organisation of art on her artist heroine. While not making a decisive leap into the professional public service ideal – it is still a commercial novel – *Ariadnê* nonetheless contributes a step along the way.

The novel is set in Rome in unspecified but clearly contemporary times. The tale is narrated by a cobbler ('one of the most successful of Ouida's creations' says the *Athenaeum* of June 2, 1877 ['Novels' 701]) who calls himself Crispin and who, though poor, delights in and has a prodigious knowledge of art and history. One day he falls asleep before a statue in the Galleria Borghese in Rome, a statue he claims is of 'Ariadnê' (the spelling adopted in the text) but which his friend, the famous sculptor Maryx, asserts is most definitely a Bacchus. He dreams that the statue comes to life as Ariadnê, followed by a host of other gods and goddesses who debate the nature of love and art. Immediately, sexual ambiguity and sex are linked to art, and to sculpture in particular; the connection is raised, however, as a question rather than as an assertion: is sex (in all its senses) really set in stone? Crispin then goes back to his stall and in a passage that explicitly recalls the Pygmalion myth but which also uncannily prefigures Jensen's *Gradiva* (so familiar to us through Freud's analysis), he falls asleep in the mid-day sun and wakes to find what he thinks is his Ariadnê alive before him. The woman is instead Giojà, a young peasant just arrived in Rome from the coast. Like many of Ouida's heroines (and like Corinne, Aurora Leigh and indeed like Ouida herself), she is a hybrid, this time half Roman, half Jewish. (Exceptionally, Ouida suspends her otherwise insistent anti-Semitism in this novel, if only as far as her heroine is concerned.) Giojà's Roman father has recently died and, now an orphan, she is looking for her Jewish grandfather. Crispin takes her to the Ghetto to find him. When her grandfather will have nothing to do with her,

Crispin takes her in. He introduces her to Maryx, and, having shown him some of her sculptures without revealing the sex of their creator, persuades him to act as her teacher. Unsurprisingly, this is against his and Crispin's belief that her poverty and sex mark her as unsuitable: 'Marble costs gold and sculpture is not for women' (Ouida, *Ariadnê* 82). Nonetheless, she delights in learning and labouring 'thoroughly as though she were a male student of the most virile of all the arts' (105). Very soon Maryx declares that Giojà has genius. He also falls in love with her, knowing well that his love is not reciprocated and that as a result he can never declare his love. Meanwhile, Hilarion, a friend of both Maryx and Crispin, returns to Rome. Hilarion is young, fabulously wealthy, 'tall, and fair, and beautiful, with something imperious and tired on his face already' (62). He is also a celebrated poet of elegant verses in a decadent French manner, which extol experience above its fruits. He seduces Giojà through his poetry because, so we later hear, he 'longed to call up [his] own image in [her eyes], as in calm waters, and trouble them for ever!' (307). She goes to live with him in Paris. He soon throws her over just as he had previously tired of other women and at least one boy, the Greek flute-player with almond eyes, Amphion. Giojà goes mad with grief and is cared for by her fellow victim, Amphion. Crispin eventually tracks them down and takes them both back to Rome where Giojà recovers her sanity. But she cannot now sculpt as once she did: Hilarion has killed her art. Meanwhile her grandfather has died and left her all his wealth. This gives her the gold that enables her to take up sculpture again as well as do good works. In order to preserve Hilarion's beauty for ever – and to force him to recognise her love – she makes a statue of him as Apollo. With Maryx's help as go-between, it takes the art world by storm. Hilarion recognises the hidden message and is, to some extent, conscience stricken, but this feeling is outweighed by his delight in reminding Parisian society that the sculptor is Maryx's protégée, and that she was also his own mistress. Maryx, incensed, challenges him to a duel and is killed. Giojà goes into a decline and dies. Hilarion finally repents and visits her on her deathbed where he confesses, too late, that he has come to love her.

As in several of her novels, Ouida has integrated autobiographical elements into this novel, despite her enigmatic defensive signature, displaying herself in her work as Giojà did in hers. We eventually find out that 'Crispin' is a pseudonym, a disguise the narrator is forced to adopt because of persecution for his radical politics. Rufo Quintilio is his real name, and he is descended, so he claims, from ancient Roman aristocracy (31, 70, 72). Parallel to Maria Louisa Ramé's recreation of herself as 'Ouida' and 'Louise (de la) Ramé(e)', such pseudonymity raises questions about the reliability of his narrative. It is also tempting to see Hilarion as partly based on the fickle Marchese Lotteringhi della Stufa, with whom Ouida had fallen in love disastrously in Florence (King, 'Ouida'). Most importantly, much of Ariadnê/Giojà's experience in the art world echoes Ouida's own in the literary. Both arrive in a capital city and by chance meet a kindly older man who introduces them to another who trains them up and introduces them to the relevant social group which ensures their success. While able to cross class from lower to upper, neither heroine nor author is integrated into any; instead they view all society with critical alienation. They remain outsiders from an Italian village or Bury St Edmunds as the case may be. Unlike many novels of about women artists of the 1890s, however, the focaliser is not the heroine herself but 'Crispin'. To the extent that Giojà is a self-portrait of Ouida, then, it is an ironic one, painted from the outside by an unreliable (if sympathetic) narrator. Giojà herself, like Ouida's escutcheon, seems designed to remain fundamentally unknown, shielded from definitive interpretation by the interpretations of those who already think they have the answers.

That does not suggest a positive model for the woman artist and *Ariadnê* is in many ways even more pessimistic about the fate of women in a male-dominated art world than de Staël's *Corinne*. Ouida keeps her heroine isolated from women except for a few warnings from Maryx's sibylline mother, so, just as in *Corinne*, sisterhood is not a solution. But at least in de Staël's work the solitary heroine is able to produce great works before she is in love with a man and does not always need to use male go-betweens. Crispin presents Giojà, by contrast, as generating her greatest work from masochistic unreciprocated love while hemmed in by men on all sides. The real art work by a woman is a love letter to an absent uncaring man which is not successful in properly communicating to him (readers who know Ouida's biography will connect this to the childhood diary she wrote for an absent father). Only Giojà's death ensures that the message actually arrives.

Such gendering and sexualisation of art is naturalised by Crispin's ingenious unfolding of the Ariadnê myth. Though the reader is encouraged early to think ridiculous his belief in the notion that Giojà is an *Ariadnê rediviva* – and Giojà herself vigorously and repeatedly repudiates the name (77, 217, 237) – it turns out to be appropriate for her after all. As Crispin several times explains, Giojà is Ariadnê to Hilarion's Theseus. But he also comes to recognise that the Bacchus who translates her to divine status when Theseus abandons her is not a person but her Art (336–7). Through the practice of her art which renders her abandonment divine ('the deifying power of the passions' as the first of my epigraphs puts it) Giojà shows that she participates in the Bacchic too. She is both abandoned and rescuer. Crispin's dream was right: Bacchus and Ariadnê are one. The ambiguity of the opening may be explained furthermore as a conflict not just of gender but of optimism and pessimism about art: the dreaming and pessimistic narrator sees the statue as Ariadnê; the energetic and optimistic Maryx sees it as Bacchus. As in Paterian aesthetic criticism, each responds to his sense impressions through his own predilections. Again, though, the woman artist seems defined by men: is there no escape?

The question remains whether Giojà has her own identity independent of any (male) observer's sense impressions. The extent to which she does can be glimpsed through ambiguities and logical flaws in Crispin's narrative. For if Giojà is the living image of an ancient statue, as Crispin thinks, that means that her body is inscribed with myth which predates any sense impressions and exists apart from them as an essence. This mythic essential narrative determines that for Bacchic Art to render Ariadnê divine, Ariadnê has to leave earthly life. Giojà's essence is thus to be abandoned, to be her own rescuer and her own killer. That we know. The important corollary is that the exclusively male artistic network she is part of, which, as the narrator dimly perceives, sees only aspects of her, is irrelevant to this mythic pulsion. This in turn has two implications: it is Giojà's/Ariadnê's fault that she dies and that her art does not communicate while the men are conveniently voided of guilt. So far so conventionally patriarchal where women are not subjects in their own right. But there are signs too that Giojà *is* an active subject. Her alienation giving her vision a peculiar acuity, she seems to know what she is doing when she falls in love with Hilarion. She instantly sees him for what he is, even making a model of him as Antinoüs, the lover of the Emperor Hadrian, as a very clear demonstration that she is aware of his homosexual practices. She is able to see into and appropriate even those aspects of masculinity where women are most excluded. And yet she chooses to follow the mythic path Crispin has laid out for her and crucially makes it her own. This appropriation of the myth is what offers the woman artist the possibility of independence from men here, however compromised that independence must be. Such compromised independence, such imperfectly crafted identity, is visible in the novel's own relations to three sibling texts, which I shall focus on for the rest of this chapter.

First, linkage of body, statue and myth has inevitable resonance with another novel set in Rome amongst artists, Hawthorne's *The Marble Faun* (1860). *Ariadnê* and *The Marble Faun* have much in common, not least their travelogue aspects (which in *Ariadnê* were highly praised by the reviewers). Both open with the direct comparison of a character's body and a statue, both offer extensive discussions of art, a cast of artists and hangers-on centring on four main characters, a strong emphasis on the effects of a failure of sympathy between them, lengthy descriptions of artists' block, and so on. Chapter 2 of *Ariadnê* even begins with a description of how Crispin plies his trade by a fountain in which he imagines a faun still lives (9–11). But Hawthorne's cast comprises two men and two women, who pair off in various ways to form two heterosexual and two homosocial couples, and the statue, body and myth belong to one of the central male characters, the Italian Donatello, who is destined to repeat the founding myth of his family: a faun in a past Golden Age falls in love with a mortal woman and falls from grace accordingly. Donatello falls into sin and the crime of murder through his love for the mysterious and hybrid Anglo–Jewish–Italian painter Miriam. The myth is in the end allegorised into the universal necessity of sin in order to gain knowledge.

The sculptor in Hawthorne is a New England man, Kenyon, while the two women artists are painters, one Miriam and the other the New England Puritan Hilda. Ouida reverses the gendering and rejigs the relationships and nationalities to create a daisy-chain of desire – the Italian narrator Crispin tells of how the French Maryx loves the Italian–Jewish Giojà who loves the German–Greek hybrid Hilarion. While one of the heterosexual couples in Hawthorne ends happily, in Ouida all ends in tragedy. Then again, Giojà sculpts Hilarion just as Hawthorne's Kenyon sculpts his beloved Hilda and, later and half unknowingly, Donatello in his fallen state. The messages of none of Hawthorne's artists really arrive (critics agree that the happy ending is archly unsatisfactory), but Ouida's change of emphasis seems to be stressing the impossibility of the woman artist's message ever arriving in marked contrast to how the messages generated by the male artists Hilarion and Maryx do hit their marks.

And yet this pessimistic view of women's doomed relation to art is undermined by the sympathy we feel for the heroine. *Ariadnê* itself debates the value of sympathy as a response, unlike *The Marble Faun* which only reiterates the importance of sympathy and condemns its absence. While both novels agree that the highest form of art is that which elicits a sympathetic response in the audience, for Ouida sympathy is what characterises *modern* art: 'The chief characteristics, the only originality of all modern art, do lie in its expressions of sympathy' concurs Maryx when Giojà suggests the idea (*Ariadnê* 95). Maryx is himself very much an artist of sympathy (120, 192), and after Giojà has suffered, she becomes so too: her particular suffering activates her sympathy for all suffering beings. It is this general sympathy that makes her art great (292). Even Hilarion knows that the correct thing to say is that 'Sympathy is the hallmark of the poet' (65), although he announces this with shocking hypocrisy just after one of his mistresses has died and he has felt nothing at all. It is only when Giojà's sculpture has a full effect upon him that he starts to suffer.

In other words, art, which is a result of sympathy on the part of the artist, is great insofar as it generates sympathy in even its hardest-hearted and most hypocritical audience. To be great the art work must therefore have an ethical effect on society; it must have a moral use-value. It creates a community of suffering, a notion that links Ouida not just to Hawthorne but to the second text I want to discuss here, George Eliot's 1862–63 novel about Renaissance Florence, *Romola*. Unlike Ouida's novel from 1881, *A Village Commune*, which explicitly refers to Eliot, Ouida only connected *Ariadnê* to *Romola* in private. In November 1881 Ouida would write to her publisher Chatto that he should bring out an illustrated edition of *Ariadnê* to compete with the newly re-issued *Romola* accompanied by the drawings by Lord Leighton. Clearly interested in the novel-as-guidebook market, Ouida proposed a quarto edition of *Ariadnê* with illustrations by Lady Paget, which was never realised (Jordan, *Writings* 37). As with *The Marble Faun*, there are clear reminiscences of *Romola* in *Ariadnê*. In Eliot's novel, Piero di Cosimo paints a wedding picture for the heroine and Tito of Ariadne and Bacchus, where the comparison between the pairs in the picture and in the novel operates as a coded forewarning to the heroine – a much simpler use of the myth than in Ouida's novel. More strikingly, it is the *Bildung* of the heroine that links the two novels. In *Ariadnê* as in *Romola*, it is through betrayal by a beloved that the heroine in the end becomes 'very tender' to little children. Giojà even becomes 'afraid of no pestilence' (Ouida, *Ariadnê* 293), a curious and unnecessary phrase reminiscent of Romola's aid to the plague-stricken village after her attempted suicide. And just as in *Romola*, in making us sympathetic to Giojà's suffering at the hands of a hypocritical man who wishes to destroy her genius, the novel aims to alert us to the fact that women, against all the odds, were able to practice – and indeed were practising with supreme success – even 'the most virile of all the arts' (Ouida, *Ariadnê* 105).[9]

Unlike Eliot's work, *Ariadnê* was openly written by a woman: even though reviewers had been using feminine pronouns when referring to her for a decade, just the previous year Ouida had granted the interview with Yates where her sex was left in no doubt. *Ariadnê* is also, as Figure 10.2 shows, dedicated to a woman sculptor.[10] Ada Colonna was so acclaimed indeed that her statue of *Pythia* was (and still is) displayed in the Paris Opera. The micronarrative of the dedication moves from friendship with a woman ('amie') through an aristocratic title to artistic pseudonym, its progression highlighted through typographic patterning. It also puts on a level the artist's masculine and feminine attributes indicating that Marcello 'has been able to/has known how to unite to all the Charm of Woman the Force of Art'. If friendship between women has the first words, Art has the last. The gender politics of *Ariadnê* are thus more declarative than *Romola* even in the paratextual apparatus the reader encounters before the narrative proper.

In this understanding, Ouida's escutcheon and aristocraticisation of her name become the result of a view of artistic practice as ennobling not only for the consumer – Arnold's *Culture and Anarchy* (1869) would have provided one of many justifications there – but also for the producer herself. This latter interpretation suggests a bourgeois – even trade – appropriation of noble titles and a daring assertion by a woman of her own value. Both are justified, as in the Arnold, by how artists carry a moral duty to society. When Maryx declares that Giojà has genius, he also announces that 'genius is nobility and like nobility is obligation' (Ouida, *Ariadnê* 92–3, cf.191). Such a profession of a woman's artistic genius which both inserts her into and separates her from society is very different from the post-Darwinian 'somatic determinism' that enabled and threatened the idea of the feminist 'woman of genius' in the

1890s as described by Boumelha, where the link of 'duty' between self and other plays no part.

The notion of the artist's social duty is key, for if *Ariadnê* appropriates elements of *Romola* and *The Marble Faun*, it uses them as opportunities to argue with a notorious contemporary text on Italy that was offering an alternative view of the function of art to either: Walter Pater's *The Renaissance* (1873). The *Saturday Review* saw traces of *The Renaissance* in *Ariadnê*, commenting in 1877 on how 'Maryx … seems to have been reading Mr Pater' (710). It ended its very negative review (including an unfair long section on what are probably typographical errors rather than Ouida's ignorance) with the following unmistakable allusion to Pater's 'Conclusion': 'Perhaps the small but lively school of New-Pagans may turn from the error of their literary ways when they find that Ouida can burn, with a hard gem-like flame, with the best of them' (710). Ouida indeed seems to have studied Pater so well that she is responding not only to *The Renaissance* but to texts important to it. Earlier in its comments on *Ariadnê* the *Saturday Review* had referred to Matthew Arnold, and it is not difficult to understand that Giojà's hybrid Jewish–Roman ancestry – a unique combination for Ouida, and perhaps picked up from Hawthorne's Miriam – echoes and reconciles Arnold's Semitic and Hellenic cultures. There is even explicit discussion of the Semitic / Hellenic binary in *Ariadnê* (128–9). Two other key texts for *The Renaissance* are also directly referred to. Very early in the novel, the narrator remarks that if 'Winckelmann was certain that the Capitoline Ariadnê was a Leucothea, so was I certain that the Borghese Bacchus was an Ariadnê' (11), and then Heinrich Heine's vision of the classical world and the death of the gods is discussed twice at length (Ouida, *Ariadnê* 140, 194). While the importance of Arnold and Winckelmann to Pater is well known (a long essay on Winckelmann appears in *The Renaissance* [see Brake; DeLaura, chap. 16]), the influence of Heine, the worldly poet of sensuality opposing Christian morality, has been less appreciated by recent critics. Heine's 1853 essay 'Les dieux en exil' for the *Revue de deux mondes* is in fact discussed in a prominent place in Pater's essay on Pico della Mirandola, which, following Heine's playful imagining of the afterlife of some of the male gods as ordinary mortals, presents Pico as a god returned to earth. This, along with the Winckelmann justification for capriciously changing the identity of a statue, is a connection which lends a new significance to the notion that Giojà is *Ariadnê rediviva*: if a male artist can be a god reborn, why can't a woman artist? But if she is, what myths are open to her? Are only Heine's ridiculous and demeaning ends available to her?

While the *Saturday Review* saw *Ariadnê* as supporting Paterian aestheticism, it is rather the opposite. It critiques *The Renaissance* in terms both of gender and of the social function assigned to art. *Ariadnê* is, first of all, keen to show up the flaws in a text where women appear only as goddesses, mothers and Madonnas, and never as artistic producers in their own right.

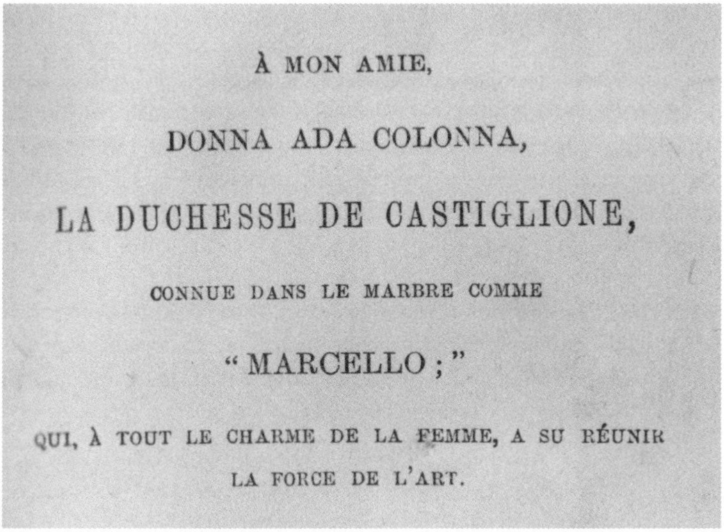

À MON AMIE,

DONNA ADA COLONNA,

LA DUCHESSE DE CASTIGLIONE,

CONNUE DANS LE MARBRE COMME

“MARCELLO;”

QUI, À TOUT LE CHARME DE LA FEMME, A SU RÉUNIR

LA FORCE DE L’ART.

10.2 Dedication to Ada Colonna taken from the 1882 Chatto & Windus yellowback edition of Ouida, *Ariadnê: The Story of a Dream.*

What are the implications for men alone having the right to decide aesthetic identity? And then is the duty of genius only to put ‘a happy world of its own creation in place of the meaner world of our common days’? (Pater 213) While accepting some aspects of the Paterian aesthetic inherited from Winckelmann – as for example, Ouida’s stress on the repose, divinity and simplicity of sculpture – Giojà’s best work shows itself thoroughly modern in deriving from a terrible passion, so unlike the aesthetic perfection that Pater described as Hellenic ‘moral sexlessness’ which ‘allows passion to play lightly over the surface’ (Pater 216, 220). Giojà’s work, ‘wearing the sharp impress of one absorbing motive’, would be, for Pater, decidedly ‘grotesque’ (216) while at the same time it refuses the term and its implications. Passion, sympathy and moral imperative constitute the root of art for Ouida.

Though elements of Paterian criticism can certainly be seen both in the narrator and in Maryx, it is Hilarion who seems the very embodiment of the solipsistic ‘aesthetic critic’ concerned only to see himself in another’s eyes, where the external object becomes merely an impression that gives pleasure of some kind or develops one’s own critical faculties, not society’s. His mixed German–Greek parentage and education in Paris of course recalls Pater’s intellectual genealogy. Yet while Crispin describes Hilarion as having ‘the temper of Heine and the muse of Musset’ (Ouida, *Ariadnê* 68), Heine is also used by the narrator to argue *against* Hilarion. The following passage in *Ariadnê* alludes to Heine’s 1829 attack on a presumptuous poet in *Die Bäder von Lucca* (translated as *The Baths of Lucca*): in the fantastical imagination of Aristophanic comedy as in the phantasmagoric creations of Hilarion's commercial cynicism, the idea of the world is topsy-turvy, not as we know it (the *Weltvernichtungsidee* that Crispin cites). Like my epigraphs, the quotation serves a multiple purpose, for we also see in it an example of the woman artist's determination in the face of casually enacted ways of ensuring she is not granted high or even equal status. Giojà's insistent, alienated but lucid questioning and refusal of gendered learning codes are (literally) spotlighted, and the masculine narrator is shown up as patronising, even equating her with his pet dog. The failings of the narrator as well as of Hilarion are all too clear here, and the apes on Giojà's statue described in my epigraph turn out to be not a generic but a specific reference, just as the dead bird in Hilarion's hand echoes the Philomel also referred to here:

> 'What poems does [Hilarion] write?' she asked me, once, in the darkness of the stairs, as I took her to her door.
>
> 'He writes as Heine says that Aristophanes did', I answered her. 'The singing of the nightingale is spoiled by the chattering of the apes that lodge in the blossoming tree of his fancy.'
>
> 'Will you give them to me to read?'
>
> 'You cannot read his tongue.'
>
> 'I can learn. Why does he let the apes come upon his trees?'
>
> 'Heine would say because the tree was set in the darksome swamp of *Weltvernichtungsidee*. There is a long word for you that you cannot translate. Not that he is the least like Aristophanes. The apes in Hilarion's tree never laugh; they mock. But, to do him justice, his nightingales are sweet and sad as Philomel herself, – who, by the by, had murder on her soul. Good-night, my dear. Palès [the dog] is quite tired; so must you be.'
>
> 'Could no one persuade him to send the apes away?'
>
> She had her hand on the latch of the door. The old, dim lamp she carried shone upon her face.
>
> 'When a man has once kept company with such apes as these, it is hard for him to forego them', I said to her. 'And it is best not to meddle with his taste: he has his hours for the nightingales. Good-night, my dear.' (Ouida, *Ariadnê* 140)

A similarly selective and strategic version of Heine by the narrator will occur later in the novel (194), again used against Hilarion. It is as if Ouida were turning Pater's own declared filiation against him. She offers a complex scenario where the narrator, himself blameworthy in terms of gender stereotyping and influenced by this new language of art, is nonetheless still able to feel for others and so see the flaws in his reasoning. If we cannot access the full reality of Giojà through Crispin's obliviously patriarchal myth-making, there is hope for him in that he does try to look after her according to his lights. The more thorough-going Paterian, Hilarion, is by contrast a moral failure: we should know even less of Giojà were he to tell her story. Rather than an Ariadnê, she would be at best a nightingale, at worst a generic and replaceable dead bird he looks at doubtfully.

Pater's vision of art was altogether too selfish, too exclusive and too androcentric for Ouida, although at this stage in her aesthetic trajectory she was not offering a viable alternative beyond an assertion of feminine genius, a vague concept of sympathy connected to a notion of the artist-aristocrat's *noblesse oblige*. She was, though, appropriating and critiquing texts, written by both men and women, not just feeding into them or slavishly following them, at the same time reminding us of the banal but frequently overlooked point that popular and élite cultures are not hermetically sealed from each other.

In my portrait, Ouida is an argumentative sister rather than just a milky mother whose texts feed *fin-de-siècle* men. She remains caught within but also empowered by networks of men (and to a lesser extent of women too) which she attempts to define just as they define her. Even while we respect her artfully constructed armour of inscrutability, we can still come to understand her professions through making visible the nature of her literary relations. And if Giojà/Ariadnê is in part an ironic and distant portrait of Ouida filtered through the eyes of an unreliable man, Ouida's act of creating this narrator, its frame and the paratextual apparatus with which she surrounds her narrative demonstrate that real women artists were by no means subject to myths men ascribed to them. Crispin makes Giojà/Ariadnê die for her message to arrive, yet Crispin's creator, like Ada Colonna, lived on. Ouida was to publish for another 30 years, materially contradicting the image of the female artist represented in her novel. The idea of the suffering and sympathetic woman artist as Bacchus/Ariadnê was a dead end, and Ouida's later actions suggest that she came to understand that.

Just a year after *Ariadnê*, Ouida started to write protest material for the *Whitehall Review* and, the following year, a stream of letters to *The Times*. By the time of *A Village Commune*, which details the dreadful descent of a peasant family into beggary and madness caused by a corrupt government official, Ouida was using art very explicitly as a call for political action. *A Village Commune* is a denunciation of the modern Italian state so ferocious that, along with her letters to *The Times*, it caused her to be banished from the Italian royal court and to be threatened by men who thought they recognised themselves in the petty tyrants she described. In a letter she tells how she was even shot at (Lee, Elisabeth 111). While it was deplored as inaccurate in some quarters (most notably by Calverley), Ruskin recommended it enthusiastically as 'photographic' in its veracity (Ruskin 30). This surely sounds like a message that arrived, but that some did not wish to receive. The idea of the woman artist that Ouida powerfully presents from the 1880s onward is that of the social activist, the idea of the artist-aristocrat now justifying strident intervention. If she did not yet pursue her politics with as little recourse to economic self-interest as she would in the last decade of her life, the effect of this shift of emphasis is still visible even in commercially successful novels such as *Moths* and *The Massarenes* (1897). By the 1880s Ouida will have found what was really important to her as a woman artist: the public service ideal that in the twentieth century came to form the ethical core of the professional.

## Works Cited

Adams, James Eli. *A History of Victorian Literature*. Chichester: Wiley-Blackwell, 2009.

'Ariadnê'. *Saturday Review*, 9 June 1877: 709–10.

Altick, Richard. *The English Common Reader: A Social History of the Mass Reading Public 1800–1900*. Columbus: Ohio State University Press, 1957.

Arnold, Matthew. *Culture and Anarchy*. London: Smith, Elder & Co., 1869.

Bacon, Francis. 'Of Simulation and Dissimulation'. *The Essays*. Ed. John Pitcher. Harmondsworth: Penguin, 1985. 76–8.

Bigland, Eileen. *Ouida, The Passionate Victorian*. Norwich: Jarrold's, 1950.

Bonaparte, Felicia. *The Triptych and the Cross: The Central Myths of George Eliot's Poetic Imagination*. New York: New York University Press, 1979.

Boumelha, Penny. 'The Woman of Genius and the Woman of Grub Street: Figures of the Female Writer in British *Fin-de-Siècle* Fiction'. *English Literature in Transition, 1880–1920* 40.2 (1997): 164–80.

Brake, Laurel. *Walter Pater*. Plymouth: Northcote House, 1994.

[Burnand, Francis]. '*Strapmore. A Romance* by Weeder'. *Punch*, 9 March–11 May 1878.

Calverley, Mary. 'Ouida's Knowledge of Italian Life'. *Contemporary Review* 40 (October 1881): 564–9.

'Concerning "Ouida"'. *Funny Folks*, 26 March 1881. Accessed through Gale's *19th Century UK Periodicals*.

DeLaura, David J. *Hebrew and Hellene in Victorian England: Newman, Arnold, and Pater*. Austin: University of Texas Press, 1969.

Eliot, George. *Romola*. Ed. Andrew Brown. Oxford: Clarendon Press, 1993.

——. *Middlemarch*. Ed. W.J. Harvey. London: Penguin, 1965.

ffrench, Yvonne. *Ouida: A Study in Ostentation*. London: Cobden-Sanderson, 1938.

Flint, Kate. *The Woman Reader, 1837–1914*. Oxford: Clarendon Press, 1993.

Freud, Sigmund, 'Delusion and Dream in Jensen's "Gradiva"'. Trans. James Strachey. *Art and Literature*, Penguin Freud Library, 14. Harmondsworth: Penguin 1985. 33–118 (orig. *Der Wahn und die Träume in W. Jensens 'Gradiva'*, Vienna and Leipzig: Hugo Heller & Cie, 1907).

Gilbert, Pamela. 'Ouida and the Other New Woman'. *Victorian Women Writers and the Woman Question*. Ed. Nicola Diane Thompson. Cambridge: Cambridge University Press, 1999. 170–88.

Hawthorne, Nathaniel. *The Marble Fawn*. Ed. Susan Manning. Oxford: Oxford University Press, 2002.

Heine, Heinrich. 'The Gods in Exile'. *The Prose Writings of Heinrich Heine*. Ed. Havelock Ellis. London: Walter Scott, 1887: 268–89.

James, Louis. *The Victorian Novel*. Oxford: Blackwell, 2006.

Jordan, Jane. 'Ouida. The Enigma of a Literary Identity'. *Princeton University Library Chronicle* 57.1 (1995): 75–105.

——. 'The Writings of 'Ouida' (Marie Louise de la Ramée)'. PhD Birkbeck College, University of London, 1995. Unpublished.

Keating, Peter. *The Haunted Study: A Social History of the English Novel, 1875–1914*. London: Secker and Warburg, 1989.

King, Andrew. *The London Journal 1845–83: Periodicals, Production and Gender*. Aldershot: Ashgate, 2004.

——. 'The Origins of Ouida's *Pascarèl*: The Combination Novel, Myths of the Female Artist and the Commerce of Art'. *Anglistica Pisana* 6.1/2 (2009): 77–85.

——. '"Army Navy, Medicine, Law/ Church, Nobility, Nothing at all": Towards the Study of Gender, the Professions and the Press in the Nineteenth Century'. *Nineteenth-Century Gender Studies* 5.2 (Summer 2009), http://www.ncgsjournal.com/issue52/issue52.htm.

——. 'The Sympathetic Individualist: Ouida's Late Journalism and Politics'. *Victorian Literature and Culture* 39.2 (2011): 563–79.

——. 'Ouida (1839–1908): Quantities, Aesthetics, Politics'. *Ouida and Victorian Popular Culture*. Ed. Jane Jordan and Andrew King. Farnham: Ashgate, 2013. 13–35.

Leavis, Q.D. *Fiction and the Reading Public* (1932). London: Pimlico, 2000.

Lee, Elisabeth. *Ouida: A Memoir*. London: Fisher Unwin, 1914.

Lee, Vernon. 'About Ouida'. *Westminster Gazette*, 27 July 1907: 2.

Lewis, Linda M. *Germaine de Staël, George Sand, and the Victorian Woman Artist*. Columbia: University of Missouri Press, 2003.

Mitchell, Sally. *The New Girl: Girls' Culture in England, 1880–1915*. New York: Columbia University Press, 1995.

Nesti, Arnaldo. *Vita di palazzo: l'aristocrazia fiorentina tra otto e novecento*. Florence: Ponte alle Grazie, 1994.

'Novels of the Week'. *Athenaeum*, 29 March 1873: 405–6.

'Novels of the Week'. *Athenaeum*, 2 June 1877: 701–2.

Ouida. *Ariadnê: The Story of a Dream*. London: Chapman & Hall, 1877; yellowback, London: Chatto & Windus, 1882.

——. *Friendship: A Story*. London: Chatto & Windus, 1878.

——. *In a Winter City: A Sketch*. London: Chapman & Hall, 1876.

——. *'Le Secret du Précepteur'. Critical Studies*. London: Fisher Unwin, 1900: 112–25. [Originally published in *Fortnightly Review* 53 (June 1893): 829–35]

——. *The Massarenes*. Ed. Andrew King. London: Pickering & Chatto, 2011.

——. *Moths*. Ed. Natalie Schroeder. Ontario: Broadview, 2005.

——. *Signa: A Story*. London: Chapman & Hall, 1875.

——. *A Village Commune*. London: Chatto & Windus, 1881.

Pater, Walter. *The Renaissance: Studies in Art and Poetry*. Ed. With an Introduction and Notes by Adam Phillips. Oxford: Oxford University Press, 1985.

Poster, Carol. 'Oxidization is a Feminist Issue: Acidity, Canonicity, and Popular Victorian Female Authors'. *College English* 58.3 (1996): 287–306.

'Reviews of Books'. *Reynolds's Newspaper*, 6 October 1872: 7.

Rose, Jonathan. *The Intellectual Life of the Working Classes*. New Haven: Yale University Press, 2001.

Ruskin, John. *Art of England: Lectures Given in Oxford*. London: George Allen, 1883.

Schaffer, Talia. *The Forgotten Female Aesthetes: Literary Culture in Late-Victorian England*. Charlottesville: University Press of Virginia, 2000.

——. 'The Origins of the Aesthetic Novel: Ouida, Wilde, and the Popular Romance'. *Wilde Writings: Contextual Conditions*. Ed. Joseph Bristow. Toronto: University of Toronto Press, 2003. 212–29.

Schroeder, Natalie. 'Feminine Sensationalism, Eroticism, and Self-Assertion: M.E. Braddon and Ouida'. *Tulsa Studies in Women's Literature* 7.1 (1988): 87–103.

Schroeder, Natalie, and Shari Hodges Holt. *Ouida the Phenomenon: Evolving Social, Political, and Gender Concerns in Her Fiction*. Newark, DE: University of Delaware Press, 2008.

Showalter, Elaine. *A Literature of Their Own*. Princeton: Princeton University Press, 1999.

Stirling, Monica. *The Fine and the Wicked: The Life and Times of Ouida*. London: Gollancz, 1957.

Street, G[eorge] S[lythe]. 'An Appreciation of Ouida'. *The Yellow Book: An Illustrated Quarterly* 6 (1895): 167–76.

Sutherland, John. *The Longman Companion to Victorian Fiction*. London: Longman, 1988.

Waller, Philip. *Writers, Readers, and Reputations: Literary Life in Britain 1870–1918*. Oxford: Oxford University Press, 2006.

Waugh, Arthur. *A Hundred Years of Publishing; Being the Story of Chapman and Hall, Ltd*. London: Chapman & Hall Co., 1930.

Weedon, Alexis. *Victorian Publishing: The Economics of Book Production for a Mass Market 1836–1916*. Burlington: Ashgate, 2003.

Wolff, Robert Lee. *Nineteenth-Century Fiction: A Bibliographical Catalogue Based on the Collection Formed by Robert Lee Wolff*. 5 vols. New York and London: Garland, 1984.

Yates, Edmund. 'Ouidà at Villa Farinola'. *Celebrities at Home*. Reprinted from 'The World'. London: Office of 'The World', 1877. 239–47.

## Notes

1 Although reference is made to the first, triple-decker, edition of *Ariadnê* from 1877 published by Chatto & Windus, unless otherwise stated, page numbers in this chapter refer to the undated Chatto & Windus yellowback back edition (Wolff in *Nineteenth-Century Fiction* (III.231) suggests 1882).

2 See, for example, Leavis; Sutherland; Keating; Flint; Mitchell; Rose; James; Waller; Adams. Curiously, Ouida does not appear at all in Richard Altick's magisterial *The English Common Reader: A Social History of the Mass Reading Public 1800–1900*.

3 More recently again, Weedon has used Ouida's writing as a case study to illustrate publishing strategies from the 1870s to the 1930s (see chap. 6). Schroeder and Holt's volume on Ouida (2008) continue Schroeder's earlier line of argument, while adding another concerned with Ouida's celebration of consumer culture.

4 See King, 'Army', esp. para. 29, for this definition of the professional.

5 See, for example, *Morning Chronicle*, 4 February 1861: 6; *Standard*, 8 May 1862: 6.

6 Stirling (17) and ffrench (3) must be right in claiming Ouida's godmother was Mary Ann, as (*pace* Lee, Elisabeth) Maria, Ouida's mother's sister, had died in 1831.

7 The device was first used on the title page of *Pascarèl* (1873). On the escutcheons added to Florentine *palazzi* because of the newly instituted habit of the carriage drive around the city, see Nesti 150.

8 'Ouida in particular was a gold mine to the firm', wrote Arthur Waugh, a managing director of Chapman & Hall (128). Chapman & Hall sold Ouida's copyrights to Chatto & Windus in 1877. A.L.O.E. (= 'A Lady of England') was Charlotte Maria Tucker (1821–1893), a very successful children's writer.

9 On this well explored theme in *Romola*, see Bonaparte; Showalter. That there may also be a memory of *Middlemarch* (1871–72) in Dorothea's interpretation of a statue of Ariadne as Cleopatra and the link made between Dorothea and Ariadne/Cleopatra by Naumann (219–20) (a connection picked up by Lewis [166]) hardly detracts from this argument.

10 The dedication is reproduced from the new 1882 Chatto & Windus yellowback edition. The 1877 first edition jointly published by Chatto & Windus and Chapman & Hall has a typographically identical dedication.

11

# 'Mady's tightrope walk': The Career of Marian Huxley Collier

*Valerie Sanders*

We are very sorry to hear of the death of the Hon. Mrs. John Collier, the wife of the able portrait painter, and herself an amateur artist of promise. ('Fine' 754)

This brief obituary notice for Marian Huxley Collier (1859–87), the second daughter of Thomas Henry Huxley ('Darwin's bulldog') and wife of the society portrait painter, John Collier, conveniently summarises all the contradictions inherent in her position as a female artist in the second half of the nineteenth century. Her name, first of all ('Mrs. John Collier') erases her own identity, and her designation as an 'amateur' despite formal training at the Slade School of Art, and paintings exhibited at the Royal Academy and the Grosvenor Gallery, together with the suggestion of 'promise', confirms that at the end of her life she still lacks recognition as a professional artist. More telling still, as a visual representation of her complex position in the Victorian art world, is her painting of 1882–83, *An Artist at Work*, which shows her husband John Collier, with paint-brushes clamped between his teeth, and both hands holding other tools of his profession, including palette and knife, half-turned towards the viewer as he completes a portrait of his wife (see Figure 11.1). As a portrait by a wife of a husband painting a portrait of his wife, it immediately raises questions of both domestic and professional authority and control. If she had merely wanted to represent him at work, as the title suggests (nor does she name him, calling him only 'An Artist'), she could easily have shown him creating a fictitious picture, or one of his many other society portraits. Lewis Carroll, indeed, photographing William Holman Hunt at his easel in 1860, leaves the canvas blank.[1] In placing herself recognisably on the easel, Marian Collier lets the viewer think – ironically or otherwise – that she is somehow an artefact of her husband's.

11.1 Marion Collier (née Huxley), *John Collier*, oil on canvas, 1882–83 [NPG 6811]. Courtesy of the National Portrait Gallery, London.

*Note*: Huxley Collier's name is variously spelt 'Marian' and 'Marion'. The National Portrait Gallery use the spelling 'Marion' for the attribution of 'An Artist at Work' but I have referred to her as 'Marian' as this was the original spelling.

Her flatness on the canvas, looking away into the distance, compared with his four-square domination of the space, his phallic palette knife angled towards her, exaggerates her passivity as a kind of Pygmalion's creation. His 'ownership' of her seems indisputable. As artist, husband, man, almost a father-figure, he guards the viewer's access to a portrait-within-a-portrait which can be seen only obliquely. On the other hand, although he dominates the picture, and she is the sitter as he crafts the flat head-and-shoulders profile on the white canvas, she is also the hidden artist painting him: a sitter himself, though portrayed as an artist confidently completing a work of his own, his staunch independence undermined by the invisible wifely gaze.

The painting's iconography is thus endlessly circular and self-reflexive, raising more questions than answers. Even the background details further complicate the viewer's understanding of the spatial geography of the Colliers' Chelsea Embankment house, and its impact on the balance of power between them as husband and wife competing in the same professional field. The grandfather clock, a large dish forming a halo behind Collier's head, and the candlestick on a lacquered and decorated chest or cupboard are suggestive not of an artist's studio, but of the couple's living-space: a sitting-room perhaps, or downstairs reception area. Given that many of Marian Huxley Collier's other paintings and drawings depict girls and women rehearsing and posing in attics and garrets, this picture suggests that John Collier's confident professional standing places him at the heart of their home, in undisputed possession of the comfort and grandeur he has earned as a society portrait-painter.

The easel-portrait meanwhile tells a story of its own, not immediately obvious to a viewer unaware of John Collier's other artistic representations of his wife. In 1883 he painted a head and upper-body portrait of Marian in a dark high-necked dress relieved only by a corsage of pink roses. The background is whitish and unspecific, so that the eye focuses on the introspective psychology of the face. Collier had already painted a three-quarter-length portrait of her in her wedding dress, sitting in a chair enclosed in a shadowy dressing screen. *The Artist's Wife* (1880), as the painting was called, clearly signals Marian's subordinate position to her husband as a new bride, her eyes avoiding direct contact with the viewer's. There is no indication here that she is an artist, though she had already attracted notice at the Slade. In his later *The Art of Portrait Painting* (1905), Collier declares himself 'a realist', who believed in rendering 'characteristic' likenesses of his sitters: 'that is, the sitters should be wearing the sort of clothes that they wear in real life, and should be in the sort of attitude that they are wont to assume' (77). While this approach could make his work seem dull and predictable, at its best it impressed viewers with its naturalness. *The Times*, for example, mentions a full-length portrait of Marian, describing it as 'the healthiest if not the best portrait' in the Grosvenor Gallery exhibition of May 1882: 'One of those easy, unaffected pictures which give every one pleasure, and possessing a vivacity and out-of-dooriness not common in Mr. Collier's work' ('Grosvenor' 4). The paper added that whereas Collier normally 'surrenders or forgets all else in the effort to be "respectable," and produces in consequence portraits of unimpeachable merit and unquestionable dullness', this picture is 'by no means dull' and 'an admirable likeness' ('Grosvenor' 4). From the date and the description, it sounds as if *The Times* is talking about a third painting, no longer in the public domain, but the reviewer clearly indicates that he likes the individuality and freshness of Marian's image in her husband's rendition. Moreover, in describing it as an 'admirable likeness', the reviewer implies that he knows Mrs Collier and knows what she looks like. Taken together, *An Artist at Work*, and the portraits of Marian Collier by her husband reinforce the sense that he manages the public reception of her image. In painting herself on his easel looking less girlish, facing the opposite way, and wearing a more matronly white lace collar, she seems to be asserting a contrary impression of herself.

I wanted to start with these images and the complex self-reflections they represent because they sum up both the difficulties we have in tracking Victorian female artists' careers in general and Marian Huxley Collier's in particular. The latest development in the unfolding history of these images is that the National Portrait Gallery recently acquired *An Artist at Work*, and in the spring of 2008 exhibited it alongside John Collier's picture of his wife. The Art Fund provided £15,000 towards the total purchase costs of £40,000, and the online publicity claims that the picture has not been seen since 1897, when John Collier lent it to the Victorian Era Exhibition. This was a major event to celebrate the achievements of 60 years of the Queen's reign, and included a section on the fine arts. As *The Times* observed in 1895, there was even a room set aside for the work of 'lady artists', but Marian Collier's name is not among those who contributed ('Victorian' 5). She had died 10 years earlier, and apart from this particular painting, her work seems by then largely to have been forgotten.

As Pamela Gerrish Nunn has noted, some female artists have proved harder to study than others, 'for reasons which do not necessarily correspond to the stature, popularity or importance of the artists' (125).[2] Marian Huxley was hailed as an important new talent when she was still a student at the Slade School, and she exhibited three drawings at the Royal Academy from 1880–84. Seven of her works appeared in exhibitions at the new and fashionable Grosvenor Gallery, including *An Artist at Work*. Yet although she sketched portraits of both Darwin and Huxley, which are now owned by the National Portrait Gallery, she never appears in studies of Victorian women artists, and has not been discussed or evaluated as a contributor to 'New Woman' aesthetics, despite her obvious affinities with this phase of late-Victorian cultural and social activity. Where she is mentioned, the information is sparse, or wrong: as in the 1934 obituary of John Collier in *The Times*, which claims she died 'soon after the birth of their only daughter' (implying death in or after childbirth, rather than three years later) ('Mr.' 17). Perversely, perhaps, most of her portraits of Victorian male scientists, historians and explorers are light pencil sketches, while her formal oil paintings are reserved for little girls engaged in trivial activities, such as poring over the contents of a jewellery box or pointing their toes in rehearsed dance steps. Moreover, though her husband's portrait of her was described by *The Times* in terms of its healthy cheerfulness, she was anything but a healthy and cheerful uncomplicated artist's wife and sitter. She was, in fact, in many ways both a classic Victorian 'New Woman' and a (pre-Freudian) neurasthenic, who struggled with the demands of marriage and motherhood, and died of pneumonia on her way to Charcot's clinic for hysterics in Paris. This essay therefore aims to identify the nature of Marian Huxley Collier's paradoxical achievement and her complex relationship to the culture she lived in, while considering why she is so difficult to trace, despite being Huxley's daughter and Collier's wife. Discovering how and where she is discussed will, I hope, help us evaluate her significance in the Victorian art world of the 1880s, while saying something about the way this world treated its up-and-coming women artists.

When the social scientist Beatrice Webb met T.H. Huxley in 1887 she noted rather brutally that 'his brilliant and gifted child has sunk into hysterical imbecility' (I.203). Marian Collier's history as an artist is unavoidably implicated in the troubled life of another man, her father, the scientist Thomas Henry Huxley. The two shared not only keen ambition about their own work, but also a depressive temperament and underlying emotional instability, combined with uncertain physical health. While Huxley was able to mitigate their effects in his own case through a happy marriage and devotion to his eight children, Marian was less conventionally satisfied, motherhood, if not marriage, exacerbating her problems. There was at the time an ongoing debate as to whether artists typically lived quiet uneventful lives, or whether they were corrupted by the bohemianism of the studio lifestyle; similarly whether the great artist was inevitably a genius tainted in some way by degeneracy or emotional instability. At the *fin de siècle*, as Julie Codell has noted, the 'discourse of heredity and environment invaded *The Art Journal*' (239), with contributors coming down on both sides of the debate as to whether talent was normally inherited. Marian Huxley Collier is part of all these debates, as the daughter of a famous man (albeit not an artist) and inheritor of his depressive temperament, while also striving in her short life to achieve an identity and independent status of her own. Beatrice Webb noted in her meeting with Huxley that he 'dreams strange things, carries on lengthy conversations between unknown persons living within his brain' (I.202). He was himself a keen amateur artist who, in the course of his travels as a research scientist on a survey ship around Australia in 1846–50 sketched human forms as well as botanical and biological specimens; then as the father of young children, dashed off pictures to entertain them before bedtime. As an established scientist, he was more than once invited as an after-dinner speaker to the Royal Academy, and Artists' Benevolent Institution, through a connection with John Everett Millais, whom Adrian Desmond calls Marian's 'old Pre-Raphaelite mentor' (*Huxley: Evolution's* 140) at the Slade. In his formal lectures and writings, Huxley liked to suggest analogies between science and art as being both actively in pursuit of beauty and truth via the use of symbolic illustration. 'The greatest men of science have always been artists', he maintained in his essay 'On Science and Art in Relation to Education' (1882), adding that the same was true in reverse of artists. In the same lecture (and elsewhere) he argued that in terms of a national curriculum for schoolchildren, he would 'provide, in the fullest sense for the development of the aesthetic side of the mind' – as he did for his own daughters, sending all five in turn to art school ('Science' 178, 186). Huxley believed that learning to draw was beneficial for everyone, not just the well-off, and apart from its other virtues, would inculcate good habits of accuracy and attention ('Science' 186).

All the indications are that Huxley was a supportive father who was proud of his daughter's burgeoning career, and actively invested in it, both financially and emotionally. In return, she provided informal records of her father and Darwin sketched in their leisure moments, outside their usual professional context. As Huxley's biographer, Adrian Desmond, reports, she was committed from an early age to sketching great men. As a child she had sat on her mother's lap at Down House, 'holding a dry pen' and trying to draw her father, while complaining that 'I can hardly make a man' (Desmond, *Huxley: The Devil's* 294). Maintaining that 'Artists are born, not made' (Huxley, 'Struggle' 220), Huxley was quick to recognise her talent and encourage it, while becoming increasingly worried about her health (diphtheria in 1878) and signs of mental instability: what Adrian Desmond calls her 'knife-edged emotions' (Desmond, *Huxley: Evolution's* 140). She followed the initial customary route for would-be women artists by attending the Slade School, and then exhibiting works at the Royal Academy, the Suffolk Street and Grosvenor galleries. In 1877 she took a composition prize at the Royal Academy for her *Death of Socrates,* which shows that painting classical subjects on a grand scale was part of her training and early repertoire. At the opposite end of the scale, she turned her hand to book illustrations for a reissue of Charlotte Mary Yonge's *The Young Stepmother* (1861). This commission, to provide three drawings for Yonge's novel of Christian family life, was more what was expected of a Victorian woman artist on the borders of a professional career, but though standardised in style to suit the Macmillan series, her illustrations bear at least some resemblance to her paintings of children. The three drawings depict moments of emotional intensity between pairs of friends and relatives, one of them a couple at the deathbed of an adult son. Nearly all of her short career was subsequently to focus on indoor scenes of portraiture, on a lesser scale than her husband's. Where pairs of sitters are depicted, there is an aspect of collusion or the sharing of a secret pleasure or forbidden activity.

As an early exhibitor at the new Grosvenor Gallery, which opened in New Bond Street in 1877, she was associated with a fashionable alternative to the Royal Academy, and a gallery favoured by 1880s aesthetes. The seven pictures she showed here were a mixture of the classical – such as *A Bacchante* (1880) – and society portraits in the tradition of her husband: as for example, *Alice, daughter of Frederick Pollock, Esq.* (1881); *Rene, son of F. Harrison, Esq.* (1882). There was also the occasional emotive landscape *By the tideless dolorous midland sea* (1884), though she was not essentially a landscape artist. Her first serious collapse in 1882 was exacerbated over the next few years by pregnancy, miscarriage, and then the birth of a baby daughter Joyce in 1884. It is always difficult to know exactly what was wrong with women that the Victorian medical establishment diagnosed as 'hysterics', but her symptoms included headaches, stomach problems, and 'melancholia' (as her father called it), which sounds like a form of post-natal depression: at her worst, she temporarily lost her eyesight, and was prey to 'gloom and horrors' (Desmond, *Huxley: Evolution's* 152). Her father, who believed that 'women are, by nature, more excitable than men', was afraid that she might suffer permanent dementia (Huxley, 'Emancipation' 71).[3] Of depressive tendencies himself, Huxley empathised so closely with her condition that it is thought to have darkened his notion of evolutionary theory. Desmond argues: 'Mady's tightrope walk would transfix him as he widened the divide between harsh Darwinian Nature and benign human ethics' (*Huxley: Evolution's* 140). His essay 'The Struggle for Existence in Human Society' (1888), written the year after his daughter's death, gloomily predicted that so long as the 'tendency to multiply without limit' drove human existence, 'the war of each against all' would determine the survival of the fittest (205–6). The unspoken implication of this and similar statements in his later writings was that highly-strung sensitive natures such as his daughter's were liable to be mown down in the competition. In the *Romanes Lecture* of 1893, 'Evolution and Ethics', Huxley focuses more directly on what constitutes 'the fittest' in society, and concludes that while this depends on the precise social conditions, 'the strongest, the most self-assertive, tend to tread down the weaker' (33). In this harsh, increasingly unsympathetic world, Huxley remained convinced that his daughter was 'a brilliant creature with a faculty for art, which some of the best artists have told me amounted to genius' (see his letter to Hooker of 21 November 1887).

John Collier twice painted Huxley, but perhaps the best known image is of the scientist gazing straight out at the viewer while holding a skull in one hand and leaning against a pile of books on a plain wooden table, his other hand in his trousers' pocket. As befitting the work of a son-in-law, this portrait of 1883 captures Huxley in a semi-casual pose, while also making a powerful statement of his professional confidence and achievement. Huxley is clearly here completely at home in a masculine scientific atmosphere with the tools of his trade about him. When Marian sketched him, it was in a domestic 'off-duty' moment, as a benign father-figure, reading with his glasses on the end of his nose, temporarily preoccupied with his own concerns. The two sketches now owned by the National Portrait Gallery are not dissimilar to the way Huxley liked to sketch himself as a young scientist: a man with a prominent nose and bushy eyebrows, absorbed in a book. While his own sketches and his daughter's represent Huxley as a bookish private man, they make a very different kind of statement from John Collier's, which asserts an entirely public version of vocational achievement and completion, with the books closed and the skull held almost nonchalantly, upside down.

There is a similar contrast of approach and style in the way the Colliers portrayed Charles Darwin, Huxley's great friend and colleague. While the formal portrait, of a rugged white-bearded Darwin cloaked to go out, with hat in hand, was financed by the Linnaean Society, and is in the heroic style also favoured by Julia Margaret Cameron in her photographs, Marian's light sketch of 1878 again looks as if it was done when Darwin was unaware of it, in a completely informal setting. As in many of her pictures, the sitter's eyes avoid those of the viewer: here they are downcast, towards Darwin's left, and he is clearly sitting indoors on a chair, with his legs crossed. Emma Darwin, however, found Marian Collier's presence in her house intrusive and disruptive. She felt the artist should have been more satisfied with her marriage, and behave with better grace, complaining:

> She ought to have been improved by marrying so nice a man – her manner is so indifferent & wanting in respect that Bessy [her daughter, Elizabeth Darwin] can hardly bring herself to call her Marian. My only aim is to be just civil enough to prevent her Jack finding out how little we like her. (Browne 487–8)

Darwin's own opinion is unrecorded. Huxley Collier was indeed a great tester of social and professional boundaries, her position as informal artist in the Huxley and Darwin homes again raising the question of her professional status, and the extent of her recognition beyond the family circle. As her artistic career developed, her more formal techniques were reserved for what look like more trivial subjects, such as *A Rehearsal* (1882) and *Treasures*, sometimes called *The Trinket-Box*. Nevertheless, Huxley as a proud father was not alone in applying the word 'genius' to her work. When the first of these oil paintings was exhibited at the Grosvenor Gallery in 1882, *The Times* was unsure what to make of what it called this 'peculiar piece', but was willing to identify exceptional elements:

> A sympathetic work this, with just that touch of genius about it which gives genuine interest to a common-place subject. As a painting it is somewhat poor and thin, but there is genuine artistic stuff in the design and in the expression of the children's faces. ('Grosvenor' 4)

The attribution of 'genius' to *fin-de-siècle* artists has a cultural history of its own, fostered by the linking of genius with insanity and degeneracy in studies such as Cesare Lombroso's *The Man of Genius* (1891) and Max Nordau's *Degeneration* (1892). In stressing the ties between artistic genius and degeneracy, Julie F. Codell argues that '[w]ithin the degeneracy discourse, genius was a force of mystery, madness, and danger, while talent encompassed social order, training, and predictability' (101). Although there was nothing particularly wild and erratic about Huxley Collier's paintings, there are unsettling overtones in her reiteration of certain themes which suggest repression of artistic instincts, in the broadest sense, while also reaching down to an apparently trivial level. Her pictures of girls and women often show them engaged in hidden acts of performance and exhibitionism, as if they are ashamed of revealing their desire for attention. Their performance space tends to be a garret or a part of the house safely closed off from access by other people, as in *A Rehearsal* (1882), where two girls dressed in black (perhaps in mourning) cautiously practise their dance steps, illuminated only by an attic skylight. To their side is a clothes rack hung with theatrical costumes, and on the floor a litter of male face masks: details echoed in *A Coming Tragedian* (1882), the subject of which the *Art Journal* for 1882 describes as 'A girl posturing before a tall mirror in an attic' ('Exhibition' 1882: 239). It omits to mention that 'the girl' is dressed like a Roman matron in an off-the-shoulder toga style, with what looks like a laurel wreath in her hair, and a disordered pile of material at her feet. Behind her is an open trunk with more rugs and blankets tumbling out, as if the woman has gone to the attic explicitly to dress up. Both this and *A Rehearsal* celebrate the pleasures of female masquerade, of which the key condition is privacy; and though *Treasures* depicts a less secretive and sparse setting, it nevertheless suggests a similar collusion between two girls (one apparently looking at herself in a small hand mirror, while her sister looks obliquely in the same direction), inhabiting an imaginative world set apart from the rest of their household. The garret is traditionally the workplace of an artist. In depicting it as the rehearsal space of girls and women with a taste for exhibitionism, she perhaps makes the dancer or actress an equivalent symbol for the Victorian woman artist: someone who must practise her art in the part of the house normally reserved for servants or lumber (or, following *Jane Eyre* [1847], the madwoman of the household). Even the more comfortable surroundings of *Treasures* are explicitly a female artistic space, packed with images of sewing and needlework, including an embroidered tablecloth and a large tapestry wall-hanging. Scissors and a bobbin on the table imply that the needlework is actively progressing, and the girls, having invaded the household sewing-room, are daydreaming over something that looks more like a sewing box than a jewellery casket.

Most of Huxley Collier's sitters were young girls and women, including her own younger sisters, implying that in the early 1880s she was relying on the family for support as well as inspiration and not employing strangers or professional models to sit for her. This may have been necessitated by her uncertain state of health. One known family portrait (exhibited at the Royal Academy in 1884) is of her younger sister Nettie, who subsequently went on to be a singer and artist/illustrator on a similar kind of amateur/professional borderline to Marian. There are clear links here with *A Coming Tragedian*, as Nettie looks dressed for a performance, but is not exactly in a public space. This light sketch can be contrasted with a more finished portrait by John Singer Sargent drawn four years later. Sargent came to know her through her husband, Harold Roller, who was a picture framer, and subsequently (1888) portrayed Nettie in a weird surreal style in a punt with J. Comyns Carr.[4] Marian's sketch makes her look more rakish and unconventional than Sargent's earlier portrait, like the *Coming Tragedian*, and again, the gaze is more downcast than direct. The *Art Journal* offered grudging praise in 1884: 'A remarkable portrait for so young an artist; and only short of being first-rate by its disagreeable flesh tones and obtrusive background' ('Exhibition' 1884: 241). Perhaps the most controversial way she incorporated her sisters into her art is in another drawing of 1880, *The Sins of the Fathers*, which shows 17-year-old Nettie and the youngest sister, Ethel, then only 14, discovering the forbidden pleasure of gambling with cards. Again, they seem to be in a shabby or hidden part of the house, which is this time a more explicitly male domain. There are no chairs and the girls in their incongruous schoolgirl dresses, crouch over a wooden box for their improvised card-game, intent on their own furtive shared experience. It provides a sharp contrast with the innocence of the Charlotte Yonge illustration from *The Young Stepmother*, facing page 200, showing two young girls comforting each other with the caption: 'You will find some one who will know how to love you'. *The Times* was somewhat more positive this time, noting on June 28, 1880: 'The look of the elder girl keenly forecasting in her sister's face the effect of a card she is about to play, is very dramatically conceived, and the whole picture shows thought carefully and artistically worked at ('Exhibition' 5). When John Collier painted the Huxley daughters, it was in a more formal, public style; in its review the *Magazine of Art* could not resist slipping in a comparison with his wife's best-known work: 'Mr Collier's *Three Sisters* has great merit in colour, characterisation, handling, and effect; and so, in a way of its own, has Mrs Collier's *Artist at Work*' (352).

Marian Collier's artistic career was cut short by her mental illness, the stages of which can be traced only through the private correspondence of her parents as it seems to have been kept successfully out of the public domain. Its extraordinary final phase involved Jean-Martin Charcot, of the Salpêtrière hospital in Paris, narrowly missing Freud's visit to the same experimental clinic. Freud was deeply interested in the neurologist Charcot's Parisian hospital as a place where hysterics were treated by a form of hypnosis: he spent several months there in 1885–86, about a year and a half before the Colliers who were on their way to Charcot's clinic in November 1887 when Marian died from a sudden attack of pneumonia. Charcot, whom Freud described as 'one of the greatest physicians and a man whose common sense borders on genius', had already seen her in England, and proposed to treat her emotional conflicts with hypnosis (Isbister 39). Charcot's public demonstrations of hysterical behaviour, in which women were hypnotised before an audience of medical men, notoriously turned hysterics into actresses, some deliberately performing on cue and feigning both symptoms and recovery, in support of Charcot's theories. The whole theatrical set-up was of a piece with Huxley Collier's fascination with scenes of female performance, though significantly her works are all of girls and women posturing for their own pleasure before mirrors or imagined audiences. In many ways she prefigures the women Freud and Breuer discussed in their *Studies in Hysteria* (1895): highly educated intelligent, middle-class women whose problems with family relationships and traumatic histories created disabling physical as well as psychological symptoms. Freud's time with Charcot significantly changed the direction of his studies, towards a fascination with the neuroses. One of the 'might-have-beens' of history is that Marian Huxley Collier could eventually have been one of Freud's and Breuer's case histories, such as 'Miss Lucy R.', the English governess who was one of their five *Studies in Hysteria*. Another, 'Anna O.', was described as suffering from disturbances of vision and paralysis not unlike Huxley Collier's; she was also 'passionately fond' of her father and her hysterical illness seemed in some ways to have developed from her relationship with him. Marian Huxley Collier's continuing legacy and relationship with her family remained as complex as her dealings with them when she was alive. When her widower John Collier decided to marry her youngest sister Ethel, he would have been in breach of the Deceased Wife's Sister Act in Britain, which viewed this kind of marriage as a form of incest. Huxley therefore accompanied Ethel to Norway where the marriage could take place away from such sanctions. Meanwhile, he became fascinated by demonology and stories of miraculous cures in the New Testament, seeking out cases of exorcism and recovery in young girls. Though scornful of primitive versions of religious belief, he nevertheless seems to have been trying to make connections between the simple credulity of ancient people and the long history of hysteria.[5] His continued care of his daughter's work and reputation was, however, curtailed by his own death in 1895. *The Illustrated London News* carrying an article soon afterwards, written by a family friend, on his homes in London and Eastbourne, claimed that all his daughters had 'artistic talent', but Marian would be especially well remembered by all those who attended the regular Sunday social gatherings held at his house: 'She was not only beautiful, with a strong likeness to her father, but she had genius'. The 'Friend' who had written the article added that *The Sins of the Fathers*, which had been sold before the Royal Academy exhibition of 1880 opened, had been 'given back to Mrs Huxley by the owner of it, who knew she longed to possess it. It hung over the big fireplace in the drawing-room there' ('Professor Huxley's Homes' 3). Huxley's widow evidently found nothing incongruous about exhibiting in the most visited room in the house a picture of her two youngest daughters secretly gambling with playing cards.

It is otherwise difficult to keep track of Marian Huxley Collier's afterlife or to ascertain to what extent her family tried to preserve her reputation as a talented artist. Two of her paintings, *Treasures* and *A Rehearsal*, recently resurfaced in auctions, *The Rehearsal* at Sotheby's in 1998, and *Treasures/The Trinket-Box* in 2002. The price is revealed only to website subscribers. In 1943 the National Portrait Gallery acquired two more of her light sketches of famous men: portraits of the historian W.E.H. Lecky (1838–1903), author of *A History of England in the Eighteenth Century* (1878–90), and of the explorer, and translator of *The Arabian Nights*, Sir Richard Burton (1821–90), sketched in 1878 and 1877 respectively. They are both enigmatic pictures, the Lecky one especially, as the ethereal, aesthetic face is turned right away from the viewer, whose gaze rests on his long, lank hair rather than on his features which can hardly be seen. The Burton sketch has a sterner, more complete look, but the eyes are resolutely downcast so that they look closed. It is difficult otherwise to find reproductions of her work, whether in books or on websites, and, unlike John Collier, she left no extant writings to explain her principles and beliefs about her art. Possibly she inspired Ella Hepworth Dixon's *The Story of a Modern Woman* (1894), whose eponymous heroine, Mary Erle, is the daughter of a Professor, 'perhaps the best-known man of science of the day', who lives, as Huxley did, in St John's Wood. Hepworth Dixon describes her heroine as born too late for a life of reading Tennyson, practising her fancy-work and waiting for her first marriage proposal, but equally born too soon for the time when parents prepare their girls as thoroughly as their boys for 'the fight of life' (2). Eventually she works at the Central London School of Art, when 'father and daughter became great friends':

> On the days when he went to lecture at the London University, she would either walk with him, or go to fetch him on those afternoons when he was coming straight home to tea instead of making his way to the Athenaeum Club. … She works now regularly with her father, acting as his amanuensis when his eyes are tired, or verifying facts in the library. (16)[6]

Unlike Huxley, however, Mary's father predeceases her, and it is her own decision to focus on an artistic career and compete for a place at the Royal Academy. Her friend and potential lover, Vincent Hemming, approves: 'Painting, especially in watercolours, he considered an eminently lady-like occupation' (26) – but Mary is determined to make it more than this. Work, she insists to him, '"probably saves some of us from the mad-house"' (27). When her stippled Laocoön fails to win her a place at the Academy, however, she is beholden to her father's reputation for a chance to succeed in journalism: 'Your late father's name carries weight with a certain section of the public' (53), says the editor of the popular weekly journal *Illustrations*. Turned down a second time by the Academy, and abandoned by Hemming in favour of a more affluent bride, Mary clings tenaciously to her independence, but there is nothing joyous or triumphant about her modest success. Memories of her father recur throughout the story, the last coming close again to a summary of Huxley's characteristics: 'the kind-eyed enthusiast who, in his younger years at least, had little enough joy, and much toil, who had been blamed and reviled and stoned by the public, and who had worked solely and single-heartedly for truth's sake' (137). As she looks at her faded image in the mirror, it speaks back to her in unmistakably Darwinian terms, phrased in the kind of bleak language the later Huxley employed to describe the competition for survival, as in the essays he wrote in the 1890s, after Marian's death: 'Nature – insolent, triumphant nature – cares nothing for the individual' (136). At the end of her battle for a career and marriage, Mary concludes: 'Human life is but a moment in the aeons of time, and yet one little human lifetime contains an eternity of suffering' (137).

The echoes of Huxley's and his daughter's lives may be only coincidental in Hepworth Dixon's novel, but this short, bitter text illustrates the difficulties experienced by a middle-class daughter of an eminent man in persuading her friends and the public to take her work seriously. Although there is no real suggestion that Mary's talents are other than run-of-the-mill, one senses that the pressures (and indeed the desire) to marry, as well as to make money and mix in the right social circles, all conflict with the ambitions of a woman artist. Ellen C. Clayton, in her two-volume collection, *English Female Artists* (1876), thought that artists' lives were on the whole quieter than authors': 'Eminently respectable, they affect little display' (I.1). Marian Huxley Collier's career, however, demonstrates a continuing fascination with performance, display and secrecy, which are revealed equally in her life and work. Throughout her life, she created family disturbances: beginning with her self-preoccupation as a child in the Darwins' drawing-room, continuing with her portrayal of her sisters as self-absorbed secret performers or gamblers' daughters, and culminating in her widower's breach of English law. She seems deliberately to have done everything differently from the accepted or expected way – for example the light sketches of famous men, the oil paintings of little girls – but of course she was never commissioned to produce the formal oil portraits that her husband was, and that makes it harder for us to judge whether the sketches of Darwin and Huxley self-consciously reinforce her sense of being a second-class artist, with informal access to them at home, but no official role in mediating their image to the general public.

Ultimately, there is an element of game-playing in much of her work which throws the responsibility of interpretation back on the viewer. Her husband, whose erotic art seems to have developed more after Marian's death, painted what were called 'problem pictures': they were problematic because the underlying moral message lacked absolute clarity, as in *The Prodigal Daughter* (1903), which shows a gaudily-dressed young woman returning home to her quiet elderly parents one evening. Has she been working as a prostitute or an actress (as her gaudy clothes suggest), or has she just been living a mildly bohemian life as an artist in an attempt to break away from middle-class respectability for a while? Either way, there is no escape from the notion of 'the return of the prodigal'.[7] Huxley Collier's paintings engage with Victorian culture in a more oblique way than this. There is no morality evident on the surface and no clear sense of what drove her to paint. The moments she captures are apparently ephemeral and trivial; they avoid direct articulation of the horror she experienced in her inner life, but portray the psychology of both men and women in private, self-absorbed postures. Overall, it is difficult to know exactly how many pictures Marian Huxley Collier produced in a decade or so of intense activity, but the brevity of her life necessarily limited her fame as well as her output. As both a daughter and a wife, she was related to famous men, and much of the way we see her, whether through John Collier's paintings of her, or hers of other people, reminds us of her unusual social position, with all its disadvantages as well as its gains. In the end, she evades neat classification: whether as Collier's wife or Huxley's daughter; as amateur or professional; as representing a male public world or a female private one; as specialising in pictures of adults or of children. Impossible to summarise, and atypical in some respects of her less privileged contemporaries, she nevertheless embodies in her brief troubled history the difficulties of the woman artist in relation to the cultural and commercial challenges of Victorian artistry and industry.

## Works Cited

Breuer, Josef, and Sigmund Freud. *Studies on Hysteria. The Standard Edition of the Complete Psychological Works of Sigmund Freud*. Ed. James Strachey. 2 vols. London: Hogarth Press, 1955.

Browne, Janet. *Charles Darwin: The Power of Place*. London: Pimlico, 2003.

Clayton, Ellen C. *English Female Artists*. 2 vols. London: Tinsley Brothers, 1876.

Codell, Julie F. *The Victorian Artist: Artists' Life-Writings in Britain, ca.1870–1910.* Cambridge: Cambridge University Press, 2003.
Collier, John. *The Art of Portrait Painting*. London: Cassell and Co., 1905.
Desmond, Adrian. *Huxley: The Devil's Disciple*. London: Michael Joseph, 1994.
—. *Huxley: Evolution's High Priest*. London: Michael Joseph, 1997.
'The Exhibition of the Royal Academy'. *Art Journal* (August 1882): 239.
'The Exhibition of the Royal Academy'. *Art Journal* (August 1884): 241.
'Exhibition of the Royal Academy'. *The Times*, 28 June 1880: 5
'The Exhibitions'. *Magazine of Art* (1883): 352.
'Fine-Art Gossip'. *Athenaeum*, 3 December 1887: 754.
'The Grosvenor Gallery (second notice)'. *The Times*, 25 May 1882: 4.
Hepworth Dixon, Ella. *The Story of a Modern Woman* (1894). Rpt. Kessinger Publishing Rare Reprints, n.d.
Huxley, Thomas Henry. 'Emancipation – Black and White' (1865). *Science and Education.* London: Macmillan, 1925. 66–75.
—. Unpublished letter from Huxley to J.D. Hooker, 21 November 1887. Huxley Papers. II.'Scientific and General Correspondence'. Imperial College, London.
—. *The Romanes Lecture: Evolution and Ethics*. London and New York: Macmillan, 1893.
—. 'On Science and Art in Relation to Education' (1882). *Collected Essays*. 9 vols. London: Macmillan, 1893–94. IX.160–88.
—. 'The Keepers of the Herd of Swine' (1890). *Science and Christian Tradition: Essays*. London: Macmillan, 1909. 366–92.
—. 'The Struggle for Existence in Human Society' (1888). *Evolution and Ethics and Other Essays*. London: Macmillan, 1925. 195–236.
—. 'The Value of Witness to the Miraculous' (1889). *Science and Christian Tradition: Essays*. London: Macmillan, 1909. 160–91.
Isbister, J.N. *Freud: An Introduction to His Life & Work*. Cambridge: Polity Press, 1985.
Lombroso, Cesare. *The Man of Genius*. London: W. Scott, 1891.
'Mr. John Collier'. *The Times*, 12 April 1934: 17.
Nordau, Max. *Degeneration*. Trans. George L. Mosse. Lincoln, NE: University of Nebraska Press, 1993.
Nunn, Pamela Gerrish. *Victorian Women Artists*. London: The Women's Press, 1987.
'Professor Huxley's Homes'. *Illustrated London News*, 6 July 1895: 3.
'The Victorian Era Exhibition'. *The Times*, 24 May 1897: 5.
Webb, Beatrice. *The Diary of Beatrice Webb*. 2 vols. Ed. Norman and Jeanne MacKenzie. London: Virago, 1982.
Yonge, Charlotte M. *The Young Stepmother*. Illus. Marian Huxley. London and New York: Macmillan, 1889.

## Notes

1 Lewis Carroll's photograph of William Holman Hunt was taken on June 30, 1860 in the Deanery garden at Christ Church, Oxford at a meeting of the British Association for the Advancement of Science: therefore not in Hunt's studio: http://www.wakeling.demon.co.uk/page 5-photo-essay.htm; accessed 22 September 2008.

2 I am grateful to Pamela Gerrish Nunn for her many helpful suggestions as to ways of developing this chapter.

3 The reference to dementia occurs in an unpublished letter from Huxley to J.D. Hooker, 21 November 1887, in the second volume of Huxley Papers, 'Scientific and General Correspondence', at Imperial College, London.

4 John Singer Sargent, *J. Comyns Carr in a Punt* (1888), was exhibited at the Tate Gallery in the opening exhibition of the Sargent Gallery in 1926: http://www.leicestergalleries.com/art-and-antiques/detail/15192; accessed 19 September 2007.

5 Apart from his obsessive writing on the story of the Gadarene Swine in the Gospel of Mark (for example in his 1890 'The Keepers of the Herd of Swine'), 'The Value of Witness to the Miraculous' (1889) discusses the alleged cure of a 16-year-old girl said to have been exorcised of a demon. These essays can be found in his *Science and the Christian Tradition* (1893).

6 I am grateful to Talia Schaffer for suggesting a possible link between Mary Erle and Marian Huxley Collier.

7 Collier's more overtly erotic art includes 'Lilith', painted the year of Marian's death (1887), and 'Lady Godiva' (1898).

12

# Living Art: Michael Field, Aestheticism and Dress

*Ana Parejo Vadillo*

Katharine Bradley and Edith Cooper, the aunt and niece who wrote together under the joint pseudonym of 'Michael Field', spent the afternoon of June 17, 1891, at Oscar Wilde's house. The visit took place at the height of a new renaissance of print and bookbinding and, unsurprisingly, the conversation turned to book design. Wilde was of the opinion that the two most beautiful books of the nineteenth century 'in appearance' were Dante Gabriel Rossetti's *Poems* (1870) and Michael Field's *The Tragic Mary* (1890). Keen readers of D.G. Rossetti, Michael Field believed, just like Rossetti, William Morris and Wilde, that art, literature and design could not be disassociated from each other. All of Michael Field's books were conceived as art objects, where form and content, design and poetry created together the aesthetics of the volume. What is fascinating, and not incidental, about this conversation (fully recorded by Cooper in the women's joint diary, *Works and Days*) is that it begins with a detailed description of the clothes that Wilde and his wife wore on this occasion:

> We visit Oscar Wilde – being received by Mrs. Oscar in turquoise blue, white frills & amber stockings. The afternoon goes on in a dull fashion till Oscar enters. He wears a lilac shirt, a heliotrope tie, a great primrose pink – very Celtic combination, ma foi! (Add.MS.46779 fols.54r–54v)[1]

Michael Field always observed closely Wilde's clothes because for the women it was not just Wilde's writings, his books or his conversation that marked him out as an aesthete but the very clothes he wore. And it is significant that they read his use of colour in the context of the Celtic revival, in which he played an important part (O'Kelly 75–83). Such was the women's knowledge of art and dress.

Michael Field's diary is full of similar entries in which discussions about books, philosophy, poetry, aesthetics and discussions about clothes, hats and other aesthetic items appear side by side. What this diary highlights is that they saw dress as a manifestation of their aesthetic personalities and of their joint authorship. They were, in many ways, the Gilbert and George of the Victorian *fin de siècle*. In an evocative and loving description of Michael Field, their friend and painter William Rothenstein pointed out that these ardent lovers of beauty were as fastidious about their writings as they were about their dresses:

> Field, wan, a little drooping, with her large eyes, clear forehead and sensitive lips, looked the poet she was; Michael, stout, with a high colour, masterful, protecting, was the active, managing spirit of the Paragon. Field again looked the poet in any dress she wore; but dress, like everything else, must for long be discussed and pondered and finally ordered from the modiste with elaborate directions. (Rothenstein II.115)

This chapter argues that for Michael Field dress was a living form of aesthetic expression, an art, just as their writing. Literary critics have recently begun to pay close attention to women's clothes mostly through the study of literary sources (novels, poetry and plays), fashion manuals and periodical publications (see Aindow; Hughes; Schaffer). And yet, while we know a lot about the theory of women's aesthetic clothes, and even more about male aesthetes, particularly Wilde, we actually know very little about how aesthetic women wore the garb. Unlike Rosamund Marriott Watson or Oscar Wilde, Michael Field did not write fashion columns. Their 'look' did not attract the attention of magazines and newspapers. Yet, not only were they the most prominent of women writers but also, as this chapter highlights, their clothes radiated aestheticism. Michael Field's case is particularly unique because their diaries and letters provide ample evidence of what dress represented in their life, what kind of clothes, fabrics and textiles interested them and the meanings they attached to wearing aesthetic clothes. As fashion historian Lou Taylor has noted, diaries allow us to examine 'emotional responses to clothes, how fabrics move, sound, smell, how clothes feel on the body and their impact on the way their wearers move in them' (102). Through their letters and diaries, we can see how Michael Field felt in those clothes, the reaction they got from male and female aesthetes and the effect those praises or criticisms had on them.

Michael Field was, of course, two women: 'Michael' (Bradley) and 'Field' (Cooper). Just like their writings, their clothing was created in collaboration. Their favourite fabrics were satin, silk and velvet; their favourite colours black, heliotrope, lilac, pink, antique gold, silver, olive green – all aesthetic fabrics and colours. They privately discussed dress, used the same dressmakers and often chose for each other clothes and hats. Their poetics of clothing expressed their aestheticism as well as their love and desire – perhaps more openly articulated by Bradley, who would write a number of lyrics about Cooper in aesthetic dress. Clothes were as much a part of their 'marriage' as their writings. But each woman wore her own garments. The poets were of different body shapes in that Bradley was stout while Cooper was bonier and taller; and their clothes were cut to fit their bodies. They did wear, however, each other's jewellery and allowed others to wear it too, most notably Charles Ricketts, because their credo was that beautiful things belong to those who appreciate beauty.

This chapter examines what the clothes of Michael Field reveal about their aestheticism. I argue here that their poetics of clothing was an anti-fashion statement, one of the many expressions of their oppositional aesthetics to mass culture. They were 'true' aesthetes; lovers of beauty and not followers of fashion. But they were also well aware of aestheticism's uneasy relationship with late-Victorian fashion, which they experienced firsthand when once at a party; as Edith Cooper noted with annoyance in their diary, Wilde snubbed them for not being fashionably well dressed:

> We were not well-dressed, as the day had begun with rain – we do not belong to the fashionable world – so Oscar rolls his shoulders towards us. When next I meet him, in my choicest French hat I will turn my back on him, and that decisively. (Add. MS.46780 fol.98r; May 25, 1892)

Bradley and Cooper were always keen to point out that their passion for clothes was not for fashion's sake. Obviously, their clothes had to express their innate sensibilities and assert their own values and cultivated tastes. In April 1902, thinking back about her development as an artist, Cooper hinted at her prescient aesthetic nature by noting how she was already caught by the craze for peacocks and aesthetic blue at the tender age of two: 'I flattened my nose at 2 years old against a shop-pane for the sake of a blue & white silk handkerchief, & my first remembrances are of blue borage & a blue peacock' (Add.MS.46791 fol. 48).

I argue here that Michael Field used clothes as a way of individualising their own aesthetic lives. Like – but also unlike – their male counterparts (Rossetti, Morris, Whistler and Wilde all designed clothes for women at some point in their lives), Michael Field also designed clothes but only for themselves. They realised their own concept of aestheticism through a poetics of clothing, which, as this chapter shows, became more personal and eccentric as aestheticism waned into the twentieth century. Their clothes personified the art of Michael Field. Henry James, so attuned to all matters of dress, gave to Madame Merle in *The Portrait of a Lady* (1881) the following words:

I know a large part of myself is in the clothes I choose to wear. I've a great respect for *things*! One self – for other people – is one's expression of oneself; and one's house, one's furniture, one's garments, the books one reads, the company one keeps – these things are all expressive. (233)

They must have read this novel at some point because Bradley wrote thus in *Works and Days:* 'To-day's dreams & desires – the tongs with wh. the angel makes living coals of our lips to-day – these are the things to be expressed in our walls, in our furniture, in our dress' (Add.MS.46781 fol.47v; July12, 1893). Michael Field's subtle but significant re-phrasing is key to understanding their fascination with the art of dress: aesthetic dress represents not just identity but also the imaginary. Focusing on dress, jewellery and hats, it is the contention of this chapter that Michael Field deliberately used dress as an expression of their dreams and desires. The chapter traces a genealogy of their clothes to argue that the choices they made about their dress evolved organically with the distinctive phases of their aestheticism and of their writings.

## Dressing for Art's Sake: Becoming Michael Field

Influenced by the Pre-Raphaelites, Bradley began to experiment with oppositional dress in the 1870s. Her departure from traditional Victorian fashion coincided with her authorial debut; Bradley's first book of poems, *The New Minnesinger and Other Poems,* published under the pseudonym of Arran Leigh, was published in May 1875. A few months earlier (January 1875) she had made contact with John Ruskin, whose critique of industrial materialism and call for a return to the artistic craftsmanship of the mediaeval ages helped to initiate the art for art's sake movement. Bradley became a 'Companion' to Ruskin's Guild of St George and committed to it 10 per cent of her income. Much has been said about Ruskin's paternalistic five-year correspondence with Bradley (1875–80). But Bradley looked up to him as a tutor in all matters of art and aesthetics, including dress. Once, for example, after she enquired about his 'orders', he replied in a letter dated June 11, 1876, that 'none' were '*positively* such' (emphasis in original): 'Even the dress order might be relaxed on occasion – unless confirmed by private word' (Field, *Works* 148). As can be expected from the philosopher and art critic who believed that art was at the core of the social regeneration of England, Ruskin rejected contemporary bourgeois fashion, preferring instead the *ascesis* of medieval styles.[2] Ruskin had been much impressed (and troubled) by St Francis's rough, simple sackcloth, which he had seen in 1874 (see Wheeler 221). He had also discussed the sackcloth in his letter 41 of *Fors* (The Guild's journal) to criticise the capitalist apotheosis of womanhood he saw in the women's fur trade in Paris (Ruskin 173–81). In a letter dated June 12, 1876, Ruskin explained to Bradley his vision of dress for female Companions:

> I don't expect my Companions to look nice: but to bear the pain of looking not nice, so far as it is necessary, as the form of 'sackcloth' – and a very gentle one surely, not expressive of monastic privation. But in a little while you will be able to teach your dressmaker to cut neatly – or, all I say is – more shame for you and more need for this law of St. George. (Field, *Works* 149)

Keen to adopt Ruskin's clothing ethos, Bradley wrote back to ask what she should do with her old clothes. In a letter dated February 21, 1877, Ruskin replied that he was delighted that she believed in his teachings but swiftly advised her to wait: 'This is one of the principles which we cannot and should not wholly carry out till the society is a practically united and acting body' (Field, *Works* 152–3).

But Bradley and Cooper could not and did not wait. By the end of 1877 their life followed the tenets of the art for art's sake movement. 'Paddington on Monday at twelve', Bradley wrote to Cooper, 'I want to buy blue china, & rare tapestries, & Morris-like garments but you say I must not' (MS.Eng. letts.c.418 fol.5v). Two years later, as students of University College, Bristol, they were known for belonging to the aesthetic set and for wearing 'aesthetic garments' (Pease 3). During the following years as they were constructing their joint authorship the women were also in parallel theorising and firming their adoption of aesthetic dress: their first joint volume of poetry, *Bellerophôn*, was published in 1881 under the pseudonym of Arran and Isla Leigh and their first book as Michael Field, *Callirrhoë/Fair Rosamund*, in 1884.

Talia Schaffer has noted that 'for the aesthetes, who attempted to introduce beauty into everyday life, British dress was an obvious target for reform' (*Forgotten* 103). Although the Aesthetic Dress Movement and the Dress Reform Movement had different aims (beauty and health respectively) both maintained that beauty could be achieved through dress. Bradley and Cooper advocated reform in dress. (Throughout their lives, for example, they always insisted on wearing fur – against Ruskin's principles – for health reasons.) In an undated letter to Cooper's father, Bradley writes about a debate on dress that took place at University College, Bristol: 'We had a very stormy debate here the other night on Reform in Dress' (emphasis in original) (MS.Eng.lett.d.400 fol.160 and *passim*). Bradley, in favour of reform, argued that 'dress was more interesting when it was made a means of self-expression'. This comment brought on a direct response from a Methodist who complained that such a view of dress would lead to 'self consciousness' and therefore 'must be bad!'. Bradley's astute response was: 'But if we dress without self-consciousness, well, it seems to me, we do not dress at all.'

An illuminating letter sheds light on how they actually looked during these pre-Michael-Field years and confirms that their style combined Ruskin's ascetic ethos with William Morris's take on design. At the International Congress for the Abolition of State Regulation of Vice held in Brussels in September 1883, the particularity of Bradley's dress prompted a woman to ask whether she was a Quaker. Bradley writes: 'I tried to explain to her the high art position, and was relieved to find she had heard of Morris' (Field, *Fowl* 101). Bradley and Cooper were regular clients at Morris's shop in Oxford Street, where they bought wallpaper, furniture and textiles to decorate their home (Vadillo 17–36). As great admirers of Morris, they also shared his belief that a new approach to clothes was essential to achieve the aesthetes' aim of bringing art to every aspect of life. A series of letters from the early 1880s reveal in particular their conscious articulation of dress as High Art. For example, in an 1880 letter to her cousin Fanny, Bradley writes how pretty Cooper looked in a 'pale rose silk kerchief' she had bought for her in London:

> This leads me to High Art. Know that now Amy [Cooper's sister] has a rich fruit yellow handkerchief, A.W.F. [Bradley] a sun-imprisoning green, & pretty Persia [Cooper], the afore-mentioned rose.
>
> These were all bought at an Indian House in London, with a rare Eastern gentleman's dressing-gown, wh. is going to be transformed into a travelling cloak. (MS.Eng. lett.d.405 fol.47)

In another letter, which the poets deliberately drew attention to by using an envelope with the inscription '"High Art" Dressing at Stoke Green' (Bristol, where the poets were living *circa* 1884), Bradley describes a carnival event the women attended dressed in aesthetic clothes. Bradley's dress, 'with its perfectly matching Liberty Satin trimming, its old gold under dress of Satine, its gold net frillings, & single accompanying ornament of coral necklace' was 'very quietly supreme in its simplicity'. 'It was made with short sleeves, sack-train & girdle' (MS.Eng.lett.d.405 fols.124–5 and *passim*). Cooper wore a 'soft Marie Antoinette scarf of Indian muslin' and a 'blue silk-dress & an arum'. Bradley's gold dress was typical of the aesthetic style. Made with Liberty's materials, she wore it without any of the heavy adornments typical of the Victorian dress – it was simply accompanied by a 'coral necklace'.[3] Cooper's scarf equally mixed one of the aesthetes' favourite styles – the eighteenth century – with oriental fabrics, just adorned with an arum, an aesthetic flower. Secretly they were the poet Michael Field but *publicly* their dress proudly identified them as aesthetes.

Even more importantly, this letter clearly highlights their public intellectual identification with aestheticism. 'We thoroughly enjoyed the evening', Bradley writes,

> but the true triumph was achieved today in P's ['Puss', Cooper] most successful defence of the aesthetic school. The warmest sympathy was shown for & with her throughout; & the applause for her was fully as warm as any ever given to the Queen. (MS.Eng.lett.d.405 fol.124v; emphasis in original)

Cooper's passionate defence of the school was a response to a very public attack on aestheticism. *Punch* cartoons depicted aesthetes as languid, enervated and affected while critics such as Harry Quilter felt that the transposition of Art into Life was unhealthy and cancerous. Cooper's passionate defence focused on herself: 'It has been said that aestheticism is enervating, look at me; aestheticism has been accused of affectation, am I affected' (emphasis in original). Using her body as a sign of 'High Art', Cooper defended aestheticism by presenting herself as its living embodiment. A photograph of 1887 (Figure 12.1) shows 'Field' inhabiting the aesthetic in a wistful pose wearing a severe, masculine shirt, much in the 'not looking nice' style propounded by Ruskin. As might be expected, this aesthetic photograph suggests that perhaps Cooper did not get away from the aesthetic wan look so fiercely attacked by critics.

There was of course only one place in London where an up-and-coming aesthetic poet could buy such clothes: Liberty's. As has been often noted, the origins of Liberty's are inextricably linked to the emergence and growth of the Aesthetic movement (see Adburgham). From its creation in 1875, 'the Liberty look' became synonymous with aestheticism and oppositional culture. Its customers included Morris, Ruskin, Whistler, Rossetti, Wilde and of course Michael Field: 'At Liberty's Sim [Bradley] got a dark blue cotton for the morning, & I [Cooper] a blue garden-party dress (not dear, very pretty) – but, alas! all the shawls were sold out' (Field, *Binary* 100).

Michael Field reached fame with the publication of the Sappho-inspired book of poems *Long Ago* in 1889. Although in some literary circles the dual authorship was known, the more general readership still believed Michael Field was a man. An intriguing 1889 photograph of Bradley (Figure 12.2), shows the poet in plain, velvet dress, adorned with smocking, ample sleeves and folds, half hidden behind a curtain, perhaps suggesting her secret.

12.1 Harold Baker, Photograph of Field (1887) [MS.Eng.misc.c.654/3 fol.16]. Courtesy of the Bodleian Library, University of Oxford.

12.2 Harold Baker, Photograph of Michael (1889) [MS.Eng.misc.c.654/3 fol.41]. Courtesy of the Bodleian Library, University of Oxford.

The poem 'My Love is like a lovely shepherdess' was written in this year too and shows how dress had become not only an expression of their aestheticism but also an expression of the women's love. The poem was composed by Bradley after seeing Cooper in a new dress, possibly chosen to match a shepherdess hat owned by Bradley. 'Edith's peach & green embroidered gown', writes Bradley, 'came home this evening; – after seeing her in it, I broke into the 1st. part of the 1st. verse of this Song; – then came down &, at my desk, in the evening light, wrote the rest of the verses':

I

My Love is like a lovely shepherdess;
She has a dress
Of peach & green
The prettiest was ever seen:
All eyes must bless
The passing of my pretty shepherdess.

II

My Love is like the first day of the spring
To everything
She gives a grace
Touching it with her tender face:
Ye lambkins cling
To her, & frolic in the sunshining.

III

My Love is like the earliest streak of morn,
Ere day is born,
So Virgin white
The sun with his transforming [top insert] transfiguring light
Fears to adorn
That tremulous, pellucid streak of morn

IV

Oh love, O spring-time morning Shepherdess,
Of my distress
I tell my flute
To thee I must be ever mute
And weeping bless
The foot-prints of my sacred shepherdess. (Add.MS.46777 fol. 87)[4]

Through this eighteenth-century inspired pastoral poem, Bradley skilfully aestheticised Cooper into a vision of love. More significantly, the poem helped Bradley transform Cooper's (eighteenth-century) shepherdess dress into a fetish and empowered her to voice her 'muted' passion for the woman she called her fellow.

## Dress for Poetry's Sake: Re-designing Aestheticism in the 1890s

Inevitably, the dual and female authorship was soon revealed in a review article of Michael Field's 1890 play *The Tragic Mary*. As the public learnt that 'Michael Field' was two women, their appearance became more gender transgressive. Talia Schaffer writes that when 'female Aesthetes wore dark, straight, unadorned, uncorseted gowns, they looked like men' ('Fashioning' 44). In 1891, during a trip to Dresden to research their next book of poems *Sight and Song* (1892), Cooper fell gravely ill with scarlet fever. As part of her treatment her hair was cut short. Michael Field's best-known photograph (see Figure 12.3), taken in Dresden, captures Cooper's boyish looks. (She would be called 'Henry' from then on.) But this dual photograph, the 'official' *carte-de-visite* of the poet 'Michael Field', is an important document for another reason too. It clearly illustrates their deliberate choice of matching dress designs to highlight the union of Michael and Field. These dresses *are* their sartorial signature.We recognise Michael Field in this photograph because of their distinctive 'Michael Field' look.

During the decadent nineties, Michael Field's dress became more distinct and highly personal and more tightly connected to art and to their own artistic production. The women had befriended the art critic and connoisseur Bernard Berenson. They fell for his art and passionately threw themselves into the poetics of art and art criticism. Out of this engagement emerged *Sight and Song*, a volume that translated into poems pictures the women had seen in their European travels. Figure 12.4 shows how during their trip to Dresden, they found in art ideas for new dresses. And just as their dress was inspired by art, the 'appearance' of their books, as Wilde so intuitively noted of *The Tragic Mary*, was now conceptualised as dress. Cooper writes:

> Sight & Song is found to be too bulky to be held by the parchment (unmounted) cover of Fêtes Galantes. Suddenly our little book is disappointed of its clothes & we do not know how to cover its nakedness. Olive-Cloth is suggested. (Add. MS.46780 fol. 62v)

They turned to two artistic couturiers to materialise their unique vision of dress: Miss Vickers and Louie Ellis. Vickers was key in creating this new look. She would be their main dressmaker until 1902. Bradley would remember in retrospect, for example, how Vickers made the 'long black coats in which, in the great year of 1890', they 'swayed through the Boulevards of Paris', interestingly picturing themselves as figures in an impressionistic landscape (Add.MS.46791 fol.21v). In another of her designs, the 'Lady-Cow velveteen dress', Cooper was framed like a portrait (Add.MS.46780 fol.46; February 12, 1892). Bradley's recollection of this dress is particularly significant for understanding the way in which dresses were now intrinsic to their art method and poetry making:

12.3 Photograph of Michael Field (1891) [MS.Eng.misc.c.654/3 fol.14].
Hugo Engler Photogaphic Studio.
Courtesy of the Bodleian Library, University of Oxford.

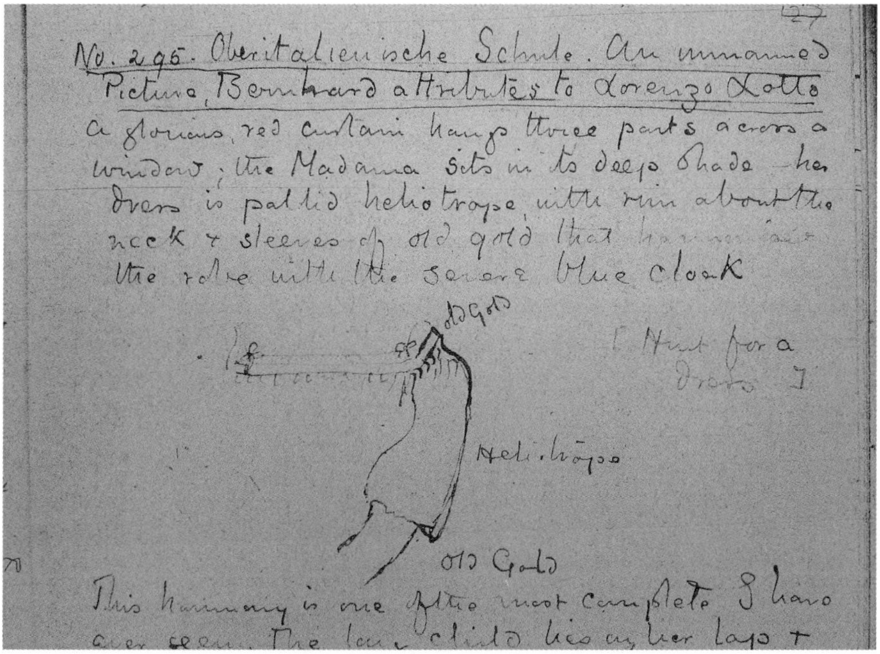


12.4 Hint for a Dress from Works and Days, 11 August 1891.
The sketch is of the Madonna's dress in Lorenzo Lotto, *Virgin and Child with the Infant St John* (1518) [Add.MS.46779 fol.70].


my Love has a gown as lustrous as the meril [sic] of the lady-cow – a burnished darkness – & in relief are knots of colour that glitter as the cherry. All this to frame the limpid water-tints of her complexion; & the pencilled springing hair. (Add.MS.46780 fol. 48v)

The entry was written while completing *Sight and Song* and exemplifies their transposition of art and the imaginary into their gowns. Just like they had used their notes on pictures to create the poems of *Sight and Song*, Bradley translated her vision of Cooper, almost verbatim, into the following unpublished poem:

Will not my Love look fair?
– For she has a gown
As lustrous as the lovely coat
Of the lady-cow –
The burnished darkness, the damask mote,
That mingle, I know not how,
In a black-green myrtle & brown;
With a cherry-knot underneath the chin,–

> The limpid, water-tints of her skin
> And the pencilled, springing hair –
> O will not my Love look fair! (Add.MS.46780 fol.49)

An equally important figure in Michael Field's new-styled aestheticism was Louie Ellis, Havelock Ellis's sister. She was a personal friend, and more importantly, someone who understood both their art and the women's incestuous passion because of her brother's incestuous feelings towards her. Ellis's artistic dressmaking was much loved by Michael Field. She had made her apprenticeship with Mrs Nettleship, well known in the art world as a maker of aesthetic dress and for being the dressmaker of the actress Ellen Terry. Michael Field nicknamed her 'Louie Quatorze' (a clear reference to the French 'Sun King' and patron of the arts), 'Orsy Cat', or simply 'Orsy' (Add. MS.46791 fol. 137; E.C.). Ellis's devotion to theatre and the stage would be crucial for the women as she later made the costumes, designed by Michael Field, for their only staged play, *A Question of Memory* (1893).

No evidence to date has emerged of when Louie Ellis actually started dressmaking for the poets but as early as 1890 she was writing to Michael Field from Paris, commenting on dresses she had seen on the stage and informing them of how she had been learning to fit clothes in the Parisian department store *La Belle Jardinière*. In a comment that could have come equally from William or May Morris (both key in the revival of art needlework in the late nineteenth century) and which also explains the women's interest in her work, Ellis writes about the 'quaint old needle work and enamelling' she had seen at the *Musée de Cluny* (MS.Eng.lett.d.407 fols.43–47). Ellis was a good interpreter of the women's poetics of clothes. The three often collaborated in the design of painterly clothes; clothes that were inspired by art and that would in turn influence the style of their books, as this example of a dress fitting for their 1892 spring clothes illustrates:

> A dress-conclave at Louie Ellis'. Sim's [Bradley] wedding-gown of soft anemone-pink with French-brown edging is enough to cause a broach of promise of marriage.
>
> My robe of black & bright olive-green veiled with black lace is severe and rather dark. Louie herself was worthy of Sargent's brush – a fine green tea-gown, boldly embroidered with damask-velvet thread & the high-lights flashed across it with brilliant blood-red beads. (Add.MS.46780 fol.62v; E.C.)

They went directly from Ellis's to the Bodley Head, where they selected an olive-green cloth for the cover of *Sight and Song*. Ideas for dresses were sent to Ellis styled in Paterian prose just as if they were poems, paintings or symphonies: 'I dream of an evening frock to wear at Asolo', Bradley writes to Ellis. 'It is of a soft black, frail and billowy, and its sleeves are in part of this, with silvery white satin ribbon tied about. If you have a better dream, send work' (quoted in Sturgeon 48). After receiving this dress, Bradley thanked her for 'that *perfect* silk gown' but asked if she knew 'where in the city' she could 'get a big shady hat to wear with it in Italy? Not a monster, but of a kind Theocritus would admire' (quoted in Sturgeon 48).

Wanting a hat admired by Theocritus, the Greek poet and creator of pastoral poetry, might seem eccentric but this letter demonstrates the key role of their hats in their overall aesthetic style. Their hats expressed their admiration for Greek poetry, Elizabethan dramas, Bacchic paganism, and even for the 'olive-green' art of *Sight and Song*. Their favourite hat designer was Madame Véréna, an artist in her own right, as Cooper noted on June 2, 1892:

> Bought from Madame Véréna a lovely hat, wreathed in Bacchic fashion with ivy, & bright with scarlet bows. Sim's [Bradley] hat is olive-green with wingy velvet bows, & a cluster of bobbing, black-heart cherries erect between them. Madame Véréna has had much sorrow – she forgets it all when she has a hat in her hand – true artist & lover of beauty! (Add.MS.46780 fol.101)

The women had a private income and could afford Véréna's expensive hats, some of which were as much as two pounds. Their relationship was clearly uneasy, with Michael Field openly disagreeing at times with Véréna: 'Anglo-French-ribbon-&-felt turmoil at Madame Véréna's. The hats this year are little worlds, where animals, birds & flowers all have their parts in the Creation wh: finds its crown in woman' (Add.MS.46784 fol.12; E.C.). But Madame Véréna created some of their most outlandish looks.

Indeed by the time of publication of *Sight and Song* their highly stylised hats and art dresses were clear signs of their confidence in their aestheticism. They became critical of Liberty's ready-made dresses (and of fake aesthetes who followed aestheticism as a fashion). For a literary lunch party on May 2, 1892, at George Meredith's, who had also invited Richard Le Gallienne and his wife, the women chose matching looks and wore their most artistic clothes. Influenced by the Exhibition of the Old Masters they had seen the previous year, Bradley wore her 'Velazquez dress & black plumed hat', Cooper her 'new dress of black cloth faced with olive silk' that was 'darkened by black lace; black hat with olive bow, a lilac spray, & black & lilac baby-ribbons' (Add.MS.46780 fol.81v and *passim*). Cooper's comment about Richard Le Gallienne's wife shows how far they had come from the 'Liberty look':

> Mrs. Le G. is a boneless heap of green Liberty stuff & smocking – over her heapy aestheticism she pokes her chin. Her hair is light & frizzled – her features common – queer & yet commonly so; & her eyes seem to curve like blue bays, monotonous and convex. … She is much below him – of the type of the artist's wife. (Add.MS.46780 fol.82v)

But as Michael Field's aesthetic code grew into a more audacious – even eccentric – fashion, their style increasingly came under scrutiny and attack.

One of the most painful moments was in the summer of 1892, when they went to Paris to stay with Berenson and his partner, Mary Costelloe, also an art critic. 'He does not like our dress', Cooper writes on June 24, 1892, 'can it be he is small enough to retreat merely from folds & colours that try him?' (Add. MS.46780 fol.118). Berenson particularly disliked the women's hats, which they had chosen specifically to blend with the Parisian bohemian context, and which they ended up altering after feeling deeply humiliated:

> "Miss Cooper, you will forgive me – I like everything about you, but your hat – those flowers in front are too dreadful; they try my nerves every time I look at them". He then takes the occasion for bullying our hats & "the vegetables" we wear in them ... He wheedles me into the promise I will take out the offending bunch. (Add.MS.46780 fol.121v;E.C.)

Not only did Berenson criticise their aesthetic look but he also tried to redefine them to fit his own conceptualisation of the aesthetic woman. Cooper arrived in Paris wearing a hat that threw, as Berenson put it, 'delicate green' onto her face. Although the women aspired to look like pictures, she was made to feel that 'the tints of the hat [were] only demonstrating Bernard's [impressionistic] method' on her face (and thus not her own artistic expression). She was, Cooper noted with some anxiety, 'but a living example of what the New Salon can show in paint' (Add.MS.46780 fol.107v and *passim*). At a bohemian *soirée*, they even felt obliged to change clothes. They arrived looking like a couple of 'draggled Partlets'.[5] '[T]hinking that in Bohemia one needed no evening attire', Cooper had put none in her suitcase. She quickly put together a traditional aesthetic look: a 'parti-coloured blouse of pink & rose, over a long black cloth skirt', which Berenson very much liked (Add.MS.46780 fol.115v and *passim*; E.C.). As he remarked to one of his friends: 'Does not Miss Cooper wear pretty colours – don't you like that fold at the waist?' Of Bradley's looks, which he both masculinised and re-historicised as old and stuffy (like Guy Fawkes), he was downright critical. 'At afternoon-tea', Cooper writes, 'Mary suggests we should go in blouses, because of the heat. Bernard turns to Sim [Bradley] – "You will not go in yours", "Why not?" "Well, you do not want to look [like] a guy[.]"' (Add.MS.46780 fols.129v-130r; E.C.).

Berenson's attack was emotionally upsetting because it was during this trip that Cooper realised she had fallen in love with him. But his critique was particularly damaging because it was directed towards their mode of aestheticism. He saw the poets as an ekphrastic representation of their poetry and thus his critique was as personal as it was aesthetical. On their return to England, Bradley noted their frustration:

> we are back in Durdans, with every feather plucked from our wings, convinced of folly in dress, of poverty and affectation in English, of false method in art (see S[ight] &S[ong]), of taking things personally, of being Anglo Saxon, of living away from Life. (Add.MS.46780 fol.132)

Although they had been shaken to the core, they 'resolved' not to make any changes to their lives (Add.MS.46780 fol.132v; K.B). Undeterred, they visited Berenson and Costelloe the following year in Italy, strutting about their outrageous style. Wearing 'a heavy fur about her neck on the hottest days "to keep [her] cool"', 'Miss Mike' attracted the attention of passers-by 'with her flowzy flowing hair'. As Costelloe explained: 'I told the people they were Poets like Dante and Ariosto and Tasso and they were immensely impressed' (Berenson 53). To be sure the poets' response to Berenson's critique was not a rejection of their style but a total re-affirmation of their *love* and their *art*. Michael Field's poem 'Second Thoughts' is of this period. Written by Bradley in 1894, and first published in 1895, it is a declaration of their love and art through dress. It's a modern poem with a modern theme – two lovers saying goodbye at a train station. Bradley, about to kiss Cooper, decides to stay behind after seeing her at the station in her fox-fur scarf:

I planned – O more – I had almost started; –
I lifted her face in my hands to kiss, –
A face in a border of fox's fur,
For the bitter black wind had stricken her,
And she wore it – her soft hair straying out
Where it buttoned against the gray, leather snout:
In an instant we should have parted;
But at sight of the delicate world within
That fox-fur collar, from brow to chin,
At sight of those wonderful eyes from the mine,
Coal pupils, an iris of glittering spa,
...

For the shining lamps, for the clash of the play –
O madness; not for a single day
Could I leave her! I stayed behind. (Field, 'Second' 545)

At the peak of the decadent nineties and fighting against the tide of very bad reviews, the women remained true to their clothing aesthetic. 'Freedom', wrote Bradley in January 1894, is 'to escape the mechanical in study, & art, to impress one's own individuality on all things – not to wrinkle into anything' (Add.MS.46782 fol.3v).

## Performing Aestheticism: Becoming Art

William Rothenstein introduced Michael Field to the painters Charles Ricketts and his partner Charles Shannon in January 1894. Both couples were of similar sensibilities. Indeed Cooper once referred to them as their 'male-doubles'

(Add.MS.46787 fol.142). Like 'Michael Field', Ricketts and Shannon lived together in 'fellowship' and were devout followers of the Cult of Beauty. Their friendship flourished at a difficult period in the poets' lives, when London's aesthetic world was most critical of their writings. Ricketts and Shannon convinced the poets to relocate to Richmond (London) to be closer to them and advised them to buy an eighteenth-century pillared house named Paragon (see Vadillo 17–36). But it was Ricketts's versatility and genius as a designer that would have the biggest impact on the women's life and art: he published their works and designed their books and jewellery, today considered key masterpieces in the Arts and Crafts movement. Crucially, he loved clothes.

After 1895, and as a consequence of the Oscar Wilde trials, London's aesthetic world was in turmoil. Michael Field's reaction to this crisis (both in art and in dress) was not to return to a more popular and less problematic form of aestheticism. Dress became a symbol of their art and of their resistance. They bought 'blue & white' gowns from Liberty but as Christmas presents for their maids (Add.MS.46790 fol.173; E.C.). They also became dissatisfied with Ellis, whose designs were becoming more fantastical and popular:

> Louie Ellis cannot succeed in the things she makes for us – It is vanity to let her continue. The new summer jacket she has sent for Michael is pure phantasy, conceived too in a popular vein. Michael looks like Mistress Harebell in it, or some such elfin lady's maid to Queen Titania. (Add.MS.46786 fol.35; E.C.)

By 1897 their dress was so different from art's early days that it prompted Cooper to write: '[w]e tried to remember how we were dressed 10 years ago & could not remember' (Add.MS.46786 fol.75).

As might be expected from these *enfants terribles*, their response was an extreme re-affirmation of their aesthetic lives magnified through a re-staging of the eighteenth-century world of grace, elegance and poise. This is how Cooper described one of their afternoons on September 12, 1903:

> Michael is sitting a sweet little Vision out of the Eighteenth Century, with the glow of the Rickettics on lip & cheek, while [Berenson] lies in the cradle of the great arm-chair as if he had been dropped there out of the moon. (Add.MS.46792 fol.150)

Their inspiration for new dresses came from Pre-Raphaelite paintings, the Renaissance, Ricketts's jewellery, their own plays (lyric poetry was a private affair during these years, in which they devoted themselves to historical verse drama), and particularly the eighteenth century. And yet, as their aesthetic clothes became more historical, they looked significantly more modern. Harold Baker's photograph of Cooper pictures her in a Renaissance-like pose wearing an embroidered shirt (see Figure 12.5). The photograph underscores Cooper's passion for medieval embroidery and makes her look particularly modern.

Vickers, 'the loved dress-maker', by now a close friend, made a number of stunning pieces for the women (Add.MS.46791 fol.10; E.C.). One such dress was the 'Sidonia gown' (for Cooper), most probably inspired by the gown worn by Sidonia von Bork in Edward Burne-Jones's 1860 painting (Add.MS.46788 fol.27v; K.B.). The last garment she ever made was a 'little eighteenth-century bodice of brocaded black silk with elbow-frills of white, lemon, & gold stripes & a ruching of dead-white' (Add.MS.46791 fol.17v and *passim*; E.C.). Vickers, fatally ill, made it for Michael, who wore it at a special aesthetic dinner with Ricketts and Shannon. Her closeness to death made Michael Field realise the emotional quality clothes brought to their aesthetic lives. Cooper in particular was very touched: 'So intimately sad to wear a thing she has just made', she wrote. Cooper's definition of art, 'The corner-stone of Art is I, because its material is emotion', explains the importance they gave to dress (MS.Eng.misc.d.333 fol.70) (emphasis in original). Their aesthetic style might have been eccentric and bizarre but they believed their clothes were Art precisely because they were personal. After Vickers's death, Bradley encapsulated in true aesthetic form what Vickers had meant for the women: 'I shall miss her, as one misses a very quaint & beloved piece of old china' (Add.MS.46791 fol.21v.).[6]

During her illness, the women had begun to use other couturiers such as Mrs White, Pile and Madame Cann, and most notably Miss Wells, from Sloane Street, who became their main dressmaker at the death of Vickers. Louie Ellis was 'persuaded' to undertake more work (Add.MS.46791 fol.138; E.C.) and made for Bradley an eighteenth-century 'divine' dress 'of grey satin and old silver' that triggered in Cooper an intense symbolist experience. She wrote thus of the dress: 'a thing one admires like a work of nature – a silvery sea or the dew drenched cloud of a mountain' (Add.MS.46791 fol.147v). Their passion for the eighteenth century was also evident in their hats (see, for example, Figure 12.6). The hat made possibly of fur or velveteen was made by Madame Véréna, still their main milliner. This is the only authenticated photograph of Cooper in a Véréna hat. It was cut out of a group photograph taken by Oscar Browning in 1895. Bradley wrote thus of her look: 'It is Henry in the world, half grand-dame, half fascinating demon' (Add.MS.46783 fol.124v).

Perhaps more interestingly, like other late aesthetes and early modernist writers (for example Edith Wharton), the women began to use *haute couture* to play up their exuberant eighteenth-century style, now almost taken up by the colour black. They engaged the services of Kate Reilly. 'Once a year', William Rothenstein tells us, 'a visit was paid to Kate Reilly, a Dover Street milliner, and imperial hats were chosen; purple with superb feathers, that drooped over Field's small ear, and waved proudly above Michael's head' (Field, *Works* xii). Renowned for her clothes and hats, Reilly is recognised today as one of the founders of modern *haute couture*.

12.5 Harold Baker, Photograph of Edith Cooper, c.1898–1901
[MS.Eng.misc.c.654/3 fol.42].
Courtesy of the Bodleian Library, University of Oxford.

12.6 Field in a Véréna hat (July 1895) [MS.Eng.misc.c.654/3 fol.32]. Courtesy of the Bodleian Library, University of Oxford.

Among her apprentices were Madelaine Vionnet and Coco Chanel, who began sewing at the age of eleven at Reilly's shop:

We are, as ever, in black. Michael with black tulle hat bound in with eighteenth century blue & 3 rose-lilac roses (Kate Reily [sic]) & rose lilac, black-veiled scarf: I bear my black picture hat with two plumes of warmest brown a'dangle & brown net scarf. As soon as I enter the Palace Fay [Ricketts] exclaims "What a lovely hat you are wearing! Tres swell!" (Add.MS.46799 fol.101v [June 29, 1909; E.C.])

Ricketts loved their hats, regularly offering advice on colours and style: 'Fay has said I [Cooper] shd. wear black, white, indigo or dark green – I get [from Véréna] one hat in black & white, one in dark green & indigo' (Add.MS.46791 fol.64v). Because he was a painter his recommendations were taken as strict aesthetic orders, which was more often than not how his advice was given.

Versatile as ever, he was just as happy editing their poems, as he was altering their hats, which he often did. When in 1906 Ricketts took Wilde's *Salomé* to the stage at the Literary Theatre Society, he paid the ultimate tribute to the women's style: 'the headdress of Herod', he wrote to Bradley, 'is to be played as a recognizable imitation of you upon the stage' (Add.MS.61723 fol.9) (see Figure 12.7). After seeing the production, Bradley wrote to him: 'You really think that burning Herod rose wreath could be worn by me. How fascinating!' (Add.MS.61723 fol.16).

Ricketts, whose varied talents included stage and costume design, also collaborated in the design of their dresses. He adored Cooper's style, adding now and again touches of his own to enhance her aesthetic presence. Cooper writes in April 1902:

> My folded soft black corsage is what Ricketts if he were a poet wd. always wear – just what he had thought of for me for so long. But my thread of cardinal velvet wants a brooch & blood-drop to hold it gracefully round the throat. (Add.MS.46791 fol.37v)

He loved this dress so much that he designed

> sleeves for it, & the line of a sinuous skirt, that will have the necessary serpentine effect. I must keep throat & shoulders bare, twist scarves about the arms & waist, wear buckles, long chains, brooches at the wrist, long gloves – even a large ring outside them. The seams of corsage & sleeves may be marked in gold or white. (Add.MS.46791 fols.40r, v; E.C.)

Ricketts's design reflects an important change in the women's (and Ricketts's) conceptualisation of dress: the reconfiguration of aesthetic clothes as costume. The couples celebrated aestheticism in special dinners and tea parties much in the style of the eighteenth century. They took place at Michael Field's home or at the Artists' (as Ricketts and Shannon were affectionately named). Dress, mostly historical, always played a key role in these soirées. When the dress code was broken, criticism would follow. Once, for example, when Cooper was wearing a 'black Sloane Street evening dress of unimaginable plainness', probably designed by Miss Wells, which made her look as if she was 'ready for execution', Ricketts noted with contempt that she 'should be in such a black dress, with a breviary, a snake twisted in [her] hair, &, for colour, only a narrow red line of velvet round the throat, to prompt the knife' (Add.MS.46791 fol.33v. [March 27, 1902]). And vice-versa, after preparing a special aesthetic dinner for Ricketts and Shannon on May 28, 1902, the women, all dressed up and wearing Ricketts's jewellery, were tremendously disappointed when the men turned up 'not dressed for dinner'. They had 'dared to depart from rule, without even excuse'! (Add. MS.46791 fol.79v; E.C.) Through these dresses, Michael Field re-enacted aestheticism by becoming the aesthetic:

12.7 Charles Ricketts, Costume design for 'Herod', c.1920 [N04684]. Courtesy of the Tate, London.

The Artists arrive in full evening dress, as ordered. I receive them. "And your fellow?" says Rickets & begins to look round the curtains & furniture, as if she inhabited a nutshell.

Then she appears in grey satin [Louie Ellis']

"It is the Eighteenth Century"

So he praises

... Michael, descending to dine, says she is going to forsake the 18th Century just as she is clothed in it, & try to become of the Renaissance! (Add.MS.46791 fol.148r, v. [September 18, 1902; E.C.])

There is one particular event worth mentioning here and this was the first visit of Berenson to Paragon. After his critique in 1892, this was one moment of vindication for Cooper:

The truth of Bernhard's visit.

Well Sweet, it was a perfect triumph for Hennie & Paragon!

Hennie in Renaissance dress looked beautiful.

"Good-bye dear Field, be as beautiful when I come again" – he said at parting – and when Field came down he exclaimed on the quintocento gown. "I see elegant ladies – I have never seen one in so beautiful a dress." (MS.Eng.lett.424–1fol.55)

By the turn of the century, the women were leading a life modelled on art, and Cooper, in particular, was conceptualised by their circle as a living artwork. 'In my black folded corsage & braided hair', Cooper writes, 'I am much observed by the Artists'. Bradley told her she looked 'cool', like the sixteenth-century poet 'Vittoria Colonna' (Add.MS.46791 fols.42v–43). Many came to Paragon just for the sake of seeing her. Havelock Ellis, for example, paid a visit after hearing from his sister about her beauty (Add. MS.46791 fol.150v). Even Berenson agreed. When he and Costelloe visited the poets on June 30, 1901, Cooper was wearing a 'simple white blouse of finest lawn, with Ricketts' ornaments' (the jewellery Ricketts had designed for Cooper):

"Field has become very beautiful" – "Like an Italian picture" Mary responds. "Like the head of the Poldi Pezzoli," he continues. '"Yes, Field, you are very beautiful." And I reply quite simply. "Then it is due to the white river light and my white walls." (Add.MS.46790 fol.87v; E.C.)

Clothes, jewellery and hats were part of a unified aesthetic. Nothing testifies more clearly to this than the women's intent to wear Ricketts's stunning jewellery with clothes specifically designed for the jewels. Thus, for example, for the 'Blue Bird' brooch (1899), a present to Cooper by Bradley, Vickers designed 'an evening blouse ... coloured in every blend' of the brooch (Add. MS.46789 fol.38v). For the 'Musico' pendant (1901) Vickers brought along ivory silks for a new dress that would form the background to the brooch (Add.MS.46790 fol.6v). Both couples exchanged, shared and gave each other lavish *objet d'arts*, presents that were much cherished by the women: an antique Persian veil (Add.MS.46792 fol.8v; E.C.); a fan 'Rubenesque in colour & mounted on golden-tone mother o'pearl, backed with chicken-skin' (given by Ricketts to Bradley because she did her hair well, in eighteenth-century style) [MS.Eng.lett.c.421–1 fols.92v–93]; a handkerchief precious for its needlework to be worn by Cooper as in a Velazquez portrait (Add. MS.46792 fol.180; K.B.). Wearing these art objects, Michael Field performed aestheticism and, in the process, they transformed themselves into pictures, into living art. And their home, Paragon, was the stage of the living art of Michael Field: 'it is exquisite to see Henry', Bradley writes in 1902, 'in his black gown & jewels, moving about – a quiet-coloured thing, among the shadows & lights of the sun-room – something attained, the perfect – figure in the perfect home' (Add.MS.46791 fol.74).

In 'The Truth of Masks' Oscar Wilde defended the importance of historical dress on the stage because, he argued, the 'stage is not merely the meeting-place of all arts, but is also the return of art to life' (216). At Michael Field's house, or indeed at Ricketts and Shannon's, the couples staged aestheticism. In a paradoxical way, just as their dresses had become art, the performativity of these clothes brought their art and aestheticism to life.

## A Fitting End

Distraught by the death of their beloved dog Whym Chow, Bradley and Cooper converted to Roman Catholicism in 1907. The poets threw themselves into Catholic life with the utmost devotion but they resisted the Catholic dress order. Dress had been a powerful signifier and amplifier of their aesthetic life and they were not willing to convert their sartorial style. Cooper writes in 1909:

> Michael's dress for the occasion has not been delivered … I have to stich her up in an 18[th].Cen. net Blouse of 4 years ago … She apologises for a garment the chères pères [their priests] wd. so disapprove of. (Add.MS.46799 fol.110v)

But Cooper was diagnosed with cancer in 1911. After the painful realisation of death and separation, they firmly prepared themselves for death. And this preparation, of course, involved dress. Bradley suggested Cooper should be buried in the brown nun habit Cooper's sister Amy, also a Catholic, wore at her death. But Cooper had other ideas: she wanted to be dressed in the white wool of the Sisters of Penance, because thus lying dead, she could make an appeal to God for all her sins (the wool making 'penance white'). Bradley was delighted. Their new Catholic life, which was at the centre of their new Catholic poetics (*Poems of Adoration* and *Mystic Trees* were published in 1912 and 1913 respectively), needed a new kind of 'wedding' and they decided to be buried together dressed in the St Dominic's white wool habit worn by one of their Renaissance idols, St Catherine of Siena: 'We have new nuptials of love within the Church. We shall lie in the Earth together two little woolly-bears – We call ourselves St Domenic's [sic] woolly bears' (Add.MS.46801 fol.26v). Just like their 1891 *carte-de-visite* had proclaimed their joint authorship through their clothes, the women decided to depart from life married, once again, through the same dress ethos. In a paradoxical way, their final sartorial choice was closer to Ruskin's ideal of the sackcloth than they would have ever anticipated.

But the habits were received without the hoods. Bradley, without Cooper's knowledge, duly asked for them and in their reaction to the hoods we can truly appreciate the women's negotiation between the new Catholic beliefs and their aesthetic personalities:

I open a parcel & find in it 2 regular nuns' hoods & face-bands, & two coarse handkerchiefs. I read a note: the handkerchiefs are to cover the face in the coffin. Under pressure from Michael the nuns have sent the veils … I put on the terrible stiff linen that only comes down to my nose instead of down my chin – the sight is pure nightmare … I look so much more than a corpse – a harpy of the graves, a vampire. It is the full revolt of a face against a surrounding for which it has no vocation. Nothing answers this stiffness, this death that the spirit has taken on while the body is still alive. No, there is nothing cloistral in my being. The robe of penance is my due portion – the veil of the spouses of Christ, who are dead to the world, is a lie round my face of a wild poet[,] makes a false appeal & condemns me as a wolf in sheeps' clothing. I cannot escape from the horror of the sight. And when, at night, Michael & I try the linen again, I toss it on the floor in my revolt longing to burn it. I never asked for it & I have been tricked into having it sent to me. I know part of my revolt is due to the sheer ugliness of the crude, stiff-white – but far deeper than any aesthetic protest, is the sense that I have nothing to do with the life this linen symbolises & evokes … but I had better put it away & apart from the habit, & without any trouble about it settle not to wear it, as I have not even taken the Vow of Chastity & feel the veil expresses no truth of my being, no truth of vocation. (Add. MS.46801 fols.72v–73v; E.C.)

In this remarkable entry we see Cooper's staunch defence of the history of her clothing identity as an aesthete, poet and lover and her revolt against the self suggested by the hoods. After a life devoted to poetry, beauty and sumptuous fabrics, she could not accept the 'stiffness' of the veil or what it symbolised: a chaste, ascetic life dedicated to Christ. The vampiric body of this 'wild poet' refused the veil because it was ugly and coarse and, more significantly, because it did not evoke her aesthetic being.

Cooper's last discourses on the art of dress confirm the importance the women placed in dress as a signifying system which produced a visual definition of the aesthetic as well as the art of 'Michael Field', and of 'Michael' and 'Field' as women writers. Ricketts and Cooper would discuss the new aesthetic experiments in the art of dress as they were happening 'in or around 1913' (to rephrase Virginia Woolf's well-known dating of modernism). They talked about post-impressionist and futurist fashion, particularly Bakst, whose work for the Ballet Ruses revolutionised modern dress, noting incredulously how the latest experiments with clothes were taken up by traditional French commercial couturiers like Jeanne Paquin (who introduced the catwalk and the mannequin into the fashion industry). These radical aesthetes found it ironic that the most traditional side of the *haute couture* industry was now involved in creating the modern. These comments are important because they evidence the transformation of aesthetic dress in modernism, particularly as they note the hermaphroditism of modernist dress:

[Ricketts] is full of couturiers & of their living art, that, like Renaissance art of all kinds, is united to life – variable, needy, exciting life … He tells the last sensation in the Sartorial World that Bakst … has confided his work to the now old-fashion Paquin – Madame Paquin, who holds her own for "safe" dressing with those who still seek the Paquin model. Imagine! The last audacities of post-impressionism & futurism in clothes confided to Paquin! … For one of the new men has made women's dress "hermaphrodite" for the sake of "sports"[.] (Add.MS.46803 fols.41v–42r; E.C.)

Cooper died in 1913. Bradley, who also died of cancer, only survived Cooper by a few months, during which time she continued to write about clothes, now an emotional part of Michael Field's aesthetic history. But without 'Field', Bradley found it hard to 'dress':

So I get back to beauty and to art. Mary, just now I am being "broken up" by the need of one of two fresh garments for the spring, especially hats. But I cannot wear things she has not passed, and approved. All our lovely old hats of every summer are brought down and I surmise the exquisite face beneath them. How hats must always be associated with Field! (Add.MS.61723 fol.191)

Bradley's insistence on hats as Cooper's final sartorial signature is touching, but it is more than that. It is a reminder that their vision of dress had the power to create 'Michael Field'. Her insistence reminds us that we must also read those clothes as part of their aesthetic legacy. In Flaubertian style, Cooper wrote on June 17, 1898: 'Brussels Lace is the only lace that is me' (Add. MS.46787 fol.48v). Those hats with feathers were the pen of Michael Field, and the intricate but delicate Brussels point lace, the lyric framework of Michael Field's poetics.

## Works Cited

Adburgham, Alison. *Shops and Shopping, 1800–1914: Where, and in What Manner the Well-dressed Englishwoman Bought her Clothes*. London: George Allen & Unwin, 1964.

Aindow, Rosy. *Dress and Identity in British Literary Culture, 1870–1914*. Farnham: Ashgate, 2010.

Berenson, Mary. *A Self Portrait from Her Diaries and Letters*. New York: Norton, 1983.

Buck, Anne. 'John Ruskin and Dress, 1882'. *Costume* 32 (1998): 80–81.

Field, Michael [Katharine Bradley and Edith Cooper]. *Binary Star: Leaves from the Journal and Letters of Michael Field*. Ed. Ivor C. Treby. Bury St Edmonds: De Blackland Press, 2006.

——. *Callirrhoë/Fair Rosamund*. London: George Bell & Sons, 1884.

——. *The Fowl and the Pussycat: Love Letters of Michael Field 1876–1909*. Ed. Sharon Bickle. Charlottesville: University of Virginia Press, 2008.

——. *Long Ago*. London: George Bell & Sons, 1889.

——. *Michael Field, The Poet. Published and Manuscript Materials*. Ed. Marion Thain and Ana Parejo Vadillo. Ontario: Broadview Press, 2009.

——. *Mystic Trees*. London: Eveleigh Nash, 1913.

——. *Poems of Adoration*. London: Sands and Co., 1912.

——. *A Question of Memory*. London: Elkin Mathews and John Lane, 1893.

——. 'Second Thoughts'. *Atlantic Monthly* 76.456 (October 1895): 545.

—. *Sight and Song*. London: Elkin Mathews and John Lane, 1892.
—. *The Tragic Mary*. London: George Bell & Sons, 1890.
—. *Works and Days. From the Journals of Michael Field*. Ed. T. Sturge Moore. London: John Murray, 1933.
Hughes, Clair. *Dressed in Fiction*. Oxford: Berg Publishers, 2005.
—. *Henry James and the Art of Dress*. Basingstoke: Palgrave, 2001.
James, Henry. *The Portrait of a Lady*. London: Macmillan, 1883.
Leigh, Arran [Katharine Bradley]. *The New Minnesinger and Other Poems*. London: Longman, Green, and Co., 1875.
Leigh, Arran, and Isla [Katharine Bradley and Edith Cooper]. *Bellerophôn*. London: C. Kegan Paul & Co., 1881.
O'Kelly, Hilary. 'Reconstructing Irishness: Dress in the Celtic Revival 1880–1920'. *Chic Thrills: A Fashion Reader*. Ed. Juliet Ash and Elizabeth Wilson. London: Pandora, 1992. 75–83.
Pease, Marion F. *Some Reminiscences of University College, Bristol, 1942*. University of Bristol Library, Special Collections, DM 219.
Rossetti, Dante Gabriel. *Poems*. London: FS Ellis, 1870.
Rothenstein, William. *Men and Memories: Recollections*. 3 vols. London: Faber and Faber, 1931–39.
Ruskin, John. *Fors Clavigera. Letters to Workmen and Labourers of Great Britain*. Ed. Dinah Birch. Edinburgh: Edinburgh University Press, 2000.
Schaffer, Talia. 'Fashioning Aestheticism by Aestheticizing Fashion: Wilde, Beerbohm, and the Male Aesthetes' Sartorial Codes'. *Victorian Literature and Culture* 28.1 (2000): 39–54.
—. *The Forgotten Female Aesthetes: Literary Culture in Late-Victorian England*. Charlottesville: University of Virginia Press, 2000.
Sturgeon, Mary. *Michael Field*. London: George G. Harrap, 1922.
Taylor, Lou. *The Study of Dress History*. Manchester: Manchester University Press, 2002.
Vadillo, Ana Parejo. 'Aestheticism and Decoration: At Home with Michael Field'. Special Issue: Female Aestheticism. *Cahiers victoriens et edouardiens* 74 (2011): 17–36.
Wheeler, Michael. *Ruskin's God*. Cambridge: Cambridge University Press, 1999.
Wilde, Oscar. *The Complete Works of Oscar Wilde: Volume IV: Criticism: Historical Criticism, Intentions, The Soul of Man*. Ed. Josephine M. Guy. Oxford: Oxford University Press, 2007.

## Notes

1 I am most grateful to Leonie Sturge-Moore and Charmian O'Neil for copyright permission to quote from manuscripts held at the Bodleian Library (material from the following deposits: MS.Eng.misc.d.333; MS.Eng.lett.d.400; MS.Eng.lett.c.418; MS.Eng.lett.d.405; MS.Eng.lett.d.407; MS.Eng.lett.c.421-1; and MS.Eng.lett.424-1), and at the British Library (material from the following deposits: Add.MS.46777 – Add.MS.46804A;B [Michael Field's 30 volumes manuscript diaries, titled *Works and Days*] and Add.MS.61723). I would also like to thank them for giving me permission to reprint Figures 12.1–7. Thanks are also due to Clair Hughes for sharing her knowledge of the nineteenth-century dress world with me. Quotes from manuscript sources are cited in the text in brackets. I have always included in the main text or in the citation the date and the author of the entry (K.B. [Katharine Bradley]; E.C. [Edith Cooper]). All punctuation, including dashes, apostrophes and quotation marks appear as in the original manuscript. All transcriptions are mine.

2 Ruskin was in favour of reducing the labour of dressmaking but he also thought that women could dress finely when the occasion demanded it (see Buck 80–81).

3 There are many portraits and photographs of Pre-Raphaelite models and Aesthetic women wearing the typical aesthetic dress only adorned with a necklace. See for example Emery Walker after John R. Parsons's 1865 photograph *Jane Morris Seated on a Divan, Three Quarters Length.*

4 Bradley drafted two other endings for the last stanza: 'To my distress / I tune my flute / Before thee I am ever mute / And bashful weeping bless / The foot-prints of my sovereign shepherdess' and 'In my distress / I tune the flute / To thee I must be ever mute / And weeping bless / The footprints of my sacred shepherdess' (Add.MS.46777 fol. 86v).

5 The reference here is to Thomas Hood's satirical poem 'Ode to Rae Wilson, Esq.' where a proud peacock attacks the chickens in the farm for their ugly looks.

6 Bradley praised her craftsmanship in the poem 'A dead workwoman': 'She laboured: Bands / Of toilers, groaning through the lands / that toil will never cease, / Lo, I would tell you, I have seen her hands / Folded in peace' (MS.Add.46791 fol. 22).

# Index